GUARD WARS

GUARD WARS

THE 28TH INFANTRY DIVISION IN WORLD WAR II

Michael E. Weaver

Indiana University Press

BLOOMINGTON AND INDIANAPOLIS

This book is a publication of

Indiana University Press
601 North Morton Street
Bloomington, Indiana 47404-3797 USA

www.iupress.indiana.edu

Telephone orders   800-842-6796
Fax orders   812-855-7931
Orders by e-mail   iuporder@indiana.edu

Library of Congress Cataloging-in-Publication Data

Weaver, Michael E., [date]
  Guard wars : the 28th Infantry Division in World War II / Michael E. Weaver.
     p. cm.
  Includes bibliographical references and index.
  ISBN 978-0-253-35521-8 (cloth : alk. paper) 1. United States. Army. Infantry Division,
28th. 2. Pennsylvania. National Guard. Infantry Division, 28th. 3. World War, 1939–1945—
Regimental histories—United States. 4. World War, 1939–1945—Campaigns—Western Front.
5. United States—Armed Forces—Organization—History—20th century. I. Title.
  D769.328th .W43 2010
  940.54'1273—dc22
                                                                                2010012447

1 2 3 4 5 15 14 13 12 11 10

*Dedicated to those who
sacrificed their lives for the
United States of America
during World War II*

Contents

Map Key

XXXX

Army

XX

Airborne/Parachute Division

II

Infantry Battalion

XXX

Corps

XX

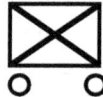

Motorized Division

II

Mechanized Battalion

XX

Infantry Division

III

Infantry Regiment

I

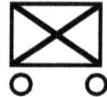

Motorized Company

XX

Armored Division

X

Combat Command

XX

Mechanized Division

III

Cavalry Regiment

Maps

Acknowledgments

I have accumulated many debts during the writing of this book. The project originated in graduate school, and my parents, Fred and Evelyn Weaver, contributed much to its completion. During my time at Temple University, Russell F. Weigley encouraged my production of this work's foundation, a dissertation that examined the Pennsylvania National Guard's development from 1939 to 1944. Richard H. Immerman taught me a great deal about writing, as did William H. Leary at the University of Georgia. Harold W. Nelson has continued to encourage my efforts to produce a full-fledged book. Edward Rouze assured me that my most difficult chapter was written clearly, while Harold Winton helped me refine its content. Thanks go to many archivists. William Weible, Mike Sherbon, and Linda Shopes as well as their staff at the Pennsylvania Historical and Museum Commission provided irreplaceable help, including a fellowship in the summer of 2000. The Military History Institute's David Keough and Larry I. Bland at the George C. Marshall Library assisted with numerous materials. Charles Oellig of the Pennsylvania National Guard Museum provided some unique documents, and William Mahoney of the National Archives walked me through the Archives' labyrinthine cataloging system. Because Attie Ward gave me access to her guest room I could afford to make multiple trips to the National Archives. David Armbruster helped me with Excel and persuaded me to finish graduate school a semester earlier than I anticipated. Dale Hayden, D. Mark Husband, Richard Muller, Charles Costanzo, Bert Sparrow, Budd Jones, and Zoë Hale of the Air Command and Staff College made sure that I got some time to rewrite the first nine chapters, write five new chapters, and turn this project into a book. Indiana's anonymous reviewers helped to make this a better piece of scholarship, and Mary Kathryn Barbier read and critiqued the final draft. Robert Sloan, Daniel Pyle, and Carol Kennedy eased me through the publication of my first book. My wife, Christine Weaver, from the day we met has endorsed my efforts to finish what I started years ago. Many thanks to all.

GUARD WARS

1

Introduction

BACKGROUND AND ISSUES

Ever since the founding of the United States, policy makers have wrestled with numerous national security challenges. Among the most persistent has been the organization and manning of the army: should the country field a "regular" army composed of full-time well-trained professional soldiers, or should it rely on a militia system of civilians called to arms only when the country faces a military threat? Which organization is better suited for defending the country: the militia/National Guard or the United States Army? Should the institutional culture of the Army take precedence over that of the militia/National Guard? Who performs better in combat: the professional regular army soldier, who is trained in the craft of war, or the civilian-soldier of the militia, who answers the call to arms when foreign armies threaten the nation? For many decades arguments surrounding these questions played out in a rivalry between the United States Army and the militia, which was later known as the National Guard. World War II merged the two into a single body and resolved the issue in favor of the U.S. Army, but without eliminating the National Guard's existence or distinctiveness.

This professional versus militia soldier debate began prior to the establishment of the United States. American colonists came to despise the soldiers of their own British Army during the years preceding the American War for Independence, finding them at best an annoyance and at worst a threat to liberty. When British regulars shot to death their fellow subjects during the Boston Massacre and at Lexington and Concord, those actions verified in the minds of many the warnings of radical pamphleteers that a standing army of professional soldiers was an instrument of governmental oppression.[1] Once the war began, many asked, "Did not the militia defend the cause of freedom against regulars at the Battle of Bunker Hill?" and before the war was over, Americans commonly believed that the "national virtue" of the people in arms, not the regular soldiers of the Continental Army, had defeated the British Army.[2] Many citizens had concluded that a people's army of civilian soldiers—the militia—was the most appropriate military institution for a democracy. Concurrently a reliance on the militia implied that there would be no standing army available to oppress innocent citizens. And besides, so went the story from the Revolution, militia soldiers were militarily superior to the automatons of a professional army. Those who had seen the combat performance of both, however, saw great merit in the establishment of a regular professional army in order to exploit the technical expertise inherent in a professional corps.[3] By the time the states ratified the Constitution, the people of the United States were perpetuating a form of the militia system from their colonial days and at the same time were reluctantly funding a nascent standing army.[4]

Both kinds of armies performed inconsistently during the United States' next major conflict, the War of 1812. After some false starts, forces of the U.S. Army finally defeated British regulars in close combat on July 5, 1814. Months of rigorous training made possible the Americans' achievement at the Battle of Chippewa, but militia forces never trained with the commitment of the U.S. Army. It was challenging to even get them to fight,[5] but during the war's final battle that seemed to make no difference. After all, Andrew Jackson's motley crew defeated a force of veteran British regulars in the Battle of New Orleans. The argument for the superiority of the militia gained more credence.[6]

Many national leaders nevertheless concluded that the War of 1812 confirmed the country's need for a professional army of some sort, if for no other reason than to form the basis for a larger army, one that would train men taken from civilian life during a time of national crisis and turn them into soldiers. In pursuit of that goal, President James Monroe's secretary of war, John C. Calhoun, borrowed a method from the French whereby he could reap many of the benefits of skilled military professionals without inflaming American fears of a standing army. The national government could use the Army to provide a cadre of officers, especially the graduates of the United States Military Academy, knowledgeable in the management of armies and the art of warfare to form the nucleus of an American army that volunteers would fill out in wartime: an "expansible" or expandable army.[7] The United States did not follow Calhoun's organizational model precisely during subsequent generations, but through the mid-twentieth century the country adjusted the model's principles to its security needs.

For the next few decades after the War of 1812 the War Department did not make first use of militia to fill out the expanded Army, but instead relied on volunteers.[8] During the Mexican-American War, for example, trained regulars provided the skilled backbone of the Army, but most of the soldiers were volunteers. Not the most ideal of armies, the regulars despised the lack of discipline and unmilitary manner these soldiers displayed.[9] Furthermore, the continuation of the militia tradition of soldiers electing their officers (some of whom had no military experience) appalled the professional officers. A few of those so elected were men who had failed to complete their studies at West Point years before but received commissions through their states, often with the purpose of furthering partisan political power.[10]

The need for a mass army during the Civil War shoved aside the militia–regular army debate during the 1860s, but afterward the question of their respective places in American military policy arose once again. Following the Civil War, the National Guard (NG) perpetuated the militia tradition.[11] For instance, during the Spanish-American War, many of the Army's volunteer soldiers came from National Guard units.[12]

This postbellum institution acquired several characteristics that endured until the mid-twentieth century. National Guard units commingled the attributes of sports clubs, fraternities, and military formations. The states used their National Guard formations primarily as police forces, although that subsided somewhat in the twentieth century. Guardsmen risked losing their jobs if they reported for extended training, and the only way officers could protect their men from being fired was by convincing employers to allow them time off. The National Guard rank and file tended to be native-born skilled workers from urban areas, and turnover in the ranks was "constant." Senior officers seldom used their offices to dispense patronage, but a unit's local identity was of great importance to its members. There was never enough money for the National Guard companies and batteries; some soldiers even had to pay out of pocket for their uniforms.[13]

The War Department began to gain bureaucratic supremacy over the states and the National Guard, with their concurrence, following the inept mobilization for the war with Spain in 1898. Soon thereafter Secretary of War Elihu Root reorganized the United States' military structure with the Dick Act of 1903, whereupon the National Guard became the Army's primary reserve force, with the U.S. Congress, not state legislatures, purchasing their weapons. The Guard leadership welcomed this change.[14] Congress allocated more money for training, and the National Guard Association, a lobby, asked the states to conform National Guard units to U.S. Army standards. Most guardsmen, however, wanted to be treated as equals to the Army and opposed greater federal authority. A few, such as Georgia's General Walter Harris, asserted otherwise and argued, "We are a national militia."[15] The National Guard was becoming an institution with both local and national characteristics prior to World War I.

Even though Congress was appropriating money for the National Guard, underfunding remained the Guard's primary challenge. Even if all guardsmen wanted to become as proficient in warfare as Army soldiers, they did not have the money to do so. The consequences were not surprising. The Army was unimpressed when it conducted its first-ever field training with the Guard in 1903. Guardsmen therefore welcomed full-time instructors from the Army, because the states' soldiers respected and valued the expertise of Army officers, even though they were often condescending toward the NG troops.

The Guard's solution to another challenge—recruiting—rankled their Army counterparts. National Guard units emphasized the fraternal and social aspects of armory life, which clashed with the Army's emphasis on tactical skills in combat, weapons use, and battlefield performance.[16] The requirement from time to time to break strikes harmed National Guard recruiting efforts, so the Guard pressed to be relieved of strikebreaking duties. It found ready allies in the Army for the establishment of state police forces, because the War Department realized that if governors had their own law enforcement apparatus, National Guard units could devote more efforts to military training. But only Pennsylvania established its own police force, so "the National Guard clung to its local ties, its traditional social and fraternal activities, and its reliance on state, local and private financing."[17]

The era of the First World War was one of great change and exposure for the National Guard. Its units were not combat-ready when roused for federal service in 1916 for action along the border with Mexico. Furthermore, the mobilization demonstrated that many NG volunteers did not even comprehend their service obligations; they did not understand that the government really could force them into active service. Many soldiers did not answer the call because they believed that as volunteers they had the right to decide whether or not they would go on active duty. Married guardsmen resigned in droves after the Mexican border affair because active service was so disruptive to family life.[18] Words like "worthless" and "hopeless failure" characterized regulars' comments.[19]

The National Guard gained more federal money in exchange for greater conformity to federal standards with the passage of the National Defense Act of 1916,[20] but the deployment to the Mexican border and the extreme demands that came with the declaration of war against Germany in 1917 put the careful implementation of that act on hold. When the United States set out to field a mass army for the war in Europe, that action threatened the National Guard's goal of maintaining local and state distinctiveness. For instance, the Army broke up a number of NG formations in order to create various types of units that better conformed to the kind of structure the Army wanted for the American Expeditionary Force. Then the Army renumbered the National Guard divisions. Assimilation appeared to be complete when the Army declared that there was only "one army," "the Army of the United States," although Guard divisions were at least able to wear distinctive shoulder patches.[21] The Army then poisoned relations between the two institutions when it relieved a number of National Guard officers and replaced them with regulars, generating deep resentment within the NG officer corps. They believed that the stated reason—"fitness"—was nothing more than a smokescreen for a scheme to provide regulars with more regimental and division commands.[22] In the summer of 1918 General Peyton C. March reiterated that "there would be no formal distinction between Guardsmen, regulars, and draftees."[23] After the Armistice, "the War Department de-mobilized Guardsmen as individuals and sent them home one by one." National Guard units had to be re-created virtually from scratch in the 1920s.[24]

Congress provided clarity regarding the place of the National Guard in national defense with the National Defense Act of 1920. The overall "Army of the United States" was organized into nine "corps areas," each of which gained an Army division, two NG divisions, "and three Reserve infantry divisions."[25] The Army and the Guard enjoyed a more amenable relationship in the 1920s and 1930s than they had before the Great War. The Guard even won a "legislative victory . . . by creating the National Guard of the United States under the Constitution's army clause," meaning that the institution was now "the constitutional state militia and a reserve component of the Army governed by federal law and regulations" at the same time. Fiscal stability characterized the 1930s, and more money for pay meant an end to recruiting shortfalls. By the late 1930s the National Guard provided the majority of the infantry divisions for the Army of the United States, and large-scale maneuvers became an annual occurrence in 1935.[26] Even with these improvements neither the National Guard nor the Regular Army was in good condition as war in Europe loomed, and both had to crawl toward combat readiness together.

During World War II some in the Army saw the National Guard as a wasted effort. The commanding general of the U.S. Army Ground Forces, Lieutenant

General Lesley J. McNair, wrote, "One of the great lessons of the present war is that the National Guard, as organized before the war, contributed nothing to national defense.... The structure of the National Guard was pregnant with disaster for the entire nation."[27] Since he was a key architect in the mobilization and expansion of the American Army, one has to take his criticism seriously. The National Guard, however, fielded eighteen half-strength divisions when war broke out between Germany and Poland in 1939; the Regular Army possessed but three at half-strength.[28] Was the National Guard really worthless, or was McNair's memo another example of the Regular Army chauvinism the National Guard had feared since World War I?

Pennsylvania's National Guard, comprising the 28th Infantry Division and several additional units, stands as an exceptional case study for the role of the National Guard during World War II.[29] Most National Guard divisions combined units from two to four states, but the 28th Infantry Division was virtually synonymous with a single state. Its commanding general from 1939 through the beginning of 1942, Major General Edward Martin (who was simultaneously adjutant general of Pennsylvania) was also the president of the National Guard Association and thus was deeply involved in the politics of the National Guard beyond the borders of Pennsylvania. The division's experience highlights National Guard–Army political relations, civil-military relations at the state and local levels, the time-consuming process of building a mass army, and the difficulties in preparing infantry for battle. Two famous generals served as its commanding officer following Edward Martin's tenure. The commander of the 12th Army Group in 1944–45, General Omar N. Bradley, reorganized and trained the 28th Infantry Division in 1942 while a brigadier general. Brigadier General Norman D. Cota provided critical leadership to men of the 29th Infantry Division (ID) on the beaches of Normandy, then commanded the 28th ID from August 1944 through the end of the war.

In *The Search for Order, 1877–1920*, Robert H. Wiebe illustrates several themes in American history that have influenced this analysis of the 28th Infantry Division.[30] Wiebe explained how the forces of nationalization, consolidation, and rationalization gained ascendancy in American life by the 1920s. When one uses these trends as lenses of analysis, it becomes easier to understand the character of the changes that happened to the Pennsylvania National Guard (PNG) from 1939 to 1945. Just as more and more aspects of American life were becoming singularly national in character, the local and state character of the PNG was becoming epiphenomenal to the accomplishment of its military mission and to the ethos of its soldiers. In World War II the 28th Infantry

Division was one of eighty-nine *American* combat divisions. A subset of the consolidating trend in America was the assimilation of the National Guard into the U.S. Army. This was so complete that by 1944 there were basically no more references to the Pennsylvania identity of the 28th ID nor to its National Guard origins. That stands in marked contrast to the constant references to state identity in the narrative of the Civil War less than a century prior. A key aspect of a rationally ordered world is the treatment of persons as objects, as components of a "machine," if you will, rather than as individuals. The institution of the Army perceived soldiers and National Guard units as bureaucratic components. They were to be moved about and utilized in whatever manner would most efficiently complete the task at hand. That made good sense during the planning, mobilization, and even the training phases of the war effort, but rationalization produced deleterious results when applied to men in combat. For example, General Cota treated the 28th Infantry Division as a military unit to be managed during the Battle of Hürtgen Forest in November 1944, instead of a formation comprising men to be led. He consequently wrecked his division. Having learned from that debacle, he led men during the Battle of the Bulge, and the 28th ID may have created the conditions necessary for the Allied victory. In the end, the National Guard was a latecomer to all of these trends, but they dominated the course this institution took during the war.

John Sloan Brown's *Draftee Division: The 88th Infantry Division in World War II* directly inspired this book.[31] Like *The Search for Order*, *Draftee Division* has influenced this work more than the footnotes imply. My examination of a National Guard division's development functions as a counterpart to his study of a conscript division. Michael Doubler's *Closing with the Enemy: How GIs Fought the War in Europe, 1944–1945* greatly assisted my analysis of the 28th Infantry Division, as well, even though Doubler's book is barely mentioned in my text.[32] My research supports his conclusion that the American Army was an institution with a steep learning curve during combat and that it fought skillfully. *Guard Wars* joins the growing number of Second World War division histories published in recent years, but concentrates more on the developmental pre-combat phase—and even the three years prior to America's entry into World War II—than do the others.[33]

From the beginning I decided to rely as much as possible on primary sources as a practicum of the craft of history as well as an effort to arrive at some original conclusions inductively. Because no one else had examined the majority of these sources, this method was in the end entirely appropriate. From that point on, the extensive first-rate scholarship on World War II, from the U.S. Army's official histories to works such as Peter Mansoor's *The GI Offensive in Europe: The Triumph of American Infantry Divisions, 1941–1945,* firmed up and disciplined my analysis.

Although the book concludes with chapters on the Keystone Division's exploits in battle, research into a combat division illustrates much more than battalion movements on a battlefield. The manner in which a country goes to war provides insights into the nature of that country. For example, the men who were fondest of the state and local identity of the Pennsylvania National Guard valued the fairness of a national draft and the expertise of professional officers of the United States Army so much more that they lobbied for both, even though they knew the Army would consolidate National Guard units into homogeneous organizations. Local civil-military relations were of vital importance to the success of the National Guard during peacetime. In his role as adjutant general, Edward Martin was particularly adept at gaining support from the Pennsylvania business community and at reassuring the parents of his recruits as to the honorable character of the National Guard. He traveled to and fro across the state persuading businesses to be tolerant of their employees who needed adjustments in their work schedules to allow time for military training, gaining their support as a result. With his community relations efforts he ensured that locals in New York, Virginia, and North Carolina welcomed his soldiers as their own when the Guard conducted military maneuvers in those states. The United States was a segregated society in the early 1940s, so the PNG resisted efforts of black Pennsylvanians to form or join local units. Finally, the division's poor state of combat readiness reveals that the people of the United States at their core did not take military preparedness seriously prior to Pearl Harbor. But once roused, the people of this state, like those of the rest of the country, put forth unceasing efforts toward achieving victory over the Axis powers.

2

Relations with the Army and State Identity

American national defense efforts in the late 1930s were hesitant and reluctant. They centered on the defense of North America; only a minority of Americans sought intervention in the crises in Europe and Asia. Feelings of contempt for the Old World in the aftermath of the First World War combined with the crisis of the Great Depression resulted in an inward focus within the United States. Preferring to rely on the protection of two oceans and the United States Navy, the country had not maintained a well-equipped or well-trained army, and the National Guard was not prepared to contribute to the defense of the country in a timely manner.

Indeed, the Pennsylvania National Guard remained in a number of ways an institution even more local in its character and outlook than the general mood of the country. In the opinion of some in the Army, the local character of the National Guard was an impediment to the accomplishment of one of its foundational tasks: developing the basic skills of soldiering. The requirements for an enlarged Army, the desire for maintaining the local distinctiveness of the Pennsylvania National Guard, coupled with the Guard's need for Regular Army expertise, generated conflict between the two institutions. National Guard leaders worried that a loss of a distinct National Guard identity would be a consequence of the Army's plans for expansion and greater readiness. Interestingly, the reaction of Pennsylvania guardsmen to the erosion of their local and state identity by their interaction with the Army was relatively mild, and illustrated that by the mid-twentieth century, localism was an emotional affinity of its officers, a preference—not a deeply held political conviction. Long-service PNG officers commingled local pride and identity with an appreciation for the Army's knowledge of the craft of modern warfare in a manner that would over time yield to the national Army's consolidating impulse.

Local Pride

Pennsylvania National Guard officers valued the local character of their units and the state distinctiveness of the formations in the PNG, but they feared that given the chance, the Army would break up and disperse guardsmen among the homogenized Army out of pure spite. The guardsmen also considered themselves to be the personification of the citizen-soldier ideal: the citizen who remains true to his civilian values, yet performs well in combat. Peacetime maneuvers and post-mobilization training from 1939 to 1941, however, proved this to be far from true. The guardsmen often lacked basic war-fighting skills and were eager for instruction from professional soldiers out of a desire to overcome that deficiency.

The men of the United States' eighteen National Guard divisions received that training from the Regular Army following the mobilization of the National Guard in 1940 and 1941. Concurrently the Army slowly assimilated the 28th Infantry Division and the other divisions into itself during 1942–1943, resulting in the divisions' loss of state identity. The ease of this assimilation resulted from the fact that members of the National Guard had already internalized the values of rationalization, centralization, and standardization that characterized American life during the first half of the twentieth century.[1]

National Guard leaders nevertheless worked against this loss of identity. Even before war broke out in Europe, they were lobbying for their special interests in an effort to resist the consolidating trends within the Army. Not only did the Guard want to be treated as the Army's principal reserve force, it also wanted National Guard units to retain their local and state identities even as they received the benefits of the Army's professional expertise. Major General Milton A. Reckord, the adjutant general of the Maryland National Guard and the chairman of the legislative committee of the National Guard Association, clashed with Army chief of staff General George C. Marshall over Army Regulation 130-10, *National Guard: Call and Draft into National Service.* Reckord believed it did not pay proper respect to the National Guard: "Whoever is responsible for the draft, in my opinion, lacked the proper conception of the position the National Guard now occupies as a part of the Army of the United States."[2]

He had reason to worry. One clause in the regulation did imply the elimination of National Guard state distinctiveness. During a presidential "order," guardsmen merged with the Army into a single body "without unnecessary distinction between individuals or units based on their component state of origin."[3] Complaining about the regulation, Reckord embarked on a letter-writing campaign to adjutant generals in other states. Marshall beseeched him to be circumspect, since animosity between the Guard and the War Department harmed both services, and bluntly reprimanded him for fostering distrust between state and federal authorities. From Reckord's perspective, no plan was satisfactory unless it allowed the National Guard to participate as it saw fit.[4] Reckord insisted on a distinctive National Guard presence that would not result in the loss of state identity.

Marshall subordinated state identity and regimental pride to efficiency and rationalism. The first manifestation of this change began modestly: the loss of state insignia on uniforms; National Guard soldiers were going to wear the same insignia as regulars.[5] The Army did intend to make some effort to protect the NG from complete amalgamation into the larger "Army of the United States." As much as possible during the coming expansion, it would fill NG officer slots with NG officers, but if that proved impossible after a month of trying, the Army would fill them from other sources. Promotions would "be based as far as practicable upon demonstrated fitness and capacity," not seniority or one's state of residency.[6]

Marshall did not wish to cast aside the National Guard, and he even asserted that because it formed 75 percent of the Army, "the National Guard must be considered as the first line of the Army." He admired the dedication of its long-service members, and wanted to help it overcome its shortcomings, especially its training deficiencies. His chief goal was to meld the National Guard, the Organized Reserve, and the Army into an efficient fighting force; this three-component system could not, however, function efficiently and maintain complete segregation among the three. One of Marshall's ideas for improving the capabilities of the National Guard was to associate Guard units with Regular units, not just Regular instructors. The Army could station, for instance, a company of Regular combat engineers plus a regimental headquarters with a battalion of National Guard engineers. They could train together, and such affiliations would lend themselves to later Army expansions.[7]

National Guard officers took the policy of being the country's primary combat-ready reserve one step further and saw themselves, as citizen-soldiers, as *the* first line of defense. To them, the Regular Army existed to provide instructors who would train volunteers and draftees.[8] Guardsmen took pride in not being as spit and polished as the regulars, as demonstrated when an anonymous Pennsylvania colonel mused, "Dear, dear, what will the Regular Army say? It's only the State Militia, only the damned State Militia that's won all the wars the United States [Army] has nearly always lost."[9] Some of the

PNG scoffed at federal inspections of their troops. After all, a leavening of veterans of the Great War in France still manned their companies and batteries. Keepers of the flame proclaimed that, for example, the 42nd "Rainbow" Division had not received any additional training prior to fighting the Germans, and it chased them out of France. Those Germans, however, were war-weary and chose to retreat. Others argued that their long service together alleviated many of the shortcomings that resulted from their limited number of training days.[10] Secretary of war Harry H. Woodring did not share the guardsmen's optimism. He cautioned that even though 40 percent of the Guard's officers had war experience, age and physical challenges were forcing many of them out of the military.[11]

Major General Edward Martin, the Pennsylvania adjutant general and the commander of the 28th Division, and Marshall were in agreement on a number of measures to improve National Guard units in ways that promoted both institutions' achieving their goals. In September 1939, Marshall looked forward to increasing the number of NG drill nights to sixty per year, facilitating weekend target practice and field exercises, gaining authorizations for 320,000 enlisted guardsmen, and adding two weeks of summer field training. He even wished to allow units in larger cities to recruit beyond their authorized strengths.[12] Martin welcomed the guidance from the Regular instructors assigned to the PNG. He held them in high regard; not once did he complain about the instructors the Army provided to his National Guard division.[13]

Expertise over Purity

Edward Martin wished to reconcile the contradictory goals of maintaining local esprit de corps and improving combat effectiveness through close relations with the Army. He crowed about the local identity of Pennsylvania Guard units, but at the same time he envisioned an even greater level of integration between the two services than did the chief of staff. At the 1939 Pennsylvania National Guard Association Convention, he conceded that the National Guard suffered from significant deficiencies and proposed "that we gradually place some regular army officers in positions of command and on our regular staff assignments" because he valued the expertise of those officers more than he coveted command billets for Pennsylvanians. Martin recommended that the PNG nominate the regulars it wanted and that the governor appoint them, but he did not explain how a state agency would exercise such authority over federal personnel.

With these proposals the Keystone State general revealed his priorities for his military organization: professional expertise over localism. Martin's suggestion calling for the blending of Regular and National Guard forces would cost the Guard some of the distinct identity it valued so dearly.[14] Martin even assigned his Regular instructor, Major Leo T. McMahon, as his G-2 (chief of staff for intelligence). That was an unusual move, since NG commanders seldom put regulars in senior positions over and above one of their own state residents.[15] He asked for three more regulars for the division, but they were in such short supply that there was no way the Army could loan him any more.[16] Marshall's staff had discussed placing regulars in the positions of executive officer and chief of staff in Guard divisions, but had not gone so far as to propose that regulars command NG regiments.[17] Momentarily the great tide of rationalization caught General Martin in its currents.[18] He placed a greater value on Regular officers' professional skills than he did on the retention of state identity and exclusiveness in the PNG officer corps.

The Pennsylvania National Guard Association also coveted the expertise of active duty officers and sergeants, so it asked for another Regular officer for each regiment, and for more Regular NCOs.[19] Endeavoring to encourage teamwork between the two institutions, Martin in December 1939 promised Marshall that the National Guard Association would support whatever legislation and policy Marshall desired.[20] Of a like mind, a few months later Marshall sought to assign relatively young regulars as the chief of staff for each NG division and as the executive officer for each regiment. Training and the development of staff work would be their raison d'être. Because these regulars would have no authority in promotions or responsibility for relations with the local community, they could remain aloof from those political minefields.[21] By August 1940 the War Department authorized sixty-seven more instructors for the Guard nationwide.[22] Marshall found the chief of the National Guard Bureau (CNGB) supportive, as well. He asked the CNGB to help him decide who would be exempt from service upon mobilization.[23] Furthermore, both agreed that they needed to convert nondivisional units of cavalry, infantry, and artillery in the Guard, which used 17,224 men and cost $3 million a year, to "essential corps, army, and GHQ [General Headquarters] Reserve and harbor defense units" in anticipation of the coming Army expansion.[24] This led to the eventual breakup of the Pennsylvania 22nd Cavalry Division, but Martin never voiced a strong protest against this decision. He was not the only Pennsylvanian to propose a closer relationship between the Army and the Guard. Colonel Eric Fisher Wood suggested that the Army use PNG assets to help create two of the new smaller "triangular" infantry divisions the Army was developing.[25]

As the United States expanded its armed forces during 1940 and 1941, individuals from outside the National Guard saw a downside to the National Guard's localism. After conscription began in September 1940, a number of Selective Service men argued that localism fostered cronyism and nepotism. These complaints from a number of National Guard divisions across the country filtered back to General Marshall. The new men asserted that discipline was poor in these divisions because the officers and men knew each other too well; consequently, the officers were too lax in maintaining standards.[26] Draftees at Camp Hulen, Louisiana, for instance, watched as promotions were awarded exclusively to National Guard boys from the hometown.[27] In some divisions, according to Marshall's sources, soldiers spent the bulk of their time planning for the weekend and rolled out of bed Monday morning too tired to perform. Newly drafted men found that many Guard officers did not know enough about their profession to teach others. Marshall reacted harshly to these reports. Although he stated that some of the NG divisions had "reached a high standard," Marshall demanded in a letter to each NG division commander that they raise the performance level of their divisions "immediately." By comparison, Marshall noted that he had not received a single complaint of low standards from Regular divisions staffed mainly by Reserve officers.[28] Martin denied that familiarity interfered with discipline in the PNG: "I do not feel in the 28th Division that acquaintanceship in home localities has interfered with discipline. The good soldier in the National Guard . . . will not permit personal friendships to interfere with duty."[29]

Federal Ascendancy

State, federal, and National Guard reactions to the fall of France in May–June 1940 illustrated federal ascendancy in national defense issues. The invasion grabbed front-page attention of Pennsylvania newspapers.[30] As a result of the French defeat, more and more Americans supported military preparedness, and the military crisis galvanized determination for upgrading the military's strength.[31] Already in session trying to solve the problem of the state's dwindling unemployment relief funds, legislators in Harrisburg reacted to the collapse of France with alarm. Their deliberations did not focus on military affairs per se, but instead centered on the economic contributions the state would make to rearmament. Deferring to the federal government, for example, the state gave its aircraft navigation beacons to Washington "in the interest of national defense."[32]

The fear of a German bomber attack alarmed many, so Pennsylvania's General Assembly appealed to the War Department to take the steps necessary to build up the country's air defenses. In particular, the assembly asked for air defense bases for the protection of the state's steel mills, and then appointed a committee to investigate the condition of the state's air defenses.[33] In a panic, the committee concluded that the state would be Germany's primary target and warned of German bombing attacks from either Canada or Mexico. The report also divided state and federal responsibilities for defense. "The state cannot be expected to furnish military planes. It is a job for the Army and Navy and they now have worlds of money." Pennsylvania instead promised flight schools and airports, evacuation plans and bomb shelters.[34] Frightened of air attack, the mayor of New Kensington demanded antiaircraft batteries, since the nearby Alcoa aluminum plant was certainly a target. The Pittsburgh Commission for Industrial Expansion called for a ring of twenty-three airbases, while Philadelphians demanded additional protection.[35]

Actually, there was no threat of aerial bombardment. Even if Germany defeated Britain in 1940, its bombers lacked the range to cross the Atlantic and attack American targets. The Germans' longest-ranged warplane, the FW-200, could fly only 1,100 miles. General Marshall knew this and briefed Congress that the proper air defense of the United States required the prevention of the establishment of German air bases on North American soil, not local defense against bomber aircraft.[36]

Military preparations had passed into the purview of federal responsibilities once and for all. States could help provide some of the military infrastructure and deal with the civilian population. Pennsylvania set up a state Council of Defense with local chapters to coordinate with the federal Council of National Defense. They coordinated defense endeavors outside the jurisdiction of the War Department, such as agricultural, industrial, and financial concerns, leaving military preparations to the federal government.[37]

Costs and Benefits of Mobilization

The threat of the German Army, the realization of the need to thoroughly train the National Guard, and, more than anything else, the shock of Germany's conquest of France combined to make a one-year mobilization of the National Guard in order to alleviate its weaknesses an obvious next step in the country's defense buildup. Just how to do so was one of the significant policy debates and bureaucratic challenges of the early 1940s.

Several factors commingled for the National Guard as the country geared up for war: mobilization, training, conscription, volunteering, NG-Army relations, and even civilian employment. When Marshall asked Congress for the immediate mobilization of the National Guard so that it could train adequately in July 1940, some Guard leaders, such as Milton Reckord, feared that mobilization would result in the end of the National Guard's existence, and that the Army would assimilate it and impose its own identity on the state formations, if not break them apart entirely. That is what Marshall had in mind, but not as a means of destroying a rival institution. Melding the National Guard into the Army was a rational and necessary step for creating a larger army. If further growth was necessary, he would break down both the Army and the National Guard divisions and use those trained men as cadres for the next larger wave of infantry and armored divisions.[38] He would then build a much larger Army. In this way the Army could expand in size from twenty-two divisions to sixty-six, or more. Such a policy would have terminal consequences for the state identity of NG forces.

Edward Martin also wanted a larger Army and called for a half-million-man Army in an April 1940 speech to the Pennsylvania Chamber of Commerce. He believed that an Army of that size would alleviate the need for intervention in the war.[39] Americans disagreed, however, on how to expand the Army: rely on volunteers, initiate a peacetime draft, or mobilize the National Guard.[40] That summer Guard and Army recruitment efforts were suffering alike. National Guard muster roles stood at over 96 percent, but the inflow of recruits was sufficient only to maintain strengths, not enough to man additional formations.[41] While 47,000 men joined the Regular Army, it netted only 15,000 in the first half of 1940 because 32,000 left.[42] The Army was meeting its quotas that summer only because it first set quotas it believed it could reach.[43]

Leaders of both services realized that a reliance on volunteers was not going to meet the nation's manpower needs and was going to result in an unfair exploitation of National Guard volunteers. Martin told the National Emergency Committee in Allegheny County: "I've never been for conscription, but it is the only thing we can do. We are not getting enough volunteers."[44] Likewise, Brigadier William E. Shedd, the assistant chief of staff for personnel, explained to Congress that without conscription, "the willing, and the willing only" would endure the sacrifices involved in defending the country.[45]

While conscription would result in a more equitable distribution of the burden of military service, mobilization would make it possible for guardsmen to concentrate on training to a degree that the peacetime pace of training did not allow. This they welcomed. Testifying with Marshall before Congress, Major General Milton Reckord spelled out the great amount of time it took to accumulate enough weekly drills at 1.5 hours a week to match just eight months of active service—six *years* in the Guard. When Marshall endorsed Reckord's conclusion, adding that the Guard lacked training, Senator Robert R. Reynolds, a North Carolina Democrat, gave the chief of staff a great opportunity to ruin NG-Army relations: "Then why have the National Guard at all if it is wrong? Why would it be unfortunate then to disband the National Guard, since you have said it is a wasteful and long drawn out operation?" When Marshall evaded the senator's question, the committee pressed him to move with them into a closed-door session so that he would feel free to speak his mind. The general realized that the image of him retiring with leading senators to a private meeting would have sent the ever-suspicious National Guard Association into a tailspin of worry and distrust. Circumspectly, Marshall reminded the committee that the Army was itself inefficient in many ways and that he could achieve remarkable results with National Guard readiness if he could just require its men to attend a standardized basic training course.[46]

Equity, Military Service, and National Guard Identity

Many National Guardsmen resented idea of being mobilized without a concurrent conscription act because of the issue of equity. An indeterminate number of Pennsylvania officers and men (the *Pittsburgh Sun-Telegraph* estimated them to be a majority) resented the threat of mobilization. They believed they would shoulder an unfair burden: "Why should we give up our civilian jobs while the rest of the country stays home and reaps the harvest of good wages?" complained one. He added that the same thing had happened during the 1916 confrontation with Mexico, when guardsmen chased Pancho Villa for $15 a month while the rest of the country took home $200.[47] Many men were finally getting jobs and feared losing them. The commanding general of the Illinois National Guard believed the crisis would have to worsen before guardsmen would cheerfully acquiesce, as did soldiers in New York a year later.[48] A Minnesota lieutenant warned the president that great numbers of guardsmen would resign if he mobilized them without first declaring a national emergency (FDR did not). What good would it be to train for a year and in all likelihood return to no job after demobilization? An Iowa officer predicted that the best men would be the first to resign.[49] These debates took place during the annual summer maneuvers, leaving guardsmen wondering whether they would return home in August, or find themselves federalized first. Many began to put their personal affairs in order, just in case.[50]

Pennsylvania's leadership encouraged their men not to complain about these issues during their summer maneuvers. Edward Martin was characteristically sanguine, stating that the PNG was "not only ready but willing to answer a call for mobilization."[51] The August 1940 issue of the *Pennsylvania Guardsman* used the fictional writer Willie Live ("will he live") to exhort their soldiers:

> Remember that you Volunteered to be a soldier. If you were tricked in, don't admit now you were a fool. You owe the gang something for the lesson they taught you. And, you know you expected to have fun and enjoy this profession . . . be cheerful! . . . why not enjoy the personal pride of being able to Take It. It builds strength and self-confidence in the man. A company of such men make a crack outfit. Now this kamp [*sic*] we'll be in competition with Regular soldiers. As Guardsmen we feel we are as good as they are—even better. LET'S PROVE IT.[52]

Colonel Eric Fisher Wood, the most outspoken of PNG officers, thought conscription could not start soon enough. Equitable sharing of the burden of military service among all United States citizens was most important to him. In an article published in October 1940, he ridiculed Congressmen "who say that they 'don't want too much American military preparedness, because it might offend Hitler.'" That summer he read about mounting delays in military equipment, bewildered that the country that led the world in automobile production let its Army suffer a 50 percent shortfall in trucks. Wood complained that American soldiers were not given enough time to train for war. He directly blamed "the behavior of a considerable minority of Congressmen who have delayed conscription by debating fatuous proposals (like 'Let's give the volunteering system a trial first')." Wood was adamant that only a draft could raise an army that was large enough, and equitable. People from all walks of life, not just the ones who enjoyed peacetime volunteer service, ought to share the burden of national defense.

> We in the National Guard feel very strongly about this. We are volunteers. Pace setters. We have given of our time and energy, at personal financial sacrifice, towards keeping alive the American military tradition over the last two decades. Now the opposition Congressmen say to us, "Suckers, YOU shall continue to hold the fort. You are hooked. You are to be called into the service. But the nation as a whole is not to be drafted to support you and back you up. We want you to be punished and

penalized for your far-sighted patriotism. You alone are to be taken away from your families and livelihoods. Moreover, in addition to your other difficulties and responsibilities you must now assume your own recruiting campaigns, to recruit your present units to war strength."

Wood concluded his tirade by quoting General Hugh A. Drum of First Army Corps Area, who had stated that the whole population had to contribute to preparedness and that the country was wasting time "by months of discussing the volunteer versus the conscription system. . . . Let us not be blind to realities. We are too few to meet the problems and must demand that all citizens be called to serve with us in preparing for the threatened crises."[53] No one writing for the *Pennsylvania Guardsman* refuted Wood's position. An editorialist for the *Allentown Morning Call* favored Selective Service as the fairest method and observed that men were not rushing to fill the ranks of the Army or the Guard.[54]

National Guard leaders knew that Selective Service would send large numbers of men from a variety of states into their units. Conscription would erode the state and local character of the PNG, as the National Defense Act of 1920 had made plain. That law stipulated that the National Guard would be subject to the "laws and regulations for the government of the Army of the United States," and the Army was now moving individuals around based on its manpower needs, regardless of the preference for unit cohesion.[55] For a National Guard officer such as Eric Fisher Wood, whose esprit de corps revolved around state and local pride, to demand national conscription illustrates that national defense had taken precedence over state identity and the preservation of state formations. That is a natural conclusion today, but the American past contains a number of examples of loyalty to states and distrust of the national government.[56]

Milton Reckord, however, feared that Selective Service would kill the National Guard. Preserving its distinctiveness was paramount in his mind. He worried that since conscripts were going to enter the Army Reserve following a year of training, some in Congress would see the NG as redundant, even though the National Defense Act of 1916 recognized the NG as the Army's primary reserve. If those soldiers could be filtered into National Guard units instead of Reserve formations, he believed that the Guard's future would be more secure.[57] The Army realized that extended active duty would result in a loss of identity for National Guard units.[58] Centralization threatened the National Guard, a collective of local institutions that favored state identity and distinctiveness from the United States Army.

Reckord had reason to worry. Under Selective Service, a soldier's skills, not his state of origin, would determine his duty assignment. If a division could not fill its vacancies from its own state, the Army could assign men from any source to it.[59] The War Department intended to pool selectees into a central reservoir, and then use standardized tests to ensure that it matched each man with a duty commensurate with his aptitudes and skills.[60] The priorities of centralization and rationalization (making the best use of an individual's abilities) clashed with the essence of the National Guard's priorities—local recruiting, local armory training, and the primacy of units being filled by men from the same town. Once the War Department began to federalize NG infantry divisions in September 1940, it did make efforts to assign men from a unit's state to that unit.[61] The Army supported allowing soldiers to reenlist in their National Guard units, "insofar as practicable," but the units also had to absorb conscripts from outside their respective states.[62] Although the War Department made efforts to send draftees from Pennsylvania into the PNG, the influx of draftees steadily diluted the state character of the 28th Division through 1941.[63] Furthermore, mobilization relieved NG soldiers of their duty to their state and suspended the governor's authority for a time. The units still existed, but "[d]uring the period of service in the Federal Forces, the organizations merely cease[d] to function as activities of the states."[64] Once in federal service, the National Guardsmen belonged to the federal government and could be sent to any units the Army saw fit.[65]

As early as March 1941, National Guardsmen nationwide were fast becoming a minority amidst the flood of conscripts entering their ranks. That month there were 255,000 enlisted guardsmen, and there were already 213,000 draftees. By June enlisted conscripts far outnumbered National Guardsmen: 542,000 to 269,000.[66] In 1941 men from the Officers Reserve Corps from around the country also began filling National Guard officer billets.[67] Full assimilation of Guard divisions into the Army became inevitable when Congress passed a law making soldiers subject to transfer without consideration for the component to which they belonged. The Army could transfer guardsmen to any unit it wished and was glad to be able to do so. The War Department adopted this "one army" concept on September 18, 1941.[68]

The Army's growth was not a hostile takeover; the Army and the National Guard Association met each other half way. For example, the Army took the fall 1940 meeting of the NGA seriously, sending Marshall and three additional generals to attend. During the proceedings, Edward Martin cited the merits of universal military training both militarily and in terms of citizenship. While he bluntly said that the NG had to be loyal to the War Department and to General Marshall, one has to ask why he felt compelled to state the obvious. The NGA also called for its enlisted men's pay to equal that of the Regular Army and urged Congress to assure that it would continue "as a first-line component of the Army of the United States after its year's training." Other resolutions included a request for the National Guard to be able to submit its views on the Guard's future role in national defense, an insistence that guardsmen be treated as the equals of regulars, and a condemnation of press reports that fostered distrust between the Army and the National Guard.[69]

As the war in Europe worsened, the PNG along with other National Guard organizations received new procedures on mobilizing for federal service in May 1940.[70] On May 31, 1940, President Roosevelt asked Congress for authority to call portions of the National Guard and Reserve to active service.[71] As of June the chief of staff was not quite ready to ask the president to mobilize the National Guard. Marshall wanted to expand the Guard and the Army in a manner that would not induce a political backlash, and would not nullify their training and their ability to divide and expand into a much larger army. He hoped to fill out the Army to its war-authorized strength of 400,000 by relying on unmarried volunteers. Marshall preferred an expansion of the Regular Army because he could train men faster in the Army than in the National Guard. Delaying NG mobilization would ease the pressures on guardsmen with jobs and families.[72] Besides, guardsmen were going to require "extensive" training to become battle-ready, a reason for their eventual call-up. Marshall wanted in due course to mobilize the Guard so that it would be reasonably well-trained when draftees started to enter their units.[73] In June, Marshall counseled Congress against a call-up for the time being, but a couple of weeks later, the War Plans Division suggested to Marshall that he ask for the federalization of the Guard. Since 85 percent of the public supported federalizing the NG, there was no longer any reason for public opinion to intimidate President Roosevelt into further mobilization delays.[74]

The War Department accelerated the steps necessary for mobilizing the Guard when the secretary of war authorized National Guard units to increase to Regular Army peacetime strength and authorized 110 more officers for Pennsylvania.[75] The NGB directed National Guard units to sift unfit soldiers from their ranks, particularly those who were too immature for the challenges of war, were physically not up to Army standards, were munitions workers, or were of the rank private first class or below with dependents.[76] Low-ranking guardsmen with dependents would have to resign because they would not make enough money to support their families while mobilized.[77] In October 1940 the 107th Field Artillery Regiment (FA) lost sixty-six men to discharges, including married men, those with other dependents, and individuals who held key jobs in industry.[78] Indeed, between July 23, 1940, and the induction of the divisions in the fall and winter of 1940–41, the NG discharged 94,000 men, mostly because they were married. The War Department also allowed them to resign voluntarily.[79] Now that was amazing. As soon as talk of mobilizing became serious, thousands of men ran for the exit. The National Guard was a part of the Army and existed to prepare for mobilization, full-time duty, war, and fighting. It would seem that the NGB had not thought through its enlistment policy and that many young men failed to consider the consequences of joining. The NG signed up other men it could not use in war, men aged 18–21 who joined without their parents' permission.[80] Not all was lost, however. The armories usually found new recruits, and they were often of better quality. Colonel Charles A. Curtis of the 213th Coast Artillery Regiment (Anti-aircraft) asserted that the recruits of 1940 were "the finest we have had in our service. They are intelligent, ambitious, and eager to learn.... They are tough."[81] Curtis was not the only one to be impressed by the new soldiers. Statistical studies found the 1940 recruit much healthier than his counterpart of 1917 in terms of chest size, weight, and IQ.[82]

Along with the NG mobilization debate, the country weighed the merits of enacting peacetime conscription. The Burke-Wadsworth Selective Service Bill was introduced in Congress on June 20.[83] Three weeks later the War Department approved a plan for a phased mobilization of the National Guard to begin on September 16. Those Guard units would mobilize at "present authorized strength."[84] After a summer of reticence, Roosevelt expressed unambiguous support for conscription on August 2, and on the 8th, Congress authorized him to mobilize the National Guard.[85] He mobilized the 30th, 41st, 44th, and 45th NG divisions with Executive Order No. 8530 on August 31. The PNG's 213 Coast Artillery Regiment joined six other mobilized anti-aircraft artillery (AAA) regiments.[86] The poor readiness for war and the consequent need for training were the primary reasons President Roosevelt mobilized the National Guard in 1940–41. Although he comprehended the threat to U.S. security better than many Americans, the president could not press for rearmament at a pace greater than the public would accept, or he would face an anti-interventionist backlash that would have left the country in greater danger than if he continued with modest increases in the Army and Navy.[87]

The 28th Infantry Division mobilized on February 17, 1941. Once federalized, the PNG lost its authority over who joined its regiments, but the Pennsylvania guardsmen looked forward to embracing conscripts as members of one team. The 109th Infantry identified them as fellow soldiers, not as outsiders. They were "entitled to every courtesy and respect." Do not call them "selectee, trainee, [or] draftee," just "soldier."[88] Conscripts began arriving on April 5, 1941. Private Alexander H. Lindsay, a lawyer from a prominent Pittsburgh family, was the first Selective Service product to join the division. Since he was an amateur radio expert, the Division Radio Operators School snatched him up immediately. The 104th Cavalry's forty-four conscripts arrived that month, mostly from Philadelphia and New York.[89] In June the influx of draftees turned into a flood when 6,956 were sent from Camp Croft, South Carolina, along with 904 from the Field Artillery Replacement Center at Fort Bragg. These men showed up having completed basic training, so they raised the quality of the PNG, and their arrival brought the division to approximately 18,000 soldiers. Greatly impressed with their bearing and quality, the Pennsylvanians welcomed them. They had been thoroughly trained in the use of the rifle, machine gun, automatic rifle, mortars, and pistols—generally ahead of their PNG brethren. The 109th FA exclaimed, "The selectees which we have recently received are indeed a promising group. They run the gamut from concert artists to truck drivers. We know that they will quickly orient themselves and become one of us." The Pennsylvanians planned to teach the new men the glories of their regiment so that they would begin to revere it.[90] Henry Fluck remembered that selectees and guardsmen got along well during 1941.[91] Pennsylvania esprit de corps was flexible enough to welcome men from outside the state. Most of the 194 conscripts who joined the 109th Infantry were from New York and New Jersey, with a mix of a few Southerners.[92]

The PNG did not distribute the new soldiers within the division rationally. Surprisingly, "the selectees were given their choice of regiments," whether or not they had received the appropriate training.[93] Because they assumed duties for which they had not been trained, commanders considered some of them poor soldiers, but the blame lay with the division. In confronting Martin over this problem, Marshall demanded that the standards of discipline, morale, and training at units like his exceed that of a replacement center.[94]

Although the PNG soldiers welcomed the conscripts, the quality of the new soldiers and ORC officers embarrassed the National Guard. Indeed, the War Department ranked National Guard personnel behind conscripts and Reserve officers. Speaking before Congress on April 22, 1941, General Marshall exposed his true assessment of the Guard in what he did and did not say. Asked whether the NG and the ORC had a feeling of unity with the Regular Army, Marshall said nothing about the Guard and praised only the products of ROTC, noting that "the most valuable single measure of national defense we had available was the Reserve Corps built up by ROTC."[95] He never ridiculed the NG in the manner Lesley J. McNair did, but his silence and obfuscation when Congress asked for his opinion is telling. Marshall's staff had completed a study of ROTC's successes and found that campus culture in the late 1930s into the early 1940s had made participation in the ROTC "Advanced Military Course" a high-status accomplishment, attracting the best male students at campuses across the country. Students and faculty did not consider someone an outstanding student unless he had taken the class, so there was intense competition for enrollment, which benefited the Army greatly.[96] Of the Selective Service men, undersecretary of war Robert F. Patterson wrote, "Opinion is unanimous that they are unusually intelligent and alert . . . many of them are superior in leadership to many officers of the National Guard and Reserve Corps."[97]

PNG officers were not jealous of the skills of Reserve Corps officers. Quite the contrary, they appreciated their abilities and potential and got along well with them during maneuvers. After the 1939 summer maneuvers in Manassas, Virginia, for example, Martin expressed every confidence that the reservists would be "very satisfactory" within the year.[98] Previous interactions between Guard and Reserve Corps officers had not always been so cordial. Guardsmen looked down on Reserve officers as novices with nothing but textbook answers for military operations, while reservists considered guardsmen good at getting along with their troops, but not at leading soldiers in tactical problems. This time, however, they saw expertise and "amazing esprit de corps and enthusiasm" among the guardsmen.[99]

Demobilization?

Even while war continued in Europe and Asia, Congress threatened to disembowel the Army by sending the National Guard and Reserve troops home in September 1941, a specter *Time* magazine called "terrifying."[100] The one-year mobilization was set to expire that month, just as the reservists, and active-duty forces for that matter, were gaining proficiency in the craft of war. Marshall turned to Edward Martin for advice about how to brief the president on the matter, asking him as early as May for his prediction on the Guard's reaction to a possible six-month extension of active duty.[101] Martin replied that NG soldiers supported building up the Army to a level sufficient to deter other nations from attacking, even as they longed to return to civilian life. He added that sentiment for extended active duty was more favorable in the PNG than elsewhere because it had not been federalized that long. Martin wished, however, that FDR would speak plainly to the American people about the severity of the security threat to the United States. He was confident in the Guard's willingness for an extension "as long as the emergency exists."[102] Marshall advised the secretary of war that the president needed to make the case for extension, emphasizing the need for a quick decision. Returning to civilian life required planning, he noted. Soldiers needed to sign apartment leases, register for college, and so on. Employers urgently wanted to know if they were to get their employees back. States needed a decision so as to know whether they should go forward with "home guards" or halt their creation.[103]

Guardsmen from other states, namely those of the 44th (New York) and 29th (Maryland) Divisions, were clamoring for demobilization. The front page of the *New York Times* indicated in mid-July that two companies of the 174th Infantry Regiment had telegraphed Senator Burton K. Wheeler, a Montana Democrat, to protest against extended active duty. In fact, the entire regiment appears to have been ready to return to civilian life immediately.[104] Some guardsmen were bitter since they had not made plans to be away from their businesses longer than twelve months.[105] Milton Reckord of the 29th Division had promised Congress that 90 percent of his enlisted men supported the extension, but actually they were in terrible spirits, and said, "s____ on him," whenever they referred to the general. Soldiers at some camps were openly drunk, cussed at and intimidated their officers, and in general rejected the Army as a worthwhile use of their time.[106] Soldiers hated marching, resented the extreme weapons shortage, and wondered what purpose their sufferings served. The best solution many officers could think of was simply to work the soldiers to exhaustion so that they "would be too tired to gripe."[107] The chief of the National Guard Bureau visited most of the NG camps himself to study the men's thoughts on extended active duty. He found no protests from soldiers busy in the field. When he floated the possibility of an extension to ten thousand men of one of the divisions, they cheered.[108]

Theodore Huntley of the *Pittsburgh Sun-Telegraph* warned that if the Guard went home, the government would probably federalize it again shortly after demobilization.[109] As the threat of demobilization peaked, Martin insisted that the PNG's morale was "very high."[110] Concerned, the War Department asked the *New York Times* to assess NG and Army morale across the nation. Hilton H. Railey, the *Times* reporter who investigated and wrote the resultant report on morale, discovered that morale was awful in the extreme. He and his publisher, Arthur Sulzberger, found the data so alarming that they kept their promise to the Army not to publish it. Marshall went one step further and classified his report "secret."[111] Wherever the exact median lay, the solid morale the 28th Division exhibited during the interminable crisis may have been Martin's greatest accomplishment. Low spirits plagued much of the rest of the Army, but there is no evidence of similar feeling among the PNG.

Demobilization of the Guard, Reserve officers, and conscripts would have been an unmitigated disaster for American security, resulting in two-thirds of the Army's soldiers returning to civilian status, the breaking up of combat units, and the wrecking of the combat capability of what remained. Demobilization would have affected the whole Army, not just the NG. For instance, most of the officers in the 1st Infantry Division were reservists. Send them home, and the division existed only on paper. Undersecretary Patterson noted that statutes [Public Resolution No. 96, 76th Congress] supported an extension: "Whenever the Congress has declared that the national interest in imperiled, such twelve-month period may be extended by the President to such time as may be necessary in the interests of national defense."[112] Marshall warned that even without further expansion, the U.S. ground forces could not function without the National Guard's "special supporting units—antiaircraft, heavy artillery, engineers."[113] FDR appealed to Congress on July 21 to extend the active duty time of guardsmen, reservists, and Selective Service soldiers.[114] A Gallup poll eight days later revealed that just 51 percent of the public supported the extension.[115] The Army was in real danger of being gutted, but fortunately, the House passed—by one vote—a law that permitted the president to continue the time of active service for six more months. The only qualifier was that the Army release men with dependents.[116] Democrats had expected to pass the measure with greater support.[117] FDR extended the time of federal service another six months on the 21st of August with Executive Order No. 8862, and morale improved.[118]

The debate over conscription and National Guard mobilization in 1940–41 was a profound window into United States military policy. With Hitler brandishing his weapons in the background, the federal government first debated the federalization of the NG, and then essentially had to lobby National Guard soldiers and the American people for their permission to do so. Here lay a great contribution of the National Guard to the country's preparation for war. The complexities of mobilization forced the government, the people, the Army, industry, and the civilian-soldiers themselves to stop, count the costs of mobilization, and arrive at a solution acceptable to all.

"Swimmandos" on maneuvers in
Louisiana, 1942 (facing top)

Barracks for 1st Battalion,
109th Infantry, Penclawdd, Wales,
February 1944 (facing bottom)

Troops in Percy, France, August 1944

110th Infantry in Paris, August 29, 1944

28th ID soldiers marching through Paris, August 29, 1944

28th ID armored car on the march through Paris, August 29, 1944

109th Infantry in Arlon, France, September 1944

Infantry combat in France, 1944

Sherman tank with extra protection from *Panzerfausts*

3

Readiness and Training

1939–1941

Mobilizing the National Guard along with the Regular Army was a basic assumption of national defense planning, and as far as the war plans were concerned, making use of National Guard forces was not as optional as the debates of 1940 and 1941 made it appear. The United States was not ready for war when the security crisis in Europe worsened in 1938 and 1939, nor after mobilization began in 1940. America had some war plans and a few hundred thousand soldiers at that time, but these served as only a starting point.

National Readiness

Unjustified optimism characterized the nation's war plans in 1939. The 28th Division formed a significant portion of the "Initial Protective Force" under the War Department's Protective Mobilization Plan (PMP) that was supposed to field 420,000 soldiers, the majority of whom were to be National Guardsmen, to meet a national emergency. The nation's defense plan that year could not, however, field combat-ready forces in a timely manner. For instance, the core of Regular and Guard forces totaled only 260,000 troops. Assuming at least thirty days between mobilization and the outbreak of hostilities, the PMP envisioned 300,000–400,000 volunteers rushing to National Guard armories, followed by 200,000 a month until the federal government enacted conscription about sixty days later.[1] War Department plans required Pennsylvania to recruit 48,000 volunteers within two months.[2] This force was to be ready to fight within a month and at the same time enter training—two contradictory goals.[3] Moreover, it had to be able to wage combined-arms warfare against a capable enemy, a capability that required many months of sophisticated training to acquire.[4] These plans reflected an unrealistic attitude toward preparedness. The month that war broke out in Europe, divisions in both the Army and the National Guard were more than a third below the minimum strength necessary for effective operations.[5]

Neither the 28th Division nor the National Guard at large was ready for war in 1939, even though the chief of the National Guard Bureau (CNGB), Major General Albert J. Blanding, claimed that the eighteen divisions could go to war immediately if necessary; in the same breath, however, he admitted that they were inadequately prepared for such a situation. Blanding failed to explain how his forces could be ready for action and at the same time needed to receive equipment so they could carry out their mission.[6] Speaking before Congress in February, the assistant chief of staff of the Army, Brigadier General George C. Marshall, testified that both the Army and the National Guard badly needed refitting because of their "antiquated" weapons.[7] Even two years later Marshall had complained that he almost never found a National Guard artillery 2nd lieutenant who had fired more than one artillery shell.[8] For its part, few of the PNG soldiers managed to become qualified with their basic weapons.[9] An unnamed officer who evaluated the 1939 Manassas Maneuvers was livid over the lack of modern equipment. Losing his temper with a repetitive veracity, he fumed, "There was not a single 37mm anti-tank gun, there was not a single 37mm anti-aircraft gun, there was not a single light divisional howitzer, there was not a single long range heavy field gun, there was not a single light machine gun."[10] The First Corps area commander, Lieutenant General Hugh A. Drum, claimed that the Army was deficient in every kind of war materiel except armored fighting vehicles.[11] Seven months later Congress refused to appropriate enough money for trucks for the National Guard, even though General Marshall testified that the Guard had only a third of its necessary vehicles.[12]

The lack of proper weapons approached the absurd. Company D of the 110th Infantry Regiment, for instance, was supposed to possess a whole platoon of mortars, but it did not even have a single tube. Instead, the platoon had to rely on the largess of the steel mill where one of the officers worked. He fashioned ersatz mortars from steel pipes, with rubber bands with which one could launch little sacks of flour to simulate shell bursts.[13] During the 1939 field exercises, the Guard used cigar boxes and blocks of wood as stand-in mines. The 1903 Springfield rifle remained the soldier's primary weapon. Mortars were inaccurate and obsolete, and field artillery battalions relied on the French-designed 75mm cannon from World War I.[14]

The country had underfunded weapons production for many years. In 1933, for example, the Ordnance Department produced only fourteen 105mm howitzers, and no artillery of any larger size. Substantial increases in appropriations did not begin until fiscal year 1939 (FY39) because of public opposition and legislation such as the Neutrality Act of 1935. Most of what was accomplished up to this time involved planning, not weapons production. A significant portion of the FY39 upturn in appropriations was to help industry gain experience with weapons manufacturing techniques, not necessarily to turn out finished materiel in large quantities.[15] Indeed, the production base literally needed retooling. Machinists at the Springfield Arsenal found that their machine tools, some of which "antedated the Civil War," needed to be replaced before production of the new M1 infantry rifle began in earnest.[16]

Another reason that the World War I–era weapons had not been replaced was "a philosophy of perfection held by many members of the General staff," as well as the infantry branch, the artillery branch, and the Ordnance Department. They wanted all of the bugs eliminated before beginning mass production. As a result, soldiers were "immediately enthusiastic" over the M1 Garand semi-automatic rifle, the replacement for the very popular M1903 Springfield. Although work had begun on the M1 in 1901, the Army did not "standardize" the design until 1935, and only two thousand had been produced by 1938.[17] Mass production of Garands did not commence until the end of 1940, following tests and trials against three other rifles.[18] Other weapons, such as the .50 caliber machine gun and the 105mm howitzer, were designed and produced more quickly. The Army's 37mm antitank gun, however, was "obsolete before it was standardized" in 1939 because the Army designed a highly mobile weapon to defeat existing tanks, not those that would be produced a few years hence.[19]

Just as a fiscal parsimony had hindered weapons development, a lack of money had long been a main contributor to poor National Guard readiness. While states were responsible for the oversight of their National Guard formations, the federal government was supposed to provide most of the money. States certainly were not going to make up for the shortfall in federal funding, and Congress during the interwar years had no incentive to ensure that the National Guard had modern weapons and equipment. For their part, governors wanted the Guard only for riot control and disaster relief.[20] Even with a world war looming, the Army failed to keep the National Guard accountable for war readiness. Inspections focused on the storage facilities in armories and on readiness to suppress rioters.[21] In October 1939, Martin and his colleagues rightly blamed Congress for the paucity of funds for the National Guard, but the Army had made a policy choice that made it also culpable.[22] Given the choice during the 1930s between spending money on weapons research and preventing the Army from going below a minimum number of personnel, the Army chose to hold on to soldiers. It did not wish to rearm until funding allowed both the maintenance of its personnel needs and the money for new weapons production. Modernization therefore lagged throughout the decade.[23] The division of allocations between the federal and state governments did not result in a sharing of responsibility, but instead provided a convenient means for both parties to pass the buck ad infinitum.

The PNG before the War

As Congress refused to fund national defense with any great seriousness during the lean years of the Depression, members of the Pennsylvania National Guard approached their duties with varying levels of seriousness, especially before Germany's invasion of Poland. One of the PNG's own inspectors chided his fellow officers for being overweight. Almost one hundred officers exceeded weight standards and were not going to be able to handle the rigors of field operations. Too old and too fat, some wore corsets, others promised to take off the pounds next year, and the remainder excused themselves as "naturally big." Some looked ridiculous, "[l]ike the overhang of a barn door in the Pennsylvania Dutch Country." One insisted that nature was just storing energy in case he got sick, and besides, the walking the doctor recommended was mind-numbing. Several were recruited as Santa Clauses, and women said their men were so huge that they had two boyfriends.[24] Secretary of War Harry H. Woodring was not laughing. He sent letters to the states' governors urging them to whip their officers into shape; too many had broken down physically twenty years prior during the Great War. The PNG did not respond with any sense of urgency, even though Governor Arthur H. James promised compliance.[25]

If the men had no weapons or time for training for war, they found time to form sports leagues. The Guard supported these pastimes because it believed they fostered esprit de corps and teamwork as well as successful recruiting.[26] Soldiers in the 111th Infantry suffered injuries from football, while each regiment fielded a basketball team. Intramural leagues were common, and armories changed their sports with the seasons.

Articles in the *Pennsylvania Guardsman* covered the games and high jinks thoroughly and with plenty of inside humor. During one inspection by the Army a soldier asserted that the Articles of War "tell how to pitch tents." An artilleryman allegedly used a 155mm howitzer to kill groundhogs. A man who later became a first sergeant initially thought his unit was a local club and asked how much dues were when he enlisted.[27] Recruiters assured another young man that in uniform he would get more dates. He mused:

> I think I'm goin to like this army life. Drill lasted only an hour and a half. Wasn't hard work neither. Got a big kick out of foolin around with the gun. They called it a 37 or something. . . . A guy by the name of Sgt. Winkler got up and told how to shoot over the top of a hill without hitting the hill. . . . Capt. Browell got the company a new ping pong table. Boy is it a honey. Had to wait two hours before I got to play.[28]

Reports on deer-hunting excursions, tournaments, and general silliness rivaled in scope stories warning that war was imminent and that the men had to improve their combat readiness. At times, cavalry training took on the character of a weekend outing. During one such winter excursion, men of Troop A, 103rd Cavalry, from Philadelphia rode to Valley Forge and back, spending the night at a farm in Lafayette Hill. The cabin for the soldiers "[p]rovided comfortable and luxurious accommodations and the atmosphere provided by the open fire place gave us a peace never found in the city."[29] Inauspiciously, the 103rd Engineers lost a shooting competition to a Philadelphia rifle club. Fraternal life like this exerted a strong pull on many in the PNG, as with one sergeant who wrote a poem about enlisting again because of the joyous experience of the annual summer encampment.[30] It is no wonder that the National Guard historian Jim Dan Hill later wrote, "These qualities gave most units many of the characteristics of a civic welfare organization and a fraternal order."[31] Only the officers and some NCOs were longtime members, so one could characterize the ethos of the mid-twentieth-century National Guard as akin more to the institution of the volunteer fire department.[32]

Calls for Greater Preparedness

Change took place slowly in the months following Germany's invasion of Poland, and Congress began to pass legislation supportive of greater readiness. Even though anti-interventionist members waged a filibuster during October, the tide was turning and the majority of Congressmen were beginning to favor greater preparedness.[33] Fed up with the absence of appropriations for military equipment and weapons, the Pennsylvania National Guard printed an open letter in June 1940:

Dear Mr. Congress,

I am only a soldier in the National Guard. It's my duty to defend my country with my life in time of war. But, Mr. Congress, this I cannot do, unless I have weapons and equipment with which to meet all comers. I also need training to fit me for this noble career (defending the nation). So please Mr. Congress, in as much as you control the funds which can make my job much more secure and efficient, won't you give this matter your urgent attention and consideration? Remember, without equipment and training, our defense is no stronger than our weakest units.[34]

Once Germany overran France, some in the PNG lost patience, incensed over Congress's earlier refusal to allocate greater appropriations for the National Guard so that it could conduct "[d]rills which are sorely needed to keep our soldiers and new members up to snuff. Congress should realize that these are serious days for guardsmen. It's upon their shoulders that the first burden of National Defense shall rest, if war should occur."[35] By the time this guardsman's complaints were printed, the budget included money for a six-day period of voluntary supplemental training.[36] Meanwhile, PNG units tried to complete what training they could in the limited time they had.

Training

Sound military training is a prerequisite to readiness for combat operations, but some in the PNG believed that they were trained so well that federal inspections were unnecessary.[37] Others in the National Guard asserted that the institution consisted of "shock troops," but Regulars asked how they could be so good if they trained only an hour and a half a week?[38] In comparison with the Regular Army, National Guard training was far from sufficient. Guardsmen did not have to go through an intensive basic training course. They instead trained at a snail's pace at their local armory one and a half hours a week for forty-eight weeks over the course of a year. Instruction was elementary, emphasizing parade-ground marching and rifle-range marksmanship. Tactical instruction amounted to thirteen hours of squad and platoon tactics.[39] By law they could not train more than twelve hours a month.[40] The CNGB had believed in 1938 that this was not an impediment to training and readiness.[41] Following the National Guard's 1939 field maneuvers, however, Maryland's adjutant general, Milton S. Reckord, noted that "National Guard Units are not well-prepared for field maneuvers. By that is meant that the Armory training does not fit them for field service"—a stunning comment from the National Guard's most vociferous defender.[42] Among the most serious problems was that the PNG had to keep training raw recruits; it could never build up an adequate mass of trained veterans. Edward Martin admitted that "it is believed that in the National Guard where *the turn-over is about one-third of the strength annually*, preliminary training should be limited to perfecting the Battalion in action and training in staff functioning" [italics added].[43]

Several Regular Army officers served as training advisors to the PNG, and they played a key role in driving it toward some modicum of combat capability. Some were outstanding, such as Maurice Rose, who functioned as the instructor for the 103rd Engineers from 1937 to 1939. He later commanded the 3rd Armored Division until he was killed in action in March 1945.[44] The Army claimed that they were "specially selected" men, but it had not chosen any to attend the Army War College. Of the 424 Regular instructors on duty in 1939–40, only 175 had completed the Command and General Staff School or better. Collectively their morale was "very low." A couple of proposals to improve their status included making new lieutenant colonels NG instructors so that they were junior enough to still be eligible for promotion, and ensuring that some officers on the War Department General Staff had NG instructor experience, thus making Guard assignments desirable for Regulars. Another idea was to let National Guard commanders rate their Army instructors.[45]

Pennsylvania's senior Army instructor, Colonel Ralph H. Leavitt, proposed an impossibly ambitious ideal for peacetime training, asserting that the NG and Regular Army were "one" and that the Guard should utilize "the same methods of training as the Regular Army."[46] General Marshall knew, however, that the Army was not the ideal model for armory drills. Guardsmen often took three hours to teach a task when one was sufficient, and National Guardsmen had no time to waste. For that reason he wanted Army training guides to be written so as to take into account the guardsman's time constraints.[47] General Martin wisely suggested that the Guard limit itself to training in units no larger than battalions because of the limitations of time. He wanted his division to gain proficiency in small-unit operations first before tackling larger goals.[48] Even Marshall was overly ambitious, desiring to provide Guard units with money and authorization for them to train not only as battalions, but also as regiments and brigades.[49]

1939 Supplemental Training

President Roosevelt knew that both the Army and the Guard were in poor shape, so twelve days after the German invasion of Poland he raised the Army's authorized strength from 210,000 to 227,000 by voluntary enlistment and allowed NG forces to expand from 200,000 to 235,000 men, with a proportional increase in officers.[50] Marshall hoped to fill out the Army and National Guard to 250,000 and 450,000, respectively, by February 1940.[51] The War Department also realized that the National Guard was poorly trained, so as a first step to alleviate that shortfall, it authorized seven additional days of field training near units' home bases and an extra 1.5-hour armory drill per week beginning in September 1939.[52] The Army also tightened its scrutiny of the guardsmen. No longer would regulars assigned to Pennsylvania inspect the state's units, for instance; instead, officers from Third Corps Area would evaluate each formation.[53]

This supplemental training paid great benefits, which the soldiers noticed and appreciated. It was pretty rigorous, as well, involving fifteen- to twenty-hour days.[54] The PNG took these efforts to heart during the fall of 1939 when it began the supplemental training on October 28. Soldiers practiced simple tasks. The 166th Field Artillery Regiment, for example, concentrated on learning to fire the 37mm cannon, firing five hundred rounds. Its Regular Army instructor also led it on a lights-out night march. Later in the week it practiced communications with an observation aircraft from the 103rd Observation Squadron.[55] At the Tobyhanna military reservation, the 109th Infantry and 109th Field Artillery Regiments practiced for a week.[56] Company C, 112th Infantry, from Ford City had its two platoons fight a simulated battle against each other. Company D from Butler found that the frigid weather did not prevent the field exercise from being a great success. In Bradford, Company K exposed its soldiers to tear gas so that they would learn how to use their gas masks properly. Over in Kane, Company M taught its men night patrolling, prohibiting smoking cigarettes, using flashlights, and speaking out loud.[57]

Headquarters company of the 110th Infantry concluded that it had learned more about setting up telephone communications between two battalions during this encampment than it would have in five years of armory drills. New Brighton's B Company saw a spike in its enthusiasm and performance. Other units reached the same conclusion. The men did not just "pitch tents": they practiced night combat, horsemanship, firing, care for battle casualties, and ceremonies. Studying how to handle large formations, the division and brigade staffs drove automobiles to the theoretical positions of their imaginary troops, analyzed their problem, and explained their solution—an innovative training method for the 28th Division. With only a tank company and no accompanying air support, however, the exercises were similar to a World War I battle sans trenches, but everyone agreed that they learned more from one solid week of training than from three drills over weekends.[58] The only live fire came from nearby deer hunters, whose stray bullets made the soldiers of the 112th Infantry from Kane nervous: "[W]ith the opening of deer season, hundreds of ambitious (and probably near sighted) hunters were gunning the Allegheny National Forest surrounding our field training area. . . . Combat troops reported scattered rifle fire throughout the sector, but no casualties."[59]

These training exercises showed that National Guard soldiers could do many of the tasks required of them if just given the time to learn how to do so. The basic training they had to conduct, however, functioned to expose the shortcomings of armory training. At least they did not spend their time on the parade ground. The PNG's commanders and soldiers agreed that the fall training was a resounding success. Soldiers were universally enthusiastic in their participation and over what they learned. Because the PNG staff officers had to plan and execute the exercises, they learned more about making site surveys, obtaining land-use leases, and arranging for transportation.[60]

Units in other states had similar experiences. High attendance nationwide surprised the War Department because it came during a period of growing employment opportunities.[61] Colonel Charles C. Haffner of Illinois, however, warned Marshall not to be misled by the outburst of support for this seven-day training experiment. People in the Midwest, he argued, were skeptical of the need for greater readiness.[62] Some members of Congress, such as Georgia's Senator Richard Russell, doubted the benefits of the training and accused the Guard of going "off to the seashore for a couple of weeks." Yet the War Department deputy chief of staff, Brigadier General Lorenzo D. Gasser, defended the extra training days' value. All the reports he had received were "uniformly enthusiastic." General Marshall testified that the absence of parades, ceremonies, and visitors helped to make the short exercises the most effective training the Guard had ever had. He also noted that the world situation caused the men to take their training more seriously.[63] Martin noticed that good weather had made it possible for the guardsmen to accomplish more than expected for that time of year, but he did not want to make cold weather training the norm.[64] The PNG witnessed an attendance rate of 87 percent and full support by the soldiers for additional weekly drills.[65] What is more, the soldiers were attending half of their armory drills without being paid for them.[66]

1940: Catching Up

With the onset of winter, armory activities returned to their more mundane pursuits, even as General Martin urged an emphasis on basic drill and weapons training. With the coming of spring, he held a division and brigade staff school at Indiantown Gap April 5–7. Ninety officers of the 28th Division and the 22nd Cavalry Division also conducted a "terrain exercise," postulating a defense against an invasion of the East Coast. It provided practice in writing orders and plans, as well as a walk-through of the problem, with a discussion of solutions.[67] In a briefing for the PNG at Indiantown Gap, Army officers who had been observers of the war in Europe passed on their evaluation of the German Army, noting that the infantry division remained the foundation of their army. Combined arms warfare, decentralization, and an absence of detailed directives characterized the Wehrmacht command philosophy.[68]

For its part, the U.S. Army shortened its staff courses for National Guard officers to twelve weeks in order to cycle more officers through a minimal curriculum.[69] To help make up for this shortfall, Third Corps Area established a General Staff College for Guard officers at Fort Meade, Maryland, for March 1940. Pennsylvania sent ten lieutenant colonels. The PNG also sent twenty-one officers and a sergeant to the Army's "service schools"—mainly the Infantry School at Fort Benning, Georgia. There they would gain expertise in infantry and artillery operations.[70] Three hundred twenty-six Guard officers attended service schools during fiscal year 1939, a dismal 2 percent of the officer corps.[71] That same year thirty-three Pennsylvania National Guard officers and seven enlisted men attended, with six of them going to Fort Benning.[72] By 1940, however, only 6,800 National Guard officers out of a total of 21,074 had completed any of the service schools during their careers.[73] Considering that the country had been enduring a severe economic depression for ten years, this percentage is commendable, because few men could afford to get away from their jobs for the training. In anticipation of large-scale maneuvers in the summer of 1940, the War Department provided funds to send National Guard division commanders and staffs to field maneuvers with Regular Army divisions. This joint staff training was of immense help to the guardsmen.[74] The chief of staff hoped that guardsmen could complete their basic training prior to the summer 1940 maneuvers. The War Department's goal was for its divisions to be able to enter combat with little notice and wage modern warfare, but the Guard could not achieve these goals learning at a pace of 1.5 to 3.0 hours per week.[75]

In addition to armory and field training, many Pennsylvania National Guardsmen pursued the Army's correspondence courses in order to acquire classroom knowledge of tactics, strategy, and command. Nationwide, 13,153 out of 14,306 Guard officers were enrolled in the Army Command and General Staff School's "extension courses," while over 19,000 enlisted troops took courses to prepare themselves for commissions.[76] The Army geared these courses toward preparing a citizen-soldier army of guardsmen and Officers Reserve Corps men for war, a wise choice since the National Guard Bureau expected 80 percent of the Army to come from the civilian sector. There were six courses, one for each of the grades 2nd lieutenant to colonel. In anticipation of exponential growth in the size of the Army, the NGB recommended that officers take the course for the grade above them—a captain would take the major's course. The Army assured prospective students that the courses would not take up a great amount of time, but the series for captains of infantry required 163 hours of study.[77] For men working full-time, caring for families, and completing armory duties, only the most conscientious National Guard officer could complete these courses. Some did. In 1938, 561 officers and 1,023 enlisted men nationwide completed at least one extension course.[78] Although the NGB could not force officers to complete these courses, several states required their guardsmen to do so if they wanted to be promoted.[79] The Army urged guardsmen bound for the Command and General Staff School to complete the extension courses through major as a prerequisite.[80] By 1940 almost all NG officers were enrolled in extension courses.[81]

Anticipating an expansion of the Army due to the crisis in Europe, the adjutant general streamlined the extension courses in 1939 so as to move more National Guard officers through the Command and General Staff School, as well as offering a fifteen-day in-residence course for Guard officers whose private business affairs prohibited them from taking off time to attend the complete course. Pennsylvania sent twelve officers to the short course in January 1939.[82] Marshall really wanted guardsmen who were successful civilian businessmen to attend a service school, but the most accomplished were also the ones who could least afford to leave their occupations for months at a time. Even with the shorter courses, how many employees in the late 1930s could ask an employer for two months off?[83]

Privates and sergeants in the Guard did not make the best use of the extension course program. Instead of improving their knowledge as noncommissioned officers—masters of the tasks of infantry combat—many focused instead on taking courses so as to qualify for officer commissions. These enlisted troops could obtain commissions in the "National Guard of the United States," whereupon they would be commissioned as 2nd lieutenants when the government federalized and mobilized the National Guard. A result of a 1933 amendment to the National Defense Act of 1916 that granted the Guard dual status as both the militia of the states and the permanent reserve of the Army, this was a way of opening the wartime officer corps to more citizens.[84] The only qualification requirements were that the man be in the active National Guard and that his application include "evidence of professional qualifications," although the regulation offered no suggestion as to what those might be.[85] In practice it would harm the 28th Division's efforts to field a proficient unit. These relatively experienced men would leave the enlisted ranks for the officer corps just when the division needed them the most: during mobilization and the influx of brand-new recruits in need of the guidance of experienced sergeants. For instance, when Company F of the 112th Infantry Regiment entered federal service on February 17, 1941, it had only four sergeants, and one of them was commissioned that day as a 2nd lieutenant. He was an unemployed machinist with a high school diploma and five years of experience with the regiment.[86]

The Army found such officers short on ability when the 28th Division was federalized in 1941.[87] Pennsylvania lost fifty-one enlisted men, many of whom were those much-needed experienced sergeants, to commissioned service in this way during the mobilization of 1941.[88] These newly commissioned 2nd lieutenants then often left their units for other assignments, further denuding the Guard just as it was about to receive great numbers of conscripts.[89] The acceptance of sub-par officer candidates was nothing new. A year and a half earlier Martin had been asked to "waive military ability qualifications for one year" for two desirable officer candidates.[90]

After the German invasion of France, preparing for active federal service became the National Guard's primary training mission.[91] Congress appropriated $5,469,962 for additional drills in March 1940, and added $19,309,100 the following year.[92] During fiscal year 1940, 675 National Guard officers and 144 enlisted men attended service schools, almost double the number from the previous year. The Corps Areas' abridged courses trained 169 staff officers in the use of combined arms and in the functions of divisions.[93] The Command and General Staff School (CGSS) formed a two-month-long accelerated course mostly for National Guard and Reserve Officer Corps officers, which emphasized division-level staff work. Of special note was a course at Fort Benning for National Guard division and brigade commanders, division chiefs of staff, and division G-3s if the chief of staff could not attend.[94] In the summer and fall of 1940, Pennsylvania sent twenty-six officers and enlisted men to service schools, all on a volunteer basis.[95] Edward Martin informed General Marshall that the guardsmen found this program challenging and instructive. They dove into it with enthusiasm, finding that it taught combined arms tactics well. The guardsmen were even learning how to become instructors themselves, which they appreciated since they knew they were soon to receive thousands of conscripts.[96]

This mad dash for military training revealed both how stagnant and insufficient National Guard peacetime training had been and the magnitude of what it took to build a massive army from what was in early 1940 a force of 227,000 regulars and 235,000 National Guardsmen into something exponentially larger.[97] Even though National Guard drills were increased to sixty per year, and even though they completed two weeks of large-unit field training in the summer of 1939 and three weeks in 1940, Guard units were spinning their wheels. They still needed an intensive round of basic training.[98]

Individual companies intensified their training during the fall of 1940 since their commanders knew that the War Department was going to federalize the 28th Division in early 1941. For instance, the antitank company of the 110th Infantry conducted night patrols to get used to winter conditions, and Company D practiced marching, tactics, and communications in Scranton's city park. One hundred men of the 104th Cavalry completed a 320-mile road trip in twenty-one vehicles to practice road discipline.[99] The regiments conducted officer candidate schools and trained new recruits.[100] To make federalization more efficient, the War Department authorized National Guardsmen two weeks of voluntary temporary duty with their divisions; consequently the 28th Division set aside February 3–16 for that duty. The division sent fifteen to a school for adjutants and seventy-five company-grade officers to the Infantry School at Fort Benning.[101] Generals Martin, Edward A. Stackpole, and John Aiken and Colonel Benjamin C. Jones upgraded their knowledge of combined arms warfare in a course for high-ranking National Guard officers at Benning. Martin told the press, "From a military viewpoint, the two weeks were the most interesting I ever experienced."[102]

The entire PNG officer corps was so inexperienced and in desperate need of elementary training that on January 26, 1941, it sent seventy-five company-grade officers to a thirty-day course at Valley Forge Military Academy, a boys' prep school. The academy's faculty trained the lieutenants under the assumption that they knew "absolutely nothing"—seven days a week.[103] Pushed to their limits, the officers made their way to the division's new barracks at Indiantown Gap to instruct the newly federalized troops. Martin was pleased with their progress and thankful for the training from Fort Benning. Realizing that his officer corps was sorely lacking in expertise, he pressed General Marshall for permission to send a second class through Valley Forge. Marshall agreed that the PNG needed to cycle another class through the school, but instead he set aside more slots for National Guard officers at the service schools. It was time for the officers to train their men.[104]

The kinds of training PNG soldiers had to repeat over and over proved that their peacetime regimen was unable to prepare them for their mandated mission of producing "units prepared to take the field on short notice at existing strength under the Protective Mobilization Plan and capable of conducting combined operations against an enemy with modern means of combat."[105] In fact, the Army found during the height of the war that it needed at least forty-four intense weeks to train new men in fighting divisions.[106] The PNG could never compensate for absence of a basic training course. At 1.5 to 3.0 hours a week, armory drills could not provide enough time for recruits to learn the rudiments of soldiering. The training course at Valley Forge, as useful as it was, was also the nadir: officers of an infantry division in a major industrial state had to go to a boarding school to learn the basics of warfare. Such was Congress's commitment to military readiness and to the National Guard in the years prior to World War II.

On Active Duty

The division received mixed reviews when it entered its year of federal service at Indiantown Gap on February 17, 1941. Major Generals Lesley J. McNair and Henry C. Pratt, along with several staff officers, began inspections even before then. They found its officers of varying quality. The 28th's operations officer, the "G-3," Lieutenant Colonel George W. Philips, had prepared an inadequate training program, so several inspectors, including the VI Corps and First Army G-3s, had to walk him through a revised syllabus. They nevertheless considered him qualified to supervise the division's training, noting that he had served as G-3 for five years and had graduated from the National Guard and Reserve Officer Course at Fort Leavenworth in 1935.[107] Brigadier General Eric Fisher Wood, however, proved to be unteachable, arrogant, and undisciplined. Major Thomas E. Lewis, who inspected Wood's 53rd Field Artillery Brigade, informed

McNair that Wood had acquired a reputation as a troublemaker while a student at the Command and General Staff School and was known to harbor bitter hatred for the Regular Army, probably out of National Guard chauvinism. Lewis added that "[v]ery little was accomplished in my conference with him as he insisted on doing all the talking. He has very strong ideas, many of which are contrary to training policies. . . . His conversation indicated a lack of knowledge of training directives."[108] McNair subsequently mused that Wood might "need a severe crack in the head" if he did not mollify his attitude. Major Leo T. McMahon, one of the PNG's Regular Army instructors, defended Wood's brigade as superior to most Guard field artillery brigades.[109] Captain Norman R. Mills, commander of the Signal Company, appeared to be incompetent, while the division signal officer, Captain Alfred H. Anderson, a manufacturer of electrical products as a civilian, left another inspector well-impressed.[110] Evaluators found the 62-year-old Colonel Horace J. Inman, commander of the 103rd Engineers and an employee of the Veterans' Bureau, too old for command. They also concluded that World War I veterans, especially those in captain's billets, were too aged for the demands of the job of company commander. Worse, the 103rd Regiment had no training plan in place.[111]

The PNG was not prepared for mobilization. Second Corps' G-3 directed numerous changes to the division's syllabus, and soon the 28th had to start basic training all over again, which would remain its primary task for some time.[112] A great number of the 28th's ranks had been recruited too recently to receive sufficient training at their armories. Most of the officers were pleased with the orders for basic training, for even veterans needed refresher training— a poor endorsement of their armory instruction program.[113]

McNair wanted NG divisions to complete a round of basic training before they received Selective Service men.[114] For the 28th Division, basic training began the week of March 15 and emphasized conditioning, small-unit training, scouting, patrolling, marching, and map reading. Bad weather, particularly ten inches of snow, drove the men indoors to learn about weapons care, truck maintenance, and "citizenship." Even though they had spent the previous month conducting road marches and parade drills to toughen the men, as many as 10 percent were in the hospital the first few weeks after arriving at Indiantown Gap.[115] Some of the public, such as Representative Sterling Cole of New York, thought conditions were too rough on the soldiers, but Marshall found the harsh conditions useful. After all, since the men were going to have to live and fight in snow and mud, they needed to become inured to that kind of life before entering combat.[116]

Along with toughness, independent thinking and initiative were charac-teristics the Army wanted to instill into soldiers. As a matter of policy, Brigadier General Francis B. Wilby of First Army, insisted:

> It is imperative that the execution of training be decentralized in ever increasing degree[s]. In combat, commanders of all grades must frequently act on their own initiative without reference to higher authority, and it is therefore essential that every possible effort be made to habituate them to make their own independent decisions and to act accordingly. Honest mistakes will not be made the basis of action that can be construed as censorious. Prompt action is what is required, even though including minor errors of judgment or technique.

Wilby ordered officers to permit "honest mistakes as a part of the learning process." He also wanted to see the division develop the ability to fight in a coordinated manner—"combined arms"—in which the PNG's infantry and artillery knew how to fight with armored and aircraft units, under a cohesive and flexible command and control system.[117]

Division personnel were creative in their training efforts. For instance, medics practiced finding "wounded" men in the dark and returning to camp with them without getting caught. Instructors used loudspeakers to narrate tactical demonstrations to large formations. Truck drivers for the 111th Infantry drove a seven-hour convoy at night through narrow mountain roads without using any lights.[118] Such initiative had support from the very top. In June, Marshall commented, "We are basing discipline of the individual on respect rather than on fear; on the effect of good example given by officers; on the intelligent comprehension by all ranks of why an order has to be, and why it must be carried out."[119] These ideals translated into an advantage when the division entered combat three years later.

Inspections

Army evaluators kept close tabs on the PNG during 1941. An inspector returned in March and found high morale and hard-working troops, and observed that "both administration and command situations are satisfactory." Lieutenant Colonel H. S. Clarkson's only serious concern was over the abilities of the quartermaster, Colonel Leo A. Luttringer, who appeared "old and frail." Clarkson concluded that at sixty-two, it was time for Luttringer to retire in favor of an officer in better physical condition.[120] General Drum was pleased: "General Martin and his command are progressing very well indeed. Excellent officers and men are very interested and are going at it with a serious approach."[121] A

June 1941 inspection was sanguine. Focusing on administration and the condition of facilities and equipment, the inspector rated nothing less than "satisfactory," and he graded troop appearance and training "highly satisfactory." He concluded that field work and marching "has shown improvement and the leadership is steadily improving. The Division is being developed as to morale, discipline and condition in a manner that is HIGHLY CREDITABLE [boldface in original]." He never subjected the division to a test of its battlefield capabilities, however, and offered no recommendations. The commander of II Corps Area, Major General Pratt, added his comments and passed on the opportunity to make himself look good by whitewashing the situation. Instead, he concluded that the division's proficiency and progress in training—its main priorities— were not yet good enough. "Considering all circumstances involved, the development of this division has been SATISFACTORY." In other words, the 28th had developed well given the circumstances of an inadequate cadre training a large number of new soldiers, but it was not yet a competent combat unit in his eyes. The adverse conditions to which Pratt referred included undermanning (772 officers, 9,865 men), a severe shortage of equipment, officer and NCO corps that were undertrained, and a low level of skill that necessitated a second round of basic training that summer. Martin's division had tried hard, but it was not combat ready, which is the only time a division should really be considered "satisfactory."[122] Finally, mobilization plans had not accounted for bringing National Guard cadres together soon enough so that they would be masters of their craft by the time conscripts arrived.[123]

Slow Progress

Once the basic training program concluded, one can see from regimental reports that the 28th Division worked diligently, if slowly, toward developing small-unit war-fighting skills. It had to complete combined arms training and division-level training by September 30, 1941. It had to learn to fight as part of a corps during October, then as part of an army in November.[124] The regiments made strides toward that goal. In May, for instance, the 112th Infantry moved from the firing range to squad tactics, while the 111th began battalion-level tactics in May, as well as machine gun and mortar firing, trench construction, and barbed wire use.[125] Soldiers even trained for gas warfare by donning their masks and walking through clouds of phosgene and mustard gas, by playing sports with the masks still on, and by firing artillery pieces and telephoning aiming coordinates through their masks over the phone.[126]

The 112th Infantry completed its longest march to date, a fifteen-miler, in late May. Soldiers of the 111th and 112th Infantry marched as far as eighteen miles to attack Troop C, 104th Cavalry, perched atop Mount Graetna.[127] Learning night tactics, the 111th taught its men how to judge distances by seeing a lit cigarette and by hearing a machine gun being cocked. Later, soldiers of the 112th traveled in their trucks at night without lights to a site where they practiced defenses against armored forces and air attack.[128] During more advanced three-day field exercises the men learned how to find new sites for artillery pieces and how to register fire. During a rainstorm one night, men of the 103rd Engineers assembled a 300-foot pontoon bridge. Martin commended them when they deployed another 300-footer in only eighteen minutes.[129] Quartermasters showed men from each unit how to load vehicles onto railroad flatcars, because every unit had to know how to do so on its own. Combat engineer training was a priority, and no one was to detail them away from their commanders and their training agenda. In fact, they often had to borrow men from combat arms units and provide supervision and guidance for engineering tasks.[130]

By June, however, many soldiers had not yet qualified with small arms. In the 109th Infantry, for instance, approximately 25 percent had qualified on the World War I vintage Springfield 1903 rifle, 59 percent on the new M1, 65 percent on a heavy machine gun left from the Great War, 47 percent on the 60mm mortar, and 86 percent with the bayonet.[131] Physically the men were becoming tougher. When the 110th Infantry marched to Mt. Graetna in the rain, not a single man fell out. Soldiers of the 112th spent two weeks on patrolling and truck loading. In the middle of the night on June 20, they went to Mt. Graetna and attacked a hill that the 111th Infantry held. Its writer noted that even though basic training was done, "There has been no noticeable let-up in the pace of our learning. The value of thorough seasoning [physical toughening] as demonstrated by the war [against the 111th Infantry] has not been lost on us."[132]

Continuing shortages of weapons and equipment forced the Pennsylvanians to improvise. The division endeavored to add some realism to its training by using klaxons, rattles, banging metal bars, blanks, smoke, tear gas, and TNT charges to simulate the battlefield environment.[133] A few modern weapons began arriving in March, including sixteen lightweight .30 caliber machine guns and 1,200 M1 Garand rifles. Both enhanced the soldiers' firepower and mobility. They could carry the new machine guns by hand and fire them from the much more survivable prone position. Only nine hundred men, all from the 109th Infantry, got to fire the new M1s.[134] These numerous materiel shortages stymied training. The division lacked enough antitank and antiaircraft guns,

105mm and 155mm artillery, motorcycles, and larger trucks because policy makers had decided to give the Navy, the Marines, and the British priority for receiving new weapons.[135] Working day and night, the 103rd Ordnance Company crafted "dummy" weapons, such as thirty-six 37mm antitank guns fashioned from metal tubes on wheels to be towed behind trucks. Making do, the division passed around its few real 37mm guns for practice firing, then used the fake ones on tactical exercises for transporting and positioning the weapons in the field. "Therefore, for tactical training purposes, a stick of wood or a length of steel pipe will have practically the same effect as a real gun."[136] Doubtful. Pennsylvania National Guard soldiers also strapped Springfield rifles to the barrels of the dummy guns and fired them at empty gas cans that trucks towed behind them. The cans simulated enemy tanks. Water-filled bottles served as makeshift Molotov cocktails, and wooden sawhorses substituted for .50 caliber machine guns.[137] Charles A. Corcoran recalled these months as the most satisfying of his career because of the demands the equipment shortages and inexperience placed on his creativity. There were few specialists or experienced NCOs. "You made something out of nothing."[138] Still, it was an appalling embarrassment. At least Corcoran and his NCOs did not waste their soldiers' time. If they had completed a portion of training and did not "have anything that was worthwhile let's not insult their intelligence by dragging it out."[139] If they did not have anything better to do, they ordered the men to don their packs and go for a hike so as to toughen their physical condition. They got in very good shape.[140]

The PNG's training program never gained enough momentum in June and July. Phase two of its training was supposed to begin on June 30 and focus on regimental and brigade training, but the Army corps commander pushed that back to July 12 to correct deficiencies. He then said that the delay was no reflection on the division's progress. Officers claimed that the 28th was advancing faster than expected and complained about the postponement.[141] For his part the chief of staff was losing patience. Of the entire NG, Marshall commented, "Views of enlisted men obtained from circulating press correspondents indicate that they know very little of what is going on and therefore derive little instruction from the maneuvers and feel that they are losing needed basic training."[142] On a hot July day, for example, several men in the 111th Infantry passed out from the heat. By comparison, Reserve officers for the most part staffed the new Regular Army divisions, along with as many as 85 percent conscripts, and complaints of incompetence were few.[143]

Continuing to try to advance its capabilities, the division opened its own one-week school for one hundred junior officers in late July. They were to learn instructional methods and the tactics of combat teams. Meanwhile, the headquarters conducted another command post exercise that walked through planning and communication procedures. It later made good on the Army philosophy that men had to know the duties of those in grades higher than their own when it had the headquarters-enlisted men conduct a command post exercise alone.[144] They were about to undergo weeks of intensive large-scale exercises in Virginia and North Carolina, so they needed all of the preparation they could get.

4

Peacetime Maneuvers

1939–1941

Starting in 1935, National Guard units gathered with their Regular Army counterparts during the summer to conduct large-scale maneuvers.[1] The Pennsylvania National Guard participated in four such exercises: once in 1939 and in
1940, and twice in 1941. The manner in which the NG participated revealed
an institution full of esprit de corps and commitment to military service, but
short on war-fighting skills. Regular Army formations also participated, and
the maneuvers demonstrated that neither institution was ready for war. Fiscal
starvation and anti-interventionism had emasculated both in regard to their
ability to fight. They were, however, in better condition than they had been in
previous years. In 1926, for example, the Army consisted of "paper divisions."
Although authorized 19,997 men, "peacetime" divisions numbered 9,200. They
retained the basic "square" organization from the Great War: two brigades,
each containing two rifle regiments.[2]

Individual armories geared up for the exercises in a variety of ways on
their own initiative. In May 1939 the 110th Infantry, for instance, practiced air-
to-ground communications with the 103rd Observation Squadron employing
visual signals and voice radio at the Duncansville airport.[3] It demonstrated the
PNG's poverty when it dropped bags of flour, simulating bombs, on members of
the 112th Infantry.[4] Regimental, brigade, and division commanders scrambled
to design and script the war games, because First Army failed to provide the
28th Division with planning orders until June 1. For that reason PNG officers
had to take off time from their civilian jobs to travel to Manassas and scout the
area, paying for the trip themselves.

While the German Army readied its invasion of Poland, the PNG spent
two weeks in August 1939 on maneuvers as part of Third Corps, First Army, at

Manassas National Battlefield Park, Virginia. Major General Milton Reckord's 29th Division, consisting predominantly of Marylanders, with a leavening of Virginians and men from the District of Columbia, also made the trip.[5] A provisional division of Army Regulars rounded out the participants and served as the adversary force for the exercise. Altogether 17,000 enlisted men and 2,200 officers—including 707 Reserve officers—participated.[6]

The maneuvers' purpose was originally to provide battle practice for large units, and to evaluate the divisions' mobilization, transportation, supply, and organizational proficiency. Commanders changed their goals to training, troop instruction, and leadership development because their soldiers were so deficient in basic skills. Soft-pedaling the issue of his men's performance, the III Corps commander, Major General James K. Parsons, did not write a critique of the maneuvers, assuming that the men could recognize and correct their mistakes.[7]

Just getting to Manassas was a learning experience. Convoys required 1,700 vehicles, and the rest of the soldiers arrived in 136 railroad cars.[8] Once they arrived, the two NG divisions busied themselves with exercises from the battalion to division during August 6–12.[9] Guardsmen always arrived at field training out of shape and unprepared for the physical demands, so the leadership set aside time for exercise and physical training.[10] The ideal was for them to arrive having completed basic and small-unit training, but that was impossible given the circumstances of the interwar NG.

Military attachés from twelve countries, including Germany and Japan, watched the maneuvers with keen if bemused interest. They joined Governor James, the chair of the House Military Affairs Committee, the chief of the National Guard Bureau, the acting chief of staff, General Marshall, and a press corps of seventy-four reporters representing thirty-eight newspapers and wire services.[11] First Army's commander, Major General Hugh A. Drum, took advantage of the abundance of press microphones to appeal to the public for help by noting the shortage of soldiers and weapons. He pointed out, for instance, an 83 percent shortage of a basic artillery weapon, the 155mm cannon for the Regular Army, as well as a 77 percent shortage in Regular soldiers.[12]

The Manassas maneuvers exposed weaknesses and shortages and helped to form the War Department's training, equipping, and military mobilization goals for the next two years. Their climax, a battle between the two NG divisions in III Corps and the Regular Army Provisional Division, took place from August 13 to 17. The mock combat between the two forces was "free"; movements were not scripted. Commanders, not exercise evaluators, directed troop movements.[13]

Map I
Manassas Maneuvers
August 1939

XXX
III
Manassas ∎

XX
⊠ 29

XX
⊠ 28

Broad Run ∎

II
⊠ Flying

Signal Hill ∎

Bristow
III
⊠ 34

Ocoquan Creek ∎

Buckhall ∎

Cabin Run ∎

III
▧ 3

Blands Ford ∎

Spriggs Ford ∎

∎Hoadly

I
⊠
o o

Brentsville ∎

III
⊠ 12

Independent Hill ∎

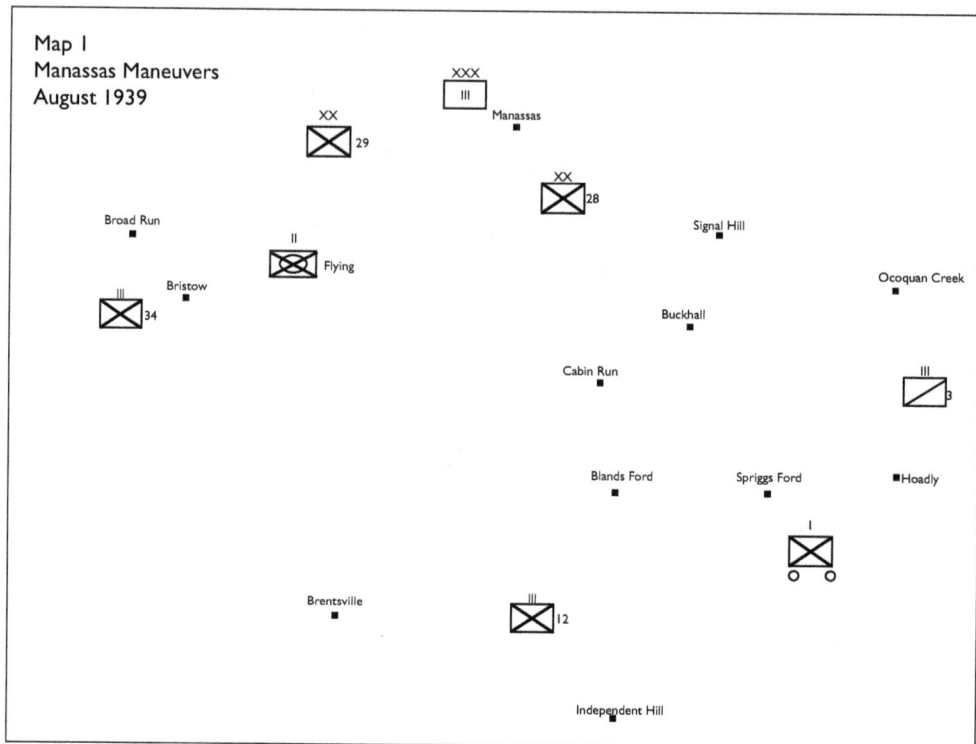

The war game tasked III Corps with the job of protecting Washington, D.C., from an attack by the "Black Force," the Provisional Division.[14] There were plenty of artificialities: raised flags signified artillery fire, since no one used live or even blank ammunition. The scenario was contrived as a teaching tool, not as a reflection of security threats, and aircraft were almost completely absent. It all required a lot of imagination on the part of the troops. Radio, telephone, and written communications were all real, as were troop and vehicle movements. One innovation was a reserve "flying battalion" of infantry and artillery, a first for the Keystone Division, all transported on twenty-three trucks. General Martin had decided to create it for the maneuvers back in the winter. His creativity followed the current teachings of the Infantry School, and this mechanized reserve proved effective in thwarting mechanized attacks against the division's flanks.[15]

The exercise began with the Black Force 12th Infantry Regiment advancing north to gain a bridgehead southeast of Brentsville, while the 34th Infantry Regiment swung to the west to attack Bristow from that direction.[16] Although

Blue infantry repulsed the attacks of the Black 3rd Cavalry Regiment, the Blue infantry were sufficiently distracted to allow the main Black force to wage a successful attack against the main bodies of the 28th and 29th Divisions, closing to within a mile and a half of the III Corps headquarters.[17]

Martin's flying battalion (the mechanized reserve) saw action against the Black cavalry in a strange skirmish that mixed a Civil War–era cavalry charge with the modern use of firepower. While on the move, the flying battalion saw two squadrons of adversary horse cavalry emerge from the woods near Bristow, about 300 yards distant, and deploy for a charge. Reacting quickly, the motorized soldiers dismounted, deployed, and aimed their machine guns, 37mm and 75mm cannon, which easily convinced the watching referee to declare that they had halted the horse cavalry charge. After the defenders were under way in their trucks, the surviving cavalry appeared again. The motorized troops were able to deploy and "fire" all of their weapons before the cavalry were even able to gather themselves in a formation. The cavalry fled.[18]

Later that morning the flying battalion found a column of forty-four Black tanks in time to deploy its guns on the flanks of the road on which the tanks were advancing. Seizing the initiative, they parked their trucks to form a roadblock. When they brought the enemy tanks under fire the umpire ruled in favor of the motorized reserve.[19]

The infantry also beat back tank and motorized infantry attacks.[20] The Maryland and Pennsylvania divisions coordinated their next attack on August 15. The 29th Division constructed a pontoon bridge over Cedar Run, crossed, and prepared to make the main attack. Meanwhile, the 28th Division launched its assault in the area of Blands Ford Bridge with one brigade and supported the 29th Division with artillery. General Martin also formed an impromptu truck-mounted force of thirty infantry, thirty machine gunners, an engineer platoon, and two 75mm batteries, which harassed the enemy to good effect.[21] The PNG forced the 3rd Cavalry to withdraw south of Spriggs Ford. In the end, Martin's efforts against adversary mobile forces failed, for Black Force tanks captured 350 prisoners.[22]

During the night of August 15–16 Black Force conducted a wide withdrawal to reposition itself opposite the Blue line near Buckhall Church and sent a small diversionary force just south of Bristow.[23] By the next day, General Parsons concluded that Black was preparing to attack from the east, so he ordered the divisions to hold their lines along state highway 234. Meanwhile, a corps reserve of Marylanders with a provisional tank battalion readied themselves near Bristow.[24] Attacking from Buckhall Church toward the southwest on the morning of the 16th, Black threatened the left flank of the 28th Division. By the afternoon, however, the Black force was on the defensive along Crooked Branch, Buckhall Church, and Signal Hill.[25] A detachment of their armored scout cars still managed to capture a battery of the Pennsylvania 213th Coast Artillery, and other Black forces attacked the 29th Division.[26] In response, Parsons reinforced the left flank of the 29th with his reserve, the 91st Brigade. Even though Reckord's division had to retreat in order to regroup, the two NG divisions used a pincer movement to repulse their adversary and throw the regulars back on their heels.[27]

For the final day, III Corps ordered a dawn attack, with the 28th Division attempting a single envelopment of the enemy's left flank. Martin sent the motorized reserve on a fifteen-mile jaunt to flank the adversary from the south with the goal of destroying rear-area encampments.[28] The PNG reached its objective, the line from Signal Hill to Spriggs Ford, but the umpires terminated the maneuvers at noon, shortly after the two sides made contact. This last attack saw the tanks of the two divisions combined into one force.[29] Before the action ended, the 5th Engineers, Regular Army, spied the 28th's motorized reserve and engaged it in a mock firefight. Even though the umpires brought the clash to a premature conclusion, the Pennsylvanians consoled themselves that they had tied up an entire Regular Army regiment far behind enemy lines—an encouraging victory for the guardsmen.[30]

Before the Pennsylvanians left for home, General Martin praised them for their enthusiasm, endurance, and discipline. In particular, he singled out the performance of the mobile formations.[31] Satisfied with staff work at all levels, he also believed that the maneuvers proved that his officers were ready to function at higher levels of command, that is, majors could move successfully into lieutenant colonel duties. He found that orders were clear, adequate, and timely. Map overlays were a great improvement over the previously verbose written orders. Privately, however, Martin confessed that his division was not yet ready to concern itself with fighting in a shooting war against a well-equipped enemy. His men had needed the first week to be "seasoned" for outdoor conditions. The division did not have enough vehicles, antitank guns, or heavy weapons, and he believed infantry divisions ought to receive their own motorized reserves with enough trucks and artillery. The exercise against the Provisional Division showed that his own mobile reserve always made successful counterattacks against mechanized units and that immobile formations of soldiers were of no use at all against a mechanized and thus mobile enemy. Martin suggested that the Army mount 37mm antitank guns on vehicles from which they could be fired and that it equip divisions with a reconnaissance detachment of horses, scout cars, and light tanks. Mobility, fire-power, voice radios, and time for training were the keys to preparing National Guard divisions for war.[32] By comparison, Martin's vision of mobile warfare was more forward-thinking than current Army doctrine.[33] Likewise, Milton Reckord concluded that the great lesson of the maneuvers was the superiority of motorized forces over foot infantry.[34]

The maneuvers forced the PNG's men to recognize that they had a long way to go.[35] Enthused by their experience, other soldiers commented, "What with the war and everything, the 109th will be digging into training with greater zest than ever, confident that *if* and *when* the Day should arrive, we shall *not* be tried and found wanting."[36] The Regular officer in charge of NG affairs noticed that even though the soldiers found the maneuvers more strenuous than expected, they "thoroughly enjoyed" them and knew that they were getting training better than in previous summers.[37] The NG troops had the right attitude; they were there to learn. "One theme stands out above all others—you have heard it voiced on every hand, from all ranks—that is, 'I learned a lot.'" Manassas was "for many Guardsmen, the outstanding adventure of a life time."[38]

The 28th Division made at least a portion of the Regular Army look inept, scoring a windfall in the areas of radio intelligence and deception. Pennsylvania's 101st Radio Company intercepted many of the unencrypted orders and reports that Black Force transmitted. When, for instance, Black Force tanks threatened the division's flank, the listening post transmitted bogus orders for them to conceal themselves in the woods just ahead of them, shut off their engines, and maintain radio silence for thirty minutes. Well, the Black tanks obeyed the false orders![39] Other Regular Army officers were not the sharpest tacks, either. An umpire attached to the 3rd Cavalry stated flatly that "Third Manassas again proved conclusively . . . that the mounted man is still indispensable on the field of battle" due to his mobility. He admitted that because they did not operate against an enemy firing bullets instead of blanks, he was unsure how well cavalry would have done under fire.[40] An observation aircraft pilot from New Jersey noted that tracking units was easy, because "almost every unit, upon going into position had been followed by a dazzling WHITE ICE CREAM TRUCK which . . . parked in the open close to the unit position and told the intelligent aviators all they needed to know."[41] Black's senior umpire, Colonel Bruce Palmer, noted that although the Provisional Division was mo-torized and mobile, its commander kept his vehicles idle throughout most of the maneuvers. Palmer decried the lethargy of the regulars, adding that the maneuvers exposed "the pitiful inadequacy which exists in the United States Army, of means and methods of combat mechanization."[42] General Marshall briefed the press; while the Guard had made "impressive advances" in its ability to move men from one place to another, he stated that it still required much more training, especially when compared with foreign armies.[43]

Plattsburg Maneuvers

The Keystone State's guardsmen began planning for their next big field exercise in December 1939. They anticipated the next summer maneuver would consist of three weeks in upstate New York. General Martin pressed his men to finish basic training before August 1940; there would be no time for it once they reached New York.[44] A look at all the skills they needed to acquire, at a pace of three hours per week, makes it clear that there were too many tasks to learn, too many soldiers with minimal training and experience, and not enough time to master basic soldiering skills.[45] They arrived at the maneuvers capable of anything requiring enthusiasm, but ignorant of the many details necessary for surviving in a combat area. The 28th joined six other National Guard divisions: Pennsylvania's 22nd Cavalry Division, the 26th Division (Massachusetts, Maine, New Hampshire, Vermont), the 27th (New York), the 29th (Maryland, Virginia, District of Columbia), the 43rd (Connecticut, Maine, Rhode Island, Vermont), the 44th (New York, New Jersey), the 16th Infantry Brigade, and the regulars of Major General Karl Truesdell's 1st Division.[46]

General Drum began with a conference on August 7, 1940. Commenting on France's defeat, he and others concluded that combined arms doctrine lay at the heart of German success and blamed France's fate on the defensive doctrine of her army. National Guard company commanders and NCOs, however, should have already been instructing soldiers in much of what he discussed. Drum's favorite tactic, pinning down an enemy with firepower while flanking and encircling him, was a mirror image of Irwin Rommel's methods. Drum urged them to combine the firepower of all available weapons. It might be appropriate, for instance, to use antiaircraft cannon against ground targets. He added that small units working together were the primary means through which armies won battles. This required that everyone understand the commander's objective. Drum preached a method somewhat like *Auftragstaktik* (mission-type orders): the overall objective constituted the foundation of an order, and subordinates were to decide on the specifics when executing their commander's wishes.[47] The maneuver's deputy director, Brigadier General Irving J. Phillipson, wished

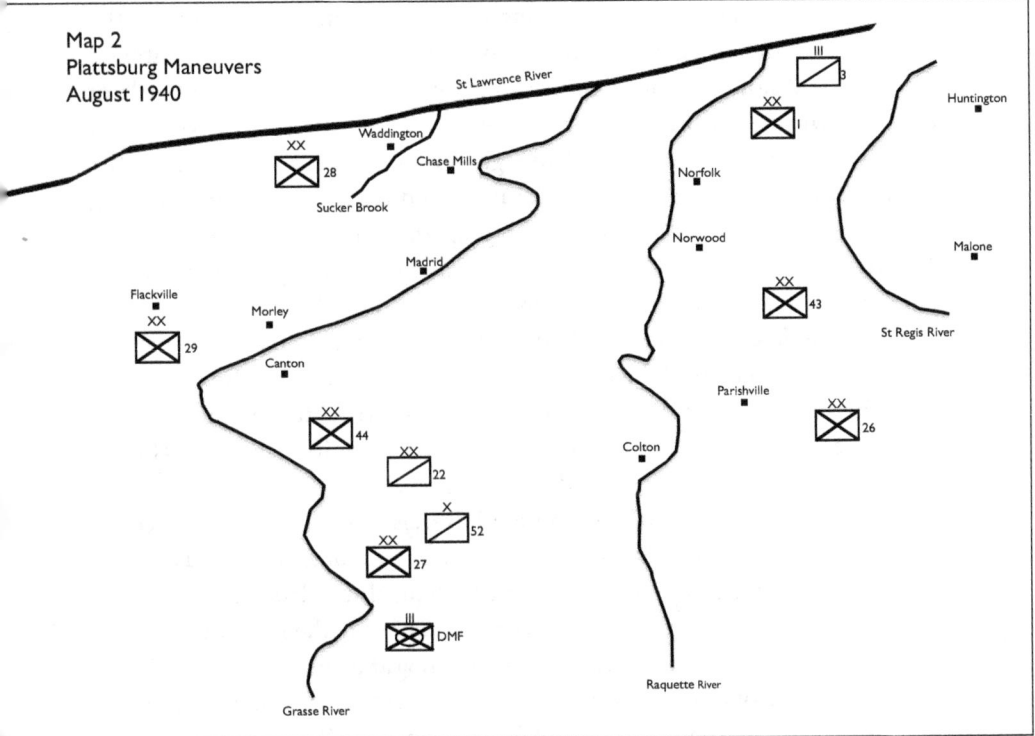

Map 2
Plattsburg Maneuvers
August 1940

that American soldiers could recognize and exploit fleeting opportunities in combat as well as the Germans had done in France.[48]

This doctrinal philosophy, keying on small-unit combat and carrying out the commander's intent away from his immediate oversight, was decisive over the next four years in turning the American Army into a first-rate fighting force. Often dismissed as a second-rate force of cautious infantry over-reliant on indirect firepower, American infantry—the 28th Infantry Division no less— over time became more than a match for the German Army. But the march to the Rhine began on the shores of the St. Lawrence River. Once again they had to contrive much of their training that summer, because the Army still lacked the vehicles and weapons of modern warfare.[49]

The maneuvers kicked off on August 8 with five days of small-unit train- ing, followed by two days for brigade training and a couple for individual divisions to put themselves through the paces, and concluded with the army- level exercises August 19–22. Marshall had hoped that the soldiers would have been advanced enough in their training to permit more time for large-scale maneuvers, but the low skill of the men denied him his wish.[50] During the first stages of the exercises, infantry and artillery improved their combined arms methods and put into practice some of the lessons from the Battle of France.[51] During the brigade-level maneuvers on August 13, the PNG waged a nighttime battle and completed an eighteen-mile hike, and gunners of the 166th Field Artillery clashed with the 103rd and 104th Cavalry in a meeting engagement.[52] After setting up to defend against air attack, the 213th Coast Artillery (Anti-aircraft) commented that "all participating really got a kick out of the problem in spite of the arduous work required."[53]

The simulated firefights resulted in some situations devoid of all practical realism. When soldiers of the 111th Infantry "attacked" the 110th Infantry, they were able to drive past a defensive position and "destroy" the regimental command post because they failed to raise colored flags signifying weapons firing, and thus their opponents hesitated in putting up a fight.[54]

Next came two days of division-level exercises, when the 28th faced off against the 29th Division. Even in the absence of weapons, tanks, and aircraft, the maneuvers at least provided everyone with much-needed experience with command problems, particularly the confusion of war. The 110th Infantry, for instance, had to send its 3rd Battalion through a bog and other rough country before it settled into its fighting position. Once again, raised flags signified "shooting," and improvised vehicles stood in for real weapons. The 110th's mobile unit shot up six 29th Division tanks, captured eight truckloads of its troops, and held the 5th Infantry Regiment "at a standstill for nearly six hours." On the evening of August 15, the 1st Virginia Infantry forced the 110th to move its command post three times in five hours and drove them from Flackville to Red Mills.[55] Horsemen of the 103rd Cavalry were pleased with their forty-five-mile trek during the battle and with their seizure of a crossing over the Grasse River in the towns of Russell and Pyrites. They also took three hills overlooking the crossings, covered the PNG infantry during its river crossing, and delayed a Black Force attack.[56] In the opinion of the II Corps commander, however, the cavalry was handled poorly and without regard to prioritizing missions.[57] On the other hand, several companies of the 103rd Engineer and Quartermaster Regiments and the 111th Infantry displayed enough flexibility to practice maneuvering a new type of reconnaissance detachment, in which they had to switch from scouting to seizing advanced positions to protecting their flanks.[58]

The absence of modern equipment was a disgrace. The guardsmen had to use ersatz wooden artillery pieces and pretend that trucks were tanks. On rented civilian dump trucks they hung signs with "This is a tank" inscribed.

Wooden logs attached to discarded carriage wheels served as antitank guns. The handful of observation aircraft on site stood in as dive bombers.[59] Soldiers even had to simulate machine guns and mortars, the latter with simple metal tubes.[60] The nadir came when a soldier of the 109th Infantry "threw a lemon which struck the scout car squarely, simulating a hand grenade." The regiment's chronicler noted dryly that "[a]ctual warfare under these conditions would have been vastly different."[61]

Before the beginning of the large-scale maneuvers, the president, the secretary of war, and Prime Minister Mackenzie King of Canada inspected the troops on August 17.[62] Their presence lent weight to the significance of the exercises and signaled to all that the president and the secretary thought them important enough to review in person. The trip also ensured that the press corps that accompanied the president would highlight the Army's strengths and deficiencies without Roosevelt himself having to raise criticisms.

The multi-division maneuvers lasted from August 19 to 22. The 28th and 29th Divisions formed III Corps in the northwest portion of the maneuver area, with the 28th's left flank up against the St. Lawrence River. II Corps included the 44th, 27th, and 22nd (Cavalry) Division on the right of III Corps. Major Generals Walter C. Short and James K. Parsons commanded the II and III Corps, respectively.[63] Together they formed the "Blue Force" under the command of General Drum. The 26th and 43rd National Guard Divisions joined the regulars of Major General Karl Truesdell's 1st Infantry Division in the adversary "Black Force," under the command of I Corps's Major General J. A. Woodruff.[64]

The Plattsburg Maneuvers assumed that an invasion from the Canadian side of the St. Lawrence River threatened. General Drum set out to block the river crossings by setting up defensive positions along the south bank of the river all the way to Montreal, and by taking the railroad centers along Huntington and Malone. U.S. forces were, of course, prohibited from entering Canada.[65] Drum used the 22nd Cavalry Division to protect the south flank of the Blue Forces, while a mobile force under Brigadier General Brice P. Disque, the "Disque Mobile Force" (DMF) was to counterattack any Black Force effort to envelop II Corps from the south.[66]

Drum ordered III Corps to push straight ahead and cross the Grasse River between Madrid and Morley. The 29th Division was to advance fifteen miles and take a bridgehead over the Raquette River near Norwood.[67] The Black Force intended to protect its south flank while driving straight ahead with the 26th Division to take crossings over the Grasse south of Canton while the 43rd Division seized bridgeheads between Canton and Madrid. The 1st Division and 3rd Cavalry Regiment operated on the north flank against the 28th Division.[68]

Wasting no time, the 1st Division attacked the Keystone Division on the morning of the 19th, holding it west of the Grasse, but the rest of the Blue forces advanced almost as far as the Raquette.[69] After fifteen miles on foot in a "cold driving rain," the 109th Infantry defeated an attack by the 3rd U.S. Cavalry. Although the cavalry captured the 109th's command post truck, the plans drawn on the maps were no longer valid. Along with the 107th Artillery, the 109th fought off 1st Division armored cars.[70] After advancing from Waddington, the 110th Infantry had to retreat through the miserable rain to Sucker Brook.[71] To the south, the PNG's 52nd Cavalry Brigade took the high ground three miles east of Canton and waited for the 27th and 44th Divisions to relieve it.[72] Drum was spring-loaded to unleash the DMF if the opportunity arose, envisioning sending it along Black's south flank all the way to Parishville, almost 25 miles, and on the night of August 19–20, he turned it loose.[73] At the same time, the 52nd Cavalry Brigade eased through a gap in the 26th Division's line undetected, and at dawn it charged the bridges across the Raquette, preventing Black Force engineers from destroying them. Within an hour, it and most of the accompanying 166th Field Artillery were secure a mile east of the crossing.[74]

On August 20, the 28th and 29th Divisions crossed the Grasse River, with the PNG attacking the 1st Division in the front while the 29th maneuvered to the rear of it southeast of Madrid. The Marylanders attacked much of Truesdell's motor transportation, forcing the Regular Division to carry out a costly daylight withdrawal.[75] Pennsylvania artillery displayed significant skill during the advance. Each battalion of the 107th FA always had one to two batteries providing fire support while the rest of the guns pressed forward to new locations. It even sent teams ahead to survey sites for their cannon.[76] By nightfall the 109th Infantry had reached Chase Mills and encamped, then tried to get some sleep under a pouring rain in wet blankets and clothes.[77] That kind of misery did not dull the guardsmen's spirits: "The Blitzkrieg on Tuesday night and Wednesday morning will be long remembered, when, with the cavalry riding the interference, we rode right through the Blacks and captured the bridgehead at Colton."[78]

Late on the 20th the 110th Infantry boarded trucks and rode to an area along Trout Brook, from which it moved to East Norfolk for the next day's river crossing. General Drum ordered a 4 AM start for the August 21 war games. He wanted pontoon bridges in place by 9 AM and under the cover of smoke screens and antiaircraft artillery protection. The general also ordered what air support he had to bomb roads and bridges well behind Black Force lines. Drum gave his subordinates permission "to pursue the enemy on their own initiative."[79] Not interested in a slugging match, Drum told the DMF and 22nd Cavalry Division to reconnoiter the best way to cut off the main Black units from behind and to sever the railroad near Malone.[80]

No one completed their pontoon bridges in time on the 21st. The 28th Division shuttled two of its four regiments across the Raquette just south of Norfolk by about 6 AM—no mean feat as Black Force aircraft were dropping flares to illuminate the ground and expose the Pennsylvanians.[81] The 109th Infantry and 107th Artillery slammed into entrenched troops, who halted them for a time. All of the 112th Infantry, at least, crossed the river by 6:30, after which it captured a machine gun and several squads from the 18th Infantry Regiment.[82] Neither the Keystone nor the 29th Division made great progress against the 1st Division prior to the end of the exercise. At 1 PM on August 21, the director terminated the exercises.[83]

The next day General Drum chaired a debriefing at the St. Lawrence University stadium at Canton, New York. The maneuvers' evaluators praised the National Guard for the enthusiasm and effort of its troops, but found that the armory training programs had not resulted in soldiers with enough proficiency in the craft of warfare. The shortages of weapons and equipment were simply deplorable, and Drum witnessed a "lack of manpower organized and trained for modern combat."[84] The G-3 section added, "The inadequacy and insufficiency of armament and equipment is so obvious as to need no comment."[85]

The First Army chief of staff commended everyone's staff work, especially since the staffs had worked together infrequently or not at all. He found that the guardsmen's orders "were models of brevity." As had happened during the Manassas Maneuvers, radio intelligence was again a boon for the PNG. Its 101st Radio Company routinely located Black and even Blue forces because neither side encoded transmissions. The Regular Army lacked enough Signal Corps troops to practice realistic communications, so it relied on the help of the New York Telephone Company.[86] Not surprisingly, a soldier at the Black Force headquarters accidentally telephoned General Drum's HQ and informed it of where the Black Force trains were. Drum's forces captured the trains.[87]

The Army noted some additional successes. General Wilby praised the use of camouflage, traffic control, and the general health of the troops, while the chief of artillery noted that field artillery moved undetected during the maneuvers.[88] The Engineer Regiment found that unexpected taskings provided excellent training, as when the 103rd Engineers had to construct ramps and repair roads due to pervasive mud. Building the pontoon bridges at night without lights was clearly a success.[89]

Drum added, "The spirit and dash of the personnel of both sides were remarkable."[90] The soldiers of the 166th FA savored the field exercises; not a single member stayed home—"we never would have missed it for a million."[91] National Guard quartermasters were universally pleased with their interface with the Army, continuing a long tradition of excellence.[92] The 103rd Observation Squadron flew 455 hours without an accident, including nine hours night flying out of a base without night-landing facilities.[93] Guardsmen surprised themselves with their stamina; two weeks into the exercise, two of the 28th's regiments completed eighteen-mile marches, whistling in spite of their sore feet.[94] Commanders from army to platoon were able to track and command their troops well. There is no evidence of units becoming lost or of officers losing control of their commands, save one. Exploiting the imaginary aspect of this war game, a lost soldier "attempted to cross a bridge and the sentry at the bridge said, 'You can't cross here, soldier; theoretically, this bridge has been blown up.' The soldier replied, 'That's all right, buddy; theoretically, I'm swimming this river.'"[95] Observers constantly commented on the men's high morale. Given a few months of solid training with sufficient equipment, the Army could translate such spirit into battlefield skill.[96]

General Drum acknowledged that the troops knew that efficient training required months, not days, of effort. "We cannot throw ground and air units into an organization just before battle and expect the two to coordinate and harmonize effectively their efforts."[97] The Plattsburg Maneuvers exposed the shortcomings of individual soldiers and small units that lacked skill in

> minor tactics to carry out effectively the operations ordered by higher quarters. Cooperation between arms, especially between infantry and its direct support artillery, had been practiced only in previous summer camps. These conditions, *inherent to our National Guard system,* were recognized and the early period of the Army Maneuvers was allotted to the training of small units. The period, however, was too short to accomplish the desired results. However, in spite of these deficiencies, there was practical unanimity of opinion that the 1940 maneuvers constituted the best training held to date by the National Guard units. [italics added]

The First Army G-3 added, "Units showed a distinct lack of preparation for employment of combined arms. This is due to the lack of opportunity for such training throughout the year."[98] The "tank" actions impressed no one. Lieutenant Colonel John C. Davis flatly stated, "No comment appears to be necessary on the suitability of improvised tanks used in this maneuver. It is quite apparent that due to the lack of this equipment in the past we have a long way to go in making the proper use of our tanks. The coordination of tanks in joint operations was not good." Similarly, ground forces made poor use of the attack aviation available, refusing to assign targets to them until the army headquarters forced them to.[99] The division was weak on antitank defenses and camouflage, and commanders depended too much on maps when passing orders.[100]

A representative from the National Guard Bureau later wrote varying assessments of the 28th. Lieutenant Colonel Don C. Faith concluded that Martin and the 28th ID staff officers had the knowledge and ability to supervise the training of the division. He also concluded that "[t]he commanding general and his staff have the necessary general qualifications and professional fitness to properly command the division in combat." Still, they needed about three months of field maneuvers to become truly proficient. Faith blamed them for making little use of close air support during the Plattsburg Maneuvers, but also noted that almost no Army Air Corps aircraft were available for their use. He was especially complimentary of Colonel John Aiken (55th Brigade) and of Brigadier General William Dunlap (53rd FA Brigade). Faith minced no words regarding Lieutenant Colonel Fred H. Kelley, who commanded the 111th Infantry during the first week in lieu of Colonel Frank A. Warner. Kelley "lacked leadership, the ability to issue orders, and to properly plan and conduct the training. He does not possess the qualities to command in combat." Major William H. Stephenson, the regimental S-3, had to take over command during the maneuver phase and performed very well. "His planning and conducting of the training was progressive and thorough. He has the ability to command in combat." Nevertheless, all of the units needed anywhere from two to three months of "intensive training."[101]

Colonel James Garesche Ord, Pennsylvania's senior instructor from the Regular Army, offered few comments. He found the 28th Division long on courage, discipline, and determination—even when marching through a bone-chilling rain—and potential. He found that many of the small units were unable to seize and hold the initiative in combat. As solutions, he suggested fast action when first meeting the enemy and quick situation reports to superiors.[102]

General Martin praised his men's verve and effort, but excoriated those who demanded written orders before taking action. A verbal order was sufficient and made a person responsible. He insisted that officers command well forward along the front lines with their soldiers. Anyone who was unwilling to accept the burdens of responsibility was unfit for command. He urged the greater use of mechanized formations for scouting, screening, and seizing tactically important points, and he was pleased that all of his units practiced local security to defend against sneak attacks. The PNG was deficient, he admitted, in combining all arms in a mutually supporting manner. "All commanders, down to the platoon, should know the value of all arms and how these arms must be used. This is no time for a division between branches of service. It is the team that counts and this includes the Air, the Infantry, Artillery, Engineers, Supply, and Transportation."[103] Martin never challenged assessments like First Army's comment that "[o]ur troops are not suitable at this time for highly intensified and accelerated warfare. I believe that is as much due to our lack of mental mobility as to our lack of ground mobility."[104]

Although Drum publicly praised the PNG for its performance in the maneuvers, the unpublished appraisal concluded that the divisions, NG as well as Regular, were not utterly incompetent, but neither were they ready for combat against a first-rate foe. Their status begged for "[t]horough tactical training of small units; teamwork of the combined arms—infantry and its supporting artillery aviation, tanks, antitank units, and engineers; speed in reaching a decision and issuing necessary orders particularly in small units."[105]

The National Guard's failure to achieve competency in small-unit tactics and even individual skills was a severe indictment of the assumptions as to what a couple of hours of training a week could accomplish. The Guard had intended for the extra training in the fall of 1939 along with the extra drills to result in men who could accomplish small-unit tactical missions. No one really expected Guard divisions to be impressive without considerably more field training, but what good was the National Guard except as a *future* army in being if soldiers could not even perform basic tasks? The failure, with extra field and training days, of the National Guard in 1940 to be ready to move straight into regimental- to corps-level operations upon arrival at summer camp raised serious questions about the viability of the American reserve system as it existed at the outbreak of the Second World War.

Autumn 1941 Field Maneuvers

Six months later the War Department federalized the Pennsylvania National Guard so that it could devote five days a week to training for war. Following six months of garrison training at Indiantown Gap, the Pennsylvania National Guard conducted one short deployment to the A. P. Hill Military Reservation in Virginia as a warm-up to the Carolina Maneuvers during the fall of 1941. Leaving on August 25 in hundreds of trucks, 17,000 soldiers journeyed through the northern Virginia countryside and a warm welcome by the locals.[106] The division spent the first week in Virginia orienting itself to camp, the second in regimental maneuvers, and the final one conducting combined arms operations. As a result of their efforts, the men brimmed with confidence, but admitted, "We have a long way to go, both in mileage and in knowledge." They knew that once they reached North Carolina they would require refresher training.[107] Life at A. P. Hill "was just one maneuver after another. We learned that modern war is full of confusion. It was a glorious release from parade soldiering"—an indictment of the training at Indiantown Gap. Individual regiments fought each other day and night.[108]

Nine hundred miles to the southwest the Army was holding the massive "Louisiana Maneuvers." Nine divisions (472,000 troops) and three hundred aircraft participated in war games in the late-summer heat. Initial planning for these "enormous army-versus-army maneuvers" began in 1939, and formal orders left General Headquarters in January 1941. The exercises in Louisiana were the largest, while the ones that followed in the Carolinas were almost as big. Goals included fielding a "battle-worthy Protective Mobilization Plan Army" and training conditions as close to combat as possible. The maneuvers would be unscripted and range over thirty thousand square miles of territory.[109]

Life did not ease up when the guardsmen returned to Pennsylvania. They readied themselves for a longer trip to Lilesville, North Carolina, for a huge military exercise: 300,000 soldiers in all. It took over 2,500 vehicles to transport all 18,000—a first for any division.[110] Right away the PNG soldiers realized that previous experiences were "child's play" by comparison, but that did nothing to dampen their enthusiasm.[111] Unlike the exercises in 1939 and 1940, the Army subjected the soldiers to repetitive maneuvers that went on for weeks, not days, so the soldiers learned more than ever. The men learned to pack up, move, deploy, and fight, necessary preliminaries before the army-level maneuvers that began five weeks later. Even though weapons shortages hounded the NG and the Army, both were still able to learn many of the procedures necessary for fighting.[112] General Drum wisely commented that the greatest benefit of these maneuvers was the chance they offered everyone to try to function in as "near utter chaos and confusion as the ingenuity of man can conceive."[113] He wished that air, armored, and infantry forces could be better coordinated, a bothersome "weakness" that the maneuvers highlighted.[114]

The preliminary "training exercises" within Major General Lloyd Fredendall's II Corps commenced on October 6. The 28th, 29th, and 44th Divisions practiced moving to a defensive site and occupying and organizing their defenses, after which they defended themselves from attack by an imaginary foe.[115] For instance, the troops had to contrive solutions to the problems of refugees clogging the roads and damaged bridges. II Corps then used an attack by the 28th Division to "relieve pressure on our main forces."[116]

Building to more advanced scenarios, the next one was a two-sided "free" maneuver; officers could move their forces as they saw fit to fulfill their commander's objectives. Here the 28th Division solved river-crossing and road-traffic problems.[117] The divisions switched back and forth between being the defender and being the attacker. In Exercise 5, for instance, the 28th functioned as the Red Force spearhead. On October 16, the Keystoners crossed the Lynches River, completing a twelve-mile hike in the process. Then they took the high ground at Pageland, from where they covered the crossing at Highways 906 and 9. Counterattacks by the 44th and 29th Divisions against them brought the last day to a close.[118] Evaluators found that the troops were failing to carry out many of the detailed operations so important to field operations. Some failed to conceal their command posts. Members of the 104th Cavalry did not display "exemplary" marching discipline until an umpire showed up. They then tried to capture prisoners instead of carrying out their reconnaissance mission. One of the 28th's artillery commanders set up his guns right behind trees and then noticed that he could not fire his guns through tree trunks.[119] The maneuvers functioned to give the novices a chance to fail publicly, after which lessons were burned into their collective knowledge on war fighting.

Prior to the climactic "Carolina Maneuvers," the 28th Infantry Division participated in Field Maneuvers 1, 2, and 3, scripted exercises within First Army involving 262,000 soldiers.[120] They gave commanders and troops further practice at managing and commanding huge formations in a dynamic environment and in making decisions under pressure.

In Field Maneuver 1 on October 20, for instance, Fredendall's II Corps defended near the town of Wadesboro against an enemy advancing from the southwest.[121] II Corps planned for the 28th Division to spearhead an attack, but First Army ordered it to pull back instead. Ordered to attack the 9th Division on the 21st, General Stackpole refused to move his brigade until he was ready, but once under way, the division fought well.[122] Like before, these exercises exposed failures and shortcomings. For instance, 58 percent of II Corps's artillery hit nothing at all. Several of the 110th Infantry's officers tried to ignore the rules of the maneuvers to gain an advantage, for instance, as when Colonel Albert O. King argued with umpires that he could drive his regiment right through enemy troops even though he was surrounded.[123]

The exercises made it clear that the soldiers still had not mastered the basics of the craft of war. Umpires rarely singled out individual units for their critiques, but instead detailed the discrepancies according to branch of service, which helped meet the goal of using the maneuvers for training instead of evaluation. The artillery displayed a multitude of shortcomings. For instance, worried about armored attacks, they placed their command posts in locations inaccessible to friendly forces. Artillery commanders knew little of what the infantry were doing at the front and failed to explain to infantry combat teams how they could offer support. Some commanders were too passive and waited for fire support requests when they ought to "get up to the front and get in the battle with the infantry." Umpires found many men so exhausted that they could barely wake up when shaken. One infantry regiment tried to defend too wide a front. Another held nothing in reserve, while others made little effort to maintain "contact with adjacent units." A battalion even kept its soldiers in parade marching formation until within two hundred yards of the enemy.[124] Everyone tended to ignore the marking of artillery fire, since it was done by dropping sacks of flour, which burst in white clouds.[125] On October 22, Martin sent his 56th Brigade on an attack to the north without knowing the location or disposition of enemy troops.[126] At one point companies from the 112th and 182nd regiments fixed bayonets, sat down in a field, and just glared at each other.[127] Even the normally upbeat *Pennsylvania Guardsman* noted that infantry refused to dig foxholes, that soldiers of the 110th Infantry exchanged prisoners under truce flags, and that NCOs and lieutenants showed a lack of knowledge in basic infantry tactics. The various arms did not coordinate their efforts, but fought separately.[128]

Evaluators made note of bright spots, commending antitank units for their "alertness and the spirit of realism," as well as their selection of gun emplacements.[129] First Army commented, "Generally tactical actions were sound." By comparison, the 28th ID nearly cut off and isolated the Regular 9th Infantry Division.[130] Staff work was the division's strong suit. The officer in charge of G-2 always confirmed the correctness of his information and consulted closely with the division G-3.[131] During one skirmish a collection of cooks, mailmen, and truck drivers captured an airport, if only momentarily, and in another a PNG battalion captured a platoon of the 176th Infantry.[132]

Field Maneuver 2 lasted from October 26 to November. The 28th and 29th Divisions struck north against enemy infantry at the bridges crossing the Rocky River on the morning of October 28, capturing a bridge in the process.[133] Men of the 112th Infantry quickly pushed their opposition out of the way, employing mortars, for example, to destroy defending machine guns. Their success allowed the 109th Infantry to cross before sunset.[134] First Army evaluators complimented the regiments' plans for the crossing as "sound" and praised the 109th's "proper advance guard." Then on the afternoon of October 28, the 110th joined the Old Grey Mare (the 109th) to drive their opponents to the base of Cedar Hill by nightfall.[135]

All three II Corps divisions attacked VI Corps the next day. Martin's division was especially effective, foiling VI Corps's hostile intentions for the 44th Division.[136] The PNG's attacking regiments secured bridgeheads on October 29, with the 110th's crossing being "made in good shape and efficiency." When the division renewed its attack that afternoon, Martin forwarded orders to his brigades in just five minutes, an "excellent example of simple concise orders quickly given." He maintained contact with the corps and his brigade commanders and went to the front to confer with his staff and ensure that officers were carrying out his orders. "MOST UNUSUAL," remarked the evaluator. On the other hand, General Martin maintained almost no liaison with the adjacent 44th and 29th Divisions, a serious deficiency.[137]

An umpire with the 109th Regiment observed a theme of the maneuvers: combat proficiency depends on mastery of a thousand details. Specifically, the regiment's 3rd Battalion sent men across the river in full view of the enemy without first laying a smoke screen. He also noticed that formations smaller than a battalion normally charged straight ahead, rarely employing maneuver.[138] Thirty-nine percent of artillery fire hit nothing. Fortunately they were not firing real shells, for umpires ruled that 10 percent hit their own troops.[139] Brigadier General Henry Terrell Jr. urged his officers to remember the lessons the French had taught them in 1918: be aware of what is happening in front of you, and know where the units on either side are; otherwise you have "lost control of the situation and anything can happen."[140] General McNair closed his comments with the encouraging words that "general improvement and many excellent specific performances were noted."[141]

Field Maneuver 3 took place from November 3 to 6, pitting the five divisions of II and VI Corps (Blue) against I Corps (Red). Blue attempted a double envelopment using the 1st Division against the northern flank of the Red Force and the 29th Division against the southern flank, while Red planned to use its 1st Armored Division to attack Blue's southern flank. At first Martin permitted his forces to repeat a previous mistake of allowing a gap to form between his division and the 44th. At the same time, traffic jams and a lack of aggressiveness delayed the 1st Armored Division, and its adversary caught wind of its intentions. On November 5 Martin corrected the mistake and made grudging progress against the 30th Division toward the town of Lancaster.[142]

The Pennsylvanians acted with aggressiveness and toughness. The 112th Infantry crossed the Rocky River in water up to their shoulders in forty-degree weather under cover of smoke. Then the 109th and 110th followed at once instead of waiting for the engineers to come and aid their crossing. This gave the II Corps the speed necessary to gain an advantage and drive back the 26th Division's advanced guard four miles.[143] The Blue army attacked again on the 6th using VI Corps and the 28th Division. Meanwhile, Red moved its 1st Armored Division to its northern flank in a well-executed seventy-mile trek at night. That withdrawal freed the Maryland-Virginia division to attack in the south. The exercise ended on November 6 with the armored attack under way.[144]

General Drum was "thoroughly satisfied with what occurred," even though he believed the Red Force wasted time switching its armored attack from the south to the north. He added that the 1st Armored Division never would have been able to disengage if the 29th Division had locked onto it through aggressive fighting. Still, he commended the troops for trying to improve their awareness of battlefield events, even though they overwhelmed themselves with information.[145] Evaluators testified that artillery remained underutilized and that troops continued to fight even when umpires ruled that they had been captured. On the positive side, artillery rounds that hit nothing at all dropped to one-third of all firings, and fratricide fell to 5 percent.[146] Lieutenant Colonel Burton Lucas considered the II Corps's combat efficiency "excellent."[147] The soldiers' efforts pleased the evaluators. Commanders and their staffs were learning, and "[w]ithout the interest and enthusiasm of the individual soldier together with the general aptitude displayed by subordinate leaders such progress would have been impossible."

The guardsmen still had a ways to go. For instance, a group of two generals and several other officers conversed within plain view of the enemy, and infantry remained in marching columns within range of enemy small arms. Soldiers at times fought to amuse townspeople while cavalry congregated at gas stations and diners. Artillerymen needed much improvement in cleaning their howitzers and positioning their guns, and in general knowledge of the tactics and techniques of their weapons. Seven battalions never even fired. It is difficult to discern how well the PNG performed since the evaluators discussed problems by branch, not unit. The 28th never received great praise or censure.[148]

The soldiers remained innocent of war. Whenever aircraft flew over, the men invariably ran out into the open to watch them fly around and attack.[149]

One astute observer, Lieutenant Colonel Thacher Nelson, argued that the Regular officer instructors would have to take into account cultural differences between themselves and other "citizen officers." Regulars would have to make special efforts to articulate what was obvious to them but not readily apparent to the NG and Reserve officers. Regulars needed to impart their knowledge more quickly. There simply was not enough time to allow it to slowly and deeply penetrate young officers over time as had been their peacetime habit.[150]

The field exercises put the soldiers in situations that exposed their tactical ignorance, which thus offered teaching opportunities. The three field maneuvers revealed that developing an effective army was going to require months of repetitive work. Battlefield operations consisted of endless important detailed tasks, all of which took time to learn.

GHQ Maneuvers

The final army-level maneuvers promised to be the most arduous the men had faced so far.[151] Over the course of November 16–23, the 28th Division steadily pushed its opponent, the 43rd Division, back thirty miles from Wadesboro to Monroe. Its success was no surprise, for First Army, to which it belonged, boasted 195,000 troops to its opponent's 100,000 soldiers who comprised the Red Force.[152]

On the first day II Corps used the 28th as bait, having it cross the Pee Dee River and advance along Route 74 toward Monroe, drawing in the adversary forces so the 44th Division and VI Corps could envelop them.[153] The success of the crossing surprised commanders, who had expected Red Force aircraft to bomb the bridge. The 28th also blunted an attack by the 2nd Armored Division and then pressed forward with the assistance of tanks and artillery.[154] Evaluators remarked that Red Force counterattacks were not disrupting the division's coordination with II Corps. Martin had his Pennsylvanians advance at night, exploiting the cover of darkness.[155] On the morning of the 20th, the Keystone and 44th Divisions launched an attack against their IV Corps opponents, who continued to "disintegrate."[156]

II Corps renewed its attacks on the morning of the 21st. Drum's larger army was crushing IV Corps, and since nothing more was to be learned from that, the exercise director ended this phase two hours later.[157] Both sides studied the results and regrouped for another round, in which IV Corps (Red) defended Camden, South Carolina, from Blue's I, II, and VI Corps.[158]

Map 3
Carolina Maneuvers
October-November 1941
As of November 16

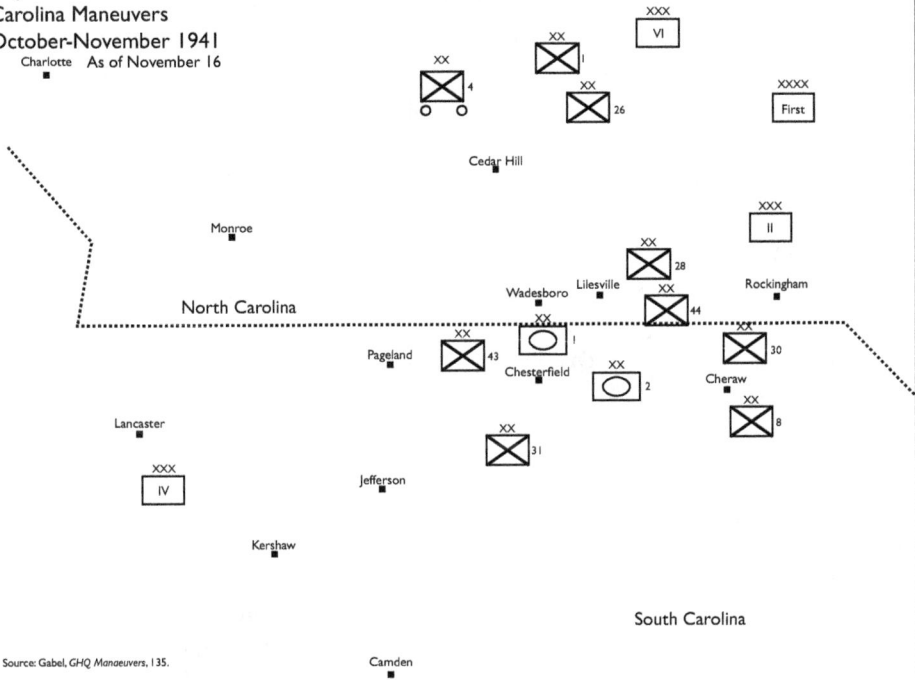

Charlotte ■

XXX
VI

XX
I

XX
4
○ ○

XX
26

XXXX
First

Cedar Hill

Monroe ■

North Carolina

XXX
II

XX
28

Wadesboro ■
Lilesville ■

XX
44

Rockingham ■

Pageland ■

XX
43

XX
I
○

Chesterfield ■

XX
2
○

XX
30

Cheraw ■

XX
8

Lancaster ■

XX
31

XXX
IV

Jefferson ■

Kershaw ■

South Carolina

Source: Gabel, *GHQ Maneuvers*, 135.

Camden ■

As before but on a larger scale, First Army employed II Corps as bait to draw the Red Force into a trap.[159] The PNG's role was to seize Wadesboro on the morning of November 25. The absence of enemy resistance there eased its task, and the division pressed forward until an umpire ordered a halt at 9:00 PM.[160] However, Red tanks got into the 28th's rear areas. "The huge machines disrupted communications and supplies, caused units to become widely separated, but eventually they were cut off and their resistance worn down."[161] The division advanced eighteen miles in spite of the 2nd Armored Division's efforts.[162]

The next day II Corps pivoted on the 44th Division toward the southwest, making for the high ground between Jefferson and Pageland.[163] Martin's division captured Chesterfield and cut off the 31st Division from the rest of the Red Force.[164] Meanwhile, with the help of a GHQ task force and tanks from II Corps, the 28th beat back a mechanized attack employing only two regiments and then advanced six miles, with some soldiers reaching Route 9 toward the southwest.[165]

During November 27, Martin aimed the 28th's main effort toward Kershaw, which moved ahead five miles by dusk.[166] Tanks continued to annoy the division, and Red Forces continually "destroyed" bridges as they fell back. Nevertheless, a task force of the 111th Infantry with the 191st Tank Battalion captured Kershaw and with it the 43rd Division's command post.[167] The 1st Armored Division, however, split the 28th from the 44th Division, and the distraction of that threat cost Drum his chance to defeat General Griswold completely.[168]

On the maneuvers' last day, the PNG spearheaded an advance two miles beyond the Lynches River. Martin credited the 103rd Engineer Regiment for making the crossing possible.[169] General Headquarters halted the exercise for good shortly thereafter. Drum's larger forces had manhandled Griswold's, but IV Corps successfully defended Camden, its primary mission.[170]

General McNair commended the results of the Carolina Maneuvers. "All must marvel at the progress made. I cannot praise too highly the intensive and intelligent collective effort which has brought about so great an achievement. *Men came to combat units directly from reception centers, knowing practically nothing of military life* [italics added]. They were trained individually in basic duties and in handling their weapons and special equipment."[171] In other words, NCOs told the recruits, this is a rifle. Point this end at the enemy. Two years after the onset of World War II, the United States still had to throw raw recruits into military exercises without the benefit of systematic training.

What really impressed McNair was "[t]he irrepressible cheerfulness, keen intelligence, and physical stamina of the American soldier." They were not ready to fight German soldiers, but, because the Army now possessed exceptional personnel, he expected they would exceed the abilities of the regulars of the prewar peacetime Army.[172] Brigadier General Mark W. Clark believed that officers would now be much more eager to concentrate on the details of small-unit tactics and training. McNair decided that he wanted to devote the first four months of 1942 to small-unit training.[173]

General Martin added his own criticisms about his division. He admitted that his squads, platoons, and companies had not received enough training prior to the maneuvers, which frustrated him because of his conviction that small-unit proficiency was foundational to success in combat. Martin believed that each of the combat arms branches in his division needed to coordinate more effectively. He accused the officers of the attached 191st Tank Battalion of an unwillingness to attack and take risks. Modern infantry divisions required many more trucks than they had, lest he starve his artillery of ammunition by moving his infantry around in what trucks he owned. Martin considered the aviation support "entirely inadequate." He believed the corps and even his own headquarters decided to take away too many battalions for use as reserves. Routinely during the maneuvers, he noted, only four battalions out of twelve attacked on behalf of the whole division. To streamline command, he suggested eliminating the brigades, but he wanted to retain all four regiments. Among his many other suggestions, Martin insisted that the division receive its own mechanized reconnaissance forces. On the one hand, he commended the PNG for marching seventy-five miles in five days, and he ordered a pass in review for the seven men who had died during the maneuvers. On the other hand, that was not good enough. Martin concluded that the maneuvers had not provided enough tests of the troops' ability to march long distances.[174] He was probably right.

A long trek in the soft North Carolina sand exhausted the men of the 110th Infantry. One of its company commanders, 2nd Lieutenant Henry Fluck, rested his men when they began collapsing. When a brigadier general stormed up and ordered the lieutenant to get his soldiers on their feet immediately, Fluck replied, "You can just go straight to hell." Nonplused, the general repeated himself and Fluck enunciated where he thought the general should go. He disobeyed so that he could get his men to their destination late rather than not at all. The general stomped away in a huff, and the men made it. Soon thereafter Martin fined Fluck two hundred dollars so that he could avoid court-martialing him and admitted that he too would have disobeyed the general.[175]

The chronic problems that the Carolina Maneuvers revealed proved that the Army was not ready for combat. Still stumbling after two years of effort at improved readiness, the 28th Infantry Division's performance called into question the wisdom behind the National Guard system of the 1930s. It also showed the inappropriateness of the expandable army concept for responding to mid-twentieth-century security threats within just a few months of mobilization. Pennsylvania had failed to adequately train, retain, and field a highly skilled nucleus of officers and NCOs around which new recruits could coalesce—one of the foundations of the expandable army. In light of the structural problems and the chronic underfunding of the National Guard during the 1930s, the PNG's performance in 1941 was a logical outgrowth of congressional policies on military funding, staffing, training, and procurement. The officers and men of the PNG had done their best considering the meager appropriations of the Depression years. Clearly, fielding an effective mass army during the twentieth century was a task requiring years, not months.

5

The Pennsylvania National Guard and American Society

Soldiers in the Pennsylvania National Guard interacted with society in ways distinctive from the manner in which the Regular Army related to the country and its people. Guardsmen had an unsettled and insecure relationship with their employers, who were ambivalent about adjusting work schedules to allow for National Guard training. Since they were civilian-soldiers, the public responded to them with greater warmth than they did to regulars. Because they were civilians first, recruiters approached them with appeals to civilian and local values. Although the PNG leadership expressed a desire for a cross-section of the state's young men as recruits, the social profile of the PNG volunteers did not match the profile of the state. Neither fully civilian nor fully military, the PNG leadership evinced a set of values that influenced its relationship with the War Department.

Relations with Employers

National Guardsmen had to navigate between the time needed for training and the work schedules of their employers. With unemployment at 17 percent, the country was still in the grip of the Great Depression in 1939 and 1940. Workers were easy to come by and jobs were at a premium.[1] National Guard soldiers needed to gain some scheduling leniency from their employers in order to attend their drills. When summer maneuvers approached, a guardsman had to persuade his employer to give him two weeks off in order to attend. Gaining cooperation from employers demanded constant attention from the Pennsylvania National Guard, especially from General Martin. This experience added another dimension to the term "civil-military relations," which normally refers to relations between the military high command and civilian leaders, particularly between the Joint Chiefs of Staff on one side and the president and the Congress on the other. Martin used his dual position as adjutant general of Pennsylvania and commanding general of the 28th Division with his political talents to ease the development of the division from a local civic institution to a war-fighting organization.

In the middle of 1939, the greatest NG-employer challenge was time off for summer maneuvers. For someone who was an invariably young employee with no seniority to ask his boss for two weeks off in 1939, even for as noble a task as military training, was a somewhat risky proposition, considering the economic environment. Pennsylvania National Guard members learned during the 1939 maneuvers that they needed plenty of lead time to make arrangements with their employers to be absent.[2] When the War Department announced the special seven-day field training program for the Guard in the fall of 1939, unit commanders worried about the impact on their troops' jobs. Companies were used to granting guardsman employees two weeks off in the summer, but this supplementary training cycle did not follow the pattern to which they were accustomed. The economy had enjoyed an upswing and, with it, a demand for workers and products. Businesses therefore could less afford to grant the men time away from their shifts. Many of the soldiers had little seniority and were reluctant to ask for leniency. Fortunately, commanders paid visits to employers to seek their cooperation and printed articles in newspapers explaining the need for time away from work. Commanders did not always have to beseech employers for understanding. The Kiwanis Club of Coraopolis, for example, asked the commander of the Service Company, 103rd Medical Regiment, to describe their operations at the Kiwanis's first meeting of the fall, which gave the medics a chance to convey the importance of their duties. Kiwanis members were "the men who employ our boys, and the more they understand about our work the easier it is going to be to obtain their cooperation when we need it."[3] Governor Arthur H. James asked businesses for their understanding in November. Guardsmen also had to find time for another drill per week.[4]

The week away from work that fall was a sacrifice for the men. Their wages averaged about twenty dollars a week, but field training paid only seven dollars a week.[5] Employers could have replaced them had they wished. Since NG service cost employers and employees time and money, patriotism played a role in their generosity and motives. Many employers, both corporate and small business, actually paid their soldier-workers their full wage while they were away on maneuvers that fall. Many of the remainder made up the difference between the PNG's one dollar a day pay and the soldier's normal wage.

A few offered no financial assistance, but still allowed the employees to miss work.[6] Furthermore, many business owners personally encouraged their workers in the PNG to attend their camps, and reassured General Martin of their advocacy. They wanted to support the strengthening of national defense.[7] The Berwick Car and Foundry Works, where many of the 3rd Battalion of the 109th Infantry were employed, released its shift workers for National Guard duty without a second thought.[8] Martin suggested that the men express their appreciation to their employers personally, since he had done so himself.[9] During the holidays he added, "I wish to take this opportunity of expressing my appreciation and admiration for the totally unselfish and intensely patriotic way in which corporations and individual employers have, without hesitation, allowed their employees time off from their employment to undertake the additional training."[10]

Commanders who thought seven continuous days of field operations would hurt their soldiers' relations with their bosses, or would prevent them from attending at all, opted for a three-day exercise followed by a four-day excursion at a later date. Other commanders were able to train their units in a single week.[11] Across the country larger businesses had been cooperative and morale was high, but in the opinion of New York's Major General William N. Haskell, most guardsmen would not be able to continue the pace of two drills per week.[12]

General Marshall shared these concerns. Following the invasion of Poland, he warned against pulling guardsmen away from their civilian occupations until national security demanded such a drastic action.[13] He understood that the Guard's greatest challenge was providing adequate training for its soldiers without taking them away from their civilian jobs so frequently that the men got fired.[14] The sudden upswing of support by employers was short-lived, however, for the PNG received consistent reports in the winter of 1940 that businesses not only discouraged employees from joining the Guard, but also threatened to fire them if they did. The *Harrisburg Telegraph* agreed that enlistment posed a difficulty for employers, but argued that dissuading enlistment was a choice with consequences far worse than lower productivity. The *Telegraph* called for an end to "lip service" patriotism and asked businesses to make the necessary sacrifices on behalf of preparedness.[15] The chief of staff also found that by December the initial enthusiastic employer support was waning and that the imposition of Guard service on work schedules was "becoming a matter of serious concern." He recommended that the Guard and War Department make fewer requests for additional training, but inexplicably

Marshall wanted to extend the two-drill-per-week policy to March 1, 1940, a direct contradiction.[16] When he brought in National Guard commanders and staff officers to join Regular Army divisions for special training in the winter of 1940, he flew them to their assignment on Friday afternoon and returned them home Tuesday morning so that they would not miss an entire week of work. The Guard officers had to do this over the weekend because they could not be away from their jobs for that long—a constraint the Army had to bear in mind.[17] Back in Pennsylvania, as production increased in Erie, Company E of the 112th Infantry saw drill attendance fall because many men had to work the night shift.[18]

When the Guard and the War Department entered discussions on the length of the summer 1940 maneuvers, training and employment collided. Conflicts between jobs and PNG duty had for months been forcing some Pennsylvania guardsmen to leave the service throughout the middle of 1940.[19] The Army wanted a whole month, but Martin feared that even twenty-one days would harm the Guard unless the government supported the effort by spelling out the danger to the country and the need for training. Three weeks of maneuvers would be hard on enlisted men because they would require three weeks of generosity from their employers. National Guard adjutant generals agreed that a proposed four-week field exercise would be catastrophic. It would force the best officers and men to choose their livelihoods over the Guard. Adjutant generals asked the men and their employers for their opinions, and the great majority could justify only a three-week maneuver. In Illinois, for instance, one-fifth of the men knew they could not endure a one-month summer exercise.

A good public relations campaign was going to be necessary to ensure that soldiers got to attend without fear of retaliation from their bosses. Martin argued that even a twenty-one-day maneuver required the declaration of a national emergency, and he believed the security crisis justified that completely. He also believed that the War Department would have no trouble convincing the populace of the need for three weeks, and that employers would readily acquiesce once they realized the seriousness of the German menace.[20] Scuttlebutt from the troops was mixed. They were ready and willing for three weeks of field training, but they also knew that many employers across the country opposed maneuvers of that duration. One guardsman commented that some of them had been preparing for mobilization for two decades and ought not to complain when the call came.[21] E. H. Kent, a former captain of the 107th Field Artillery writing from Wilkes-Barre, warned that many would resign and the

Guard would have to replace them with less-desirable men who could not find jobs.[22] The chief of the National Guard Bureau supported no more than twenty-one days of field training.[23]

Anticipating the August 1940 maneuvers, Marshall once again appealed to employers not to threaten the jobs of men in the National Guard. Martin made the same petition before the Pennsylvania Chamber of Commerce, calling the protection of guardsmen's jobs an employer's duty. He agreed that businesses were going to suffer for letting employees attend field training, but found the Chamber supportive. Martin also found some allies among the state's newspapers. The *Harrisburg Telegraph* supported his challenge, as did the *Punxsutawney Spirit,* the *Allentown Morning Call,* and the *Uniontown Genius.*[24] When Troop I of the 103rd Cavalry ran into difficulties maintaining full strength, the *Spirit* called on local businesses to pitch in out of patriotism: "Not only should the employer eagerly acquiesce in permitting time off for the training periods, but he should arrange a pay differential that would cause his trooper employee to suffer no financial hardship as a result of the time taken from his civilian duties."[25]

When Martin spoke before the Pennsylvania Chamber of Commerce in April, he asked that businesses assure guardsmen that their jobs would be waiting for them when they returned from summer field training. The Chamber responded with overwhelming support, wrote every member, and urged them not to threaten guardsmen's jobs.[26] By May the National Association of Manufacturers endorsed the extended field training and wrote letters to each of its members encouraging them to "permit employees who are members of the National Guard to attend without loss of pay such maneuvers as may be required by the War Department."[27] Marshall told the press on May 6 that because the National Guard constituted 75 percent of the Initial Protective Force, it had to increase its field training to three weeks.[28] Martin continued to lobby the Pennsylvania business community in May for leniency for his soldiers. Many businesses complied, offering to continue to pay their PNG employees during the field exercise.[29] The Pennsylvania Edison Company, for instance, decided to pay its guardsmen's salaries for two weeks, and pay the difference between their Guard and civilian pay for the third. Its president, J. Harry Shearer, encouraged other businesses in Altoona to do likewise: "It is the duty of industry and commerce in every community to cooperate as much as possible with the National Guard in any manner possible."[30] Just before the Plattsburg Maneuvers, guardsmen from the Pittsburgh area found out that they were not going to lose pay or vacation time during the exercise, thanks to the Retail Merchants Association.[31] Such support extended outside the state. Colonel Robert A. Roos, an Army reservist and San Francisco businessman, won the support in July of the National Retail Dry Goods Association and the National Association of Retail Clothiers and Furnishers, who were prepared to offer sixty-day leaves.[32]

When discussion switched to building a mass army and mobilizing the National Guard following the fall of France, the need for training, burden sharing, and the growing economy collided. Prior to congressional action, thousands nationwide left the Guard because they were afraid they would be mobilized for a few months, return to civilian life, and find that they had been fired from the job they had worked so hard to obtain.[33] This was a great fear among the PNG's leadership before induction into federal service. In all likelihood, the men with the greatest expertise—those with the most years of service—had families who were financially dependent on them. Resignations for this reason were frequent.[34]

Protecting jobs required continued effort after the Plattsburgh Maneuvers. In the fall of 1940, members of the Pennsylvania National Guard Association passed a resolution calling for laws protecting guardsmen's jobs during the one year of active service that was by then imminent.[35] Later that fall, Congress wrote into law protections for soldiers even though they faced a year of mobilization. By statute, employers had to rehire mobilized guardsmen once they returned from duty.[36] In addition, Congress equalized pay between National Guard and Regular soldiers.[37]

Relations with Locals

The public's opinion of the National Guard underwent great change in the three years prior to America's entry into World War II. During the inauguration parade for Governor James in January 1939, isolationists in the crowd harassed the PNG without mercy. They counted cadence to throw off the marching troops and yelled, "Left shoulder arms," which new recruits obeyed by mistake. The reporter had never seen such a hostile crowd.[38] Around Carnegie, Pennsylvania, at least, the average citizen believed the PNG existed to break strikes and that it was not truly an integral part of national defense policy.[39] Before the war the 103rd Quartermaster Regiment urged community involvement. National Guardsmen needed to join and speak to civic organizations and schools on the nature of patriotism so as to instill more pride in their country.[40] In August 1939, about four thousand people turned out to see the retirement parade for Major General Edward C. Shannon in Columbia, a speaking program, and a drum corps performance.[41] A year after the poor reception at the inauguration, the PNG made use of Army Day (April 21) and Memorial Day celebrations to improve bonds with the local population and convince people of the necessity of military preparedness. In Franklin, Company L of the 112th Infantry achieved near-perfect attendance for the Memorial Day celebration, which reflected that its members were "appreciative of the civic obligations not comprehended in the oath of enlistment."[42] The 109th Field Artillery participated in several Memorial Day parades and noticed that it was under constant public scrutiny.[43] On its own, the 112th Infantry participated in several parades with organizations such as the Veterans of Foreign Wars and the Salvation Army.[44] Just after its return from the Manassas Maneuvers in August, the 110th marched in the parade for the Grand Army of the Republic in Pittsburgh.[45]

Sometimes companies and batteries invited the local community to examine their encampments up close. During the June run-up for the August 1939 Manassas Maneuvers, Company H and Headquarters Company, 110th Infantry, invited the people of Washington to tour their bivouac. They treated over 500 people to presentations on machine guns, rangefinders, radios, and defense against chemical attack.[46] At Oil City, the 112th Infantry staged a set-piece demonstration, while several thousand people watched as Company L attacked Company M. It was here that citizens saw aircraft drop sacks of flour as simulated bombs.[47] A couple of months later it did the same at Johnsonburg, during which it demonstrated the taking of a machine-gun nest on a hill opposite the town—at night under the light of an aerial flare. A hundred locals crammed into the Howitzer Company's armory in Oil City in order to see a demonstration, while over in Ford City, Company C held a "Regimental Day Celebration" for 250 civilian and military townspeople.[48] At Clearfield, 3,000 people viewed the 103rd Cavalry's retreat ceremony one evening, and the whole town turned out on another afternoon to watch it pass on its way to night operations training.[49] When the 109th Infantry departed for the maneuvers, the largest crowd to jam the Jersey Central Railroad Station in Scranton since World War I saw off the troops. "One thing is decidedly conspicuous, that is the keen interest manifested in our regiment by the civilian population . . . the public is interested and will cooperate."[50] During its November 1939 field training, the people of Pemberton, New Jersey, welcomed the 111th Infantry with open arms, convincing one soldier that it was "the friendliest town they ever got into."[51] In Scranton, "dense lines of civilians" watched the 109th Infantry march on December 9.[52] These public events continued in the spring of 1940.

Company E of the 110th drilled before a large crowd in Mount Pleasant, and Company A held a parade and open house in Monongahela.[53] General Martin was at the head of the Valley Forge Military Academy cadets during their Army Day parade.[54]

These efforts paid dividends, at least in Bloomsburg, which looked "with great favor upon the" 22nd Cavalry Division, recently stationed there. The locals had assisted "materially" in efforts to get the new formation up and running.[55] The Pennsylvania soldiers found ways to remain connected to civilian interests. Although one hundred vehicles of the 104th Cavalry completed a 200-mile round-trip trek to Cockeysville, Maryland, they stopped to watch the Maryland Hunt Club horse race along the way. Then two of its men managed to compete in the Radnor races outside of Philadelphia. A few days later, Captain J. B. Stauffer won four blue ribbons in the Lancaster Horse Show.[56]

The PNG made a concerted effort during the spring of 1940 to reach out to each community. Company M of the 110th hosted a dinner on April 6 and invited Latrobe city council members and representatives from local businesses.[57] PNG infantry companies and artillery batteries carried out a social function in their local communities, particularly because of the space available in their armories. The 109th Infantry sponsored a track meet for several high schools in the Scranton area.[58] In May 1940 the 111th Infantry's NCO Club saw large crowds attend their two "very successful dances."[59] Company D of the 110th Infantry even featured the Harry James Orchestra, one of the era's most popular, at its armory.[60] That same month "an abnormally large turnout" surprised the 112th Infantry at its dance. "The people of Meadeville are whole-heartedly behind the company in their social events, which has been our aim for quite some time."[61] When the 213th Coast Artillery hosted its annual regimental day for nearby residents, prominent members of Allentown also attended.[62] Two former PNG commanders, two congressmen, seven mayors, and many city leaders and state assemblymen from the seven cities and Lehigh, Northampton, and Lebanon Counties were on hand. During the speeches, Colonel Charles Curtis, the commanding officer, asserted that military training had made better citizens of its 1,200 men. The gathering highlighted American political-military life. It drew great attendance from significant political leaders—prior to the wake-up call the invasion of France soon provided. Patriotism, not class solidarity, formed the common ground for everyone from the political leaders to the urban working-class soldiers.[63] For the civic leadership to enthusiastically arm the young men of the working class was noteworthy in light of experiences elsewhere.[64]

At the same time he reached out, Edward Martin believed local communities ought to shoulder more responsibility for the care and manning of regimental companies. Each region in the state needed to know the contributions its units had made to national defense, and "[t]he community must realize that the responsibility of replacing those [soldiers] long identified with local units is a community duty." Martin echoed the aspiration of community "ownership" of its militia–National Guard duties, which had always been an unreachable goal.[65] Here Martin echoed another value of the National Guard, that of "community spirit."[66] To his company commanders he added, "Your organization must continue to be a cross-section of the communities in which they are stationed."[67] One guardsman in Montrose suggested that Martin establish a unit in that town if he sought greater community support. That way he and twelve other guardsmen would not have to drive so far to their drill.[68]

During the Selective Service debates during the summer of 1940, Martin attributed the need for conscription to "laziness." Speaking before the National Emergency Committee in Allegheny County, he lectured his audience that everyone was responsible for national defense. Martin believed that a draft would not be necessary if everyone took that responsibility to heart.[69] Martin also believed that distinctions between military and civilian responsibilities were misleading. The PNG needed to convince the people of Pennsylvania that in a democracy "the people" fought the wars and that they could not leave defense to the soldiers themselves.[70] On Memorial Day 1941, he reminded visitors to the PNG's Indiantown Gap cantonment that individuals on the home front were going to have to make sacrifices.[71]

Close ties between the Pennsylvania National Guard and individual communities were of great importance to Edward Martin and other long-service guardsmen: "A military plan in which all the people take part is a melting pot for democracy."[72] Nationalism was the companion of localism in the PNG's set of values. A National Guard Bureau officer believed that the guardsman's place was as a component of a *national* force, "the Army of the United States." Nothing in the pages of the *Pennsylvania Guardsman* disputed this. Guardsmen also took pride in fulfilling roles as both civilian and soldier. The citizen-soldier ideal—competence and involvement in both the civilian and military worlds—formed the basis of NG service.[73]

Characteristic of the parades and exhibitions was civic approval of the soldiers from their own communities, even though most of the soldiers had served for only a short time. Some in the Army recognized the National Guard's character as a local institution: "These local groups, partly military and partly social in character . . . are the cream of the countryside localities, maintaining traditions of their own vicinities, fostering public service for high patriotic effort."[74] That assessment was far more generous than that of some civic leaders, who often "viewed the Guardsmen as just another group of fraternal order devotees who happened to join the local volunteer Militia unit instead of the Elks."[75]

Recruiting Methods

The Pennsylvania National Guard overcame a variety of challenges in recruiting men to its units. It had to compete against increased civilian job opportunities and against the federal military. Localism and personal choice were two themes of the recruiting drive that took place as the NG expanded. Jim Dan Hill argued in the 1960s that the majority of armories had "waiting lists" of potential recruits from which they could select the best volunteers. Whether that was true or not, the PNG had to go out and recruit soldiers.[76]

When the War Department increased the division's authorized strength to 13,392 men in the fall of 1939, it had to recruit 2,200 more soldiers. Recruiting took off quickly, as the state enlisted 206 during the first week of October. Pennsylvania reached 94 percent of its personnel requirements by November 12, and four companies attained 100 percent manning by the 15th. By Christmastime, fifty-two companies, detachments, and batteries had reached 100 percent. The state's aggregate shortfall was 567 men, which put it within 96 percent of its goal.[77]

The regiments employed a variety of inducements. The 109th Infantry appealed to patriotism and pointed to its distinguished history. It proudly noted that all of the regimental staff officers save one had fought in World War I. It had sent several of its men to West Point as cadets.[78] The 112th Infantry's Company G from Erie was not impressed. It boasted that it had sent more cadets to West Point than any other company in the country; theirs was the company to join.[79] Radio broadcasts were often used. An officer of the 176th Field Artillery was a disc jockey and always put in a nightly plug for his regiment.[80] The PNG also promised listening mothers that competent officers would train their sons and that they would not return from war "ruined" men.[81] In May 1940 the 28th Military Police Company from York began a series of thirteen weekly broadcasts on the radio station WORK highlighting the company's history.[82] In the fall of 1940 the 111th Infantry broadcast four "half-hour dramatizations" of training maneuvers over Baltimore's WLIF.[83] The 109th Field Artillery interviewed its members on the air.[84] Armories appealed to young men's patriotism; the 109th Infantry called for "good, red-blooded Americans."[85]

The Guard had to use creative recruiting methods because competition from the Army, Army Air Corps, and the Civilian Conservation Corps made it difficult to reach full strength.[86] Those services were competing ruthlessly with the National Guard for manpower, pirating men who had already joined the Guard. From September 1939 to January 1940, 3,500 across the country left the Guard for the Army, Navy, and Marines.[87] Some units complained that "for every three we get we lose four."[88] The 176th FA's Company E lost one out of every three to the Army.[89] It was all legal, within the bounds set by Army Regulation 600-750. All that was necessary for transfer was for the NG to discharge the soldier first.[90] In Scranton, the Army obtained almost 10 percent of its recruits from the 109th Infantry.[91] The regiment thanked God when the Army recruiter reached his quota: "Now maybe we can keep a couple of men. We never saw such an insatiable appetite for recruits."[92] The 110th Infantry lost a parcel of men to the Army Air Corps, and some companies found recruiting their quota of eighty-three a challenge.[93] Company A of the 109th Infantry enlisted four men one day only to lose them when the men decided to join the Army or the CCC.[94] The PNG signed up nine men in Bradford after setting up a recruiting tent, but the Army had several recruiters combing the town.[95]

In a spirit of cooperation, the 107th FA paraded in Lebanon to assist in Selective Service registration, but this was the exception.[96] Recruiting competition remained a sore spot between the PNG and the Army. Regiments could not maintain their strength following federalization in 1941, even though more and more Selective Service troops arrived, because the Army continuously recruited men away from it. When the 109th Infantry left for the Virginia Maneuvers in August 1941, it departed with 2,230 men when it was supposed to have at least 3,000. Although it was short of the required strength, the unit was also a victim of an Army campaign, which had already lured away 120 men that month.[97]

Continual losses prevented the division from grouping the same soldiers together for a long period of time so as to build proficiency. The Army Air Corps was the worst rival for manpower. The division lost 437 men to it by July 1941.[98] Recruiters brazenly drove into the Indiantown Gap Military Reservation, located a regimental recreation hall, and set up a recruiting station with a loudspeaker right in front of it. Colonel Robert Morris of the inspector general's office wrote that NG officers found that that kind of behavior not only produced ill feelings toward the Regular Army, but also wrecked the morale and team spirit of the draftees. The Army Recruiting Service gave them the impression that the 28th National Guard Division was by nature a second-class outfit for which they should develop no affection. Morris reminded his superiors that the War Department was trying to build *one* army and that recruiters should not be allowed to raid "one component of the army for the benefit of another."[99]

A recovering economy took away one reason for men to enlist. Around Berwick, Pennsylvania, the shoe, underwear, and railroad car factories were finally humming, and for that reason young men had less of an economic incentive to join the military.[100] Out-of-town job opportunities were taking men away from Company C of the 110th.[101] The PNG units also lost soldiers to discharges, but some, like the 109th Infantry, had no difficulty in recruiting replacements.[102]

The Personnel Section of the PNG State Staff provided funding for recruiting posters, pamphlets, letters, and speeches. To add an air of mystique, it suggested that "[s]ocial affairs and ceremonies attended by local officials, wives, mothers, and prospective recruits **On Invitation Only** have a distinct value and must be arranged by the local officers" [boldface in original]. Advertisements with a "help wanted" approach were undesirable and may have made the Guard come across as simply a second job. Instead, units should sell its camaraderie and advantages. The staff suggested using home movies of Guard life, as well as open houses at armories, radio advertisements in quiz format, and outdoor drills during warm weather.[103] The 112th's Company E in Erie invited prospective recruits to its Christmas party, while Allentown's 213th Coast Artillery Regiment (Anti-aircraft) portrayed its second annual military ball as a posh, exclusive affair.[104] After Company A of the 110th in Monongahela held an open house and a parade on Army Day, seventeen men signed up.[105]

With this backdrop, the PNG employed two primary arguments in their recruiting drive. First, they asserted that NG service was superior to conscription into the Army. Regiments also encouraged young men to exercise some control over their futures by enlisting now instead of waiting for the draft.[106] Once the PNG was federalized, no one could volunteer to join it.[107] A man could join a nearby infantry company or artillery battery and serve with men from his hometown, or wait and take his chances with the draft board.[108] Time was of the essence, since President Roosevelt had mobilized four National Guard divisions on September 16, and voluntary enlistment was certainly superior to the draft.[109]

In addition, PNG companies often cited the fraternal nature of armory life as a recruiting inducement.[110] Furthermore, the 111th Infantry argued that by joining before federalization, men would gain a leg up on later recruits. Taking the long view, a guardsman was obligated to fulfill only two years of Reserve service after the year of active duty, while the conscript would face an inconvenient ten years in the Reserves after a three-year obligation. One would even learn a useful trade, and if one desired military service, what advantage was there in waiting for one's draft notice?[111]

Localism formed a central theme of the recruiting drive. For instance, the publicity campaign of the 107th FA stressed the advantages of serving in one's hometown unit.[112] Similarly, the 109th Infantry exploited that as its main selling point: "Enlist with us and be with your friends."[113] The 107th FA concluded that its "publicity campaign, stressing the advantages of service in home town units, has brought dozens of men of draft age to it."[114] When supporting the PNG recruiting campaign, newspapers emphasized: "Young men joining the 109th will be among friends and commanded by officers from the region. They will be more at home than in other outfits. These considerations, aside from the training and discipline they will receive, should weigh heavily in any decision they may make regarding enlisting."

"With the regiment brought up to its full strength of 1,900 men and officers, enlisted from local communities, it will retain its identity," wrote the 109th Infantry.[115] The *Canonsburg Daily* wrote, "By volunteering for the National Guard, he will be able to pick his associates."[116] Volunteers would remain in the state at the Indiantown Gap Military Reservation in Annville, where they could visit family members and girlfriends on weekends.[117]

Relations with Locals during Maneuvers

During deployments out of the state, the PNG made every effort to leave a good impression on locals. The Army paved the way at the Manassas Maneuvers when in January 1939 it met with local leaders in northern Virginia to ask their permission for trespass rights. The Army needed to find a way for troops to maneuver on private land surrounding Manassas Battlefield Park in order to run the maneuvers properly. When the Army showed the estimate of the money that the military would spend in the local area, the citizens' groups were easily convinced and persuaded local farmers not to require the Army to pay leases for trespass rights.[118]

At a lull during that exercise, the 28th Tank Company made some friends when it allowed locals to pose for photographs on one of its tanks.[119] When soldiers of the 103rd Medical Regiment encamped on a farm, the neighbor's children stopped, stared, and exclaimed, "My Gawd would you look at that! There's cousin Eddie talking to those damn Yanks!"[120] Master Sergeant W. F. Kennedy of the 111th had been warned that the soldiers would encounter sectional animosity in Virginia, but he found that everyone was friendly and polite. One "charming young lady" gently instructed him on the Southern version of "the war between the states."[121] On the last day, the area's local businessmen invited the PNG to return the following summer for another round of war games.[122] Following the exercise, Martin could not say enough about the positive attitude and helpfulness of the northern Virginia farmers. Municipal authorities were profoundly helpful, and the division promptly settled all property damage claims.[123]

Martin knew that the deployment to Plattsburgh, New York, the following summer was another public relations opportunity, the division's only chance to make a good first impression. He was pleased when the Pennsylvania Railroad complimented the "excellent" conduct of the 110th Infantry.[124] He implored his troops to minimize the wear and tear they inflicted on farmers' land during the maneuvers and to remember that they were their state's ambassadors. To add to their wholesome image, Martin asked the guardsmen to attend church on July 28 in uniform.[125] Martin himself met with officials in upstate New York and beamed when the mayors of Lisbon and Ogdensburg told him that his men behaved in an "exemplary" manner.[126] The 103rd Cavalry band coordinated concerts with the Rotary and Grange Clubs of Canton, while the 213th Coast Artillery (CA) did the same for four to five thousand people in Cortland, along with a display of its artillery pieces.[127] The PNG received a tremendous outpouring of interest and support from people along their way to the maneuvers in St. Lawrence County. Cortland welcomed the 111th Infantry with "a grand reception. They took us right to their collective heart."[128] Lisbon was the division's base camp, and many of the women there offered to do soldiers' laundry, gave them coffee, cakes, and pies, and displayed all manner of hospitality.[129] The 109th Infantry even arranged for CBS radio to broadcast the training of its troops on August 7, 1940.[130] The people of upstate New York identified with the PNG forces as *their* army.

A year later the PNG received an even warmer welcome on their way to an exercise at the A. P. Mill Military Reservation in Virginia. Convoying through Emmetsburg, Maryland, the guardsmen waved back at the people lining the streets.[131] One soldier remarked, "Pardon my Southern accent, but we've heard 'you all' so often of late that we are beginning to wonder if this is a Yankee army after all. The Southerners have lived up to their well known hospitality.

It was heartening to witness the genial ovation we received when we passed through Southern towns en route here."[132] The 112th's Antitank Battalion found half-priced meals waiting for them in Middlesburg, Virginia, and the mayor sponsored another dinner in their honor. "Southern hospitality has not been exaggerated."[133] The division continued its efforts to form congenial bonds with the locals, as when the 104th Cavalry put on a dance for more than two thousand people in Fredericksburg. It left behind a "splendid reputation."[134] Churches, Elks, Rotarians, Lions, Kiwanis, and the Salvation Army provided reading rooms, billiards, and entertainment for the men.[135]

General Martin was shrewd in orchestrating these kinds of events and impressions. When the War Department began federalizing National Guard units for a year's training in the fall of 1940, tens of thousands of soldiers began to inundate the small towns near their training camps. Liquor, prostitution, and apartment price gouging became troubling problems.[136] The Army received terrible publicity from a *Life* magazine article in December 1940, which included photographs of soldiers visiting a strip-tease club, and which claimed soldiers could visit red-light districts the Army had inspected as long as they stopped "at a prophylactic station on the way home."[137]

Martin initiated contact between his soldiers and the people of Virginia when the division staged a firepower demonstration for locals during their August 1941 deployment. Hundreds of civilians gathered to watch the latest in antitank defenses, but a close examination was discouraging. PNG soldiers assured them that .50 caliber machine guns could slow down a tank blitz by forcing the tank soldiers to close their hatches, rendering them blind. Good PR, mines, bangalore torpedoes, Molotov cocktails, flamethrowers, artillery, and 3-inch antiaircraft guns joined in to reassure the crowd that tanks had met their match.[138]

When the Pennsylvanians embarked for the Carolina Maneuvers just three weeks later, they witnessed yet another outpouring of grass-roots support. Children of Martinsburg, West Virginia, were let out of school so that they could wave at the passing convoy. Had they looked closely, however, they would have noticed that the antitank unit trucks towed a parade of sheet metal connected to wooden sticks with just eight 37mm guns interspersed "that lent a little dignity to our columns."[139] Similarly, their machine guns were often nothing more than wooden replicas.[140] When the division stopped in Greensboro, North Carolina, families went out into the streets and took soldiers into their homes and private parties; the city's mayor and civic organizations had already coordinated the welcome.[141] Restaurants did not raise their prices, and "[e]verywhere the soldier seemed welcomed, in marked contrast to conditions during other Summer maneuvers."[142] Guardsmen stared at each other in disbelief at the generosity. Not only did the usual civic clubs bend over backward for them, but individual households had also prepared spare bedrooms for them and invited the soldiers to stay the weekend. Towns erected showers, and colleges listed dance partners.[143] "The farther south we go, the greater the hospitality, until . . . it reached near hysteria in a veritable eruption of dances for the boys."[144] Martin had "never seen such a display of patriotism and cordiality."[145] The PNG returned the favor by putting on a dance of its own.[146] The division probably organized entertainment with the cities behind the scenes so as to keep the men away from trouble. The medical corps published warnings against venereal disease with the purpose of steering the men away from the source.[147]

Another *Life* article may have set up the guardsmen for this surprise. Its August 18, 1941, issue had published the way in which "nice girls" in Fayetteville, North Carolina—right where the maneuvers were going to take place—"shunned" young men in uniform, many of whom were gentlemen.[148] Relations between regulars at Fort Pope and Carolinians had not been amicable during the 1930s. A Fayetteville pastor had warned his congregation, "Never let your daughter be seen with a soldier."[149] Perhaps the Tarheels had read the article, too, and decided to give the Yankees the benefit of the doubt, recognizing that these were civilian-soldiers, not long-service regulars. The civilians' actions show that they considered that this army was theirs and that the soldiers were like their own relatives and friends. Because the majority had just recently joined the PNG, they were still more civilian than military in their habits and demeanor—much more so than men of the interwar Regular Army.

The Carolina Maneuvers were so demanding that they left little time for mingling with locals once they began. Still, when they climbed aboard their trucks on December 7, the Pennsylvanians took with them fond memories of the South and its people.[150] "We received the grandest treatment from all the good people that we came into close contact. Not by the farthest stretch did any of us expect the fine 'all-out' treatment extended by the citizens of the South."[151] Annie B. Johnson of Marion, South Carolina, wrote, "We have never had more courteous, thoughtful, and appreciative young people in our home. . . . They seemed to have the makings of good South Carolinians in them."[152] Onlookers cheered them as they motored north, but then the guardsmen sensed a change in the tone of their behavior. When Henry Fluck's convoy stopped in Madison, Virginia, on December 8, they learned of the Pearl Harbor attack.

At another stop they heard that they were in for the duration of the war. The men older than twenty-eight were stunned, for they had been on the verge of being discharged. Morale fell for a few days before rebounding.[153] To lift their spirits, General Martin ensured that as many as possible got to go home for the holidays.[154] Half remained at Indiantown Gap and practiced small-unit tactics. The "over twenty-eights" gathered themselves and pressed on.[155]

Relations with Pennsylvania Locals

Local institutions offered their support to the Pennsylvania National Guard in a variety of ways. Muhlenberg College, for instance, offered three full scholarships to eligible enlisted men of the 213th Coast Artillery. The regiment found this exceptionally beneficial, since many of its soldiers would not otherwise have had a shot at a college education.[156] The Pro-To Club of Wilkes-Barre showed its appreciation when the mayor and several city officials held a fund-raiser to buy the 109th FA stoves and coffeepots for their road marches.[157] As induction day, February 17, 1941, approached, civic and business leaders made elaborate preparations to send off their soldiers with a great flourish. In Bradford, for instance, the Board of Commerce fed the men at a huge banquet. All of the military and civic organizations joined together in a parade commemorating the departure of the 112th Infantry's Company K. The Veterans of Foreign Wars in Warren planned a similar celebration for Company I.[158] Crowds in other towns also venerated their soldiers as they left. Over a thousand, for instance, watched a review of the 109th FA.[159] Nicholas Kafkalas recalled: "When Company D left Monessen, the people in Monessen knew that something different was happening. They were aware that the United States of America felt that they had to mobilize, or partially mobilize. The fact that Company D, which was then up to a strength of about 95 people, including officers and enlisted men, was leaving—left a mark on Monessen."[160]

Civilians supported the PNG during its year at Indiantown Gap. The General Assembly provided funding for recreational facilities. The Harrisburg Senators baseball team played several benefit games to raise money for the camp and played the Pittsburgh Pirates at Indiantown Gap on August 12 for free.[161] Harrisburg's Catholic recreation center hosted a dance for the 109th Infantry, while an Episcopal women's organization from Wilkes-Barre gave the 109th FA a large brass cross. Harrisburg's Jewish community provided a menorah to the division.[162] Once baseball season began, the Harris Amusement Company of Pittsburgh paid for the 107th FA's baseball uniforms.[163]

During the 1941 encampment at Indiantown Gap, the division made every effort to be up-front regarding the conditions of the garrison. When they arrived in the middle of February, snow, gray skies, and partially completed facilities greeted them. Buildings were unpainted, trash was scattered everywhere from the recent construction, and roads were still unpaved.[164] These conditions were understandable since construction of the 23,000-man facility had not begun until September 1940.[165] Commanders immediately took steps to clean up the cantonment.[166] To avoid accusations of a cover-up, General Martin then made sure the press was fully informed. He led twenty-two reporters on a tour of the camp—before it was presentable—and made every effort to keep it as accessible as possible for family and friends. "Nothing, absolutely nothing, in this camp is suppressed."[167] He knew that he had to be frank in his disclosure of the poor conditions there, or the press would have accused him of hiding them from the public. Consequently, he also welcomed York's Rotary Club and invited them to sample the soldiers' food. On Army Day, visitors watched the parade and toured the camp.[168]

Martin also argued that training in the winter weather had the advantage of toughening the men.[169] Because the soldiers trained in the bad weather, accusations of mistreatment continued to reverberate. The 111th Infantry took public relations matters into their own hands, broadcasting a series of radio messages called "We're in the Army Now" to explain the reasons for the miserable outdoor training, to connect with the public, and to assure Pennsylvanians that the division was run competently.[170]

Since the mobilization of National Guard divisions was to be for one year, followed by a return to civilian life, Martin had to pursue several simultaneous objectives. Naturally, he had to see that the men received basic and intermediate level military training, but he decided that he could not isolate his soldiers from the civilian world. Wishing to civilianize their military experience, he therefore went to considerable lengths to help the soldiers maintain contacts with their families and loved ones. Every weekend hundreds of the soldiers visited home. Families trekked to the Gap to see their sons. The division even raised several buildings just for visiting friends and relatives.[171] Indeed, Martin wanted the men to go home on weekends as much as possible as long as they returned by midnight on Sunday.[172] He was trying to find alternatives to the strip clubs and prostitutes *Life* had publicized in the fall of 1940. Martin called for colleges and churches to encourage "home life" both in the camps and when the guardsmen visited their hometowns. The 28th Division emphasized high morale and athletic recreation as alternatives to drunkenness and prostitutes, for it knew that soldiers would turn to meretricious diversions if they got bored.[173] "Unhealthy collecting places," presumably brothels or at least seedy bars (the article did not specify), had sprouted on the outskirts of the camp and in neighboring towns. By August 1941 the division had had sixty cases of venereal disease, but on the whole, the division's men avoided prostitutes.[174] A month later the division was down to ten cases.[175] Here the PNG differed from the Regular Army, which held a more relaxed attitude toward soldiers' off-duty behavior. Still, an Army physician warned, "Flies spread disease, so keep yours buttoned."[176]

As individual armories had done before federalization, the division organized dances. The 109th Infantry entertained "100 of Harrisburg's fairest daughters in one of the most highly appreciated 'Defense of America' gestures to be offered." It promised to be a very "busy social season."[177] Women from the surrounding towns ensured that other dances succeeded, and the first USO show arrived in June.[178] Mothers and girlfriends visited the camp.[179] Tommy Dorsey, a famous band leader, visited the 109th FA Band.[180] Martin credited these actions with keeping the division's morale high.[181] His overall efforts were in step with War Department policies designed to maintain soldiers' morale.[182]

To encourage greater contact between the PNG and the public, division components made public appearances across the state. Soldiers paraded at Johnstown's Americanization Day in front of twenty thousand people. Even regulars complimented the guardsmen's precision. Wearing their new khaki uniforms and helmets and rifles with bayonets fixed, men from the 109th Infantry and Field Artillery Regiments marched before 60,000 in Scranton for the city's diamond jubilee celebration. As the men made their way back to the camp, women cried and girls waved from the roadsides.[183] Regimental bands entertained surrounding towns and were treated to church suppers in return.[184]

Martin was almost as concerned with preparing his soldiers for the work world after they returned to civilian life as he was with preparing them for fighting a war. About five hundred of the state's guardsmen were unable to complete high school because of the call to active duty, so Martin persuaded the state superintendent of public instruction, Francis B. Haas, to waive the last three months of high school and award them "certificates."[185] Enough time remained in the evenings for the guardsmen to pursue continuing education after supper. Up at six and to bed at ten, the work day apart from meals was only about ten hours.[186] The general formed an educational committee consisting of a principal, a teacher, and a former judge to set up college prep courses.[187] It managed to recruit twenty teachers, including five Ph.D.s from Princeton, Elizabethtown College, Lebanon Valley College, and Hershey Junior College.[188] Available classes included automobile mechanics, stenography, sign painting, mapping and sketching, math, accounting, German, Spanish, welding, and business courses. The latter three were the most popular, and more than five thousand men applied.[189] By the time the program ended in August, two thousand men had been taught in almost one hundred classes.[190] Given that the Second World War was raging, this was an odd use of time, but schooling with post-mobilization civilian employment in mind was in accord with the National Defense Act of 1916.[191] The PNG should have used that time to prepare for war, but America's involvement was not assured until the Pearl Harbor attack ten months after the 28th Division was federalized, and most Americans hoped against hope to stay out of the war.[192]

Team sports were another way in which General Martin endeavored to civilianize the PNG's year of active duty. Division engineers completed a baseball field in April.[193] With the realities of the Depression in mind, he opened participation to everyone. Many of the young men had sacrificed the chance to play sports in high school because they had to take jobs to help their families reach a living income. Some might even be able to use the sports leagues as a springboard to athletic careers once the mobilization ended. Rumors abounded that baseball scouts were going to reconnoiter the military reservation with their own agendas. In addition, the men boxed, played volleyball, and saw no end of pick-up baseball games, as well as organized games.[194] In addition to the intramural tournaments, the PNG formed teams for competition against college athletes. Finding a 440-yard specialist from Penn State in their midst, it sent a track team to the Penn Relays.[195] In June, the 28th Division and 104th Cavalry Regiment fielded teams of former high school and college stars, including the world champion hurdler Frank Fuller, for the Amateur Athletic Union meet at Franklin Field. Soldiers from the 109th Infantry took second and third in the 100-meter dash.[196] The 104th Cavalry sent twenty-one equestrians to a riding competition and held a benefit for the Junior Red Cross in Harrisburg.[197] In April the men suddenly ramped up their work during their spare time, leaving Martin moved by their dedication. Actually, they were completing work early so that they could make it to opening day of trout season.[198]

6

Social Class, Recruiting, and Ideology

Recruiting and Social Class

A close examination of the soldiers who volunteered for the PNG prior to its induction into federal service highlights several issues surrounding American military service before the United States became fully involved in the war. Starting with an examination of the 1,988 PNG enlistment records remaining from 1939 to 1941, one can construct a social profile of the PNG volunteers. This collection, held in the Pennsylvania State Archive, is fortuitous, because the bulk of the Army's enlistment records were burned up in a 1972 fire at the National Personnel Record Center in St. Louis.[1] Each PNG enlistment record contains data on the volunteer's residency, employment, years of employment, years of education, birthday, and dependents—enough information to allow one to draw conclusions on the soldier's social class and reasons for joining the National Guard.

Conscription affected the PNG's recruiting efforts in 1940–41. As debates over Selective Service raged, enlistments in the PNG climbed somewhat in June 1940, then fell for the rest of the summer as young men of the state waited to see whether conscription might be in their future. Before the year was up, Selective Service provided a direct boost to Pennsylvania National Guard rolls. Upon enactment of the Burke-Wadsworth Selective Service bill on September 16, 1940, draft-age men began enlisting in the PNG in greater numbers in October.[2]

This proportional relationship between conscription and volunteering was nothing new. The United States exploited the threat of compulsory service to boost voluntary enlistment during the Civil War, when people considered being drafted a badge of shame. During World War I, the Army did not use the draft just as a prod to persuade men to volunteer; it drafted millions. The PNG took advantage of the World War II draft to encourage men to volunteer for National Guard service instead.[3]

There was a direct relationship between world events, domestic policy, and volunteering for the PNG. Enlistments rose briefly following the invasion of Poland in September 1939. A similar increase occurred when Germany conquered France. A short, sharp spike in Pennsylvania enlistments followed the implementation of the draft in the fall of 1940, but the relationship between the draft and volunteering became most evident as the 28th Division's federalization date of February 17, 1941, approached. Once it became public knowledge in October that the War Department was going to mobilize the PNG that winter for a year of service, enlistments picked up.[4] Personal preference was the deciding factor for many. January and February 1941 were the last opportunities for men to choose to join the 28th Division of their own volition, and volunteering skyrocketed during the six weeks leading up to its federalization. Volunteering for the National Guard was a last act of personal sovereignty for these men in a country moving systematically toward full mobilization.

The Social Profile of Pennsylvania National Guard Volunteers

The citizens who volunteered for the Pennsylvania National Guard shared a number of characteristics. Above all, the great majority came from the urban working class. Of the entire sample, 1,345 (67 percent) worked as unskilled laborers, while 33 percent (643) held skilled, clerical, or professional jobs. Rough comparisons reveal that in terms of employment, the enlistees diverged significantly from the rest of Pennsylvania's working population. U.S. Census records, which provide labor information in much greater detail than simply "skilled" or "unskilled," show that 44 percent of Pennsylvania's male labor force consisted of skilled labor.[5] Only 8 percent, or 161 individuals, of the PNG volunteers were skilled. More specifically, just 18 recruits had been electricians, only 20 worked as carpenters, while 60 had been mechanics. Twenty-three percent of the PNG-enlisted force, numbering 458, worked at white-collar jobs, compared with 17 percent holding such jobs statewide.[6] Two percent (40) held professional or executive jobs, as compared with 5.6 percent for the state. Within the unskilled segment of the recruits, 398 listed "laborer"—the most commonly listed job. Clerk was the next most frequently held position at 158, followed by student (120), truck driver (102), and salesman (69). Only 29 enlistees were farmers—1.4 percent—compared with 4 percent of the state's population who engaged in some sort of farmwork. Nine (0.4 percent) of the volunteers were lawyers, matching closely the 0.3 percent statewide. Small numbers of recruits held jobs in numerous other fields. There were, for instance, two bartenders, a milkman, and a steel miller.[7]

The high percentage of unskilled workers among the enlistees can be explained at least in part by their youth. Normally one enters wage labor at the apprentice level, working one's way up to skilled positions.[8] Thus, many of the young enlistees who held unskilled jobs would have ascended into skilled labor later in their thirties and forties. Therefore, their actual social class leaned more toward skilled labor than the employment statistics indicate. Reflective of their youth, the soldiers averaged only 3.9 years of work experience, with a mode (the most frequent answer) of one year of work experience.[9]

Data are unclear on the number of soldiers who were unemployed, because many recruits wrote nothing regarding their employment status. While some marked "unemployed," others suggested that they were out of work by not listing a job. Those who filled in nothing for their career have been counted as unemployed, because if they had had a job, they would have noted it. On the other hand, some may have written the title of the last job they held. An unemployed truck driver could have written "truck driver" as his trade. Therefore, 227 jobless recruits—an 11 percent unemployment rate—is probably a low figure. The state unemployment rate at the time for males fourteen and over was 17.7 percent.[10]

Perceived another way, as many as 89 percent of the recruits had jobs when they enlisted. Most men did not join for economic reasons, and in fact, enlistments increased even as the demand for civilian labor grew.[11] Enlistments did not correlate with employment opportunities. Instead, enlistments increased after the invasion of Poland and the later implementation of conscription, and subsided the most during the 1939 and 1940 holiday seasons. These figures indicate that men were not exploiting the National Guard as a last resort means of employment, and that the PNG's rolls were not filled with the chronically out of work. Their behavior contrasts sharply with previous wars. From the Revolution to the Civil War, economic incentives were a key aspect of recruiting. The Army offered bounties to potential soldiers, in the form of either land grants or cash signing bonuses.[12] The employment status of the 1940–41 troops combined with the growing economy and the proportional relationship between the worsening of the war and the rate of enlistment indicate that the PNG soldiers volunteered so as to participate in national defense, especially after being drafted became likely, and a one-year mobilization for the PNG became certain. Money was not an incentive for joining the Pennsylvania National Guard in 1940 and 1941, as volunteers received no signing bonus at all.

Indeed, a man enlisting in the PNG, knowing it was about to be mobilized for a year, was accepting a huge cut in pay. Mobilized privates made $21 a month. If inducted to federal service after four months of weekend Guard service, they received $30 a month.[13] While the wages PNG soldiers had received as civilians varied among regiments, the men's civilian earnings put them above the state's average. Soldiers in the 109th Infantry Regiment, for instance, averaged $52.88 a month in their civilian jobs, while Headquarters troops averaged $105.84, even though there was little variation in the types of jobs they held. The overall average in civilian wages for the PNG was $86.40, but this is a deflated statistic because enlistees in Troop A of the 104th Cavalry did not report their wages. Since its members held high-paying jobs, the actual PNG average was higher. The mode of the division's monthly civilian wage is more informative at precisely $100 a month. This was considerably higher than the wages of many Pennsylvania men. In 1939, the census showed that the highest number of employed urban males statewide (545,854) reported an annual wage of under $100, and the next highest number of workers (253,647) earned $600–799.[14] Thus the average civilian annual wage of the PNG enlisted man was higher than that of many urban wage earners in their state. The 1938–41 enlistment data confirm assertions that as far as the PNG was concerned, the World War II American military underrepresented the lowest socioeconomic strata of the population.[15] The Pennsylvania National Guard was not an army of the underclass, but instead consisted of solidly educated working-class men, virtually all from urban areas.

The soldiers the PNG recruited were well-educated for the day. They had completed on average eleven years of school, while the mode was twelve. Forty-eight of the sixty-seven companies, troops, and detachments examined also had a mode of twelve years of schooling. Exactly 50 percent of the soldiers, 993 of 1,988, had finished at least a high school education. In comparison, only 11 percent of males statewide aged twenty-five and older had completed four years of high school.[16] Eighteen percent of the enlistees had achieved education beyond high school. Seven percent, comprising 150 soldiers, had graduated from college. One-fourth (37) of these men were in Troop A, 104th Cavalry. PNG volunteers compared favorably to the prewar Regular Army, in which "some 31 percent had less than an eighth grade education."[17] Only 3 percent of the PNG enlisted men had less than an eighth grade education. Overall, the Pennsylvanians were following a national trend; the educational level of new soldiers throughout the Army was on average much higher than that of the established peacetime enlisted force.[18]

Troop A offers an unusual study because its enlistees averaged fourteen years of schooling. The mode for Troop A was sixteen, which equates with completing college. Most of its soldiers were, in fact, college graduates. Fifty-five Troop A men out of ninety-eight for whom there are enlistment records signed on between November 1940 and February 17, 1941. Judging from their neighborhoods, jobs, and education, nearly all were from affluent families. Like the rest of the recruits, they lacked previous military experience. Seventeen of the ninety-eight were from locations as far away as Phoenix, Arizona, and Palm Beach, Florida, suggesting that the troop held a nationwide attraction among a certain class of individuals.[19] In fact, it had long been an upper-class unit. *Time* reported that "its rolls are almost synonymous with the Philadelphia social register."[20]

While the PNG had long claimed that it had scores of troops with many years of military experience, the training and longevity of its soldiers were in fact limited. Thirty percent of the Pennsylvania guardsmen enlisted in the six weeks prior to mobilization in February 1941. Forty-two percent of the 109th Infantry, for example, consisted of soldiers who joined in January–February 1941. Actually, the experience level was even lower than these data suggest, for many soldiers joined in October, November, and December of 1940, which certainly did not allow them enough time to gain anything but the most rudimentary military knowledge.[21] Of the 447 guardsmen serving a second enlistment or greater, the average year of their first enlistment was 1934. Those with more than a single enlistment comprised just 22 percent of the PNG. At 11 percent, the number of sergeants matched that of the Army precisely, but their proficiency did not approach that of their counterparts in the Army.[22] The press reported these deficiencies when the *Lebanon Daily News* wrote that the division ranked "no better than a recruit outfit in the eyes of the United States Army," and that it was going to have to go through thirteen weeks of basic training starting March 10, 1941.[23]

The Officers

There is less information available regarding the PNG officer corps, but clearly they were not the equals of their Regular Army counterparts. The most striking statistic is the high percentage of officers who were commissioned in the six weeks prior to federalization: 176 out of a total of 867.[24] Of these, 88 were sworn in on February 17—10 percent of the corps. Not surprisingly, 2nd lieutenant was the mode rank in 1941, and the overall average rank at federalization was 1st lieutenant. Eleven had enlisted as late as 1941, and 44 joined in 1940 prior to being commissioned from the ranks. The PNG officer corps averaged five years of experience as enlisted troops prior to receiving commissions.

The *Official National Guard Register* contains no information on the number of years of schooling the officers had completed, but it does contain data on their college education. Twenty-eight percent had graduated from college, and 8 percent were alumni of Ivy League universities, along with the occasional Duke, Johns Hopkins, and Chicago graduate. Since 72 percent of the corps did not hold degrees, it seems that merit as an enlisted soldier drove commissionings. Although it was laudable that most of the PNG guardsmen therefore had a shot at an officer's commission, the fact that nearly three-quarters of the prewar PNG officers did not have college degrees offers another explanation as to why West Point graduates, among others, viewed their abilities and potential with suspicion, if not disdain. By comparison, all members of the Officers' Reserve Corps had college degrees. One concerned NCO who had been in the National Guard wrote the CNGB in 1938 regarding this disparity. He had attended service schools with both Guard and Reserve officers, and his observations led him to conclude that Reserve officers were far superior to NG officers.[25] The one commodity the PNG had in abundance was artillery officers, who comprised 34 percent of the corps. At the same time it was deficient in infantry officers. It needed 452 of the latter, but had only 298 on hand.[26]

The PNG had boasted about the great number of officers who had fought in World War I, but by the Second World War, only 151, 17 percent, had served on the Western Front. More bothersome was the low percentage of officers who had completed any professional military education, such as the Infantry School or the Command and General Staff School, prior to 1940. Only 117 officers, or 14 percent, had done so. These factors did not prevent them from gaining promotions during the war. Three-fourths got promotions by 1943. Four reached colonel, and one, Charles A. Curtis, put on brigadier general's stars. Captains Thomas J. Noto and Adam J. Dreibelbies rose to lieutenant colonel by 1943, with Noto becoming the commander of 3rd Battalion, 109th Infantry.[27] The irascible Eric Fisher Wood made brigadier general and served on Eisenhower's staff.

The *Register* does not list the civilian occupations of the Guard officers, but anecdotal evidence suggests that the PNG leadership, at least, was exceptionally successful in their civilian pursuits. Lieutenant Colonel J. Victor Dallin, for example, was manager of the Philadelphia Airport.[28] Colonel Stanley F. Coar, commander of the 109th Infantry, was a lawyer.[29] Edward Martin was first among many politically active officers. His predecessor, Major General E. C. Shannon, had been both lieutenant governor and a delegate to the 1932 Republican National Convention.[30] Eric Fisher Wood was a prominent architect.[31] Typically, the cavalry drew from the "better sort" of men, families of higher status in their communities. In 1939, the Headquarters Troop, 22nd Cavalry Division, had noted that "[m]any of the young men who enlisted in the Troop are representatives of the best families in Bloomsburg."[32]

A number of guardsmen made considerable financial sacrifices to enlist in the PNG, such as a lawyer from Greensburg who joined the 110th Infantry as a private.[33] Another attorney signed on with the 112th Infantry's Company D while France succumbed to the Germans.[34] Not only did hundreds of men decide to join the Pennsylvania National Guard after FDR decided to mobilize it for a year, numerous PNG soldiers with dependents chose to remain in the Guard rather than remain with their families, suggesting further that patriotism was more important to them than mere economic concerns. In February 1941, 157 married soldiers (7.9 percent of the sample) mobilized, even though National Guard policy allowed men with dependents to avoid the call to active duty by accepting a discharge without any further service obligation.[35] Many left, but these men with dependents remained, such as the unmarried machinist from Allentown with four dependents. He may have chosen active duty to retain a guaranteed income, out of patriotic concern for his country, or because the mobilization was scheduled to last only a year.[36] A married laborer from Lyndora joined seven days prior to federalization, without claiming his wife and son as dependents. He may have done so for nationalistic reasons with their blessing, or he may have filed for divorce on his way to the recruiter.[37] Although the PNG leadership interpreted this behavior as an outgrowth of patriotism, some commanders refused to allow soldiers with dependents to go on active duty, believing the soldiers had insufficient funds to support their wives and children without the earnings from their civilian jobs. The soldiers would worry so much about their destitute families that they would be of little use to the military.[38]

Wives of Pennsylvania guardsmen were willing to make sacrifices to see that their husbands remained in the Guard. Several signed legal documents testifying that they were financially independent of their husbands. There was no monetary incentive for this action because, again, a private could not make enough money to support a family on his active duty pay, and jobs were becoming more available in the civilian sector.[39] Wives who rearranged their lives on behalf of the mobilization impressed Brigadier General Charles A. Curtis of the 213th Coastal Artillery Regiment: "Many, that we thought could not get along, however, showed remarkable ingenuity in cutting corners, and their wives came through 100 percent. Many of the women are going back to work so their husbands can do their bit for their country."[40] The wife of a machinist in Company K of the 112th Infantry took an oath that she was not a dependent of her husband when he enlisted two days before Christmas 1940, as did the wife of a salesman who joined on the same day. The salesman's wife stated, however, "It is my desire that my husband shall make proper arrangement to assist in the support of his child and son."[41] While these may have been marital separations, it is more likely that service to the country factored considerably into the decisions of these men and their families. The increasing availability of better-paying jobs for women made these choices available. On the other hand, the PNG was not going to publicize instances of soldiers resigning in response to pressure from their families.

Another characteristic that distinguished the PNG from the Army was the preponderance of native-born enlistees. Of the 1,988 recruits for which records remain, less than 1 percent (16) were foreign-born, and only 158 were born in states other than Pennsylvania. During World War I, a full 18 percent of the U.S. Army had been foreign-born.[42] With 92 percent of the enlistees being native Pennsylvanians, the PNG met one of the primary goals of its recruiting drive.

Major General Martin had sought a National Guard that was a cross-section of the male population of Pennsylvania, with the unspoken exception of blacks. Overall, four male groups were either missing or present in only small numbers in the PNG. There were no blacks, very few whites from the lowest economic strata, almost no upper-class whites (nearly all of those were clustered in the Philadelphia First City Troop), and a great underrepresentation of farmers and others from rural areas. While NG service was unevenly shared by male Pennsylvanians when the PNG mobilized in 1941, the cross-section among urban white males was fairly broad, even if it was not uniform.

This was a significant step toward an American ideal, whereby all groups and classes share the burden of military service.[43] The claim that lower-class men comprise the rank and file of the U.S. military has been nonchalantly assumed for some time. At times in American history that assertion has not been off the mark, and the military has fallen short of the ideal. It dismayed the Revolutionary generation when it appeared that the common soldiers of the Continental Army were disproportionately unpropertied men from the lower classes; citizens from all classes ought to be fighting for the cause.[44] During the War of 1812, individual states made great if unsuccessful efforts "to ensure equity in militia service."[45] The Union Army during the Civil War fairly represented a cross-section of the male population. For instance, the social profile of Pennsylvania soldiers during the Civil War approached the ideal.[46] Comprehensive conscription ensured a similar equity during World War I, when military service was "based upon the principle of universal obligation to service on the part of all male citizens or friendly aliens."[47] A Marine writing in 1935 opined that the soldiers and sailors of the U.S. military comprised "a cross section of the whole population."[48] This concern for equity in military service remains strong to this day. During the current wars in Iraq and Afghanistan complaints arose as months of service in remote desert posts strained the lives of National Guardsmen mustered to active duty.[49] In 1939–41, the PNG was concerned not only with recruiting equitably, training for war, and relations with employers, but also with the Nazi threat and American identity.

Values and Ideology

The pages of the *Pennsylvania Guardsman* serve as a window into the political values and opinions of the Pennsylvania National Guard's leadership, if not the rank and file. Brigadier General Edward A. Stackpole, the commander of the 52nd Brigade, was the *Pennsylvania Guardsman*'s editor, so it is reasonable to assume that the PNG leadership endorsed its content. It devoted considerable space to discussions of patriotism, the crisis in Europe, and ethnicity and American identity. Their primary goal was to improve the combat power and readiness of the military, particularly the National Guard, into a force that could defeat an invading army, not to send troops to Europe.

They considered Hitler and Germany to be threats of the gravest sort, and believed that he intended to work his way toward a conquest of the United States via west Africa and South America. Staff Sergeant Howard G. Young wrote at the beginning of 1939 that a German conquest of Europe was a direct threat to U.S. security. The Nazis threatened every political and spiritual value dear to America. Once in possession of Europe, the Nazis could then seize the Cape Verde Islands, and they would possess "a naval base . . . 1,000 miles nearer Brazil than the United States Government's nearest! Hitler is on the march!"[50] In March 1939, the *Pennsylvania Guardsman* carried a full-page ad ridiculing

Hitler's *Mein Kampf,* counterposing his peaceful proclamations with his malicious actions.[51]

The editors got the civilian W. R. Cunningham to write most of their vitriol, perhaps to avoid the constitutional taboo on soldiers publicly commenting on national policy, although not all PNG officers kept silent.[52] Cunningham was well placed socially, was a graduate of the University of Pennsylvania's Wharton School of Business, and was a 32nd degree Freemason. Cunningham favored military preparedness to protect American values and spoke with pride of the absence of militarism in America. Foreign dignitaries did not hear masses of soldiers marching past their windows, nor did the government use troops and parades to intimidate citizens.[53] In 1939, the PNG hoped the United States would remain aloof from the conflict even as it rearmed and prepared a robust hemispheric defense, just in case. "This is not our war," Cunningham concluded.[54] Preferring deterrence, he leaves the reader with the impression that he expected the United States to be drawn into the war no matter what it did to avoid it.[55]

Unlike regulars, some National Guard officers explicitly criticized the policies of the president and Congress. The *Pennsylvania Guardsman* wrote in early 1939 that after "years of asinine apathy, Americans are waking up to the need for national defense."[56] Major Henry M. Prentiss of the 213th Coast Artillery Regiment insisted that the Guard be expanded to 400,000 troops.[57] Just before the Manassas Maneuvers, the *Pennsylvania Guardsman* printed a tongue-in-cheek but serious letter to Congress begging for modern equipment.[58] An officer of the 109th Infantry ridiculed congressional defense appropriations, specifically the money denied for extra drills so that the men could train more. Reminding them of America's flat-footedness in 1917, he barked, "Can't we for ONCE BE PREPARED!"[59] Captain Karl H. Shriver rejected unpreparedness as a viable policy, reminding listeners on the radio how long it took the Army to mobilize for war in 1917–18, not to mention previous crises such as the War of 1812.[60]

General Martin himself had to wrestle with the issue of free speech in a country experiencing subversive activity. In the winter of 1939 he received a letter from someone complaining that he had seen guardsmen from Pennsylvania at a rally "favoring a foreign form of government." Martin investigated, found no disloyalty, and asked his soldiers to behave with circumspection since in America the public carried out surveillance on the military, not vice versa.[61] Cunningham commented that Americans had to protect free speech and follow the Constitution as they countered Nazi propaganda.[62] Five months later the *Philadelphia Inquirer* reported that the FBI was investigating several PNG officers for supporting Nazi activities. The *Inquirer* implied that an *active* Pennsylvania general, Major General Robert M. Brookfield, attended a pro-Germany rally at Sellersville, Pennsylvania, but Brookfield had retired in 1937. The principal at the high school where he taught ardently defended Brookfield's innocence.[63]

Other PNG officers regretted that America was not harder on fascists and communists, and wondered if the First Amendment might be providing safe harbor for subversives.[64] An unnamed solider in the 111th Infantry worried that some of the men so eager to join the Guard might be seditious Trojan horses. He cited rumors that subversive organizations had distributed pamphlets encouraging members to infiltrate National Guard units. He favored loyalty tests so as to avoid enlisting men who began their speeches with "Fellow workers," and who longed to establish "Soldiers, Sailors, and Peoples Committees."[65] Martin insisted that aliens in the state either become American citizens or be deported and that the government closely monitor individuals who preached communism, fascism, and Nazism. He found registered Communist Party members especially worrisome.[66] For his part, General Stackpole saw Nazism and communism as one and the same on essentials.[67] Colonel Charles Curtis called for American unity and for an end to "class consciousness at the expense of the general welfare."[68]

Guardsmen in Pennsylvania had no patience with any form of anti-Americanism. Major Henry M. Prentiss, chaplain of the 213th CA, dean of Valley Forge Military Academy, and an anti-interventionist, demanded that the government fingerprint everyone so as to monitor subversives and that it suppress foreign groups that donned foreign uniforms and espoused the doctrine of foreign governments on American soil. "There is no room in these United States for anybody unless he be an American. . . . We must not permit them to Europeanize us; we must . . . Americanize them."[69] Cunningham added that democracy's existence was in question as long as there was a single place on earth where it was not practiced.[70] A year later he warned that communists and Nazis were in cahoots in light of the Non-Aggression Pact. Sympathizers were dangerous sleeper cells who had to be severely punished within the rule of law.[71] The fears of Cunningham and Prentiss were grounded in reality.

Seventy fascist organizations such as the German-American *Bund*, the Italian Black Shirts, and the Ku Klux Klan were active in Pennsylvania, although membership was not widespread.[72] Klan activity declined to twenty lodges by 1940, and the Philadelphia chapter of the *Bund* numbered only two hundred members. Nevertheless, German and Italian fascists held a joint rally in nearby New Jersey in 1937, and the House Un-American Activities Committee investigated both. One sect of the Klan hoped to use terrorism and sabotage to disrupt the war effort in 1940.[73] The state police fought a conspiracy by German sympathizers and the Irish Republican Army to murder the king and queen of England during their 1939 visit.[74]

Communists were also active. In 1940, police foiled a communist effort to plant seven to eight bombs at the Philadelphia site of the 1940 Republican Convention. A tip that communists from New York City were organizing the assassination attempt led police to a "workers school" where they found a nitroglycerine bomb. Governor James was the target.[75]

In spite of these threats, the Pennsylvania officer corps retained a strong vein of confidence. At a party in New York City a contributor from the 111th Infantry found himself in an argument with a Nazi and a communist. With bemusement he pointed out the difference between the two. "The nazi will nazify you if he has to kill you to do it. The communist feels that if you're not a communist now you'll never be so it's best to liquidate you (and he doesn't mean with scotch) now." The Nazi then informed him that his party would overthrow the United States government on April 6, 1940, to which he laughed. "What would we do without such stuff to relieve the monotony of making a living?" To those who doubted his story he replied, "Just ask the FBI."[76]

To the PNG leadership, political ideology, not differing variations of white ethnicity, determined how much of an American a person really was. It condemned looking down on white Americans who were not Anglo-Saxon, condemned anyone opposed to American ideals, and welcomed everyone who supported American liberty. Cunningham asserted that anyone who held to the true ideals of the United States was an American, no matter his race, religion, birthplace, or length of time in the United States.[77] He later addressed the primacy of ideology over race at length in a March 1940 article, asserting that racial differences were "purely superficial and have no relation to behavior and to society." "Science tells us, there are no inborn mental differences, associated with physical differences which distinguish races." He noted that his humble corner grocer and Albert Einstein were both Jews; how then could ethnicity reliably predict a person's intelligence? Cunningham added that one should assess "true greatness" on a person's accomplishments, but even there he cautioned against impugning an entire group for the misconduct of a few— a common mistake. American democracy would function best when people developed respect for those different from themselves, and found the good in everyone. In contrast to Nazi ideology, Cunningham argued that America's ethnic mixing was its strength. America got the "sum total of the ingenuity and cooperative effort of all races," and because of intermarriage in America, racial differences had become "of no significance," a marked contrast to Nazi racial ideas. Although he believed that each ethnic group possessed special abilities and flaws, he argued that each should be encouraged to develop its talents to the fullest, instead of calling one or the other superior. Instead of focusing on differences, Americans should concentrate on their common ground of love for democracy and liberty. "WE ARE AMERICANS." "Let us all respect racial differences, but cast aside glorification of those differences."[78] As an example, the 103rd Quartermaster Battalion endorsed a blend of diversity, nativism, and Americanism with its participation in the "Americans All" folk festival, which was "designed to present a racial cross-section of American life in the interest of increasing national unity."[79]

Cunningham never included black Americans by name when calling for racial equality. Targeting Nazi and Japanese ideology, he mentioned European ethnic groups, Jews, Orientals, and Asian Indians. Some cartoons in the *Pennsylvania Guardsman* seemed to treat blacks with respect by the standards of the day, but another made a black man look like a chimpanzee, while a third made fun of Pennsylvania hillbillies.[80] The *Guardsman* also made use of short stories to convey the accepted views on race and ethnicity. One story rebuked an old-time sergeant for questioning the loyalty of a Russian-American guardsman named "Gregorovich." Why would the battery commander have promoted him if he was not competent and loyal? Another character recounted the exploits of "Fritz of Berlin," an obviously Germanic citizen of Wisconsin who performed heroically during the Great War.[81] Discord would wrack a multiethnic infantry division if an ethnic hierarchy played a part in its milieu. General Martin was proud of the way in which the PNG gathered the participation of all of the "races" of America, pointing with pride to the list of the 28th's fallen soldiers from 1918, which carried the names of twenty-four nationalities.[82] Another World War I feature story highlighted an amputee black soldier recuperating in a bed next to his unconscious white friend. "George" discovered in a letter to the white soldier that his friend's girlfriend had married a "stay at home." George also noticed that the attending nurse was falling for his wounded friend. George saw an opportunity to help his friend heal emotionally from the bad news and encourage the new romance with a woman he considered good enough for his friend. Any sort of agenda behind the story is unclear, but the author could just as easily have used a white character had the lesson of the story not involved racial equality. George was not treated as fully equal, but neither was he an invisible man.[83]

The discussions of race, however, did not originate from the problem of white oppression of black Americans. The issue remained in a European context, and the discussions pressed for full acceptance of non-Anglo-Saxon whites. If there were any movements toward "race liberalism" in the PNG, they were not enough to bring black men into the ranks. Not one black man was enlisted during the February 1941 mobilization.[84]

Black Pennsylvanians had tried to join the PNG, but their efforts proved fruitless.[85] On February 28, 1939, Hobson R. Reynolds, the representative for the 21st District in Philadelphia, made an impassioned plea before the Pennsylvania Assembly that in view of the long history of patriotic military service by African Americans, every branch of the United States military should grant them entrance without prejudice. The chief clerk referred Reynold's Resolution No. 22 to the assembly's committee on federal relations, since Reynolds asked the assembly to forward it to President Roosevelt and the secretaries of war and of the navy, Harry H. Woodring and Claude A. Swanson.[86] The Pennsylvania House adopted the resolution on May 24.[87] In March 1939, state representative Edwin F. Thompson of Philadelphia's 13th District filed Pennsylvania House Bill 562, "An Act providing for the organization under certain conditions of one colored battalion of infantry; and making an appropriation therefore."[88] Following referral to the committee on military affairs and two readings before the state house, the house placed the bill on the "postponed calendar" on March 29 per Thompson's request.[89] Bill 562 never reached the Pennsylvania Senate, perhaps because everyone decided it had no chance of passing.[90] The proposal might have moved forward if the PNG's leadership desired the inclusion of black Pennsylvanians in its formations, even if in segregated units.

Efforts continued at the federal level. In April 1939, Representative Dave E. Satterfield Jr. of Richmond, Virginia, introduced U.S. House Resolution 6046 for two African American battalions, and Pittsburgh's Herman P. Eberharter proposed to Congress a bill, HR 6467, for an entire black regiment.[91] Nothing came of either effort. In the fall of 1939, Dr. DeHaven Hinkson of the American Legion met with Governor Arthur H. James and proposed the integration of blacks into existing regiments so as to avoid the additional costs of segregated units. The governor replied that this was impossible: "There are certain customs in this country that are beyond law."[92]

In September 1940 the Pennsylvania Department of Military Affairs promised African American leaders that it would ask the War Department for the creation of a battalion of black troops for Pennsylvania, and General Martin promised to speak with the leader of that initiative before October. Both he and Governor James promised their support. Leadership from the National Association for the Advancement of Colored People, the Veterans of Foreign Wars, and the American Legion were all involved in this initiative. The Pennsylvania state convention of the American Legion had passed a resolution in August calling for the enlistment of blacks in the National Guard and Army.[93] Two months later the national president, Raymond J. Kelly, spoke in West Chester of his goal of the "recognition of Negroes in the Army, Navy, and National Guard."[94] The delegation of African American leaders who met with General Martin on September 12 wanted an integrated battalion. Everett Johnson of the Allied Veterans' Association, an organization of black World War I veterans, advocated enlistment of African Americans in any PNG company: "We want representation in the National Guard on the same basis as members of any other racial group, and we're tired of getting a run-around." Martin replied that the War Department forbade integrated units, and that further action depended on the state legislature, which was double-talk, since the Pennsylvania Assembly could not trump national policy.[95] Because the War Department's policy nullified the ability of Martin and James to integrate the PNG, the two could promise support to black Pennsylvanians knowing full well they had little ability to effect change.

Pennsylvania's complete exclusion of blacks from its National Guard was out of step with its neighbor New Jersey, which at least supported the formation of segregated detachments. President Roosevelt wanted blacks to make up 10 percent of the Army since they comprised a like percentage of the national population.[96] Consequently the War Department revised its personnel policy so as to fill 10 percent of the Army with African American men, and mobilized the 372nd Infantry (New Jersey) and the 184th Field Artillery and 369th Coastal Artillery (Anti-aircraft) Regiments (both from Illinois) during the National Guard's mobilization.[97] Governmental action at this time, however, did not challenge the status quo on race.[98] So in a broader context, the PNG was in line with the rest of the country. The War Department decided to restrict the few existing black National Guard units to their armories so as to avoid racial conflict.[99] The United States armed forces either ignored or actively resisted racial integration until the Korean War.

7

The October Purge

Edward Martin led his division through the Carolina Maneuvers during the fall of 1941 knowing that his days as division commander were numbered. General Marshall had notified him on September 4 that at the age of sixty-two Martin was too old for the rigors of field operations and that he would have to relinquish his command. The Pennsylvania adjutant general took his medicine graciously, if reluctantly, reentering political life as a gubernatorial candidate the following year. Martin was not the only National Guard general released that autumn. Sixteen other National Guard commanding generals, along with dozens more NG officers of lesser rank, suffered the same ignominious fate. The origins of this October purge went back months, if not years, into NG-Army relations. This purge revealed much about National Guard–Regular Army politics and shed light on the respective values and cultures of the two institutions.

Since the beginning of World War II, Army and National Guard officers had eyed each other with suspicion. Army officers nurtured growing doubts about the competence of their National Guard counterparts, attitudes that went back a century and a half. Officers of the Regular Army rejected the possibility that part-time officers with little if any formal training could lead large formations of soldiers in battle successfully, but Militia and National Guard officers had argued for generations that their patriotism and personal courage compensated for the absence of professional expertise.[1] In the process of fielding a mass army, the U.S. Army imposed its standards of professionalism on the National Guard officers in the fall of 1941 by rooting out those it determined were unfit for command, leaving a wake of bitterness and resentment.

Events during the Great War had poisoned National Guard–Army relations. The Army removed or reassigned 1,480 NG officers, 501 for failing physicals. It subsequently replaced many longtime Guard officers with regulars, leading to Guard accusations that the Army had stolen command assignments on the Western Front that were rightfully theirs.[2] So when the War Department began to mobilize the Guard in the fall of 1940, these suspicions reemerged. Some guardsmen feared that the Army's new requirement for two physical examinations might be a ploy to purge the NG of its senior officers so as to replace them with regulars. As a result, the National Guard Association demanded waivers for those who had passed previous physical exams, but not the new ones. It also demanded that NG officers comprise at least 50 percent of the examination boards. In reality, the War Department relaxed its policy to retain officers whose physical shortcomings did not "interfere with the satisfactory performance of field duties appropriate to the grade and assignment."[3] It could even readmit to active duty those who failed their physicals, providing there was a vacancy in their grade.[4] Subsequent gossip about a feared purge of NG officers led to an outburst by Marshall: "If everything pertaining to the Army has to be put on a town meeting basis, we might as well quit before we start." The chief of staff urged the vice president of the National Guard Association to keep his petty National Guard politics to himself.[5]

Some PNG leaders, however, saw the mobilization as an opportunity. Colonel Charles A. Curtis of the 213th Coast Artillery Regiment (Anti-aircraft) actually urged Pennsylvania armories to replace men who were unfit physically or professionally. He admitted that they had been retaining some "old timers because of sentimental reasons," but the war was going to be too brutal to subject any but the fittest to its rigors. He also noted that commanders needed the best men they could find. An early purge, he added, would allow time to replace those discharged with men of the unit's choosing and would at least allow for a few weeks of training.[6]

Since federalization had begun, General Marshall had seen accumulating evidence that many National Guard officers were not up to their tasks, which led him to look for a way to remove the incompetent ones. At the same time, the War Department had been pondering how to move its most qualified officers into commanding general slots. The public knew of and approved of Marshall's goal of placing younger, more capable officers into leadership positions.[7] Beginning in May 1941, General McNair and the inspector general (IG), Major General Virgil I. Peterson, discussed "immediate wholesale relief of National Guard officers," but they preferred to wait until replacement officers had been adequately trained.[8] Hoping to remove 20 percent of the NG officer corps, the IG wrote:

The situation with regard to National Guard officers is much more serious than in either of the other components. Many enlisted guardsmen, hardly above noncommissioned officer standard, were inducted as lieutenants under their commissions in the National Guard of the United States. Many captains are inactive and over-age in grade, many field officers lack energy and assurance. A very considerable number of general officers were complacent and lack fundamental qualifications for higher command. These undesirables tend to coast along pending termination of their year of service. Their number estimated at not less than 20 percent, is about equally divided in company, field and general officer grades.[9]

The IG believed that the War Department ought to apply the high standard to regulars first, then to Guard officers. This fairness may have only been a smoke screen. Although the Army planned to post the relieved generals in rear-area jobs that did not exceed their capabilities, the IG assumed that the guardsmen would be released from active duty entirely after a few months in their new assignments.[10]

The stress of the mobilization had exposed the weaknesses of many division commanders. Their responsibilities overwhelmed them. Because eighteen of the twenty-nine divisions were National Guard, the majority of the division commanders were guardsmen. To replace them with ostensibly more qualified regulars was going to resemble a repeat of the World War I purge. Indeed, only one Guard general of that generation managed to avoid "reclassification."[11] Regulars were accorded no special treatment, however. The Personnel Division recommended that the Army "reclassify" 164 Regular officers, including seven corps commanders and two army commanders.[12] Seeing a correlation between an officer's age—relative to his rank—and his ability to perform the tasks commensurate with that rank, the War Department set maximum ages for each rank. Officers who exceeded it were either moved to less strenuous duties or retired altogether.[13] Congress supported the effort to remove officers unable to perform adequately, with Public Law 190, July 29, 1941.[14] The regulation written to implement the policy applied to all components of the Army. It left the decision as to whether or not an officer was suitable to the discretion of the review boards, because it provided no guidance as to the standards to be used. Board members had to make judgments.[15]

Marshall ran out of patience by the fall of 1941, when the Regular divisions were progressing faster than the NG divisions in terms of fighting skill. He intended to put the latter through their paces again, "along with considerable change in officer personnel."[16] Even though most of Congress and the majority of public opinion supported the chief of staff's efforts to put the best available officers in charge of combat units, the removal of the NG officers, especially the generals, gave Marshall a political headache of the first rank.[17] In his opinion he had "[d]elayed the preparation of the Army to give them [the NG generals] a chance." Because they had failed to meet his standards, Marshall had to relieve them.[18]

The War Department announced the "age-in-grade" policy of removing officers who had reached an age ceiling for their rank on July 16, 1941. Major General Peterson wrote Marshall that he knew every one of the seven National Guard division commanders who were over the age of sixty and that "not one of them will ever function satisfactorily as a division commander in the war that threatens us."[19] Marshall was sincerely concerned about the relationships between age, stamina, and the ability to lead during combat. He had seen "physical exhaustion" destroy the careers of more high-ranking officers during World War I than anything else.[20] National Guard officers were often old for their ranks. The median age for 1st lieutenant was thirty-five, for colonels fifty-one, and for brigadier and major generals, fifty-six and fifty-five, respectively. Sixteen generals were older than fifty-nine. The Guard even contained 346 captains aged fifty or older.[21] McNair had no confidence in them. Referring to Edward Martin, he wrote, "No question but that he should go." He rejected most of the other Guard division commanders as well, rating Major General Clifford R. Powell of New Jersey "incompetent." While he correctly saw Robert S. Beightler's (Ohio) promise, McNair was not always sagacious regarding his regulars, wondering if George S. Patton Jr. had any ability beyond that of a division commander.[22] He also predicted "plenty of house cleaning" in the 28th Division.[23] First Army had given up on all of its general officers by June: "National Guard General Officers and staff lack necessary personal characteristics and professional training. All grades are too old.[24]

Back in 1940, Marshall found that a few of the NG divisions were in "fine shape," and had successfully cleared out some of the "dead wood," but over time his attitude hardened.[25] He concluded that one of the NG generals' greatest shortcomings was their refusal to replace poorly performing subordinates. They lacked the will to fire personal friends for the sake of combat efficiency, this even after the purge of 1941.[26] Along with removing subpar officers, Marshall wanted to buttress the Guard staffs by assigning younger regulars to the positions of division chief of staff and as executive officers in each regiment. To avoid political recriminations they would have no authority over promotions.[27] McNair steadfastly opposed promoting any of the NG brigadier generals to the post of division commander. There were too many better-qualified regulars waiting in the wings. McNair knew that political friends of the National Guard generals would berate Marshall for replacing all of the Guard generals with regulars, but he was confident the public would support the changes.[28]

Following the age-in-grade purge, McNair recommended in October the replacement of nine more NG division commanders. Although regulars commanded six of the Guard divisions by then, he noted that three Guard division commanders were "of promise, although I make no positive prophesies." McNair did not have it in for the guardsmen just to grease the career paths for regulars. The corps commanders—regulars all—concerned him even more. He fired seven of nine, plus the commanders of First and Second Armies, Lieutenant Generals Hugh A. Drum and Ben Lear, both of whom were sixty-two years old.[29]

The National Guard officer corps believed McNair had singled them out. They believed that regulars found the high command slots of their divisions irresistible and that the Army was sacking them so that its own officers could gain division and regimental commands. Indeed, according the Major General Henry D. Russell of the Georgia National Guard, regulars in his 30th Infantry Division filed unfavorable reports on NG officers in order to get them fired and take their commands.[30] Lieutenant Colonel Lloyd D. Brown, who later commanded the 28th following Omar Bradley's tenure, encouraged the firing of as many Guard officers as possible in ranks of major through brigadier general so as to replace them with regulars. In his 1964 history *The Minute Man in Peace and War,* Jim Dan Hill argued to the contrary; the majority of regulars behaved ethically. Besides, with the Army's expansion, plenty of command positions were opening up, and the confident, capable regular knew his superiors would recognize his talent and promote him.[31] Marshall himself directed that the War Department apply reasonable standards to National Guard officers.[32] He also consulted with National Guardsmen regarding whom to relieve.[33]

This controversy over whether military competency required long years of full-time service was an old one. Following the Civil War, for example, Major General John A. Logan argued vociferously that nonprofessional generals plucked from civilian life were the equals of West Point regulars.[34] He defended innate "genius," not education, as the basis of sound officership and leadership. Logan dismissed military education as "superfluous."[35] To Major General Henry D. Russell, professional military education and training was a sign that an officer lacked the savoir faire and natural ability of true military leaders. Following his dismissal in World War II he wrote, "I was not a professional soldier and had never attended any of the schools. It was perfectly natural for little men with professional training to regard themselves as highly equipped to do the job which I and many other National Guard officers throughout the country were doing."[36] The professional-amateur officer debate was also paralleling the development of the professions within the United States at large. The Regular Army sought exclusive control over the officer corps, and the National Guard civilian-officers stood in their way. Regulars considered the guardsmen to be incapable of reaching their level of competence because of their lack of experience and military education. Since they violated the Army's sense of professionalism, high-ranking Guard officers had to go.[37]

One of the National Guard's own, CNGB Major General John F. Williams, added weight to the regulars' arguments when he wrote evaluations critical of his fellow guardsmen. The chief of the National Guard Bureau rated the officers in terms of military and civilian education—their professional knowledge base—as well as their performance, physical stamina, and potential for leadership under combat conditions. He wrote that General Martin's physical condition was "poor," that he was a "slow, ponderous thinker," not what one would expect from a lawyer, and added that he had attended none of the service schools or war colleges.

Ten of the fifteen senior officers in the 28th Division whom Williams assessed had never attended a service school or war college. Only the division's chief of staff, Colonel Robert Morris, and Colonel Franklin P. Haller, commander of the 103rd Quartermaster Regiment, had graduated from the Army War College. The G-1, G-2, G-4, and the commanders of the three brigades had no professional military education. Nevertheless, Williams rated each as at least "satisfactory," with the exception of the G-1 (chief of staff, personnel), Lieutenant Colonel Fred H. Kelley, whom he considered "poor" because he had no leadership qualities. Unlike the Army IG, Williams considered Colonel Eric Fisher Wood "excellent." In terms of performance and education, however, the 28th Division staff formed a less than sterling group.[38] Nine of its senior staff officers had never graduated from college. Such low rates of higher education were the norm for the PNG officer corps. Only 21 percent had college degrees, and just 14 percent had completed any of the Army's basic or advanced professional courses prior to 1940.[39]

Civilians were unsympathetic with the Pennsylvania officer corps. Theodore A. Huntley of the *Pittsburgh Sun-Telegraph* referred to the 28th Division hierarchy as "politicians and good fellows" and wondered aloud if they would make it past the reclassification board in spite of their good records.[40] The public found the War Department's commitment to fielding the best officers it could reassuring. The *Williamsport News* hoped that the War Department would be firm with the 28th Division. In its view the only thing the division seemed to be good at was creating confusion.[41] *Time* expected the removals to improve morale because they constituted visible attempts to improve the officer corps.[42] The whole affair never gained prominence in Pennsylvania newspapers or in the national press even though the state's division commander was one of those who got fired.[43]

Martin's Moment of Truth

On September 4, 1941, General Martin learned that because he was sixty-two, too old to be a major general, the Army was going to relieve him of command of the 28th Infantry Division.[44] Marshall immediately offered Martin a staff job as president of an examination board assessing the officers under consideration for reclassification, along with two regulars and a medical corps officer.[45] Marshall's effort to place Martin in a position of influence within the Army instead of calling for his complete resignation casts doubt on the long-held assertion that the regulars were purging the National Guard division commanders just so they could take their jobs. "Such experience as yours must not be lost to the army. Your service can be used to advantage in building up the training and administration of the army."[46] Since the chief of staff offered Martin authority over personnel assignments, he did not expect him to become vindictive.

Martin would not have to leave immediately; he endeavored to complete twelve months of active duty and leave on February 17, 1942.[47] Marshall, who wanted to avoid a scene, feared that Martin would hold onto the 28th "like grim death." He was thus willing to wait until after the Carolina Maneuvers before forcing the change in command.[48] In reply Martin thanked him for asking him to remain in the Army, adding that he did not have to offer him an assignment just to appease him. Martin professed that he would continue to serve his country whether in or out of the military.[49] Polite, but with a purpose, Martin would hang on. A month later he asked Marshall if he could finish out the year as division commander, or at least until the completion of the Carolina Maneuvers.[50] Marshall did not press the issue until early 1942.

The Army was relieving officers it found wanting in ability; the age-in-grade reason was a smoke screen. The assistant chief of staff for personnel insisted in October that "[t]he efficiency of the officers involved will not be a question at issue and the Inspector General believes that the relief of these officers should be accomplished in a manner that would not only leave no question as to their efficiency but will make them feel that the sacrifices they have made while on active service have been appreciated." Fire them for lack of ability, but do not say that that is the reason. Haislip conceded that the Army had relieved some of the NG officers for incompetence but that the Army had to avoid firing them "in a manner that would tend to cause resentment and ill will toward the Regular Army."[51] Competency had been the theme of discussions over National Guard officers within the chief of staff's office. Age arose only as a superficially objective reason to remove officers who were concurrently poor performers and in all likelihood were not going to be able to endure the physical rigors of extended combat.

Fallout from the firings bothered Marshall for months. Several officers nagged the chief of staff with recriminations, and the relief of the generals of the 35th and 36th Infantry Divisions blew up in his face because they were handled so poorly.[52] When Texas senator Thomas T. Connally found out that the Army had relieved two generals from his state, he stormed into the secretary of war's office "with his hair standing up on end, full of anger and resentment because two Texas Generals of the National Guard had been retired."[53] Marshall faced similar reactions from other states.[54] Senator Bennett Champ Clark of Missouri complained to the *New York Times,* "It is, of course, the old Armygame [*sic*] which does not intend to leave a National Guard officer, no matter how efficient, in command of a National Guard division."[55] The following April senators from the states of the 30th ID—Tennessee, Georgia, and North and South Carolina—protested to Marshall over the relief of its commander, Major General Henry D. Russell. McNair and Drum both considered Russell to be ignorant of military affairs.[56] In contrast, Brigadier General John Aiken of the 55th Infantry Brigade, Pennsylvania, displayed self-abnegation. Realizing that his retirement was a forgone conclusion, he went ahead and resigned in early October to give his successor as much training time as possible. "I feel that I am performing my duty in retiring at this time."[57]

Upset as he was over his relief, Martin offered Marshall suggestions on handling the poor press the National Guard had been receiving, which the chief of staff appreciated and passed on to his staff. Marshall replied, "I feel this way about the whole thing; the Guard has rendered yeoman service and has gone about its work generally with commendable enthusiasm and with little complaint over the handicaps under which many of the units entered active service." Marshall added that he believed a wise press release campaign could raise the spirits both of the guardsmen and the Selective Service men and Reserve officers who served in the Guard divisions.[58] The Personnel Division agreed, noting that the press had reported the Guard's problems and had ignored the manner in which it had soldiered on with little complaining under difficult conditions.[59] The *Scranton Times* opined that National Guard officers, including those who had been sacked because of their age, had been necessary since there were so few regulars.[60] The Army never got around to rehabilitating the National Guard's reputation. The Carolina Maneuvers, the impending war, and then the Pearl Harbor attack overshadowed such concerns.

Secretary Stimson and General Marshall badly wanted to replace at least one of the fired NG generals with another qualified guardsman in order to avoid accusations of a purge for the sake of promoting regulars. In every case, however, there was a Regular available whom Marshall and McNair believed was better qualified than any guardsman. They believed their first duty was to the soldiers—providing them the best leaders possible.[61] Martin observed that the Army would score politically with the National Guard if Marshall would assign one of his brigade or regimental commanders as the 28th's next commanding general.[62] In particular, he suggested General Stackpole, who was only forty-seven, had graduated from Yale, and possessed a "magnificent combat record." Nevertheless, Martin promised, "It is my intention to be of all possible help to you personally and to the Army." He never explained what kind of help he had in mind, but Martin probably wished to contribute to good relations between Army and National Guard as he had done in the past.[63] Stackpole did not impress the chief, who instead had in mind a regular, Brigadier General James Garesche Ord, who had previously served as the advisor to the PNG in 1940. Marshall suggested that Martin forward a letter proposing Ord as his replacement, which would save Martin some embarrassment. Having a guardsman offer suggestions on his replacement would cover Marshall politically; he could say he was acting on advice from an outgoing Guard division commander. Martin complied, writing that he held Ord in high esteem.[64] Still, Martin tried to change the chief's mind again in December and to protect four of his older officers from reassignment. He wrote that the commander of the 110th Infantry, Colonel Albert O. King, was in "splendid physical condition and commanded his regiment in a superior manner," as did the 111th's commander, Colonel Franklin P. Haller. The COs of the 107th Field Artillery and the 103rd Quartermaster Regiments, Lieutenant Colonel John Nuckel and Colonel George J. Shoemaker, were similarly qualified.[65] On Christmas Eve he repeated that he could best serve by remaining the 28th's commander and pointed out that prior to his reclassification the Army had put him on the eligibility list for the General Staff.[66] When it was clear a month later that Marshall would not budge, Martin asked to be put on a corps staff so as to have some interaction with troops.[67]

National Guard officers, who had sacrificed much and worked hard to become the best officers they could, found the judgment "Not good enough" a pill too bitter to swallow. Taking the testimony of Colonel Louis L. Roberts of the 38th ID as indicative of the feelings of these men, these "career National Guard" officers believed they had, at great sacrifice, kept the flame of military readiness alive during the interwar years.[68] Roberts complained that he had never taken a vacation with his children, for he always gave summer field training priority, because "some of us had to keep alive that spark of national defense and preparedness in this country." He had "eaten more bad food at luncheon clubs, such as Rotary and Kiwanis, than almost anybody I know for the sole purpose of preaching this doctrine." Roberts and others like him in the Guard had laid the groundwork for the training of the present citizen army. "This business," he continued, "of sending officers who have given their all, back to their communities embittered, near-broken hearted and discarded—well, we don't even treat Army mules in the manner in which we have treated some of these officers who have given everything." Roberts admitted, however, that the Guard had failed to develop the ability to train its officers for higher levels of command.[69]

The "October Purge" removed all but one of the National Guard division commanders from their posts, but in the larger scheme of things it affected less than 1 percent of all National Guard officers. Altogether, the War Department relieved 127 National Guard and 142 Reserve Officers Corps officers out of a total of 19,542 (NG) who "had entered from the peacetime National Guard," as well as 195 officers of the Regular Army.[70] The War Department transferred forty overage officers from the PNG to administrative duties in the Army Air Forces on November 10.[71] Most were actually company-grade officers,[72] but these figures do not tell the whole story. National Guard commanding generals conducted their own purge, in addition to that of the War Department, removing even more officers with the goal of improving the quality of leadership. For instance, Ohio's Brigadier General Robert S. Beightler released 119, and Martin himself sacked 124.[73] Martin did not reflexively defend all of his officers, recommending two of his regimental commanders for reassignment due to poor performance.[74] He never named them explicitly, but it would seem that they were Colonel Edward Hubbs of the 108th FA and Colonel George J. Shoemaker of the 103rd Quartermaster Regiment, because he recommended them for either military police or provost marshal duty. That was really a better match for both, since Hubbs was the Philadelphia deputy chief of police and Shoemaker was Harrisburg's police superintendent.[75] Martin's recommendation for Colonel Shoemaker is at odds with his assessment that he was qualified to be the division's commanding general. Martin made no effort to protect the 112th's commander, Colonel Monroe A. Means, either.[76]

The fact that Martin himself was also removing officers from commands put his own demotion in perspective. He had to evaluate officers with the same frankness with which his superiors had evaluated him. During the Plattsburg Maneuvers a number of deficient officers had come to Martin's attention, and he discharged them from the PNG. In September 1941 he removed twelve more, and he was reviewing additional cases when he got his own bad news.[77] Several of his regimental commanders—he never specified which ones on paper—disappointed him during the Carolina Maneuvers.[78] Martin had already removed twelve incompetent officers from the division outright in early September: "There are cases, however, where it was necessary for us to ask [for] reclassification . . . we found they were of no further service to us." Martin moved others into less taxing duties, "with partial success." He added:

> We have too many officers in the National Guard who are too old for their grades. Unfortunately these are enthusiastic men, who have kept themselves in fine physical condition and are now producing real results. That has been one of the most difficult things I have had to solve. We are pleading for and demanding results and when these old fellows produce results it does seem that they should be retained. On the other hand I realized that some of them are working at a pace which their age will not stand and they may be casualties in the service of their country. It is really a most difficult thing to solve in some cases.

National Guard officers were not of one mind. Unlike Major General Henry D. Russell, Martin did not reject the Regular Army, nor did he see a conspiracy against state troops. Instead, the president of the National Guard Association, no less, told Marshall in his September 8 letter, "[A]s you know, personally I would much prefer seeing a professional Army than one of citizens. However, it is necessary for us to have what we can get."[79] Edward Martin had acquiesced to the forces of centralization, rationalization, and professional expertise that had washed over American society. He wanted the most technically proficient Army possible, and as he had with his previous requests for more regulars in his division, he gave way to the skills of the full-time professional officer. Martin and Marshall were not so different. Both valued military expertise, and even though Martin hoped to retain the state identities of National Guard units, he never spoke negatively of non-Pennsylvanians.

This removal of overage officers created a significant shortfall throughout the 28th ID. Of the 124 new officers it needed, it required 48 for the infantry and 33 for the artillery. Eight of 14 staff officers, including Martin, were relieved. The 110th, 111th, and 112th Infantry Regiments received new commanders, as did the 107th and 108th Field Artillery Regiments and the 103rd Quartermaster Regiment.[80] These new officers were about eight to ten years younger than their predecessors and were better educated. Two had attended the Command and General Staff School's National Guard Course in 1940. Furthermore, the new commander of the 108th FA, Lieutenant Colonel James C. Rosborough, was a 1929 graduate of the Field Artillery School's National Guard Course, and Lieutenant Colonel John L. Heilman finished the Quartermaster School's NG Course in 1936. Colonel John H. Van Vliet inherited the 111th Infantry and brought with him degrees from West Point, the Command and General Staff School, and the Army War College.[81]

Ignominy was not in Edward Martin's future. After the beginning of the year, well-placed Republican friends urged him to run for governor of Pennsylvania. None of the other potential candidates was well known, they counseled, and he was electable.[82] He also had better name recognition because of his National Guard career.[83] No one had to twist his arm. Martin hoped to put his name on the ticket, not campaign, and then resign from military service if elected—a violation of the regulations that prohibited an active duty officer from running for office. The Army corrected him on that account.[84] After he finished some projects for General Daniel Van Voorhis of V Corps Area, he tendered his resignation in March. Marshall put forth no effort to keep him in the service, released him, and expressed his deep appreciation for the loyalty and support Martin had consistently shown him.[85] Pennsylvania voters elected Edward Martin governor that fall, but he valued his military service much more: "It took me a year to become governor and forty to earn a star. Call me general."[86] Following one term as governor, he served in the U.S. Senate for two terms, retiring in 1959.[87]

According to the recollections of Henry Fluck, a member of the 110th Infantry at that time, the men of the 28th Infantry Division were not surprised by Martin's ouster. He had reached the reasonable age limit the War Department had set. "We all loved Martin, who was a good man, but there was no question." The troops believed the removal of older officers was prudent, and Fluck added that it left morale, except for that of Martin's staff and some of the regimental commanders, unaffected. He also believed that a division command is such a rare jewel that any commander, Martin included, ought to be thankful for whatever time he has to serve in that capacity.[88] The 109th Infantry briefly noted that Martin's "absence . . . was keenly felt."[89] The PNG soldiers first heard about it on November 12.[90] His dismissal attracted no publicity, only a thoughtful letter of thanks for what he had accomplished from the chief of the National Guard Bureau.[91] Pennsylvania newspapers praised him as a kind, caring general officer, but none pitched a fit that the Army was sacking a battlefield genius.[92] America was at war, so Regular Army–National Guard politics were by comparison inconsequential.

Martin may not have had the ability to be a good combat commander even had he been young enough to remain on active duty. For instance, it would have been exceedingly difficult for him to have the same understanding of the craft of war as a Regular colonel who over the span of twenty years had attended all of the Army's schools in residence and had rotated between line and staff duties on a consistent basis. On the other hand, being a successful peacetime—Depression era, no less—National Guard general may have required other talents less "military" but nevertheless important for keeping a division functioning. National Guard general officers had to compete for first-rate men. Then they had to encourage them to succeed at their civilian jobs and to devote their extra time to National Guard duties. They had to deal effectively with employers, as well as local, state, and national officials. Division commanders had to build up support for the Guard in the civilian world.[93] They had to keep their men motivated and morale high, for in the impoverished days before 1942, the Army and National Guard had little besides gumption and ingenuity for learning the art and craft of war. Neither possessed enough weapons with which to practice. A man with the proper skills for being a successful peacetime National Guard division commander may have not been naturally the type who would have succeeded as a combat commander, and vice versa.

The October Purge exposed several problems. It illustrated the mutual distrust and bitterness between the Regular Army and the National Guard officer corps. On a larger scale it showed that the poor peacetime military education of the NG officer corps had been allowed to get out of hand. National Guard officers should have made sure that they met the standards of military education of their Regular counterparts, but that necessitated a corps of men with enough private money and free time to allow for continuing study and education. Perceiving the competition for time between an officer's full-time job and the National Guard, Ohio's governor, John W. Bricker, explicitly stated that his commanding officers had to have achieved enough success in private life to permit them time away from civilian pursuits because a National Guard salary was "not sufficient for these men to devote the time necessary unless they have further means of support."[94] Martin fit the bill, but did not pursue continuing education, such as the Command and General Staff School. Neither the Army nor Congress forced the National Guard to meet standards, and Congress never provided enough appropriations so that either institution could achieve combat readiness.

Still, the National Guard made an important contribution to national defense by the time America declared war on Japan and Germany. It provided the Army with more than 200,000 men, who if they were not fully trained were at least well motivated. Retired Pennsylvania generals Kafkalas and Fluck agreed that the prewar National Guard provided a "framework on which to build" at least part of the Army, as well as officers, in the form of cadres for other divisions. Fluck, for example, helped form the 83rd Infantry Division as a company commander.[95] Along with the Regular Army, the National Guard served as a great reservoir for the expandable army.

8

Stateside Training

1942–1943

Cadres

The first half of 1942 was a dreadful and unproductive time for the Keystone Division. Chaos presided over its manning during the first months of 1942 because the country had delayed the buildup and expansion of the Army. Just after Pearl Harbor, the Army Ground Forces totaled approximately 1.3 million soldiers and officers organized in thirty-six divisions in varying states of readiness. The Army was too small to be employed as an effective instrument of policy just yet, so the War Department decided to expand it from thirty-six to eighty-nine divisions, Calhoun's expandable-army concept on steroids. By the end of the war the Army Ground Forces (AGF) would number about two million.[1]

Expanding the Army required the raiding of built-up divisions for men to cadre new formations. Growth of this magnitude required the Army to tap two sources of manpower. The great bulk of the soldiers came from Selective Service, while half-trained or even fully trained Army and National Guard divisions provided experienced and trained officers and NCOs either as individuals or as cadres around which new divisions were created. For instance, when the Army activated the 79th Infantry Division in June 1942, the source for its cadre of officers and men was the 4th Infantry Division.[2] The "Ivy Division" provided 172 officers and 1,190 enlisted men as the nucleus around which 452 new officers—Officers Candidate School and service school graduates—and 13,425 conscripts coalesced.[3] This was not an improvised plan. Marshall had already warned in the summer of 1940 that he would have to tap or even break up combat-ready divisions into cadres for more divisions.[4] This requirement for exponential expansion generated two consequences. The Army was not ready to send substantial forces into combat until the latter part of 1942, and many divisions that were on the road to combat readiness had to divvy up thousands of troops for even more cadres instead, which set back their own training programs by many months. This necessary procedure for building up a mass army took time, and resulted in the draining off of men from the 28th Infantry Division in the spring of 1942.

The Keystone Division moved from Indiantown Gap to Camp Beauregard, Louisiana, between January 9 and 19, 1942, and the changes began.[5] A sentimentalist more than an opponent to progress, General Martin made one last, albeit futile, effort to keep the PNG together. He asked for the transfer of the 104th Cavalry to the 28th Division and for its continuance as a horse outfit.[6] One welcomed change had long been one of Martin's goals: the elimination of the brigades so that the division commander exerted direct control over his regiments. Since the division was transformed into a "triangular" division with just three infantry regiments, the 111th Infantry Regiment was transferred to the Eastern Defense Command.[7] Field artillery regiments also became battalions, as did the medical and support regiments. The division's brigade headquarters were transformed into a reconnaissance troop and a "military police company."[8] The Army had been making these structural changes in its infantry divisions in order to make them more responsive to the command and control stresses of the modern battlefield and to improve their maneuverability.[9] The Army further upgraded the infantry divisions in 1942. They received three cannon companies, four more 155mm howitzers, twenty-four additional .50 caliber machine guns, and lost their 75mm guns. More trucks increased their mobility. Personnel now reached 15,514 officers and men.[10] Brigadier General James Garesche Ord quietly replaced Martin and became the division's commanding general on January 28.[11] Then in February the Army transferred the division to IV Corps Third Army, and renamed it an Infantry Division.[12]

After the Pennsylvanians arrived at Camp Beauregard, inspectors from Third Army assessed the division to be in sound condition, judging the training for its infantry "well-organized," if rudimentary. The artillerymen kept themselves and their camp "extraordinarily neat and orderly, well above average," although they suffered from a severe shortage of qualified instructors.[13] Soon after taking command of the division, Brigadier General Ord exclaimed to his mother, "I have a magnificent body of men under me. If we can complete our present training program we will be in fine shape."[14] Army policy decisions prevented Ord from achieving his goal.

In the short term, Third Army's mission was not to prepare its divisions for combat with all dispatch; instead, it had to provide highly trained soldiers

Chart I

Infantry Division, 1 August 1942

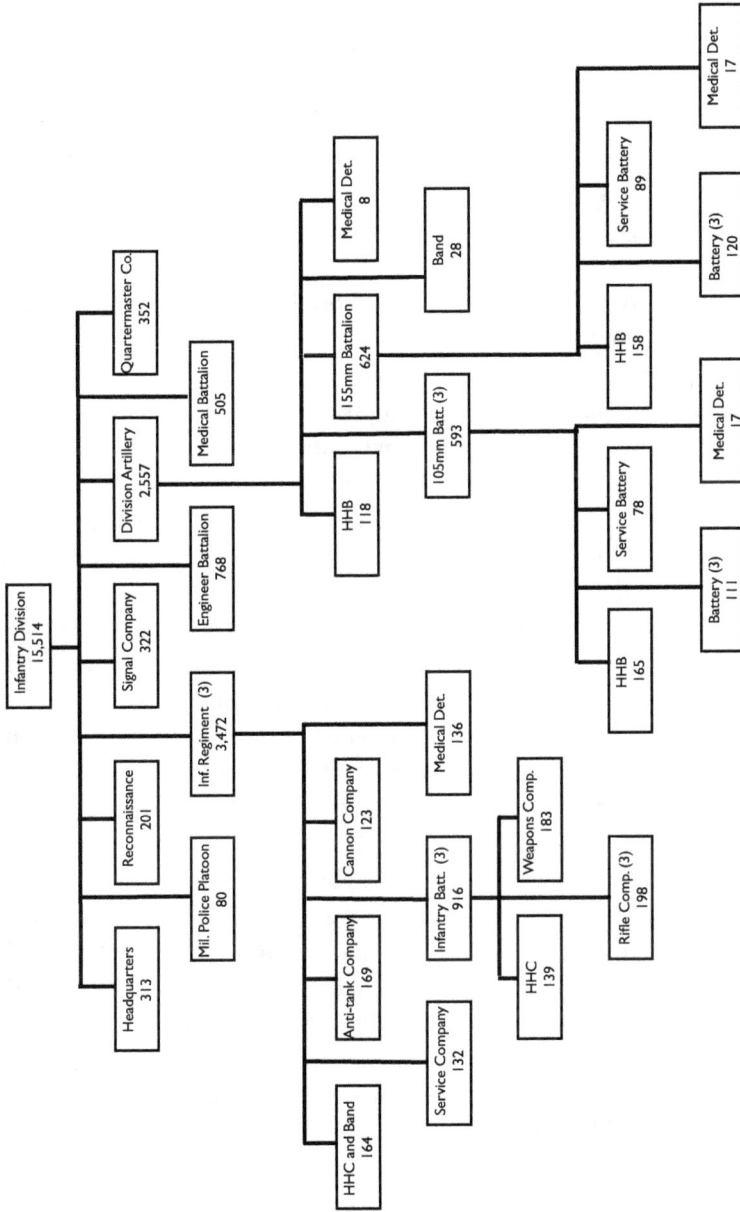

Infantry Division
15,514

Headquarters
313

Reconnaissance
201

Mil. Police Platoon
80

Signal Company
322

Engineer Battalion
768

Division Artillery
2,557

Medical Battalion
505

Quartermaster Co.
352

Inf. Regiment (3)
3,472

HHC and Band
164

Anti-tank Company
169

Service Company
132

Cannon Company
123

Infantry Batt. (3)
916

Medical Det.
136

HHC
139

Weapons Comp.
183

Rifle Comp. (3)
198

HHB
118

105mm Batt. (3)
593

155mm Battalion
624

Band
28

Medical Det.
8

HHB
165

Service Battery
78

Battery (3)
111

Medical Det.
17

HHB
158

Service Battery
89

Battery (3)
120

Medical Det.
17

Source: Wilson, Maneuver and Firepower, 162.

for action overseas as individuals, even if that disrupted its own plans and efforts to achieve combat readiness. It also provided cadres for new divisions at the rate of ten thousand men per month, a serious drain on its component divisions. Commanders were not allowed to hoard their best men; newly formed units had to receive capable personnel.[15] There was no formal training for these cadremen in how to form new units from scratch, although they did receive thirty days of training in their branch specialty.[16] The unit providing the cadres then had to train conscripts it received as replacements for those it had lost.

When the War Department forced stateside divisions to turn over equipment to formations about to enter combat, VIII Corps Commander Major General George V. Strong sarcastically commented: "Now you're beginning to cut in rather hard on this training business. I can go back, of course, to the *galvanized iron pipe and ration cards for 37mm guns*, but that's going to react rather badly on training and worse on morale" [emphasis in original].[17] The 28th ID's Antitank Battalion never even fired live ammunition until November 1942.[18]

A perusal of the division's special orders illustrates the extent of the reassignment of soldiers, a form of personnel anarchy that caused the division to regress. In January 1942, for instance, the division lost 10 men to the motor mechanics course at Fort Benning, Georgia, until April 14; lost 12 to the Third Army Junior Officers' Training Center for five weeks; received 48 conscripts into the 112th Infantry Regiment; and sent 7 lieutenants to the communications course at Fort Benning, 4 privates to OCS, and 4 officers to the battalion commander and staff course for three months. Three hundred men were taken to form the 628th Tank Destroyer (TD) Battalion.[19]

The reshuffling continued through February. Ord's division lost 162 privates to the Army Air Forces, and 61 more to the 628th TD Battalion. Ten went to the Quartermaster Corps OCS and would return in late May, as did 9 lieutenants tapped for the motor maintenance course. Then 32 officers arrived from the 32nd Infantry Division.[20] In March the division processed 1,178 new privates and sent 77 men to OCS. Nineteen lieutenants and a major traveled to Camp Bullis, Texas, for a five-week junior officer's course, while 47 remained on post for a school for bakers and cooks. Simultaneously, the 109th Infantry received 1,500 draftees straight from their induction centers, completely bereft of any basic training.[21] When all this siphoning began, the inspector general prepared to reexamine the division in the spring. At the same time, the Army's divisions had to be kept in a high state of readiness prior to shipment overseas, an impossible task under the circumstances.[22]

The bleeding continued in April and May when soldiers and officers went to the field artillery, battalion commander, and junior officers' courses. In May and June, 221 more men went to OCS, and 86 functioned as the cadre for a battalion in the 176th Engineer Regiment. Meanwhile, the 109th and 112th Infantry Regiments lost 199 men between them to the division's 103rd Engineer Battalion. Then all three infantry regiments received 166 draftees apiece.[23] This is only a sample of the personnel drain on the division. It had to continue training in the midst of losing capable, trained soldiers and incorporating conscripts. The division even had to maintain a battalion ready for combat at a moment's notice.[24]

The Army had assigned too many tasks to the 28th ID while refusing to grant it the personnel stability necessary to complete those assignments. For instance, with soldiers in a constant state of flux, the division had to ready its artillery for firing tests by late April. Indicative of its declining fortunes, it had to establish schools to teach officers and NCOs how to instruct the ways of war to their new soldiers, implying that neither the conscript nor the officers and sergeants in charge of them were ready for anything but another interminable round of basic training.[25] A better solution would have been for the Army to complete the personnel transfers in one fell swoop, leaving a more stable, if somewhat gutted, large cadre from which the division could build up its size and combat strength. Still, the 28th was comparatively lucky. Its neighbor the 29th Infantry Division (Maryland, Virginia, D.C.) was scattered hither and yon to guard strategic facilities, while the 30th (Tennessee, Georgia, the Carolinas) was drained of so many personnel that a year after Pearl Harbor it had to start training from the beginning.[26]

Even though the country was at war, many of the division's men strained to hang on to civilian comforts. When the division moved to Louisiana, more than three hundred wives followed their husbands. NCOs and officers often found housing off post for their wives. Permission to live off base was mandatory, and enlisted men had to hold the rank of staff sergeant or higher to do so. Many soldiers of lesser rank found places for their wives as well, but the Army offered no financial help. Those with wives nearby burdened themselves with another concern: they had to return to camp by midnight. Finding a place to live was difficult at first, but once the movement of men in and out of the area stabilized, Pineville, Alexandria, and other towns turned out to be large enough to house the married couples. It was just another distraction for the Army to deal with. While the families received commissary subsidies, nothing could be done to alleviate the wives' boredom. Their husbands were often absent for days during maneuvers. The United Services Organization (USO) stepped in and started classes, clubs, and socials, as did individual battalions.[27] During the heat of war and in an effort to hold onto home life, thousands of soldiers rushed into marriage. The 28th's soldiers married at a rate of "100–150 each week" and continued to do so throughout the spring and summer of 1942.[28]

The soldiers' morale received priority at the expense of battlefield training, but civilian-military teamwork took place willingly. As Martin had done a year earlier, the division offered a wide variety of sports. Nearby colleges offered to scrimmage against divisional basketball teams, and local communities pitched in to open recreational centers.[29] The USO and the Jewish Welfare Board teamed up to run their facility in Alexandria.[30] "Charming girls serve[d] as dance partners and instructors" at the service club.[31] The division even held a beauty pageant. Local businesses reaped profits as soldiers crammed stores and restaurants on weekends.[32] The soldiers were not sentenced to remain in western Louisiana indefinitely. They could take up to fifteen days of leave, but at thirty-five dollars, the cost of a round-trip ticket to Pennsylvania kept most close to Camp Beauregard.[33] Considering the growing displeasure of his superiors with the division's lack of improvement, General Ord should have concentrated more on training his division and less on propping up its morale. Although Army Personnel made it nearly impossible for Ord to accomplish training with lasting results, he was not doing everything he could to improve the division.

The Firing of General Ord

The chaos of having to take in new men, send soldiers away for advanced training, and provide cadres for other units, all while trying to upgrade the combat capability of the 28th Infantry Division, overwhelmed General Ord, and his superiors showed him no mercy. Nowhere in the record did they concede that Army policies were the root cause of the division's stagnant readiness. His failure was a surprise considering his previous assignments. Ord had a fine background of line and staff duties, including the command of the 57th Infantry Regiment, second in command of the Army's premier infantry division, the 1st, four years as an instructor at the Command and General Staff School, and four in the War Plans Division. Ord had graduated with honors from the Infantry School and the CGSS.[34] He had impressed General Martin and other Pennsylvania officers during his two months as senior instructor in August–September 1940, and Martin thought Ord would make a fine commanding general. Martin even told the Army's adjutant general that he would welcome the opportunity to "serve with or under General Ord at any time."[35] General Virgil I. Peterson, however, was unimpressed during an April 1942 inspection when he found Ord ignoring known weaknesses in the division.

Marshall had already expressed reservations about Ord's abilities the previous fall, as had Generals Drum and McNair. Drum found that Ord irritated other officers badly.[36] He also believed that Ord was somewhat lacking in "force and character," and a proper sense of priorities.[37] When the division reached Alexandria, Louisiana, he first emphasized bayonet instruction.[38] By permitting a liberal leave policy, Ord failed to instill a sense of urgency among the division's soldiers. For example, a private was noted for visiting a different state every weekend, reaching Memphis, Mobile, and points in Texas.[39] Seventeen of the division's staff officers lived off post, including General Ord and his chief of staff, Colonel Benjamin C. Jones. Regimental officers may have done likewise; the documents do not address their billeting arrangements.[40] Even though Ord worked past six p.m. seven days a week,[41] living off post hurt senior officers' connections with their men. Ord also had low expectations of his soldiers. He believed that they would not progress as well during the summer's heat as they would in March, commenting to his sister that the GIs would not "put the effort into their work when" the heat sapped their energy.[42]

Ord had not inherited the best situation. Indicative of the problems the 28th ID faced was the eight-week-long course IV Corps put together for "illiterate, inept, backward, and poorly coordinated individuals" in April.[43] Furthermore, the junior officers were providing poor leadership. In response, Third Army set up a six-week officers training center at Camp Bullis, Texas. In it, one might function as a first sergeant one day, a rifleman the next, and then serve on a mortar crew the third. Graduates then returned to their divisions to teach small-unit tactics.[44]

Marshall might, in fact, have been wiser to choose one of the Pennsylvanians Martin had recommended—Colonels Jones, Coar, King, and Haller—instead of Ord. Benjamin C. Jones, for one, was an alumnus of Princeton, the Cavalry School, and the Command and General Staff School's National Guard course. The CNGB considered him to be "excellent" with a "fine mind."[45] Among the best possibilities was Colonel John H. Van Vliet, a West Pointer who had graduated from the Infantry and Command and General Staff Schools and the Army War College. Martin had given him command of the 111th Infantry Regiment.[46] The best alternative which the Army failed to use was a "centralized command selection board," which may have been an improvement over Marshall's system, which consisted of selecting generals from the officers he had gotten to know personally during the 1920s and 1930s.[47] Nevertheless, by June, the commander of IV Corps, Major General Griswold, and Third Army Commander Lieutenant General Walter Krueger agreed that they had to find a replacement for Ord. McNair concurred, and recommended Brigadier General R. O. Baront, then with the 85th Infantry Division. Marshall decided instead to replace Ord with Brigadier General Omar N. Bradley effective June 20.[48] Ord went on to become chairman of the Joint Brazil–United States Defense Commission later that month.[49]

Bradley Shakes Things Up

Bradley was, of course, a general of the highest caliber. The men found him to be attentive, full of common sense, and able to relate to the ordinary soldier.[50] By the fall 1942 maneuvers, the men spoke of him with a commitment of feeling unseen during the Martin and Ord days. "The commanding general does not command respect; he wins devotion. That, perhaps more than anything else, is responsible for the heated loyalty of his command." He assigned soldiers their missions and got out of their way. Verbal praise from Bradley was uncommon, to be sure, so it carried more weight when a soldier heard it.[51]

Bradley put the division through a considerable reorganization before he gained its esteem. He arrived with a poor impression of the 28th when he took command, having watched from his 82nd Airborne Division command just thirty-eight miles down the road.[52] He noticed that it maintained an eight and one-half hour work day. There was no substantive difference in the time the men spent on their training now that the United States was at war. Bradley soon made far more efficient use of the soldiers' time than had Martin and Ord.[53] He spent the next month examining the division's problems and found a first-rate mess. The transfer of 1,600 men—who did not return to the division—to OCS, of hundreds more to the Army Air Forces, and of more to cadre other units had reduced the division to the status of a manpower repository. Bradley brought the manpower drain to a halt and asked for more OCS graduates.[54] He found that unqualified NCOs staffed many of the units, and that they refused to embrace their responsibilities. Officers had failed to "put their best men into NCO positions and train them properly."[55]

He also believed that familiarity between subordinates and superiors—a leftover of "Hometown-ism" from National Guard days—was rife and unacceptable. For instance, an officer might be in command of the banker who financed his business back in Pennsylvania—certainly a conflict of interest. Bradley also found that the guardsmen formed cliques that excluded new soldiers.[56] Not surprisingly, the *Pennsylvania Guardsman* had never hinted that localism had any drawbacks, although it reminded soldiers that "they no longer are separated by class distinction—they are now thrown together as a body to unite and become a strong organization."[57] The general put his foot down and forced a radical mixing of officers and NCOs so as to break up the localist connections between them. When he gave the order in a theater full of them, "a stunned hush fell over the theater." His order delighted nearly everyone, with one junior officer exclaiming, "General, this is the best thing that ever happened to this division."[58] Conscripted from New York in January 1942, First Sergeant Reynold W. Ross of the 110th Infantry agreed, noting that leadership improved once Bradley had broken up the National Guard "cliques."[59] Not all agreed that there was a problem. Harry M. Kemp, a veteran of the 109th Infantry who served in it from 1939 throughout the war, avowed:

> First of all, at least in the 109th, almost all soldiers did not know there was such a problem. So many personnel changes in and out had occurred since federalization that units had already lost their hometown flavor. Original officers and NCOs had been discharged, transferred or cadred out to the extent that a problem of "hometownism" could not be recognized. Officer replacements and enlisted selectees had been received, trained, integrated, and promoted by merit.[60]

Kemp believed that Bradley's wholesale shuffling of soldiers slowed the division's progress, for it had to reconstitute small-unit cohesion.[61] The accusation that localism impeded discipline was not new. Martin had directly denied that there was a problem the previous September.[62] Similar allegations arose elsewhere. An incognito captain at Camp Hulen, Texas, had found a year earlier that the only soldiers who had a chance at promotion were National Guardsmen.[63] Bradley tried to alleviate concerns of an anti-Guard bias by retaining the Illinois guardsman Brigadier General Kenneth Buchanan as assistant division commander and just five more from his staff on the 82nd Airborne when he transferred to the 28th.[64] National Guardsmen still dominated the division's headquarters. Along with Buchanan, other Guard officers included these positions: chief of staff, G-1 (personnel), G-2 (intelligence), G-4 (supply), adjutant general, chaplain, antiaircraft and antitank officer, chemical warfare, engineer, finance, quartermaster, and inspector general. The one Regular officer besides General Bradley was the G-3, the assistant chief of staff for operations, an all-important post. Altogether, guardsmen manned thirty-seven of the forty-seven headquarters positions, with two from the Army of the

United States and six reservists.[65] By May 1943, guardsmen filled twenty-three of sixty-two HQ desks. Regulars were then five in number. Officers from the Army of the United States jumped to twenty-three, reflecting the consolidating effect of the war.[66] Considering the magnitude of the personnel changes, the National Guard character of the division could not have been what it was a year prior, but the reaction of soldiers then and decades later to Bradley's insistence on uniformity suggests that National Guard factionalism was a problem in the division at the beginning of his tenure.

Marshall chimed in on the issue of the National Guard's distinctiveness and performance. In his view, there was a double standard: the War Department was merciless toward regulars and lenient toward guardsmen.[67] When Major General Roy D. Keehn complained to him in June that regulars were still sacking NG officers so as to take their commands, Marshall exploded:

> I do not like this. Frankly, I am irritated by it. We have leaned over backward in the handling of the National Guard officers, and I have laid myself open to severe criticism for delaying to the extent I have in a number of cases. At the same time we have been ruthless in the handling of regular officers who did not measure up to the required standards, and have relieved large numbers. However, there is no reaction to such action, while almost every relief or transfer of a senior National Guard officer provides a political or cabinet repercussion to distract me from vital business.... There has been too much thought and consideration for the individual and far too little for the thousands who are to be entrusted to his command. I feel that my responsibility to the soldier and his family takes clear precedence over that of the individual senior whose effective leadership is in doubt.[68]

Marshall was right. By failing to prevent their senators from whining to the chief of staff, several National Guard officers displayed shortcomings in professionalism. The senators likewise placed a greater value on the trappings and residency of the NG officer than on his ability and the needs of the troops. One also has to blame the War Department, for if these standards were so important, it should have ensured that they were met prior to the war.

Meanwhile, the personnel shortages continued well into General Bradley's tenure. The Army Ground Forces were supposed to supply the 28th with 706 officers, but by August it had only 440. Of these, 106 were away at schools for specialized training. Since so many of the division's best officers had been drawn off to cadre new formations, inexperienced officers had to take charge of duties for which they were not ready. Sergeants commanded most of the platoons and even some companies, functions normally reserved for lieutenants and captains. The division's leadership was thus unable to train the men properly; it was unfocused and demotivated.[69]

But Bradley was correcting these deficiencies. The training program in the spring and summer concentrated on elementary tasks. Artillerymen, for example, focused their efforts on calculating firing solutions, radio communication, and gunnery procedures. Everyone spent most of their time on small-unit and individual training, with continued focus on basic training. There were no field exercises until August 17, whereupon small units walked through eighteen different field problems, including: "night patrolling, tank stalking, assault of a fortified position, camouflage, road blocks, defense of an aerodrome, stream crossing, jungle fighting, guerrilla warfare, defense of a stream-line, night marching by compass, street and defile fighting, and night raids."[70] Bradley terminated furloughs; the men were going to concentrate on war fighting, and everyone was going to be present.[71]

Bradley thoroughly invigorated the 28th training regimen, starting with physical fitness. Daily exercise included sports, calisthenics, and obstacle courses, and worked up to a twenty-five-mile hike, which the general completed himself. Marching incognito with the 109th Infantry, he watched soldiers ignore orders to only sip from their canteens. After guzzling their water all at once in the heat, many collapsed. Ambulances picked them up, but they soon had to renew the march.[72] One who did not fall out asked Bradley, "Who the hell ordered this march?" to which Bradley replied, "I don't know, but they ought to hang the S.O.B." Bradley finished the twenty-five miles carrying several packs of men half his age.[73] One soldier recognized him and was well impressed that he completed the road march with his soldiers.[74] Some of the officers displayed similar energy, foreshadowing their leadership in combat. Lieutenant Colonel Daniel Strickler, commander of the 1st Battalion 109th Infantry, trained his men above and beyond what the Army required. He ensured that his troops knew how to breech water obstacles, for example, as well as how to attack silently at night.[75] Soldiers also welcomed the requirement for night training, even though they had to set out bright and early the following morning.[76]

Over the summer the division finally completed a systematic training program. Beginning with a twenty-four-hour regimental combat team exercise in June, it lengthened to thirty-six hours in July. Bradley did not let up during the dog days; he emphasized road marches, running through obstacle courses, and bayonet practice. The 109th Infantry soon completed a twenty-five-mile road march with only two men falling out. Instruction in air–ground operations took place in August, as did battalion and regimental schools. A division field exercise was inaugurated in September, and soon the division, having made quick progress, was ready for larger-scale maneuvers.[77]

All of the divisions that participated in the fall 1942 maneuvers had been cadred down, then rebuilt. Therefore, in spite of the Carolina Maneuvers, these were the first major war games for many of the men in the 28th ID. The chaotic personnel changes had sent away many veterans of the Carolina Maneuvers and replaced them with rookies. All of the divisions made slow progress, but at least they received considerable practice with close air support, and in that area proficiency climbed. The Keystone Division at the start of the 1942 maneuvers was approximately at the same standard it had set after completing the maneuvers in the Carolinas the previous year.[78] The tearing down and rebuilding of the division made another army-size maneuver imperative.

Louisiana Maneuvers

There would be no dinners with kind families, no dances with local girls. "The maneuver area, centering around Leeseville, La., has been called the dreariest and most uninteresting section in this country—dry, gradually rolling hills covered with pine stumps and inhabited by wild pigs, poisonous snakes, and poverty-stricken sharecroppers. There was no place for the men to go and little for them to do in what free time they had."[79] In western Louisiana one could stand in neck-high swamp water and feel the blast of blowing sand at the same time.[80] Although the soldiers looked forward to the maneuvers, their feelings changed once they commenced. The never-ending foxhole digging left them tired and frustrated. First Virginia, then North Carolina, now Louisiana— when were they going overseas?[81]

These maneuvers followed a pattern. Corps-sized forces faced off, clashed for a few days, received instruction and feedback, then switched roles and started all over again. They did so ten times in eight weeks.[82] A day-by-day narrative would be redundant, because the course of events in Army maneuvers was described in chapter 4. A review of the exercises will nevertheless demonstrate the division's substantial progress during the fall of 1942.

On October 8, for example, the 28th ID "was to advance on Hornbeck and defeat any hostile force encountered." Trailing it and awaiting orders was the 7th Armored Division (AD). While the 28th surged forward, the 7th AD maneuvered to envelop the enemy from the north. The 28th fixed the adversary in place while a combat command destroyed it. These maneuvers provided infantry and armor with welcome opportunities for combat side by side. Combat Command B, for instance, sent two columns between the 110th and 112th Regiments to strike the adversary. Unlike the case in previous exercises, tactical bombers flew in support of the ground troops.[83]

The maneuvers consisted of a series of problems that the 28th ID had to solve. Comments following the first problem of September 21–23 focused on familiar-sounding shortcomings: poor road discipline, poor security, and failures in intelligence gathering. Outnumbered two to one, the 28th endured a rough three days. During the next problem both sides showed a lack of aggressiveness and poor staff coordination at the corps level. A lieutenant who was carrying an overlay showing the troop dispositions for his side was also carrying a memo on "The Safeguarding of Military Information." He had no answer when an evaluator asked him why he was carrying the overlay in a place where he could easily be captured. The Keystone Division, at least, demonstrated communications that were "much improved." When it joined the 7th Armored Division in an attack against the 38th in problem 5, it demonstrated improvements in security, communications, and traffic control. Intelligence and staff functions remained unsatisfactory.

In a similar exercise at the end of October, the 28th had not completed its bridges across the Sabine River, although the 7th Armored had made it to the Red Force rear. During problem 9, the 28th had to defend against the 7th Armored and 38th Infantry Divisions. The only serious deficiency the evaluators found was its poor use of combat engineers. Evaluators complimented all of the troops on their "excellent spirit, aggressiveness, and physical condition." The larger force attacking Bradley's division used "splendid" infiltration tactics, but the troops were, for example, still not employing the 37mm antitank gun properly. In the final exercise, November 5–8, the 28th and 7th had to practice a withdrawal under fire. Quartermasters failed to cooperate well, and troops neglected to behave as if they were under fire.

Traditionally, exercise evaluators accentuate shortcomings and downplay successes, but overall the ones in Louisiana liked what they saw. Third Army commander Lieutenant General Walter Krueger complimented the aggressiveness, stamina, and spirit he witnessed. Most heartening, nearly all of the fighting occurred off the roads, a marked difference from the previous year.[84]

Troops received a more varied and challenging range of experiences from the Louisiana Maneuvers than those in 1941. One conclusion was that air and ground units had to train together continually if they were to gain enough skill to fight well. Unlike the Carolina Maneuvers, the 28th ID along with its occasional ally the 7th Armored Division practiced with substantial close air support aircraft.[85] The exercises exposed reticence against taking risks among many of the commanders, but because there were so many skirmishes, they had the opportunity to redeem themselves. More and more often troops fought well, and commanders made the correct decisions. The 110th Infantry, for instance, endured a well-executed counterattack by the 149th Infantry on October 10. Furthermore, the IV Corps commander, Major General Oscar W. Griswold, showed that he could make the right choice in not sending his 7th AD on a wide envelopment. It would have bogged down in the swamps and would not have made any difference in the outcome of the battle. The 7th failed, however, to conceal its attack adequately and reconnoiter the ground ahead of it. While the 28th ID did have to overcome the confusion caused by the allied 7th's Combat Command B attacking right through it, "The Blue plan of attack for October 11 was an excellent one." Krueger singled out Company C, 112th Infantry, for praise for its attack that same day. Its riflemen exploited cover well and crawled "hundreds of yards." No one had praised the troops at the Carolina Maneuvers in a like manner: "The movement of combat teams 109 and 110 through Flatwoods during the night of October 9–10 was well planned and well executed."[86]

There was always room for improvement. Krueger added: "Many more creditable actions might be mentioned, but there were not nearly enough of them." He was confident that his men would become first-rate soldiers, as long as the officers trained them diligently and did not wait for learning to happen. A healthy fear of combat led Krueger to demand that his soldiers master the details of surviving and fighting on the battlefield. Anything short of complete proficiency of their craft would result in death at the hands of the Germans, and that included general officers.[87] General Bradley, for example, never mentioned in his memoirs that adversary troops captured him on the night of November 7.[88]

The 28th ID left Lesley J. McNair well impressed. His observers noted, for example, that because the 109th planned ahead, it launched a counterattack swiftly on October 23. Its soldiers also knew to disperse and fight off road. Division units coordinated well with air forces. When his commanding officer was absent, the executive officer of the 2nd Battalion 110th Infantry displayed the initiative to attack an enemy river crossing with "prompt and vigorous action." Liaison between the regiments and the 109th FA was "well organized." Both it and the 108th FA sited and prepared their batteries well. "The performance of these batteries was particularly commendable in view of the shortage of personnel."[89]

Its soldiers were not perfect, yet. Riflemen were not aggressive enough against tanks and aircraft. They never took the exercises with deadly seriousness. After a skillful fight between the 110th and 152nd Infantry Regiments, "soldiers on opposite sides were throwing gravel at each other across a road." Nevertheless, McNair repeatedly praised the division's performance, unlike evaluators, who often pay little attention to the soldiers who know what they are doing. The details of the discrepancies they found attest to the fact that the soldiers were performing many other tasks well. The evaluators could not find enough faults to make sweeping criticisms.[90]

The division still needed to face and overcome several specific challenges. During problem C-9, the 28th ID practiced a river crossing. The crossing exposed a weakness in the division's capabilities, which is one of the purposes of field maneuvers. On November 2, the 152nd Infantry repulsed the 110th's attack that day. Defeated, it limped to its own side of the Sabine River "with severe losses." Fortunately, the 109th Infantry faced no resistance, because the bulk of the adversary forces were ranged against the 110th to the north of the Old Grey Mare.[91] It is unclear whether Omar Bradley bore ultimate responsibility for the mismanagement of the crossing, since the commanding general of the 7th AD held supreme command. Bradley did come up short when the division shifted its main effort to the 109th's sector. It did not bring adequate artillery to support the 112th Infantry, which had been diverted there because no one had planned for the contingency.[92]

Soldiers ignored the danger of capture. Out of carelessness, the 110th and the 229th FA lost "documents containing vital information," which they had no business carrying near the front line, to the enemy. General Griswold was nonetheless confident in the ability of the soldiers to improve. "The troops in these field maneuvers have demonstrated by their zeal to learn, their high esprit and fortitude, that they have what it takes."[93] The division and regimental staffs were shrewd enough to appreciate the benefits of the chaos. "The supply problems [are] actual. The motors break down. And the traffic snarls up." It all taught them how to solve problems they would face in combat.[94]

Just days later they impressed General McNair again. Even though he criticized the "higher commanders" of the 28th ID for being absent from their units during a critical juncture, he praised success when he saw it. He found the batteries of the 108th FA well dug in. "The infantry actions [the essence of an infantry division] were characterized by maneuver—generally decided in clever fashion . . . this is most praiseworthy." Even though Company K of the 109th boarded trucks within small arms range of the enemy—a suicidal practice—"The men were in exceptionally good spirits and proud of their work although they had had no food all day and only one hot meal in 48 hours."[95] The coexistence of high stress and high morale was becoming a common feature in the 28th ID. Those two traits often exist together, a surprising fact that Martin and Ord may not have comprehended. Bradley knew that he would improve the morale of his soldiers by challenging them. Another bright spot was the personal courage of the men. PFC John P. Linehan of the 103rd Engineers, for example, dove into a river to save a truck driver after the vehicle sank.[96]

After further evaluation, McNair expressed high praise, having seen numerous "examples of excellent small unit leadership." His last words on the IV Corps were full of praise:

> The improvement of units with each succeeding maneuver was evident, demonstrating attention to details of training by participants and the value of maneuver as a training vehicle. In general, performances were markedly superior over those of last year. This improvement was particularly gratifying in view of the personnel shortages and turnover experienced by all units during the pre-maneuver period. Strong leadership was evident repeatedly.[97]

As McNair just mentioned, the buildup of the Army continued to impinge on the 28th ID. In the middle of these maneuvers, the division still had to integrate new soldiers. For instance, new officers jointed the 110th Infantry in September, then on October 1, a thousand conscripts arrived from their basic training camps. Within seven days in early December, 180 more joined the regiment.[98] Although the new troops filled out the regiments, they did not necessarily add to their fighting power qualitatively, due to a systemic flaw in the Army's personnel system.

As a rule, the Army sent a below-average cross-section of soldiers in terms of physical fitness and intelligence to the infantry, a consequence of an assumption by personnel specialists that the infantry could get by with less than the best men. Riflemen were, however, just as specialized as soldiers with more prestigious duties. A private had to know how to employ twelve different weapons. He also had to understand tactics and small-unit field operations to an extent comparable to that required of junior officers. Modern dispersed tactics required soldiers to spread themselves out, which means that officers and NCOs would often not be close enough to physically force their soldiers to advance and shoot. A one-stripe rifleman had to possess the intelligence, courage, and motivation to fight well when no one was looking. Using up riflemen as cannon fodder did not lead to success on the modern battlefield. But why not use up the least intelligent men by putting them in the infantry? Everyone knows that infantry get shot to hell anyway, and why expose college graduates to an 80 percent casualty rate? Let a simpleton take his bullet instead. Archaic reasoning like that failed to account for the complexities of modern infantry warfare. The assumption that infantry formations can get by without first-rate minds and with below-average men does not stand up to close scrutiny.

During 1942–43, the Army tried to pass off "class V" men, those with the lowest aptitude scores, to infantry rifle squads. Field commanders, however, knew that class V men had no business handling weapons. Putting them in the line was "murder" and also imperiled their comrades. Infantry units in 1942 received only 34 percent of the men with the highest intelligence scores, but the Army sent 44 percent of the men with the lowest aptitudes their way. Since only 5 percent of volunteers chose the infantry that year, the quality of rifle companies was lowered even further.[99] Meanwhile, the War Department drew away more and more of the better men from the Army Ground Forces, especially from infantry units, for other duties. Furthermore, the Army Air Forces (AAF) got more of the class I and II men in 1942 because it would enter combat first. Adding to the problem, the drain of volunteers from the ranks to the AAF and to Officers' Candidate School depleted a branch already deficient in first-rate soldiers.

This disparity worsened in 1943. With good intentions, the Army sought to preclude an officer shortage by sending tens of thousands of soldiers to college for two years under the Army Specialized Training Program (ASTP). The Army lost 150,000 men to the ASTP in 1943, 47 percent of them from the AGF alone. Imagine the NCO corps the Army could have created with just half of that number. In 1943 the infantry and armored divisions received just 27.9 percent of the class I and II soldiers, while the AAF thrived on 41.7 percent. Following an established pattern, many of the class I and II men in the AGF continued to leave the ranks for OCS and return to the field in noncombat arms duties. Altogether platoons, companies, and battalions lost key individuals and had to train new, less capable men to replace them.[100] Fortunately, in February 1944 the Army began the transfer of 80,000 ASTP men to the AGF so as to fill out the NCO corps with sharp, capable soldiers.[101] During its fighting in Italy for example, the 3rd ID's adjutant general wrote: "Infantry combat requires great exertion, is subject to greater risk, and imposes greater hardship than any other branch. Certainly no combat imposes greater mental and physical strain on individuals than does infantry combat. Infantry, therefore, requires the highest physical standards and replacements must be in the highest degree of physical condition."[102] By June 1944, the Army placed 80 percent of the fittest men in the infantry.[103] But in the meantime, because of the Army's personnel practices, the 28th ID entered its next round of training less capable than it could have been.

The older divisions such as the 28th performed well in the fall 1942 maneuvers, and the Army considered any division that completed the training cycle and the large-scale maneuvers combat-ready.[104] Nevertheless, IV Corps began another round of training after the Louisiana Maneuvers: thirteen weeks of individual instruction, eleven for units, and a final eleven-week "combined training period." This was not an unusual practice for infantry divisions. The AGF found that during large-scale maneuvers small-unit tactical proficiency became stale.[105] Within a few weeks the Army transferred the division to the supervision of VII Corps, Second Army.[106] General Bradley himself moved on to serve as deputy commander II Corps under Major General George S. Patton Jr. in February 1943.

Marshall delayed Bradley's promotion several times because he wanted the 28th Infantry Division to benefit from stability for several months so that it could mature as a fighting force.[107] The division's progress left Bradley enthusiastic over its abilities by the year's end. On the eve of his promotion, he related to General Marshall that he had enjoyed his time with it and declared that it was "improving by leaps and bounds. I do believe that we are ready for combat right now and that we are better than many divisions that have already gone." He was certain that after the next month's training the Keystone would rank among the best in the Army.[108] Major General Griswold was also pleased and by December 30 deemed the division ready for amphibious training.[109] The soldiers completed the fall maneuvers in high spirits. Major General Daniel I. Sultan of Third Army commented: "[T]he men have never reached the point where they could not take still more. . . . I predict a brilliant future for you when you enter actual battle."[110]

Hell-by-the-Sea

Although Bradley may have considered the 28th Infantry Division ready to fight by 1943, there was no place to send it. The war against Japan was a relatively low priority for the AGF and never received that many infantry divisions. The Americans and British were on their way to defeating the Germans in North Africa, but shipping shortages and African geography limited the troops that could be sent to that theater. Consequently, for the time being, the Keystone Division trained to spearhead the assault on France, which might take place as early as August 1943.[111]

On January 14, 1943, the Keystone soldiers boarded forty-four trains and moved from Camp Livingston to Camp Carrabelle on the Florida panhandle, where they practiced amphibious landings and received a new commander, Major General Lloyd D. Brown, on February 20.[112] The men soon named him "cowboy," J. J. Kuhn recalled. He liked "to ride standing up in a jeep, hanging onto the windshield. He also carried a [riding] crop."[113] Information about the division's activities in 1943 is scarcer than for 1942, but the men were clearly busy. Since the Army no longer culled it for soldiers for other formations, the 28th had the opportunity to practice as an entire division.[114]

The first three weeks in Camp Gordon Johnston, the site's name from January 1943, consisted of constant briefings for the staffs covering sixty-seven topics. A single day could demand that officers learn about signal communications, field artillery, infantry, and antiaircraft artillery—all in "Shore-to-shore operations." Meanwhile the soldiers practiced searching houses, using grenades in urban warfare, moving about and concealing oneself, climbing walls and roofs, and spotting for artillery batteries.[115] They had to learn quickly and retain their lessons usually after only one trial run. Realistic and violent, the obstacle courses, hand-to-hand combat, and demolition sites "so engaged the interest of the troops that they very nearly overshadowed the amphibious features of the training offered." One course "was designed to teach the soldier how to kill with his bare hands and to condition him mentally for that gruesome task."[116] Machine guns fired bullets less than three feet over the heads of the troops crawling through the obstacle course.[117] According to *Newsweek* no one in the division was shot, but one veteran remembered differently.[118] Running around the abandoned logging town of Harbeson City, the troops practiced urban combat, which they liked best of all.[119] At that site, known as "Schicklgruber's Haven," the soldiers learned about such sinister German tactics as setting booby traps in food.[120]

Their training included an amphibious exercise, their most complex operation to date, in late February. For instance, the complexity of loading the landing craft from ships challenged everyone. The divisional headquarters would first be at sea, then change to a shore location. The boats had to force their way ashore under radio silence, breaking it only if it became obvious that the "enemy" had seen them.[121] Commanders had to assess a variety of information. A successful landing required intelligence that informed the commander of the beach defenses, the presence or absence of mines and underwater obstacles, and the day's weather. Division engineers had to determine the direction and speed of currents and routes inland from the beach. They needed to be able to detect whether the enemy had altered the channel offshore. Scouting parties had to survey the ground 1,500 yards from the beach, at night.[122] The division had to know how to coordinate with attack aircraft that would support their landing. An examination of the maps charting the courses that landing craft took to the beach illustrates the difficulty of coordinating such an operation.[123]

In the end, the division never conducted an amphibious landing under fire; it went ashore in France on July 27, 1944. Still, successfully executing an infantry division's tasks was in no way "easier" than more prestigious arms such as aviation, armor, or artillery. The 28th found itself faced with an enormously complex operation involving hundreds of interdependent, ever-changing variables. Every detail was important, and in battle mistakes caused the deaths of fellow soldiers. Consider the precise order of the battalion landing team in terms of packing the landing craft and timing their assault. During maneuvers later that year in the Chesapeake Bay, the first wave contained assault commanders, mine removal specialists, three teams of engineers, and no weapons heavier than a BAR or a rocket launcher. Eight minutes, not seven or nine, expired between the first and second waves. Every weapon and soldier was to arrive in order with precise spacing and timing. The fourth wave, for instance, saw the battalion executive officer, the rest of the heavy machine guns and 81mm mortars, more 37mm antitank guns, a platoon of 105mm artillery, and bulldozers come ashore, all of it meticulously choreographed.[124]

Their time in Florida greatly improved the division, but the only sentiment the Gulf Coast instilled in the men was a longing to go elsewhere. While soldiers had laughed in Louisiana when an armadillo crawled into bed with one soldier, they found that Carrabelle was full of cottonmouths, even in winter.[125] John R. Chernitsky remembered the typical way of waking up in the middle of the night—to the sound of yet another soldier screaming "Kill the S.O.B.," referring to a snake. He and his mate even woke up once, turned on the light, and watched six-foot water moccasins swing from the rafters, banging into the wall.[126] Mosquitoes ruled the air. Soldiers defended themselves with mosquito nets, but crawling underneath without letting the bugs follow inside was nearly impossible. A comic in the 110th Infantry instructed his friends to boast about where they were going to sleep that night with instructions on how to find that tent. Once the mosquitoes were distracted, break for your own tent, and crawl into your own bed from the outside. "This is all very shattering to the spirit of the mosquitoes. I've heard mosquitoes break down and weep great tears, after buzzing fruitlessly about the empty bed in another tent all night. . . . This is downright deceitful, and shouldn't be used on any of the friendly mosquitoes."[127]

Conditions did not improve off post. The nearby town of Sopchoppy, an Indian name supposedly meaning "Land of the Sky Blue Skunk Cabbage," welcomed tourists with a speed trap and swarmed with untended pigs. The nearest city, Panama City, was off-limits and full of prostitutes, while Tallahassee resided in a dry county.[128] Carrabelle was hell. With the stiff wind and high humidity, forty-degree temperatures on the north Florida coast chilled the soldiers to their bones. Even worse, this winter was colder than usual and completely dashed the men's expectations. Visions of palm trees and a climate akin to that of Miami Beach sank into the panhandle's mud amid the camp's primitive huts.[129] Bradley hated the place and thought that whoever picked it as a training location deserved a court-martial "for stupidity." Still, he admitted that the training they received after his departure was of great value.[130]

The division's stay in Florida climaxed with another landing exercise against a hostile beach on March 4–6. All elements were in play. Soldier-laden craft followed a bombardment by aircraft and ships, while airborne forces parachuted near bridges.[131] The 28th ID carried out the landing with skill, better than any of the other three units previously trained at the center: "at least most of the units hit the right beaches at approximately the right time."[132] General Brown praised the troops' performance, for they exceeded his expectations. They approached the entire operation with great interest and careful preparation. They were especially disciplined in remaining quiet and not giving away their locations through the misuse of lights.[133] Their landing succeeded in spite of a storm that struck, which cost them much of their equipment, and more.[134]

The amphibious exercise was as near to real combat as could be had. Fourteen soldiers perished during the storm.[135] On March 5, the commanders checked the weather and found no warnings of an approaching squall. One hundred fifty landing craft set sail, and the sudden storm swamped a flotilla at 8 PM. Because of radio static, many of the craft could not receive the frantic warnings to head for the beach immediately. One landing craft with men of the 112th Infantry hit a sandbar close in that the coxswain mistook for the beach because of the darkness. He ordered the men to disembark. Thinking they were jumping onto solid ground the soldiers discarded their lifejackets—their standard procedure. Fourteen of nineteen drowned in the dark. Boats received the storm warning two hours later at 10:30—too late.[136] The training syllabus had taken into account the dangers of ocean-borne operations, for not only had the division taught its men how to swim, but they also practiced jumping off a platform into a lake with full packs, so as to know better what to do if a landing craft sank.[137] Tragic circumstances overcame good training and forethought.

General Brown considered the drowned no less heroic than if they had died in battle.[138] The calamity was an apropos capstone to the Camp Gordon Johnston experience, a place of misery, cold, and sand.

Following the amphibious exercise, the division again returned to fundamentals, emphasizing physical conditioning. Soldiers completed timed marches carrying the equipment they would use under fire. Standards were high; anyone who could not finish twenty-five miles in eight hours was transferred out of the division. A strong sense of self-respect, along with stern sergeants and officers, ensured that most made it.[139] This indicated that the morale of the division was high, because the march was a perfect opportunity to get out of the division. The 109th Infantry spent most of April and May at Fort Rucker, Alabama, conditioning itself with fast marches and practicing shooting and night operations. One veteran exclaimed, "What a treat! A nice, new camp—and a permanent fort."[140] The Army Ground Forces expected the division would be ready for combat in July.[141]

A Summer in Virginia

The division moved its location to Camp Pickett, Virginia, on June 6, 1943.[142] Its soldiers considered it a return to civilization after life on the Gulf coast. Many officers spent July at Fort Benning, Georgia, studying advanced infantry tactics.[143] Three of the 28th ID's combat teams continued to practice landing operations in the Chesapeake Bay out of Camp Bedford, Virginia, while the rest of the division conducted two weeks of mountain maneuvers in West Virginia in August and September.[144] The 112th Infantry's 3rd Battalion, for example, camped in West Virginia mud and began a six-day exercise on August 8, followed by the "usual camp duties" from the 16th to September 3.[145] Because of the Army's emphasis on multiple qualifications that summer, on average soldiers gained proficiency in five to six different weapons or tasks.[146] Details still evaded many of the soldiers. They walked where they could be seen, did not place antitank guns on dominant ground, neglected to authenticate their transmissions, and seldom requested artillery support.[147]

As they honed their skills further, troops of the 28th ID made liberal use of live ammunition. The cracking of bullets, combined with the practice of evacuating casualties on landing craft back to ships, opened their eyes as to the nature of their business.[148] In addition to landing practice, the soldiers learned how to load equipment on transport ships, how to live on ships, proper selection of landing sites, and the reloading of men on landing craft from the beach.

Following landings in the Chesapeake, teams still had to show consideration for private property by removing trash, empty cartridge casings, and obstacles and filling trenches.[149]

The mountain warfare training in West Virginia again highlighted the connection between rough training and high morale, even though it placed severe demands on them physically and challenged even these exceptionally fit soldiers, who had been training for over a year. Battalion commanders called the course "well-balanced, progressive . . . superior as pertains to the physical hardening and conditioning of personnel. Morale is high, and there has been a minimum of illness."[150] The commander of the 112th's 3rd Battalion considered the mountain maneuvers "highly beneficial."[151] Lieutenant Colonel Thomas J. Noto, who commanded the 109th Infantry's 3rd Battalion, wrote: "[T]he period of mountain training has been as interesting as any tour of duty I have had in my period of service."[152] Comments by commanders took on an enthusiastic tone when evaluating the mountain warfare training. They realized they could really utilize what they were learning and appreciated the physical and mental challenges. Their morale consequently increased.[153]

During the summer of 1943, spirits among the soldiers of the 28th ID differed greatly from that of the rest of the ground forces. Many ground troops were mired in low morale because for riflemen, daily life was a grind.[154] By August 1943, 80 percent of infantrymen wanted to transfer to another assignment. The reasons for their dissatisfaction were clear. A foot soldier's life was dangerous, and low prestige exacerbated their discouragement. In the North African campaign, for example, infantry and armored troops bore 80 percent of the casualties, but they never approached that percentage of total Army manpower. By March 1944, 6 percent of the Army's personnel were shouldering 53 percent of the casualties. Because the AGF received less than its fair share of the best manpower, the likelihood of death in combat increased for the infantryman.[155] In order to give the foot soldier some distinction, the Army created the Combat Infantry Badge as a mark of distinction for GIs who had closed with the enemy.[156]

To Wales

The Keystoners avoided some of the "hurry up and wait" so endemic to Army life on its way to Wales, its home between the posting in West Virginia and combat in France. Previously, many divisions had languished in or near their port of embarkation waiting for ships, but the 28th ID did not suffer that fate.[157]

While the soldiers mustered at Camp Myles Standish in Massachusetts, rumors soon spread that they were bound for Great Britain, since that was where the troop ships came from.[158]

They were sailing as a smaller division because the Army had reduced the size of its infantry divisions. The United States did not have an endless supply of men, and the Allies were experiencing a shortage in shipping, so there was an imperative to strip the infantry divisions of any "excess" soldiers and equipment. Divisions lost 509 vehicles (these could be "pooled" at the corps level for use as necessary) and 2,102 men. Various service personnel were reassigned, and the infantry divisions lost 108 automatic rifles. The AGF took most of the bridging equipment from the engineer battalion, and it and the signal company "each lost about 100 men." It also deemed the headquarters staff "too large." Fifty-seven millimeter antitank guns replaced the obsolete 37mm weapons. What was left was a division of 14,253 men.[159] These reductions reflect a problem the Army had wrestled with for decades: the choice between a division's fighting stamina and its mobility. A division with more staying power was less mobile, and vice versa. One consequence was the stripping of stateside divisions for "men periodically for replacements for the divisions overseas." That weakened the capabilities of the stripped divisions.[160]

The division's first twenty months of wartime service was a microcosm of some of the problems with which the Army struggled as it expanded. In terms of the culture of a National Guard division, General Bradley concluded that cliques of National Guardsmen were detrimental to the development of cohesion and the equity of promotion within the organization. He thus redistributed the men who had started out in the PNG among the various units of the division. As a result the division's consolidation into the Army was nearly complete. The Army's requirement to build up and then raid divisions for cadres for new divisions set back the 28th ID's training program by many months. The commanding general's leadership proved critical. General Ord never gained any momentum in training the division, while Bradley whipped it into shape. The multitude of tasks modern infantry had to master validated the fact that the twentieth-century infantry division was a complex organization comprising highly skilled soldiers who could not be produced overnight. The 28th's subsequent experience with training in Wales illustrated further the myriad of tasks incumbent upon an infantry division.

Chart 2

Infantry Division, 15 July 1943

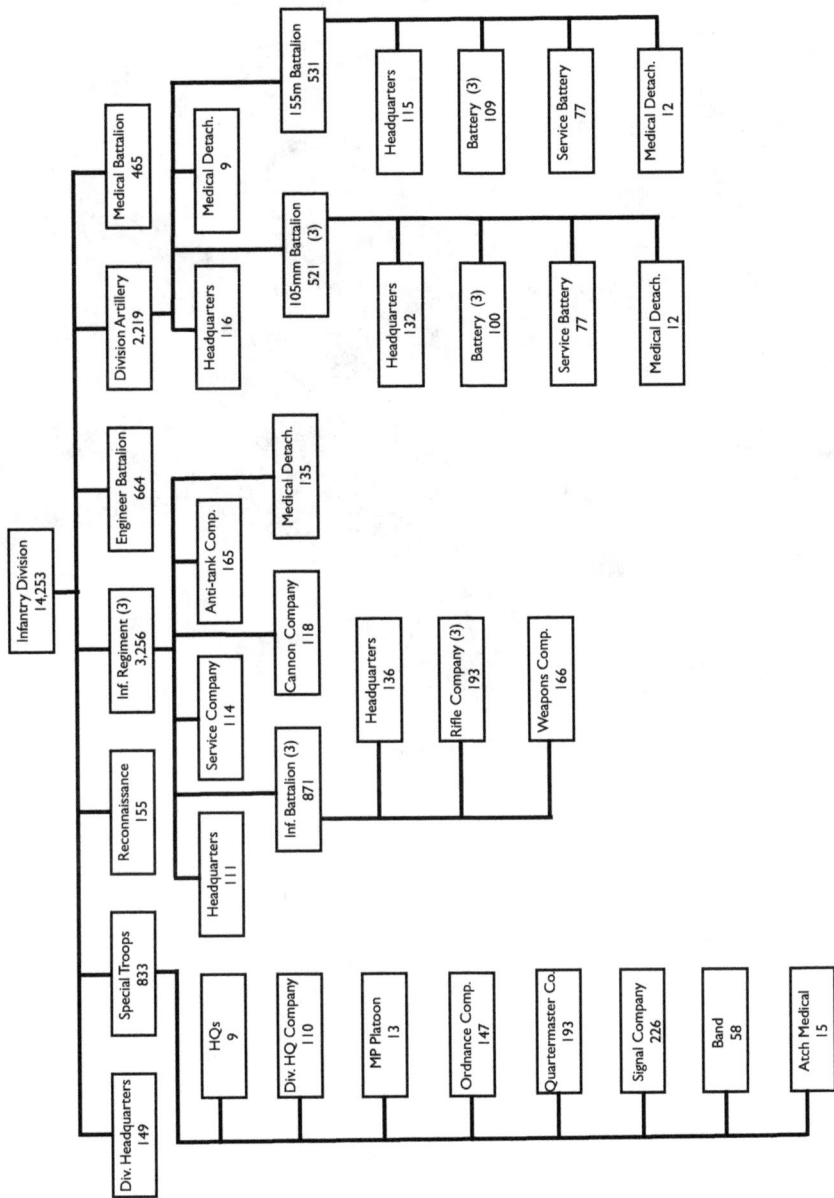

Infantry Division — 14,253

- Div. Headquarters — 149
- Special Troops — 833
  - HQs — 9
  - Div. HQ Company — 110
  - MP Platoon — 13
  - Ordnance Comp. — 147
  - Quartermaster Co. — 193
  - Signal Company — 226
  - Band — 58
  - Atch Medical — 15
- Reconnaissance — 155
- Inf. Regiment (3) — 3,256
  - Headquarters — 111
  - Service Company — 114
  - Cannon Company — 118
  - Anti-tank Comp. — 165
  - Medical Detach. — 135
  - Inf. Battalion (3) — 871
    - Headquarters — 136
    - Rifle Company (3) — 193
    - Weapons Comp. — 166
- Engineer Battalion — 664
- Division Artillery — 2,219
  - Headquarters — 116
  - 105mm Battalion (3) — 521
    - Headquarters — 132
    - Battery (3) — 100
    - Service Battery — 77
    - Medical Detach. — 12
  - 155m Battalion — 531
    - Headquarters — 115
    - Battery (3) — 109
    - Service Battery — 77
    - Medical Detach. — 12
- Medical Battalion — 465
  - Medical Detach. — 9

Source: Wilson, Maneuver and Firepower, 183.

28th passing through Siegfried Line near
Roetgen, Germany, September 1944

An American warning to American troops,
November 1944, Germany (facing top)

110th Infantry east of Orbey, France,
January 1945 (facing bottom)

Collapsed bridge at the division's crossing point
over the Rhine, Weissenthurm, Germany

Raising the flag at Ehrenbreitstein,
April 6, 1945 (facing top)

Adjutant General Robert M. Vail, Mrs. Martin,
Governor Martin, General Cota, December 1945
(facing bottom)

9

Training in Wales

1943–1944

Ships carrying the soldiers left port on October 7–8, and within two days the sea's roughness started taking its toll. Seasickness sent many to bed.[1] Cooped up and desperate to see daylight, the men on the S.S. *Santa Paula* opened its removable roof only to gaze at the depressing "dripping gray clouds of the North Atlantic."[2] By October 16 stormy weather made the men anxious for the shore. Seas were rough enough to toss dishes about the galley, but a 112th diarist noticed with envy that the pitching and roiling did not bother the Filipino stewards. Within sight of land, by the 17th seasickness subsided in anticipation of journey's end. The convoy docked at Cardiff, Wales, the next day.[3] "Welcome to Wales," barked an Army major. "If the sun is shining, it's going to rain; if the sun's not shining, it's raining!"[4]

The GIs marveled at Wales's beauty and its differences from America. The bright green grass, well-trimmed hedges, manicured countryside, complete absence of trash and billboards, and quaint stone houses all stood out. John Fairchild wrote, "It all had an air of unreality. It was like one of Disney's pictures of springtime with the colorful land, doll-like houses, happy birds, and cheerful music." The soldiers welcomed the daily two-hour hikes because they wanted to go see beyond the next hill. Most of the men had never journeyed outside the United States, so every distinction stood out. "The bi-lingual Welsh; the Main Street provincialism that 'In WALES, nothing opens on Sundays, not even parachutes,' the British accent with its rising final inflections, the friendly attitude which prevailed—these are things never to be forgotten by the men of this battalion."[5] Another wrote, that the "food is good, morale is excellent, and the country is a bit strange to everyone."[6] During the 1990s, most veterans who mentioned their time in Wales remembered the friendliness of the people and the beauty of the countryside.[7] Soldiers took advantage of two-day passes to visit Cardiff, Swansea, Aberystwyth, and even London.[8] As had been done in the past, the Army coordinated with civilian authorities so that when 14,000 American soldiers descended on a small portion of Wales, both sides would get along well. Regimental band concerts for the locals contributed to mutual goodwill.[9] The 28th ID's experience was fortuitous, for by the time it arrived, the island of Great Britain was already swelling with American soldiers. Britons were losing patience, however, and would soon "come to think of the U.S. soldier as sloppy, conceited, insensitive, undiscriminating, noisy."[10]

The 28th Infantry Division did not encamp in one location. Regiments and even companies were spread about the Welsh countryside, which inadvertently forced small-unit commanders to run their units more on their own, "a good—and safe—introduction to typical combat situations."[11] Soldiers spent the second and third weeks of November repeating personal and small-unit training so that the requisite skill necessary for the more specialized training at the Assault Training Center would be at its peak. Road marches, map reading, visual communication, and sports occupied them for the time being.[12]

After a month in Wales, the troops had "only the highest praise for the treatment . . . by the civilian populace."[13] One veteran, PFC Thomas Hickman, considered the Welsh "great," but found that the English "resented us."[14] Some of the Americans attended local churches and made friends in Carmarthen. A nearby golf club offered memberships to the division's officers, and locals from Llanelli, Burry Port, and Pembry invited men to dinner.[15]

The holiday season provided another opportunity for generosity between the Welsh and the Americans. Soldiers of the 112th's 1st Battalion found time on Christmas Eve to entertain two hundred underprivileged children who lived near their encampment. About fifty sergeants acted as "daddies" for the children, and everyone enjoyed themselves. Many other visitors from Lampeter and Llandysul joined in.[16] Company C entertained children in a nearby castle, while men of the 109th Infantry extended similar generosity to the children of Port Talbot.[17] The 109th FA participated in a candlelight service in St. Thomas's Church in Haverfordwest.[18] Many of the people of Bridgend invited soldiers of the 108th FA into their homes for the Christmas celebration.[19] Although formal arrangements were in place to match Americans who wished to have a "home away from home" with host families, local citizens and soldiers arranged a great many of these friendships on their own.[20] These were but short respites. A fifteen-mile march and a five-day field problem bracketed the 112th's Christmas turkey dinner.[21]

British-American fraternalism had a military component, as well. Following a meeting between a 28th ID combat unit and members of a nearby Home Guard unit, the British commander commented, "Probably more good has been done [for local British-American relations] by yesterday's meeting than by all the hot air belched forth by our respective national propaganda machines!"[22] The division had an exchange program with the 15th Scottish Division. It not only received observers from the Scots, it also exchanged coats of arms. Officers and men became acquainted with the 15th and its training.[23] The formation of "inter-attachment" divisions as between these two was a policy the British initiated, seeking friendly relations and understanding between the soldiers of the respective armies. Such cross-pollination not only would assist in combat, but also looked forward to a closer relationship between the two peoples in the postwar world.[24] The division's commanders enthusiastically looked forward to cross-training with the British Army, especially when offered the chance to learn the air–ground liaison methods of both armies.[25] They did not have to wait long, as a British Army lieutenant paid them a visit to see what they needed in the way of cooperating with tactical aviation.[26]

The nature of their presence brought another opportunity for friction, for the best way to practice combat was to have the freedom to maneuver without regard to fields and fences, and without having to interrupt a maneuver to settle property damage claims on the spot. Not long after arriving the division's commanders met with nearby residents to work out mutually agreeable solutions. As long as they asked for the landowner's permission, troops could set up camps on private farms. Some of the issues verged on the bizarre. Imagine having to remember to coordinate with "Mr. Davies" before opening fire on the Cilwenau range so that artillery shells would not blow his sheep to bits. Imagine writing a letter granting a foreign army permission to use one of your fields as a landing strip. Because entrenching was as basic to a rifleman's craft as shooting, troops could pockmark a field in minutes. The GIs were granted permission to do so as long as they filled the holes when finished. A few thoughtless officers ordered men to cut down farmers' trees.[27] No place was safe. One camp was next to the Ashburnham Golf Club, grounds ideal for infantry exercises.[28]

Nonetheless, tensions arose as a result of the sudden influx of GIs. Their spending power inflated prices in Britain, burdening the local people. General Brown consequently asked his men to increase their deductions for savings bonds so that they would have less cash in Wales, and he wished that the soldiers would stop receiving money from home, another contributor to inflation.[29]

A more serious problem was the racial strife that accompanied the GIs overseas. When the division arrived in Wales, encounters with black American servicemen often escalated into violent confrontations. The 28th was an all-white division, but some of the truck drivers who transported its personnel were black, and trouble erupted right away. As a result of a stabbing incident, the division leadership questioned soldiers about the assault and held meetings on how to prevent further episodes. By mid-December, First Army was trying to suppress hostility and violence between white and black American soldiers.[30]

Cordial British treatment of blacks offended white Americans and was a major source of white anger. Locals in Carmarthen, for instance, treated American blacks decently and placed no restrictions on them.[31] Throughout Britain, British Army soldiers wished to socialize with them, and Tommies resented American whites who tried to force them to treat blacks as inferiors, or discouraged interaction altogether. In response, British citizens pointed out the inconsistencies between democratic ideals and American racial customs.[32]

Name-calling and even fights broke out when white Americans witnessed the Britons' egalitarian treatment of blacks, especially if it involved a white woman accompanying a black man. Likewise, a group of black soldiers asked a white soldier from the 112th Infantry if he was from Georgia. When he replied that he was not, they told him that he was lucky, implying that they would have beaten him up if he had been. Seven blacks beat up another white private badly in Carmarthen. To lessen the opportunity for clashes, the division made every effort to billet associated black service troops away from its whites, but by the spring, race relations had not quieted. After a race riot on April 3, Burry Port was off-limits. One white private faced a general court-martial for trying to start a fight between a group of blacks and nearby whites.[33]

The "alternate-pass system," whereby the races were separated during off-duty hours, ended up creating white and black "turfs." If a soldier of one race entered a town claimed by his opposite, he was in peril.[34] The experience of the 28th ID troops was no different from that of other white troops. A patchwork solution solved the problems temporarily. The Army limited its assignment of black soldiers to Britain, and, at British insistence, instructed white GIs to treat blacks with respect.[35] General Eisenhower dictated that "*derogatory statements concerning the character of any group of United States troops, either white or colored, must be considered as conduct prejudicial to good order and military discipline and offenders must be promptly punished*" [italics in original].[36]

To the Invasion

Sight-seeing, developing friendships with the British, and quarreling with other Americans were not the Keystone Division's purposes, of course; training to kill German soldiers was. Army policy was for division commanders on down to take responsibility for the training and performance of their men.[37] In examining the training completed before the division entered combat, one can see the traits of decentralization, self-motivation, and responsibility throughout the division's training regimen in Britain. The G-3 daily log is one of only a few records from this period, and in it virtually no orders from higher headquarters as to how to manage the division's day-to-day affairs or training can be found.

Officers from the platoon on up, of their own initiative, beat the bushes for training areas and instructional courses. They knew what their soldiers needed to learn in preparation for combat. Units' scheduling their own training times was a central trait of this decentralized training program. For instance, General Brown asked for the use of the Sennybridge artillery range in the last half of March. He also directed his infantry officers to practice artillery targeting, thus improving combined arms capabilities, and effectively giving the artillery many more forward observers.[38] Foreshadowing the gravity of their task, the division asked to send three NCOs to the Mines and Booby Traps School.[39] For the most part, Brown left those decisions to his company, battalion, and regimental commanders.

They sent a constant stream of requests for specific training opportunities. Battalions wrote their own training schedules, and the regiments decided who attended assault cadre training. Rifle platoons had to draw up their own tests and create their own exercises.[40] Sometimes battalions had to move in order to facilitate their combat preparations. When the 112th's 3rd Battalion moved to Old Harbor in November, they found that "[t]he camp has the appearance of having been suddenly evacuated by several surprised coal miners."[41] After Christmas it moved to Braunton Station and "plenty of mud."[42]

Platoon leaders developed independent thinking and initiative in their riflemen. During field exercises, platoon leaders presented their soldiers with tactical problems, had everyone write solutions with accompanying orders, and "with the assistance of the NCOs" selected the best answers. The privates who wrote the best answers took turns taking command of the platoon. Soldiers and officers alike found this pedagogy "exceptionally beneficial . . . for it teaches them the difficulties involved in leading platoons and squads, enabling them to better understand the mechanics of troop leadership."[43] By late December, platoons conducted five-day exercises "entirely on their own." The soldiers considered these platoon exercises without parallel for teaching small-unit combat tactics, and eagerly anticipated them.[44] Such practices are remarkable testaments to self-leadership and maturity. American GIs regularly took their training to heart with ardor because they understood the importance of mastering the craft of warfare. Not even cold North Atlantic rains could dampen their enthusiasm.[45]

At the same time the next higher echelon, V Corps, informed the division of openings and opportunities. For example at the end of October, V Corps had two openings at the British Battle Training School, "reputed to be very good," for 28th ID junior officers. A lieutenant colonel or a colonel could go to a senior officer's battle course at Oxford if he wanted to attend.[46] When offered a slot at a joint training school, the division G-3 replied that he would like to send as many students as possible.[47] The V Corps later offered training at camouflage and maintenance schools.[48]

No sooner were the division's assets settling into their routine in Wales than new soldiers began arriving in December.[49] Yet again the division had to incorporate and train more men fresh from basic training. Wasting no time, the division got them instruction on infiltration and practice in how to crawl through barbed wire while machine guns fired over their heads. The Army planned to send 2,500 selectees to every assault division in Britain from January to March, as well as 150 officers in November. If a division went into combat it was to pool this overstrength for use as replacements.[50] Losses of leaders in platoons and companies to other assignments, an interminable problem, set back its readiness.

Once units began tactical exercises in November, their commanders designed them to harden the men physically, by, for instance, deliberately scheduling them to occur when the soldiers were tired. A march preceded an exercise by no more than twenty-four hours, and the exercise took a full eight. Soldiers trained at night at least once a week, and the tasks were the same as those required during the day. Each week included a fifteen-mile march, and one per month was extended to twenty-five miles.[51] Hard-surface roads abused the men's feet, and rain drenched them.[52] When the fifteen-mile hikes blistered the feet of the Medical Battalion soldiers, the battalion decided to schedule additional shorter marches between the long ones to toughen the medics.[53] By early spring soldiers were completing marches of almost twenty-five miles in just over six hours.[54] The 112th Infantry had to finish its day of firing in the rain despite pleas to return to camp. Then it had to begin another five-day field exercise.[55] Some of the GIs appreciated the rigors, such as practicing a battalion problem when exhausted after a road march. They knew that they would have to fight while tired.[56] Many, however, came down with the flu because so much of the training took place in rain and snow.[57] Not letting up, the troops spent Thanksgiving in the field, during which Company C of the 112th conducted "a four-hour night problem—the reason being it brings us one more day closer to victory."[58]

The 28th again had to embark on amphibious training with somewhat of a remedial agenda, when portions of it formed the 109th Regimental Combat Team and made their way to the U.S. Assault Training Center (ATC) at Braunton in Devonshire.[59] They trained in deadly earnest literally; a short round from a 105mm howitzer killed two men.[60] Three landing craft capsized and thirteen more men drowned during a "live-fire assault" on the 18th of November.[61] Soldiers trained in how to evacuate wounded.[62] All of the regiments practiced antiaircraft shooting at Aberayton. Since U.S. ground forces were shooting down too many of their own aircraft, the men had to perfect their aircraft recognition skills. Each soldier had to study three hours a week until proficient, then one hour a week thereafter. V Corps notified General Brown when aircraft would be flying overhead so soldiers could practice identifying them. Commanders in the 112th Infantry arranged with a nearby RAF base for assistance. During the weeks prior to the invasion of France, Allied aircraft flew overhead to give the soldiers a good look—"do *not* shoot at these!"—then landed for a more close-up inspection.[63]

Training in January required many men to step up to the next higher leadership level, for many NCOs were sent to Braunton for advanced instruction. The 112th's Company D was soon practicing wire cutting and demolition, among other things. The troops concentrated on assaulting pillboxes with all of the section's firepower plus that of accompanying tanks. They practiced embarking and disembarking on landing craft, and progressed from company to regimental exercises.[64]

The division practiced assaulting beaches in landing craft over and over because in December 1943, V Corps planned for the 28th to join the 29th ID as the first wave against Omaha Beach.[65] Toward that end, small-unit training remained the theme, as platoons, companies, and battalions continued to carry out field exercises lasting several days. The 112th conducted five days of platoon-level training during the first week of January, and the 109th Infantry held its own field exercise January 6–10.[66] The 109th Infantry completed a five-day "self-sustaining exercise," the 110th conducted field exercises at Mynydd in February, and then the 109th Infantry maneuvered at Black Mountain from February 28 to March 3.[67] Conditions were miserable, but high winds, sleet, blowing sand, and rain did not stop field training. Neither did safety concerns dissuade the 112th from carrying out a seaborne assault in a storm. When finished, the troops marched to their bivouac soaking wet, hungry, tired, and sore. At the end of February, the assistant division commander, Brigadier General Kenneth Buchanan, chastised them for the absence of initiative they displayed, but they were exercising in a snowstorm.[68] Maneuvers on board landing craft left every soldier thoroughly soaked, but their efforts were worth it. Even though the soldiers made some mistakes, their practice landings and assaults with tanks, artillery, and tank destroyers received high praise from ATC instructors. After the February 2 assault by the 112th's 3rd Battalion, an ATC evaluator remarked that it was the "finest exhibition of a battalion team yet seen."[69] A landing exercise later that month went well for the 112th, and its officers appreciated learning to live in the cold, wet weather.[70] Members of the 1st Infantry Division called the 112th's landing on January 29 "one of the best they had ever witnessed."[71] The veterans of Camp Gordon Johnston had trained them well.[72]

Nevertheless, by the end of February the assault teams had not yet mastered their craft. Subsequent reviews from the ATC were mixed. Soldiers' morale was very high, and efforts there were "well-received, but inadequate to produce a well-trained individual." Soldiers displayed initiative and teamwork in every task but cover and concealment.[73] Their written orders were poorly constructed, but the division finally provided a more standardized method and guidance. In late February, the division explained to its officers that orders had to be brief, clear, simple, and transmitted rapidly. Orders had to avoid telling a subordinate *how* to conduct his task. "UNMISTAKABLE clarity" was the one overriding trait orders had to possess.[74]

During March units conducted short exercises, artillery batteries went to the firing range, and the division asked that its men be sent to various schools such as the Bomb Reconnaissance School. It engaged in a continual conversation with V Corps in pursuit of these training opportunities.[75] The 112th's 1st Battalion was pleased when all but four men were able to complete a twenty-two-mile march, but recognized its shortcomings when it failed to defend a hill properly.[76]

Third Army Headquarters had some hard questions for the division. Why had General Brown changed its ready-for-combat date from March 1 to April 1?

The V Corps and the division G-3s discussed the change and decided to sweep the problem under the rug. They decided to write down "this division is ready for operations" on March 14, the day Third Army asked for an explanation.[77] Then V Corps reminded the division that its training directives had expired; when were its new ones going to arrive? Never. "Colonel [Thomas E.] Briggs stated that at the present time the division is continuing by verbal direction in whatever training the Commanders consider necessary and the division does not contemplate publishing a new directive."[78]

As the invasion approached, senior officers began devoting personal attention to the assault divisions. Lieutenant General George S. Patton's persona surprised the officers and NCOs of the division when he addressed them. He looked like a tough aristocrat according to Harry Kemp, but he also appeared small and cussed in a "high-pitched, almost falsetto voice . . . 'kill, kill, kill—or be killed.'"[79] General Dwight D. Eisenhower visited on April 1 and engaged the men about their responsibility in the invasion and asked about their hometowns and living conditions.[80] Although the soldiers had to stand in the rain for two hours before he arrived, they did not seem to mind.[81] Inspecting the men, Eisenhower asked individuals their feelings about the imminent invasion. "'How do you feel about it, soldier?' he would ask. 'Do you feel we can make a success of this invasion?' Then he'd put his hand on the soldier's shoulder and move on."[82] Eisenhower remarked that he left "filled with pride at the obvious fitness, appearance and all-around efficiency of the units which I inspected. They impress me as being serious and determined and I am well satisfied that they will give a good account of themselves in the difficult task which lies before us."[83]

Toward May, however, not everything was in order. Some of the soldiers were not yet qualified marksmen, and Brown reminded his commanders to be alert for open firing range time. By now General Brown was paying more attention to day-to-day operations. He ensured that the battalions practiced cross-country movements, daytime and nighttime. They also practiced dry runs of "marching fire–delivery" followed by the same with live ammunition. Marching fire was an infantry tactic in which soldiers maintained a steady stream of small arms fire toward enemy positions while they advanced over open ground. Their continuous shooting suppressed enemy counterfire, and greatly increased the confidence of the advancing American infantry. The division scheduled combined exercises with artillery and mortar fire over the men's heads and a variety of entrenching exercises. The 109th Infantry tried to obtain some tanks from the 712th Battalion, but none could be had.[84]

Aircraft and tanks were conspicuous by their absence. The operations journal reveals no evidence of training with the AAF in close air support at all, only in aircraft recognition so as to avoid fratricide. There is one mention of training alongside tanks at the ATC in February, and the 112th Infantry practiced with tanks in late January, a baptism of their "first experience with flat trajectory weapons firing directly over our heads."[85] Tanks from the 771st Tank Destroyer Battalion conducted combined operations with the 109th Infantry on February 28 and March 4.[86] Consultations with the 712th Tank Battalion began on May 23, and four days later the 112th practiced assaults with tanks.[87] A division history mentioned "strenuous training exercises involving Infantry-Tank cooperation" in July 1944.[88]

An absence of thorough combined arms training was a problem throughout the AGF. The Army in the European Theater of Operations (ETO) never put much emphasis on tank-infantry operations until just a few weeks before the sixth of June.[89] Leadership realized that the ground forces were going to need close air support, but days prior to the Normandy landings there was still *talk* of the need for the development of "weapons, equipment, tactics and technique and organization of air units employed in air-ground cooperation." This concept of joint warfare had been the lowest priority for the Army Air Forces, so the Americans entered the campaign with a less-than-optimum doctrine.[90] Segregating tanks and infantry had not been considered a problem because armor was to be kept separate "for massed armored action." Interestingly, two tank proponents found fault with this idea. The chief of the Armored Force, Lieutenant General Jacob L. Devers, had warned in 1942 that the pooling of tanks and tank destroyers in units away from the rifle regiments would result in poor teamwork in the field between infantry and armor.[91] George S. Patton Jr. sought to attach a tank battalion permanently to each infantry division. He believed that the mere presence of a few tanks would greatly inspire the infantry.[92] General McNair and the AGF had made some attempts to organize tank-infantry training, but there were not enough armored vehicles available for such an enterprise until late 1943, when he finally ordered corps commanders to associate tank battalions with infantry divisions for training in October of that year. Worried that attaching armor to infantry divisions too liberally would harm the distinct training of those individual battalions, McNair never fully supported their combination.[93] As a result, at least one of the 28th's infantry companies did not see an M4 Sherman up close until May 6.[94]

Planners changed the Keystone Division's role in the invasion three times. In February it became a reserve division, to follow closely on the heels of the

1st and 29th Infantry Divisions. This status as the corps reserve burdened the division staff with even greater command and planning challenges. General Brown had to prepare to be redirected during the middle of the assault toward an alternative landing zone.[95] The 28th was still going to land a 4,196-man regimental combat team on the first day, along with fifty-six tanks.[96] It also had to function as one of the elaborate decoys in Operation Fortitude, the Allies' grand deception whereby they tricked the Germans into thinking that the Normandy landings were just a diversion from the primary landing at Calais. Allied intelligence utilized existing units for the fictional deception force, the "First US Army Group—FUSAG."[97] For this reason the 28th had to practice perfect security. On March 27, however, one of the division's officers asked V Corps for a map of France right in the area of the Normandy landings, over the telephone, a "serious security violation." Since the Germans had been led to believe that the 28th was destined to land at Calais, knowledge of a request for Normandy maps may have encouraged them to suspect a ruse had they found out about it. This breach, however, did not contribute to the removal of the division from the first wave; that had already been decided.[98]

Fortitude commanders fed false information primarily through three German double agents. As part of the deception, the 28th, along with the 79th and 83rd Infantry Divisions, made up part of VIII Corps within the Canadian First Army for the supposed invasion of Pas de Calais. Indeed, the 28th was to be one of the vanguard divisions. In early May an agent reported to the Germans that the 28th was in Southeast England, right where one would expect a landing force bound for Calais to stage.[99]

On April 8, Third Army transferred the Keystone to XX Corps because Patton needed an infantry division that had completed amphibious assault training, just in case a subsequent landing under fire was necessary.[100] Once the division left the FUSAG, radio operators continued to use its frequencies, generating false message traffic as if the 28th were still a part of the FUSAG. From then on the division had to train under radio silence so that the Germans would not find out where it really was.[101] This deception operation continued past D-Day, as when an agent passed on information on the division's amphibious exercise of June 17 against the beaches of Felixstowe, trying to suggest that another invasion (at Calais) was a possibility.[102]

The division HQ left Tenby for Chiseldon Camp on April 17.[103] The locals were sad to see them leave, and watched as the soldiers sang "hill-billy songs," and made fun of Hitler. Passersby walked over and shook hands; friends bade farewell. Most of all, the children appreciated the Americans' stay. "The Americans displayed more than a kindly interest in them, and in years to come they will still be talking about the extra chocolates and gum they enjoyed in 1944. It was a great send-off for men who had won the hearts of everyone by their exemplary conduct."[104]

Life during the month of May was rough on the soldiers and often boring.[105] They engaged in mock combat with the 101st Airborne Division on May 11–12 to prepare it for the invasion, more for the benefit of the Screaming Eagles than for the Keystone.[106] As it turned out, the 28th fought it to a standstill, ruining its plan of attack and capturing five hundred of the elite troopers.[107] The division had relocated to Swindon, Wiltshire, forcing the men to live in tents. They looked forward to building shacks out of the crates used to ship the gliders the airborne forces were going to fly in. Many went without showers for two weeks and had to wash out of their helmets. Then instructors ordered the GIs to dig foxholes and get in them while tanks drove over them, the point being to prove that a deep foxhole was safe from a rampaging tank. Every man qualified to fire mortars, and by the end of the month they resumed practicing the combat loading of trucks, in which they were packed in a way so that they would have access to critical items first.[108] Fortitude exploited the divisions' training "exercises in Ipswich."[109] Training continued much as it had during the preceding months: attacking fortified positions, conducting withdrawals under fire, defeating counterattacks. The training continued into June, but the division's G-3 log had no more entries after May 10. May ended with the soldiers anxious: "We've been alerted, and still no dammed invasion. Our fingernails have been chewed off to the elbow, waiting . . . waiting . . . waiting . . . ."[110]

The men did not have any difficulty figuring out when the invasion was going to occur. Passes were limited to a twenty-five-mile radius on June 5, and they heard the constant drone of airplanes overhead all night.[111] The next morning thousands of eyes watched in awe as hundreds of damaged B-17s and B-24s limped back from France. When they realized that the 28th ID was not going to participate in the initial beach assault, the soldiers were "extremely disappointed at not having an opportunity to take part in the invasion." Another wrote, "It is useless to attempt to describe the extreme disappointment and hurt that overcame the officers and men."[112] On June 13 the Supreme Headquarters Allied Expeditionary Force removed the stipulation that the 28th be used only for a landing under fire.[113] Third Army still had no clear purpose for the division except for its continued training for imminent combat. It had to be ready to cross the channel by June 23. The XX Corps pondered three plans, either a landing in a secure port in the Cotinen Peninsula or Brittany, a landing on the beaches of Quiberon Bay, or an assault near Morlaix for an attack on Brest. The XX Corps received word on June 29th to prepare to land near St. Malo, but then Third Army, still a secret entity, ordered it to discontinue further preparations on July 12.[114]

Stuck in a now monotonous training schedule for the next several weeks, the division finally received orders on July 14 to begin marshaling for the crossing in three days.[115] When this word reached the men, their spirits brightened. "Nothing much interesting happened until July 15, when the battalion commanders received secret orders that a move was imminent. The official alert was on the 17th: the restriction of personnel, cutting of telephone lines and the holding up of mail *made morale soar immensely*" [italics added].[116] As had happened during the mountain combat training in West Virginia, morale improved as danger and the challenges of combat neared. General Brown made some command changes, transferring "strong" leaders to "weak" battalions, such as Lieutenant Colonel Thomas J. Noto, whom he switched from the 109th's 3rd Battalion to command of the 110th's 1st Battalion. Third Army, to which the division belonged for now, became operational on July 25, and the division landed on the beaches of Normandy near Bricqueville on July 27.[117] It did not, however, enter the battle with a fully mature combined arms doctrine.

Years of training had prepared the 28th Infantry Division well for certain aspects of combat, especially at the battalion level and below. Nevertheless, its training lacked thoroughness in the tactics of combined arms warfare because the men had had so little training with tanks, and even less in close air support. The Army's combat experience in 1943 had confirmed the usefulness of close coordination between infantry and their counterparts in the armored and air forces, but the Army did not fully institutionalize this lesson.[118] And as noted earlier in this chapter, the Army Air Forces and Army Ground Forces were still making basic decisions on the relationship between these two components of the Army. Therefore the 28th Infantry Division had to harmonize its tactics with armor and air in the midst of combat. Previous decisions on training priorities beyond its control meant that it did not enter combat with as much know-how as it might have had.

10

From Normandy to the West Wall

When the 28th Infantry Division reached the shores of France on July 27th, its soldiers found the Normandy beaches littered with the refuse of fighting. After clambering up from the shore, they stared at "a small green field covered with row upon row of white crosses."[1] On their way to the front the soldiers saw and smelled the consequences of the recent fighting—fields scattered with German corpses and dead draft horses. "Death, which had been a report in the newspapers, an abstract, unpleasant thought, had become a cold, hard fact."[2] Veterans of the fighting told them to "[f]orget all your past training, this is different."[3] The Keystone Division quickly marshaled northwest of St. Lo, entering combat on July 30 in the midst of Operation Cobra. It functioned as a backstop while other divisions raced east to try to cut off the German forces. During August, the American, British, and Canadian armies tried to trap the enemy in the "Mortain Pocket" after the Germans attempted to counter the Allied breakout of the deadlock around Normandy. The Allies were not able to seal off all escape routes when German forces tried to flee, and although approximately ten thousand of the enemy were killed and fifty thousand captured, anywhere from twenty to one hundred thousand escaped.[4] Brown's division (and many others) would nip at their heels all the way to the German border.

The 28th ID's combat experience was going to demonstrate an unfair reality of war in the mid-twentieth century: difficult terrain combined with dull-minded leadership trumped sound combined arms training. Once the division left the maneuver-friendly provinces of northern France, its men found that bravery and firepower could not easily overcome the defenses along the Franco-German border. By November, they would suffer debilitating casualties because of the unimaginative leadership of their commanding general and his superiors, who squandered the division's hard-won capabilities and used them up against German firepower.

Map 4
The 28th Infantry Division's Route
August-September 1944

Source:
http://www.history.army.mil/brochures/no-fran/p18-19
(map).jpg

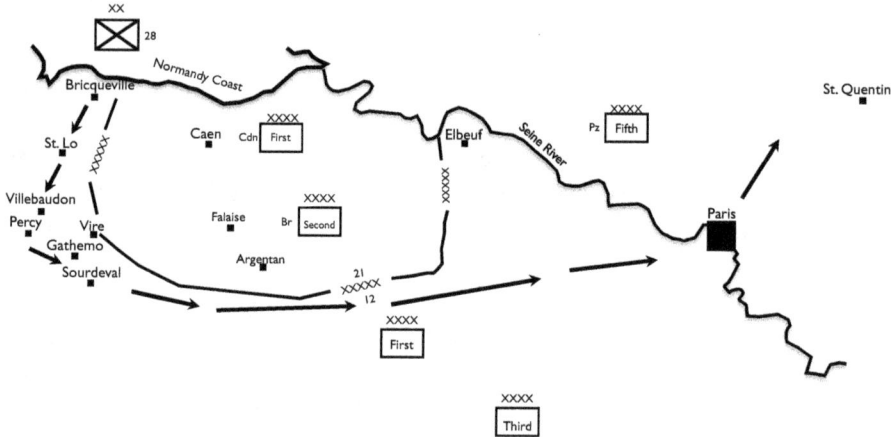

The division's first frustrations took place in hedgerow country, terrain
that had stymied the Allies for weeks. In his portion of Operation Cobra, Major General Charles H. Corlett, the XIX Corps commander, intended to drive
south. He assigned the 28th a supporting role covering VII Corps's left flank
since it was not a combat-tested division. Its baptism of fire came at the village of Villebaudon while the 29th and 30th Divisions led the attack. The next
day it moved to Percy so as to strike east toward Vire. Along the way the 28th
displayed the usual characteristics of unbloodied divisions, such as a reluctance to move and fire. It suffered a stunning 700+ casualties on August 2, but
still seized St.-Sever-Calvados two days later.[5] Hidden snipers and 88mm cannons were their most lethal adversaries, and soon the limited visibility among
the *bocage* fragmented the fighting into platoon- and squad-sized firefights.[6]
Brigadier General Norman D. Cota observed that the Germans exploited the
bocage masterfully, using the ground to protect their withdrawals while they
inflicted serious losses on the Allies. "Many officers became casualties due to
their pushing forward, trying to speed up the advance."[7] Lieutenant Julian
Farrior commented, "We came so close to the enemy that hand grenades were

tossed back and forth across the hedgerows and we opened fire at point blank range."[8] Right away the first of many replacement soldiers and officers arrived to restore the division's muster rolls to near full strength.[9] Now that they had some know-how to pass on, leaders in the rifle companies gave replacements instruction on hedgerow fighting.[10]

August saw an ominous development for the division's riflemen: high casualties. The 110th Infantry alone suffered 1,779 during August, 251 of whom were killed in action. The 109th Infantry fared better, with 698 wounded or missing and 153 killed.[11] Colonel Theodore A. Seeley informed General Brown that his 110th regiment was no longer combat-effective. Although it recovered, Seeley's regiment had lost 20 percent of its strength in five days of fighting during the first week of August.[12] Such losses were not surprising, since the division staff had never discussed tactics for hedgerow fighting during their training in Britain, much less trained its troops in the requisite methods. They had to learn by trial and error.[13] These loss rates were the norm for the U.S. Army. Over time, American infantry regiments routinely suffered loss rates greater than 100 percent.[14]

On August 5 the 109th Infantry fought a bitter battle at Forêt de St.-Sever, "hedgerow by hedgerow." The defenders had carefully gauged their fields of fire and saturated them with small arms and mortars.[15] The division nevertheless took its next objective, the crossroads at Gathemo, over the course of August 8–11.[16] After heavy fighting, the 109th Infantry occupied the town on the 10th, encountering resistance that was relatively light for two reasons: the Germans were in full flight toward their homeland, and many of the troops the 28th encountered were non-Germans who surrendered at their first opportunity.[17] By the second week of August, the 28th wheeled east around the town of Sourdeval. Fortunately, it did not face a "serious threat" after the fighting at Forêt de St.-Sever until they reached the German border four weeks later.[18]

Once in open country, "the troops for the first time saw the real joy of the liberated French, the streets of towns and roads through the country were lined with civilians passing out drinks of all nature, green apples, and showering them with flowers." The only complaint was from a prostitute who objected "that the soldiers kept on their cartridge belts."[19] Villagers shouted, "Vive de Americains!" but the GIs also witnessed the ugly treatment female collaborators received. French civilians shaved the heads of women who had partnered with Germans.[20] The next month the Americans watched a truly gruesome sight at Montmédy, Belgium, where children sang "ring around the rosy" as they danced around a pile of dead German soldiers. When the children stopped,

Free French partisans forced five women to sit on the pile as they shaved their heads.[21] A few French were not so welcoming. GIs of Company M, 112th Infantry, discovered a noncombatant who allowed a German artillery observer to use his house and made no effort to help the liberators ferret him out:

> As we approached Hill 210 from this valley, we came across this Frenchman standing in front of his house and offering us drinks of cider. He seemed friendly but very nervous and fidgety. . . . There was a German observer in the attic of the house who had a perfect view of the valley and our troops. A BAR man pointed his BAR straight at the Frenchman's head and pulled the trigger. Then the house was burned down.[22]

The GIs did not tolerate treachery. A few days earlier J. J. Kuhn and his patrol stopped a priest in the town of Percy. When they searched the small suitcase he was carrying, they found a German officer's uniform. The man said nothing. Kuhn later wrote, "I told two of my men to take the Kraut officer behind one of the buildings and shoot him. We didn't feel too bad about it, because that's what he had done to the priest whose clothing he had stolen."[23]

The story of the next month was one of trying to catch up with, bypass, and cut off the German armies before they reached the relative safety of the east bank of the Seine and Germany proper beyond. Day after day the infantry set out after the Germans, gaining contact late in the morning. They would then engage in a firefight, followed by German shelling from about five until eight in the evening. The Americans were never able to maintain contact throughout the night with their adversary, who managed to pull away a couple of hours before dawn to the next rise, beyond which they would await the next U.S. attack.[24]

General officers, the soldiers found out, were not immune from the risks of combat. Their new division commander, Brigadier General James E. Wharton, was killed by a sniper on August 13, one day after assuming command following the relief of General Brown. Omar Bradley had replaced Brown because of his poor leadership at the battle in Gathemo. Charles Scott recounted, "The whole situation was chaotic . . . he added to the general confusion by demanding allegedly impossible tasks and by several times changing his plans on the spot." Bunched up on the road, blocked by a destroyed bridge, the GIs of the 28th were sitting ducks, and "the Jerries really poured in the artillery."[25] At first, Brown had been reluctant to urge his forces forward. On July 30, for example, he "ordered Colonel Seeley not to advance in the face of possible further losses."[26] But on August 5, he ordered "a mass formation" forward to seize Gathemo, insisting over the protests of Daniel Strickler that the Germans were not lying in wait. They were. Concealed infantry opened fire on GIs crossing open ground, and his platoon of light tanks had no hope against hidden 88s. Brown also misled a company commander as to the extent of German defenses at Gathemo.[27] Omar Bradley noticed that XIX and V Corps had fought well, with the exception of the Keystone Division, which "fell on its face. The fault, we judged, was Brown's, and I relieved him of command without delay."[28]

Brigadier General Norman D. "Dutch" Cota, formerly the assistant division commander for the 29th ID, took over on August 14th and led the division through its toughest months.[29] Cota had fought on Omaha Beach, where his personal courage and leadership persuaded soldiers immobilized by fear to scale and seize the cliffs overlooking the landing zone: "Two kinds of people are staying on this beach," he shouted, "the dead and those about to die. Now let's get the hell out of here!"[30]

By August 18, it was clear to XIX Corps that the Germans were giving up Paris and were not going to fight with the Seine at their backs.[31] Small *Wehrmacht* formations turned on the Americans and inflicted losses, but for the most part they either fled or surrendered. By the 19th the division had captured 833 prisoners.[32] Because it had killed and captured so many, the Germans named it the *Blutiger Eimer*—bloody bucket—"a feared and hated outfit which the Germans would try to get some fine day when conditions were more favorable for the Wehrmacht."[33] The name came from the Germans' interpretation of the division's shoulder patch. It was shaped like a red keystone, but to them it looked like a bucket filled with blood.

Because of the speed of the German flight, the division encountered no more than a few pockets of resistance that quickly gave up, and the Americans no longer suffered air or artillery attacks.[34] Carried by six truck companies, the soldiers of the 28th ID moved 120 miles on the 20th and 21st, a lightning-fast pace during wartime. "The route was strewn with ruined German materiel (a tribute to the Air Force) and for over 50 miles the road was lined with people, cheering the advancing Americans." By August 25, the Keystone Division approached the Seine south of Rouen.[35] When masses of German soldiers tried to cross the river in barges, the first round the 107th FA fired at them scored a direct hit, destroying a barge loaded with men midstream. Then their shelling slaughtered those who remained on the west bank.[36] Because of stiffening German resistance, it took the 109th Infantry Regiment and the 2nd Armored Division seven hours to take the town of Elbeuf on August 25.[37] Completely routed, the Germans resisted more as ad hoc groupings than as organized formations.[38]

Occasionally prisoners shed light on the manner in which the Americans fought. One German NCO with five years' experience, including action on the eastern front, exposed several flaws in American infantry tactics. He noticed that they usually waged frontal attacks, neglecting to flank German infantry, who normally operated in smaller formations that were vulnerable to such turning movements. Furthermore, the Americans exposed themselves to counterfire by staying in the same place after firing at German soldiers, who learned to predict the Americans' actions. From his perspective, GIs had breakfast, fought in the morning, stopped for lunch and a nap, fought until bedtime, and then slept through the night. On the other hand, he found American artillery "terrifying," and "much heavier and more devastating than the Russian artillery." U.S. infantry, he added, hesitated to "follow up the advantage gained," allowing German troops to pick up weapons from their dead comrades and resume fighting. The prisoner gave detailed instructions about how to defeat German infantry—for example, informing his interrogators that German infantry considered it "honorable to surrender" once surrounded, but not before. Therefore, American reluctance to flank and surround German positions sacrificed many opportunities for GIs to capture more of the enemy. He also informed his captors that the best time to shell German positions was between eleven and midnight; that was when relief parties went forward.[39] Other prisoners asserted that "they would have liked to surrender, but were afraid we would kill them."[40]

The German decision to make for their border was the right choice for conserving their forces and prolonging the war. The terrain in northern France favored offensive movement; it was not a place suitable for them to stop and make a defensive stand. The flatness of the ground meant that there were no rises from which the German defenders could see Allied forces approaching from a distance and there were no ridgelines for setting up defensive fortifications. Numerous villages and good roads meant that American mobile forces could appear suddenly. American analysts encouraged their troops not to be intimidated by the violence of German counterattacks lest they encourage more of the same. GIs should instead overrun them.[41]

Through Paris

Allied forces were attempting just that, and not even Paris could slow them down. During August 28–29, members of the division, along with other Allied troops, marshaled in Bois de Boulogne, a park in the Paris suburbs, for a parade through the city. The division history noted with pride that they had required a week and several major conferences to prepare for the 1941 Memorial Day review. This time, however, the staff held a fifteen-minute meeting before issuing a page of instructions, and the soldiers formed themselves for a parade in a matter of twenty-two hours.[42] A parade, however, was not what the American men wanted to enjoy. Shaving before he marshaled for the parade, Robert L. Smith saw "a very pretty French woman peddling by on her bicycle with skirt flying high and legs showing marvelously in the morning sunshine. In my best French I shouted, 'Oo la la,' to which she replied in perfect English, 'Enjoy the view; you will find it everywhere in Paris.'"[43]

The parade was a political event staged to assist General Charles de Gaulle's bid for power in the capital. Preferring "to leave the French capital to the French," Eisenhower had refused his request for two American divisions to occupy the city and ensure order in Paris—an odd way for De Gaulle to communicate to Parisians that a Frenchman had firm, legitimate control over the city and government—but the supreme commander did accede to the marching of one American division by de Gaulle's reviewing stand on August 29, where he presided over the event as if he was the head of state.[44] The 28th received the honor, and it was the greatest parade the division had ever experienced.[45]

> The Parisians, who crowded the streets to cheer for these, the first American troops to march through the city in World War II, showered flowers, fruit, and cognac on the un-protesting Americans; jumped into vehicles to shake hands with the occupants; urged their pretty French compatriots to kiss as many of the grinning GIs as willing traffic would bear and finally linked arms with their U.S. allies and marched exuberantly to the edge of the city.[46] In a few cases, individual men were snatched from the ranks, probably not too unwillingly, to not be seen again for a day or two. So far as can be determined, those "kidnapped" all found their way back to their companies looking not too bad but in need of extended rest and sleep.[47]

The crowd gave the soldiers wine along the way, so "the division was drunk as hell by the time we got out."[48] The division marched straight through without even stopping, then deployed for battle on the outskirts of Paris at the end of the day. Eisenhower had also used the parade as means of enabling the Keystone Division to avoid traffic jams on its way after the Germans. Only a worsening gasoline shortage retarded their advance to the German border.

The 28th turned to the northeast and advanced day and night. Along with the rest of V and VII Corps, the division received gasoline at the expense of other forces so as to keep moving.[49] Quite simply, in hopes of overtaking the

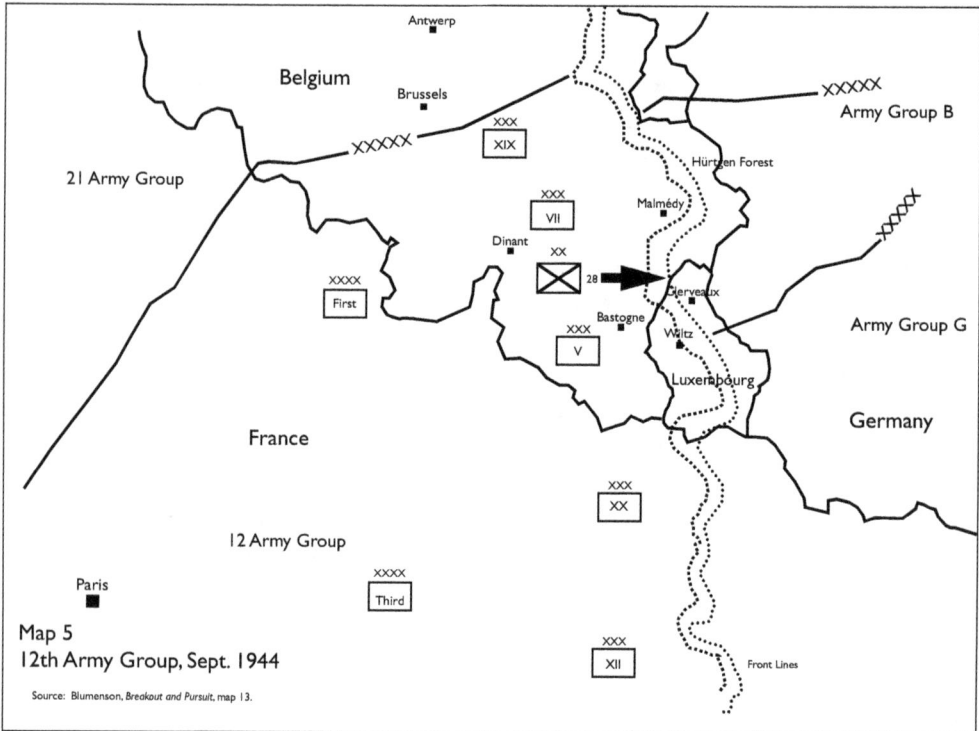

Map 5
12th Army Group, Sept. 1944

Source: Blumenson, *Breakout and Pursuit*, map 13.

retreating Germans, the Allies were going to go as far east as possible and then let their supply lines catch up.[50] Along the way the Americans got the best of their adversaries. When on September 2 an enemy company attacked the 110th Infantry at St.-Quentin, it suffered 125 killed, while the Americans lost just 15.[51] On the 4th of September Cota was ordered, along with the 4th ID and the 5th Armored, to turn to the east and "advance with all possible speed."[52] The division's men fought through other "light delaying actions" and took numerous German stragglers as prisoners. An enemy fighter strafed them just once the entire month.[53] A sniper, however, shot the 112th's CO, Colonel Henry I. Hodes.[54] As the division passed through Luxembourg, Lieutenant Randall B. Patterson, a Kentuckian in the 112th, noticed that the locals were "very friendly" even though most of them spoke German. Could this presage an early end to the war?[55] General Leonard T. Gerow, the V Corps commander, reflected the optimism of those who were not at the front by commenting that the war might be over in a few short weeks.[56] More conservative leaders forecast a complete victory before the end of 1944.[57] Soldiers who had interrogated captured German soldiers, however, expected a tough fight. Many German prisoners warned their captors of a coming fusillade of super-weapons.[58]

Both armies were racing for possession of a strategic prize: the Siegfried Line, also known as the West Wall. This series of pillboxes, fortifications, and steel and concrete barriers running along the German border was only partially manned, and in some spots it was entirely vacant. Farmers had even packed earth around the "dragon's teeth" at some spots so that they could drive right over them. If the Americans could create a substantial breech and pour forces through it before the Germans could organize an effective defense, then the last physical barrier between the American forces and the German heartland would be the Rhine River.

The German Border

By September 11, a few platoons from the 109th and 110th regiments were roaming up to three miles inside Germany proper.[59] The 109th Infantry found ten unoccupied pillboxes near Sevenig, and manned several of them. Some companies forded the Our River with ease, while small arms fire forced others back.[60] It seemed so easy that day, but American forces had advanced so far ahead of their supplies that they had little ammunition left with them. Trucks had to drive sixty miles each way to bring ammunition forward, if they could obtain fuel, which First Army was now rationing. For that reason First Army ordered its forces to avoid "a full scale engagement."[61] To comply, Cota allowed his regiments to commit no more than one battalion to the assault—not enough firepower. When 2nd Battalion of the 110th Infantry probed east, it found the pillboxes and German artillery too formidable to overcome. They shot a U.S. tank destroyer (TD), and American artillery did nothing more to the pillboxes than tear up their camouflage.[62] Still, Company I reached Harspalt, then returned to its battalion on September 11.[63] Lieutenant General Courtney H. Hodges, the commander of First Army, believed that the Germans would fight enough to save face, but he did not expect a major effort that would stymie the Allied advance for another four months.[64]

One of his opponents, the chief of staff of the German Seventh Army, Generalmajor Rudolf Freiherr von Gersdorff, believed this effort to pierce the Siegfried Line "was neither planned nor executed skillfully." Had the Americans been able to commit adequate forces, the offensive threatened the Germans with "grave danger." Instead, the fighting bolstered the morale of the German troops, who had been beaten continuously by the Americans "who were supe-

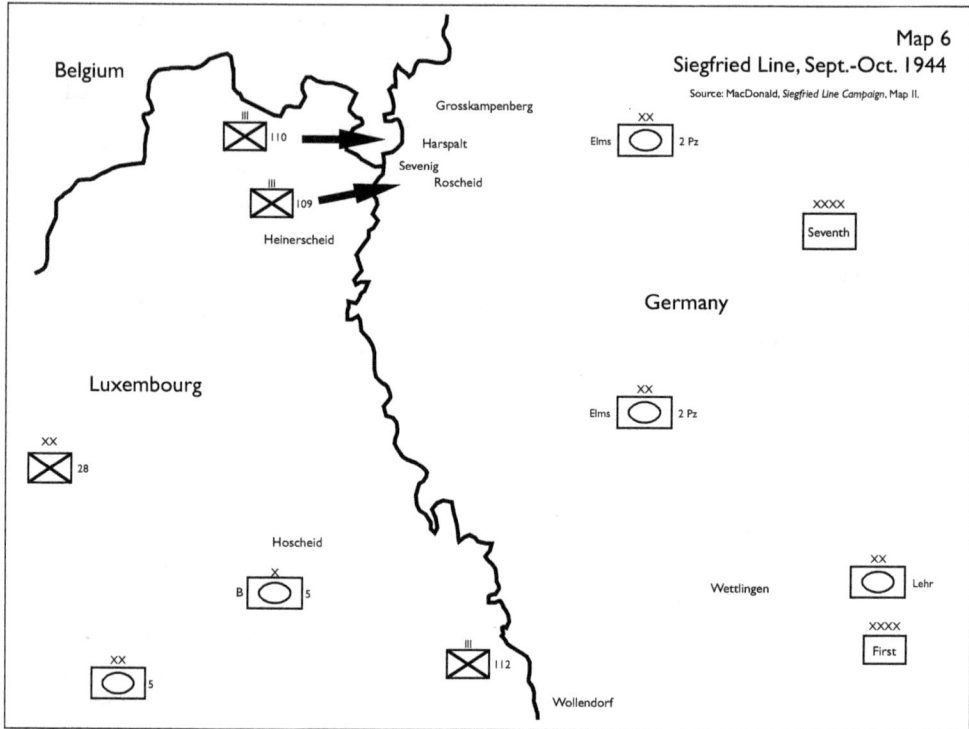

Map 6
Siegfried Line, Sept.-Oct. 1944
Source: MacDonald, *Siegfried Line Campaign*, Map II.

rior in every respect."[65] General Gerow made a poor choice when deploying his forces along the Line. The V Corps commander had ordered the 5th Armored Division, then in the lead, to spread out laterally so as to maintain contact with Third Army to the south. He thus weakened the breakthrough potential of the division that had the most organic firepower. This was fortuitous for the Germans, since V Corps had approached "the great gap between the I SS Panzer Corps and the LXXX Corps."[66]

The American forces outran their supply lines because they had moved with such great speed, resulting in the leading edge of their advance running out of steam by the time it reached Germany. Criticism of the Allies for being unable to supply their forces all the way into the Ruhr Valley is misplaced.[67] Look at what the Americans accomplished. From September 1 to 11, they advanced two hundred miles, even while turning to capture twenty-five thousand Germans near Mons, Belgium. They were 233 days "ahead of schedule."[68] Perhaps decisively, the Allied fuel pipeline "by the end of August barely reached Alencon"—a long way from the German border.[69] The U.S. failures at the West

Wall in September never would have happened had they not achieved the success of driving hundreds of thousands of Germans out of France in a matter of days. Furthermore, it was better to fight a stalemate along the German border than in the *bocage*.[70]

Nevertheless, the stalled offensive frustrated the Americans. They believed they had an opportunity to breech the border because prisoners consistently told them that the German Army was unable to man the fortifications of the West Wall sufficiently or properly. "Replacements were literally thrown in to man the fortifications." They consisted of mechanics from the Luftwaffe, stunned and sullen over the harsh realities of the front, "various *Wehrmacht* training replacements, and the SS," which "kept in line" the other troops.[71] By that is meant that "they shot anyone who ran from his position."[72] Others were "a hodge-podge of cooks, bakers, butchers, truck drivers, and other service troops," who did not know each other but were shoved into the pillboxes on the night of the 13th, given some weapons, and told to fight.[73] This motley collection, however, was under the command of the headquarters troops left from German divisions that had been shattered during the Normandy campaign, officers whose operational skills were exceptional.[74] From the 11th to the 18th of September, two of the division's regiments fought a progressively more violent battle against forces rushing to defend the border. Here the men of the Bloody Bucket division slammed into the complexities and frustrations of fighting an enemy exploiting hilly, wooded, fortified terrain, ground that served as a force multiplier to the troops defending along the Line.[75] Even though the Germans were not confident that they could succeed, local counterattacks and artillery stymied American efforts.[76]

On the 13th the 5th Armored Division received the 112th's 1st Battalion as reinforcing infantry. They then participated in a sharp fight at Wettlingen in which German artillery took a terrible toll, helped by the fact that their spotters had an "excellent" view of the battlefield. The Germans inflicted 238 casualties in four days and forced the 112th and the armored division to withdraw under fire.[77] The 110th's 2nd Battalion tried to pierce the Line at Grosskampenberg, but could not overcome the machine gun and artillery fire.[78] Hodges had authorized a "reconnaissance in force," but this escalated into serious fighting.[79]

The nature of the terrain altered combat from that of large formations to that of squads and even individuals. Before dawn on the 14th, for instance, a group of ten volunteers were trying to bring up enough explosives to blast a hole through some dragon's teeth. They were carrying fifty pounds of TNT each, when for whatever reason the explosives simply blew up at three in the morning, killing everyone. After dark on the 15th, ten more GIs carrying TNT charges low-crawled through three hundred yards of mud from a bend in a road to a barrier of dragon's teeth, which tanks had been unable to demolish. Only darkness and a few trees concealed them. After placing their explosives and pulling the igniters, they "went like hell to the rear." Their charges obliterated enough dragon's teeth to permit tanks to accompany attacking infantry. The task force then captured a nearby hill and fifty-eight prisoners and settled in for the inevitable German counterattack.[80] Company F of the 110th was able to capture six pillboxes after tanks had "punched a hole through the dragons teeth with their own guns."[81]

German forces wasted no time in plugging the breech. Company F suffered a harrowing attack on the 15th, was scattered, and two days later mustered only forty-four men, eighteen of whom were "fit for combat." Private Roy Fleming, holed up in a pillbox, witnessed the German counterattack up close. SS troops attacked using infantry and flame-throwing halftracks. A captured German said that they attacked at night because "the Americans were poor night fighters.[82]

Just as the 109th Infantry was launching its own attack toward the area southeast of Sevenig and toward Roscheid, the Germans struck again. Mid-morning on the 16th, three tank destroyers crested a hill only to be hit by German direct fire. An officer remembered, "Christ, one minute I looked and they were there, firing. The next, they were burning like hell." F and G took a wrong turn and were shot to pieces from most every angle. G Company was "routed . . . shot up completely, and fled in all directions, some returning to the rear singly, in pairs, and in small groups." Formations began to pull back that night.[83] So many officers were casualties that NCOs had to take command of two companies. The battle generated so much confusion and death that one "badly shaken" battalion commander, Major Benjamin T. Owens of 3rd Battalion, had to be replaced.[84] I Company may have suffered the worst. With only twenty-eight men left, it "formed into a provisional platoon," turned about and took back the ground it had lost. Then the Germans unleashed a terrible barrage. "The wood itself was decimated, leaves were pulverized, trunks were shattered, branches smashed. The place was practically denuded." The shelling and small arms fire pinned down the GIs in the cold rain, and no one was going to bring food or water forward under a rain of artillery shells. "The Germans came out of their pillboxes throwing grenades. They brought a machine gun out and set it up and sprayed the whole front."[85]

The hills turned into a tempest of confused small-unit combat. Infantry often did not find out where the enemy was until they opened fire. GIs replied with their rifles until the barrels were too hot to touch. The uncertainty generated rumors, and 3rd Battalion withdrew under the pressure of its fears. Daniel Strickler relieved its commander, Lieutenant Colonel Benjamin Trapani, and the assistant division commander, Brigadier General George Davis, relieved company commander Captain Andy Homanich of Company K, who broke down under the strain. Davis even sacked the 109th's CO, Colonel Blanton, because of the withdrawal of its 3rd Battalion.[86] Thus began a trend for the men of the 28th ID that continued through the Battle of the Hürtgen Forest: soldiers and commanders suffered psychological collapses when forced into extended combat on terrain that allowed little movement. Figuratively trapped, many broke, a phenomenon not nearly so prominent during the Battle of the Bulge in December. These cases of combat exhaustion were more a reflection of the toll of combat on difficult terrain than they were of the character of the individuals who broke.

Nearby armored commanders were eager to lend support, but muddy ground and enemy fire frustrated their efforts. The enemy's counterattack against the 109th Infantry continued until the 18th and drove the Americans from the dominant terrain they had seized.[87] The 2nd Battalion of the 112th admitted, "We were really caught with our pants down" by the counterattack.[88] Near Wallendorf, German troops "had completely encircled us and were attempting to rout us from the rear as well as the front," forcing soldiers of the 112th infantry to fight a battle of several hours just to survive and escape.[89] Given the success of this counterattack, it was fortunate that General Gerow had decided on the 16th not to send his forces any deeper into German territory.[90]

Although the division continued to patrol, fight, and destroy pillboxes for the rest of the month, it did not have enough reserve strength to regain the ground lost, having suffered 1,562 casualties during September.[91] By October it was worn out, having fought for two months "without a break, with no time for rest or rehabilitation aside from one or two days."[92] The Bloody Bucket faced a reconstituted and determined enemy, confident now that they had stopped the American advance.[93]

A variety of factors combined to corrode the division's opportunity. Terrain and the fortifications made it easy for a few to hold off many. The defenders combined small arms fire, machine guns, mortars, and artillery to make any movement costly. Low clouds, poor visibility, and rainy weather made it more difficult for artillery observers to see their targets, nullified the Allies' air power advantage, and discouraged tank commanders from leading attacks. The division still could not obtain enough ammunition, and the Americans' forces were too spread out. Tanks had to pull back to receive fuel and ammunition, thus forcing the infantry to stop advancing, hunker down, and wait for their return. Companies often lost 25 percent of their men to enemy fire on each assault. The necessity to bring combat engineers forward to completely obliterate the fortifications so that they could never be used again took more time, and the Americans did not have enough soldiers available to occupy (pending demolition) all of the pillboxes they captured. The Germans took advantage of that and recaptured many during night counterattacks.[94]

By the end of the month the division's soldiers "had destroyed 137 fortifications" of all types, a metric that illustrates how the fighting had degenerated into a stalemate.[95] These pillboxes were constructed of steel-reinforced concrete, with eight-foot-thick walls, and only half of the structure might protrude above ground. German laborers had built as many as ten pillboxes per mile along the line.[96] GIs developed several ways of overcoming them, with teamwork a common theme. Infantrymen and tanks worked together to reduce them one at a time. A tank would blast away at a pillbox, forcing the occupants away from the firing ports, thus preventing them from shooting approaching infantry. Infantry would then place explosives to blast holes in the steel doors or the embrasures. After blowing the charges, attacking soldiers immediately threw grenades through the holes to either kill the occupants or persuade them to surrender. The tanks sometimes managed to bludgeon their way through dragon's teeth by firing at point-blank range.[97] By experimenting with explosive charges against different kinds of dragon's teeth, the 103rd Combat Engineer Battalion developed five ways of demolishing them so that tanks could pass.[98] Another method was to attach a bulldozer blade to the front of a tank and cover the fortification—and the soldiers inside—with dirt. But sometimes the Germans dug their way through to the pillbox and brought it back into action. When GI demolition teams blew them to pieces, German infantry returned and set up machine guns and mortars among the rubble.[99] Destroying pillboxes took patience, skill, meticulous planning, and careful execution—all of which slowed the advance and allowed the enemy time to react.[100]

Although tank destroyers neutralized German antitank guns and artillery shelled any German reinforcements coming forward to help, GIs did the dirty work. A team of eighteen to twenty riflemen, accompanied by a bazooka, six "pole charges," a soldier with a flamethrower, a party with BARs, rifle grenades, smoke grenades, and hand-carried explosives swarmed over the pillbox and set charges to destroy it. Sometimes all was for naught if the GIs did not use enough explosive. Thoroughness was necessary, as in spraying the inside of a pillbox with gunfire after blowing it open. The Americans found that often several Germans inside the box surrendered, exited the fortification saying that no one was left inside, and all the while one remained hidden inside, waiting to kill the GIs as they entered.[101] One prisoner, Private Michael Salobir, recommended that the Americans attack the pillboxes at night, as only one fortress soldier manned each, and the SS was not around to prevent surrender.[102] In spite of the dangers, the soldiers of the 28th ID destroyed numerous fortifications. On September 27 alone, for instance, the 110th Infantry eliminated twenty-seven.[103]

Major Harold S. Yeager later shed more light on why the actions against the West Wall went so slowly. First, the GIs were reluctant to move about even when the ubiquitous enemy fire was inaccurate. Instead, many preferred to stay safely inside the pillboxes they had just captured. When replacement troops arrived, they were handed over to the battalion's companies and flung into combat.[104]

> The majority of the men in his battalion were replacements. Of a group of 100, 87 had been trained as Anti-Tank gun crews. Their basic combat infantry training had consisted of some two to three weeks of training somewhere in Normandy upon their arrival in France. The men had had little or no opportunity to get to know one another well, or to work together as a well-knit fighting team. They *all* lacked the thorough training in assault of fortified positions which the original men of the division had been thoroughly given at the Assault Training Center in England, in addition to long training with the Atlantic Fleet Amphibious Force while in the U.S.A.[105]

Replacements, however, were critical to maintaining the fighting power of the division. Another cruel aspect of this war was the fact that a few days of combat could quickly chew up highly proficient infantry that had required months of training to reach the level of efficiency necessary to overcome the tactical obstacles faced on the Siegfried Line.

Their tactical victories and stalemates were preferable to defeats, and the Americans had no other choice, given the terrain and their logistical challenges. Strategically, the Germans were now winning this campaign since they were delaying the Allies all along the front, largely with soldiers who "represented the 'bottom of the barrel' of German manpower."[106] The division had demonstrated a solid ability to fight well, but in the succeeding weeks, strategic and operational decisions put it in situations that either nullified its combat capabilities or reduced it to the role of speed bump.

Unable to breech the Siegfried Line, V Corps spent October fighting a holding action. Eisenhower had decided to continue to use General Bernard Montgomery's 21st Army Group for the main effort into Germany, which was a peculiar decision for a couple of reasons.[107] Montgomery's September offensive had failed. Ill-conceived, Operation Market-Garden hoped to move a congenitally slow-moving army under the command of a cautious general with great speed across several easily defended rivers in Holland in order to gain a bridgehead across the Rhine. This would be a costly offensive, but Britain had no manpower reserves for its army. Whatever troops Montgomery had, he was not going to receive any more, nor could he afford heavy losses.[108] Stretched too thin, Allied logistical capabilities could not support his offensive.[109] Furthermore, if Britain wanted to help dictate the peace with the same level of influence as the United States and the U.S.S.R., Montgomery had to ensure that he entered Germany with a large, intact army, something he could not do if he waged the bloody fighting necessary to defeat the Germans in his sector. Operational realities prevented him from achieving his strategic goals, and his manpower limitations made it impossible to achieve Britain's political goals.[110]

Stalemate personified October for V Corps. The Germans firmed up their defenses, while the American supply lines caught up with their troops. U.S. forces began rotating to rear areas to train once again in assault techniques.[111] Units that were not patrolling the front conducted small-unit training, with particular emphasis on combined operations against pillboxes and dragon's teeth.[112] Paired with the 707th Tank Battalion, the 110th found the training "excellent,"[113] but 1st Lieutenant Raymond E. Fleig, the commander of the 1st Platoon in Company A of the 707th, deemed the combined arms training abysmal. They trained together for only a few days, and the infantry never even learned that Shermans had externally mounted telephones so that riflemen could talk to the tank commander. "We married up with the infantry on the run."[114]

Simple measures such as roadblocks, felled trees, and minefields reduced the fighting to quests for square yards of ground. German patrols attacked between regimental boundaries, normally at night.[115] Fortunately, the German troops the 28th ID encountered during October continued to be second-tier home guard and fortress soldiers of the 526th Infantry Training Division.[116] Patrols from the 28th ID provoked a couple of firefights,[117] but overall the operations were modest in scope. Along with the rest of V Corps, the Keystone commenced a "reconnaissance in force" toward the east to leave the Germans no chance to rest.[118] The assault was delayed for a week, however, and then put off until the end of the month.[119] Even though October was a "quiet" period, the former PNG division still suffered 992 casualties, 106 of which were combat deaths, while capturing 125 of the enemy.[120]

The 28th ID sorely needed time for training, for it was receiving a steady stream of replacement soldiers. The 112th Infantry incorporated 378 men who either were brand-new replacements or were returning to the line after being wounded.[121] The idea was to have veterans train replacements in combat tactics and familiarize them with field operations and the combat environment and "to enable the individual to experience, and get over . . . the initial shock of combat prior to actual engagement." Veterans used them for patrols, but not as assault troops in situations where getting shot at was likely.[122]

By the end of the month, the division had taken in 1,465 replacements. These green soldiers were "extremely grateful [for the] opportunity to find out what it is all about before their turn comes to go into the line."[123] Fortunate was the replacement, such as Robert L. Smith, a medic who joined the 28th shortly after it landed, who was taken under the wing of a veteran soldier. A middle-aged man named Dave Johnson, "from one of Philadelphia's better families . . . a genuine, highly committed alcoholic," taught Smith how to survive the battle-field.[124] Not all arrived trained in how to stay alive in combat. During the Battle of the Hürtgen Forest the next month, one veteran commented, "A lot of men being new replacements, were killed because they would not keep down."[125] Marshall C. Lewis, who finished the war as a first sergeant, remembered, "I was totally unprepared for combat," reaching the front "as a raw replacement who knew nobody!" He felt "bewilderment, dismay, confusion, isolation."[126] Toward the end of the 28th's participation in the Battle of the Hürtgen Forest, replacements were hurled into intense combat without adequate training.[127] Fortunately, the division subjected replacements to that particular stress only once.

Constant rain added to the rifleman's misery: "We all agreed that this was the wettest country in the world. The only things to look forward to were chow and mail."[128] This was no exaggeration; 1944 was one of dampest and coldest years on record. As a result, the soldiers received wool overcoats, caps, and gloves. Unhappily the GIs found that when the overcoats became wet, they were too heavy to wear.[129] They did not receive enough winter footwear, which led to a serious outbreak of trench foot, a painful affliction "caused by prolonged exposure of feet to wet conditions at temperatures of 32 to 60 degrees Fahrenheit, inactivity and damp socks and boots."[130] The First Army quartermaster, Colonel Andrew T. McNamara, believed that First Army would

186 | Guard Wars

not have to fight in a snowy climate and failed to realize that 38 degrees and constant wetness would cause trench foot. Consequently, no one planned to make sure the men were properly shod.[131] General Bradley chose to give priority to gasoline over winter clothing, which he later concluded was a mistake.[132] The 28th needed nine thousand pairs of overshoes, but did not get any until November 14—after it had fought the Battle of Hürtgen Forest, during which its men suffered a "tremendous number of casualties due to immersion foot."[133] To offer some relief, regiments set up rest and recreation areas with coffee, doughnuts, and movies.[134] Optimistically, engineers practiced river-crossing methods "with a view of future assault crossing of the Rhine River."[135] The Army chief of staff, General Marshall, even paid a visit to his old division on October 11, telling them, "You are doing excellent work over here and people back home are aware of it."[136]

The men, however, limped into their next battle, having not received enough time to recuperate from the surprisingly costly fighting that began in August. One can trace their quick return to battle to the Army's decision earlier in the war to get by with just eighty-nine divisions.

11

Battle of the Hürtgen Forest

A LEADERSHIP FAILURE

While the 28th Infantry Division recovered from its battles along the Siegfried Line in October, VII Corps was carrying out an offensive to its north to try to reach the Rhine. Beginning in late September, Courtney H. Hodges and the VII Corps commander, Major General J. Lawton Collins, decided that advancing through an area known as the Hürtgen Forest was a suitable route. Collins "probably expected this [attack] to force the Germans to evacuate the forest and make it easier for the Americans to reach the Roer River," an intermediate objective. Advancing through the forest seemed so simple on paper. From October 6 to 16, however, the 9th ID tried to take the village of Germeter but advanced only a mile and a half, suffering 4,500 losses in the process.[1] These costly results did not, however, convince Hodges or Bradley to seek a different route into Germany's heartland.

On a grander scale, General Bradley sought to use First Army with Montgomery's 21st Army Group in a double envelopment. Monty's forces were to take Antwerp and then advance to the southeast, while Hodges's forces formed the southern half of the pincer. VII Corps was to lead the attack for First Army, and V Corps's mission was to take the crossroads at the village of Schmidt and to protect Collins's "right flank." Although Gerow and Hodges discussed fighting through easier terrain and avoiding the Hürtgen Forest altogether because it had already proven itself to be conducive to German defenses, they decided to attack through the forest once again—this time with the 28th ID.[2] That was an unfortunate decision because the Germans lacked the forces necessary to threaten VII Corps over open ground, and they never even considered using the forest as a base from which to mount an offensive.[3]

Hodges originally planned a larger operation, but ordered a delay in the main effort without postponing the 28th's attack, which permitted the Germans to gang up on one lone division.[4] Consequently, the 28th ID was going to have to fight alone "for nearly two weeks . . . the only attack on over 150 miles of First Army front."[5] From November 2 to 9 the Bloody Bucket made a journey to hell and back. It first sent a battalion of infantry to take the village of Schmidt, and did so with deceptive ease. The Germans quickly counterattacked with infantry, panzers, and artillery and routed the riflemen, who did not have any tank support close at hand. Cota kept trying to retake the village, which just subjected his men to more futile suffering. Meanwhile German artillery pummeled the other two regiments when they were not throwing themselves against German machine guns and mines.

General von Gersdorff later stated that the Germans considered the forest worth defending because it was a good place to keep "the West Wall from being crumbled . . . a defense in the forest was more favorable, as there the enemy supremacy in tanks and in the air would not be so effective as in open terrain." Gersdorff also assumed the Americans wanted to capture the dams across the Roer River (the Germans could have opened the dams while the American army crossed the river downstream). The forest was also an important section of the "northern flank of the [upcoming] Ardennes attack." So to hold the dams and secure their upcoming Ardennes offensive, the Germans were going to have to thwart this American operation "at all costs."[6]

The Americans had not, however, thoroughly decided on what they were trying to accomplish. Hodges did not even begin to make specific plans to take the dams until November 7, by which time the 28th ID was too mangled to contribute to that effort.[7] The battle wrecked the division, particularly the 112th Infantry Regiment. The Battle of the Hürtgen Forest became synonymous with futility in war.

The Shattering of a Regiment

When the 112th Infantry seized the villages of Vossenack and Kommerscheidt on the 2nd, they encountered little resistance. Leaving Major Robert T. Hazlett's 1st Battalion in Kommerscheidt, Lieutenant Colonel Albert C. Flood's 3rd Battalion of the 112th pressed on to Schmidt on the 3rd of November, taking the village by late afternoon.[8] They surprised the Germans, capturing some just sitting down for a meal. Others were drunk.[9] But the closest American armor could get to Schmidt was 1,500 yards, so the infantry were dangerously exposed, were overextended, and possessed no heavy firepower.[10]

On November 4 the Germans counterattacked. They rained a heavy, searching artillery barrage on 3rd Battalion in Schmidt, and then about sixty German infantry attacked from the southeast at 7:30, followed by ten tanks. The panzers quickly got in among the infantry and killed many. Bazooka rounds made no difference.[11] Then a battalion of the 1055th Regiment attacked the western side of Schmidt. Accompanied by panzers, German soldiers routed 3rd Battalion.[12] They struck with such suddenness and force that they drove Flood's battalion out of Schmidt, and cut off at least one hundred GIs. The result was a forgone conclusion, as the soldiers had no adequate defense against the tanks.[13] By attacking from two directions, the enemy surprised the GIs, and combined infantry, armor, and artillery with skill and determination. Because the American position was indefensible against such forces, the soldiers in Schmidt could either stay and fight—and die, or run away and perhaps live. During the Battle of Hürtgen Forest, Cota's GIs broke and ran from the field of battle only when subjected to specific stressors: when they were overextended and essentially defenseless, or when they were bombarded for a long period of time without the opportunity to move or to accomplish anything worthwhile with their fighting. The occupation of Schmidt without armored support was the first of those situations, and the static battle of the 109th and 110th Regiments met the second criterion.

On the 4th, one platoon "seemed to disintegrate—a few darted out of their foxholes and headed back into Schmidt—[a] few more—and then the whole platoon took off."[14] Three platoons fled to the southwest, straight toward German positions, but they had no choice, because a panzer was herding them in that direction.[15] Consequently, quite a few men were captured south of Schmidt.[16] "That was the last we saw of them," recalled Captain Jack Walker, the L Company commander. Walker added "that although he was not proud of it, they had had to leave a large number of dead and wounded to the Germans when they were driven out of Schmidt in disorder."[17] Out on a limb without any armor protection as they were, the flight of 3rd Battalion might have been cowardly, but it was certainly an act of self-preservation.

First sergeant Hank Ripperdam rationalized his own escape when he saw some of his company behind him. "I knew that they had seen us and that they would follow."[18] M Company began its withdrawal from Schmidt around 10:30, after the battalion headquarters told them to head north. Third Battalion HQ

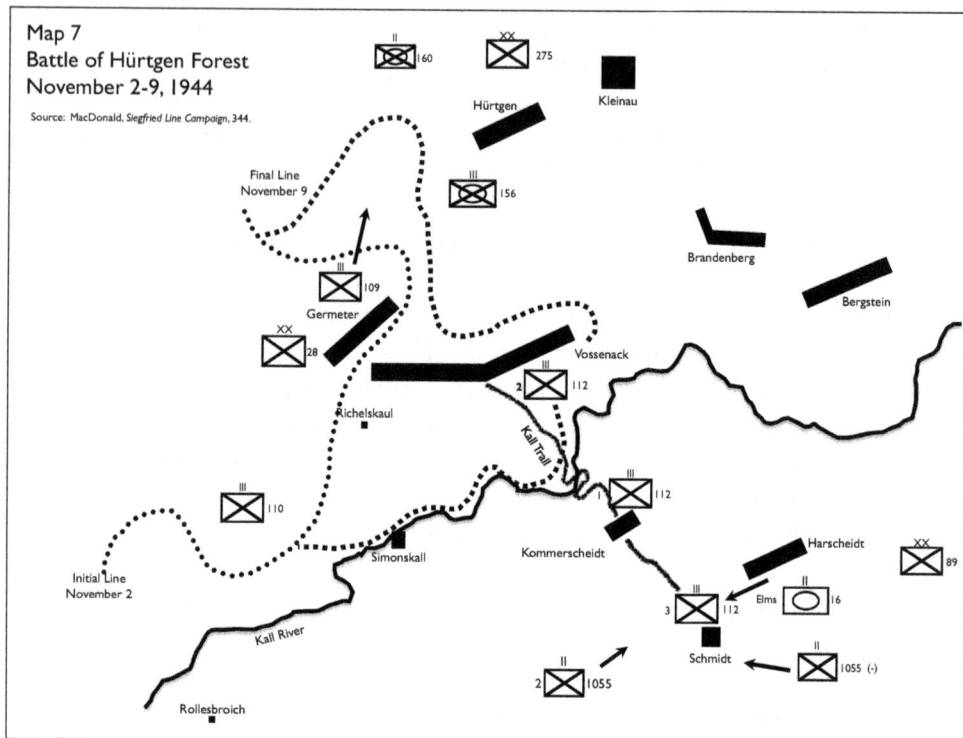

Map 7
Battle of Hürtgen Forest
November 2-9, 1944

Source: MacDonald, *Siegfried Line Campaign*, 344.

also withdrew, after disconnecting its telephone switchboard and leaving the companies without further guidance.[19]

As 3rd Battalion reached Kommerscheidt, the soldiers of the 1st Battalion "grabbed them, and put them in position. The men were scared and wanted to get out."[20] Staff Sergeant Joseph Perll watched as "some men of the 3rd Bn streamed back through our position in panic. . . . There was a lot of effort to turn some of the 3rd Bn men around after a lot of them had gone through."[21] Although disorganized and frightened, some of the soldiers rallied behind their officers and NCOs in Kommerscheidt, setting up defensive positions. P-47s bombed German armor, and it encouraged the GIs when they saw a Thunderbolt attack a nearby panzer.[22]

Two days later, men of the 112th's 2nd Battalion at Vossenack also cracked. These men, however, had been placed singly in defensive positions out in the open, alone, whereupon tanks and artillery shelled them for hours on end. The pounding drained the men of hope. Each had to endure the bombardment in isolation without the support of fellow soldiers. Just before dark on the 5th, the commanders of F and G Companies had ordered their soldiers from the protection of basements back into isolated foxholes so as to shore up local defenses, but "[t]he troops ordered into the holes, utterly fatigued, their nerves shattered, many of them crying unashamedly, would return to the dubious protection of the houses" once their officers left.[23]

A lull in the shelling at daybreak on the 6th spooked the men of the 112th Infantry and encouraged them to think that a German counterattack was in the offing. The Germans had, in fact, silenced their guns with the hope of surprising the GIs.[24] Second Battalion's company commanders already realized that their platoons were so on edge that they were on the verge of abandoning their positions and fleeing at the first provocation, so they informed the battalion commander, Lieutenant Colonel Theodore Hatzfeld, that the shelling had pushed them to the breaking point.[25] The commander of E Company had warned Hatzfeld the day before that his soldiers had had it and needed to be evacuated.[26]

All four of Company E's platoon leaders succumbed to combat exhaustion during the attack on the 6th. NCOs took command but could not prevent the rout.[27] It seems that at seven in the morning, Company F's commander saw German tanks and infantry approaching and told his platoons to pull back. Men at other command posts on the communication network heard the order, which encouraged everyone to lose confidence in the safety of his own position.[28] Panzers commenced obliterating individual foxholes with direct cannon fire and that induced the soldiers of Companies F and G to take flight. "The men in these holes started to pull out first. The others, seeing them flee, started to follow. That was the start of the retreat. They had just had too much. . . . Lt Kauffman, the F Co. commander, gave orders on his own for his men to withdraw in order not to be cut off completely. They did, at first in an orderly manner and then in a panicky fashion."[29] Once one company broke, the others were exposed, realized their own peril, and ran from their foxholes.[30] By midmorning, German forces were driving elements of the 112th out of Vossenack.[31]

Lieutenant James Condon saw the consequences of F Company's order. When he left the basement of his E Company command post, he

saw the saddest sight I have ever seen. Down the road from the east came men from "F" "G" and "E" Cos, pushing, shoving, throwing away equipment, trying to outrace the artillery and each other down the main road, all in a frantic effort to escape. They were all scared and excited. Some were terror-stricken. Most of them were running. Some were helping the slightly wounded to run, and many of the badly wounded men, probably hit by the artillery, were lying in the road where they fell, screaming for help. It was a heart-breaking, demoralizing scene.[32]

Condon and his command post (CP) evacuated as well, but he tried to stop the rout and rally the men. He later said that the rout was unjustified but understandable: "I feel that the men simply had had too much. They could not stand any more of the hell of lying in a foxhole waiting to be killed."[33] A great number of replacements had filled out the rifle companies, which contributed to their fragility under fire.[34]

After five days of combat, many soldiers were still doing as Cota demanded, staying in their foxholes, even as the panzers aimed their cannons directly "into individual foxholes," obliterating them one by one.[35] More and more, however, would sneak off and hide in cellars after their officers had led them to the trenches. "They were tired and they were scared and they were cold and they wanted no more of war for that time."[36] Lieutenant Colonel Richard W. Ripple exhorted C Company of the 112th to buttress the left side of the line, but found that both the commander and his soldiers were too rattled to do so.[37] Several factors contributed to this debacle.

Topography and Terrain

By choosing to fight here, American generals disregarded the interplay between topography and combined arms warfare. The hills, cuts, trees, and late autumn bad weather negated the Americans' firepower and mobility advantages and functioned as force multipliers for the German defenders. The dense trees restricted direct fire, and the ravines on the American side made mechanized capabilities almost inconsequential. Cota knew that the terrain was unable to support substantial offensive action; therefore, on October 29 he directed combat engineers to "[c]onstruct a road in zone of 112 Inf." That regiment was going to have to take Schmidt "without vehicles until adequate roads become available." Cota did not even know whether there were roads between Germeter and Schmidt.[38]

Following a one-day delay, Gerow had ordered Cota to take the villages of Schmidt and Vossenack in the Hürtgen Forest, commencing on November 2.[39] Even though Gerow, and ultimately Hodges at First Army, were having the division take a piece of ground, they did not take into account the consequences of having only one pathway—a narrow, winding trail—form the division's jumping-off point and route to the objective of Schmidt. This terrain meant that infantry would have to advance without close armored support. Cota, therefore, tasked Colonel Theodore Seeley's 110th Infantry with seizing and opening an actual road, the one from Richelskaul to Rollesbroich, but the regiment got bogged down in the woods. If they had gained use of that road, division forces might have been able to attack Schmidt from two directions and then defend it, but Seeley's men kept running into German machine gun fire and minefields full of booby traps.[40] Sending the troops toward Schmidt without a legitimate supply line was a terrible decision.[41] Cota realized that the Kall River gorge trail (the official history calls it "a narrow cart track") was an insufficient supply line.

Another problem was that each objective—Vossenack, Kommerscheidt, and then Schmidt—was on progressively higher terrain, which meant that the defenders could shoot down at Cota's men from higher ground.[42] Because he had three tactical objectives—shielding his left flank, seizing the second road to Schmidt, and taking Schmidt itself—Cota could assign but one regiment to the main effort.[43] As noted, only one battalion of Lieutenant Colonel Carl Peterson's regiment, Lieutenant Colonel Albert Flood's 3rd battalion, actually spearheaded the operation. Its soldiers were not optimistic: "The general feeling in the area was one of tension and apprehension of the impending attack. The area we occupied had been thoroughly covered with artillery fire and numerous enemy dead were still lying about."[44]

Cota had tanks follow the infantry down the trail toward Kommerscheidt and Schmidt during the initial attack, but the trail was so narrow and muddy that tanks kept sliding off into the ravine. When one M4 tank threw a track on a hairpin turn, GIs had to shove it down the hillside to get it out of the way.[45] After taking Schmidt on November 3, the infantry of 3rd Battalion occupied the town with only soldiers and light weapons.[46]

The trail's narrowness defeated the efforts to move tanks forward. Three Shermans reached Kommerscheidt by 9:30 on the morning of the 4th, but it took "back-breaking labor" to get them into the village to support the GIs there. Even with all this effort, two more tanks threw their tracks, slipped off the side of the trail, and stuck fast in the mud.[47] Combat engineers were repairing them, but events, the German counterattack of November 4, overtook their plans. Since the lightly armed infantry were helpless against Panzer Mark IVs and Vs, their commander told Peterson "that he absolutely had to have more tanks," but the one trail through the Kall River gorge was still in such bad shape that tanks could not reach Schmidt.[48] Three tanks blocked it in three different places, and yet another tank "had been pushed off the road and fill thrown in around it to build up the road."[49] Their efforts seemed futile; mechanics would repair a tank that had thrown a track, only to drive it a few yards and see it throw a track again. "By this time everyone of us was ready to pull out his hair, root by root."[50]

By November 5 the geography of the forest had channeled Cota's forces into fighting on three individual fronts, and they could not function in a way to relieve pressure on each other, provide mutual support, or force the enemy to disperse his own efforts. This allowed the Germans to gang up on the 112th Infantry on successive days.[51] To the west, Seeley's regiment was unable to lend significant support by opening up a second road to Schmidt.[52] Two of his companies got "lost in the deep woods and did not accomplish their mission."[53] The area's topography conspired against offensive warfare, and a single infantry division was too small to overcome these endemic obstacles.

Not until November 9 did Gerow tell Cota to stop trying to take Schmidt because the local terrain gave too many advantages to the enemy. German forces could attack Schmidt and Kommerscheidt from three directions, employing movement and firepower, while the Americans could not receive enough reinforcements over the mud trail to defend themselves. It was only a couple of thousand yards, but that one bad, undefendable pathway was all the 28th ID had to support those overextended forces that tried to hold Schmidt.[54]

Poor Assumptions

Poor assumptions and inadequate planning were the reasons behind this debacle. Cota assumed that tactical air strikes could isolate the area by finding and wrecking tanks before they could get among his foot soldiers. That assumed good flying weather, which was a forlorn hope during November.[55] The weather grounded the fighter squadrons on several different days. Furthermore, pilots had a harder time finding their targets in the Hürtgen Forest than they had during previous campaigns because the Germans were "well dug in and camouflaged."[56] No one successfully pointed out these constraints, and "[a]n air plan was drawn up and approved by higher headquarters to accomplish this result."[57] The pilots intended to coordinate strikes with the division's artillery, but low clouds, rain, and mist ensured that this effort was stillborn.[58]

Cota knew neither what was the condition of the German defenses nor whether they were reinforcing them with more soldiers. Division intelligence concluded that the few panzers in the area would not receive reinforcements.[59] Just as the offensive kicked off, however, the Germans moved the 116th Panzer Division to the area.[60] Cota also assumed that counter-battery fire could destroy German artillery hidden on the ridgeline from Steckenborn to Bergstein to Hürtgen, but he later admitted that "nothing was done about" them.[61]

American intelligence assessments were incomplete. Their opponents were not capable of launching or prepared to launch offensives against Americans in the area, but they were adequate for waging the defensive battle that the Keystone Division was about to present them.[62] Division intelligence did not consider its nearest opponent, the 89th Infantry Division, to be a formidable enemy. To the best of their knowledge, the Germans had rushed it from Norway during the summer, after which the fighting near Mons, France, ruined it as an effective fighting force. Its two main components, the 1055th and 1056th Infantry Regiments, were being rebuilt by absorbing training, fortress, and replacement battalions. The defensive measures one deserter described—numerous minefields and barbed wire entanglements the 89th had placed between itself and the Americans—suggested that the 89th would not be used for offensive movements.[63] General von Gersdorff later commented, "The personnel of the units were not soldiers. They were secondary troops and formerly assigned within the nation and had no field experience."[64] The 275th Volksgrenadier and 272nd Infantry Divisions were also in the vicinity of Germeter, although Cota was unaware of the second division.[65] The 272nd was rushed to the front before it had been able to conduct training above battalion level.[66] Other intelligence concluded that although these ad hoc forces were well led by combat veterans, they were not going to be reinforced in significant numbers.[67] Whatever subpar material these divisions might have been made of, the earlier manifestations had left the 9th ID, one of the U.S. Army's very best, bloodied and mangled.[68]

Misinterpreting field intelligence was another contributor to the catastrophe. Prisoner reports of battalions of bakers and mechanics thrown into the lines encouraged the Americans to hold their adversaries in low regard. Prisoners that the GIs captured admitted their weaknesses, which encouraged Cota and Gerow to believe that just one more attack would defeat their enemy. A prisoner told of an entire battalion composed of men released from a hospital who were considered "unfit for combat duty."[69] Another reported that his unit, Infantry Fortress Battalion 1412, had emplaced no mines or barbed wire, that its outposts did not cover all avenues of approach, nor did its soldiers patrol aggressively.[70] A prisoner revealed that the Americans, especially their artillery, were slaughtering the German troops nearby: "He stated that yesterday his company had 150 men. Today they have about 60 men. About 50 of the men surrendered and the others lost as result of casualties from our artillery fire. Stated that morale of unit varies from fair to low."[71] Daniel Strickler's 109th Infantry captured "lots of prisoners," many of whom were old veteran replacements, which further suggested that the forces facing them could not put up much of a fight.[72] A prisoner from the 983rd Infantry Regiment informed Colonel Seeley that his commander was willing to surrender his entire battalion if given instructions how to do so.[73] Two other German soldiers, charged with guarding some captured GIs, surrendered to their own prisoners "because they were tired of fighting."[74] In fact, most of the prisoners taken continued to be former aircraft "mechanics and flying personnel"—hardly the stuff that could successfully attack American forces over open ground, so it seemed.[75] A prisoner from the 116th Panzer Division told his interrogators that American artillery had inflicted "severe losses," forcing an eight-hour delay in their counterattack. He added that most of his comrades were "new replacements without battle experience. Morale is low and fifteen other men in his company want to desert." His warnings, inaccurate as they were, of an SS unit he had seen that included as many as a dozen Tiger tanks should have given the Americans pause.[76]

Leadership

The inadequate planning was the result of unimaginative and uninformed leadership. The division's command section appeared overconfident and apparently believed, for example, that Flood's 3rd Battalion would simply move forward, seize Vossenack, and "mop-up . . . any remnants of resistance," with a single company.[77] Cota believed that German resistance might be slight enough to allow a "rapid" advance and a quick seizure of Simonskall and Schmidt.[78]

In any event, Cota had no choice; General Gerow had ordered him to send his division into the forest. Three days prior to the battle, Cota and his staff expressed considerable "misgivings," with doubts centering around the fact that the ground was unsuitable for mechanized warfare or for any maneuver at all, with the abysmal roads, the density of the forest, and the fact that the enemy dominated the high ground surrounding the division's tactical objective. The Army historians who visited the division command post on October 31 found that "[n]one of the officers to whom we talked regarding this operation was in the least bit optimistic. Many were almost certain that if the operation succeeded it would be a miracle." General Gerow had warned Hodges of all of these difficulties, but to no avail.[79] At the outset Cota had few choices: "the placing of the regiments had been practically specified by higher headquarters, based on previous experience."[80] Cota later revealed that he thought the division "had only 'a gambler's chance' of succeeding."[81]

After the assault's initial gains, Cota did not handle success well. The ease with which they took the villages on the first day deluded him into thinking that the next operation would be easy. Flood's battalion had captured Kommerscheidt and Schmidt with little difficulty, and readied itself for the move against Steckenborn, which lay to the southeast of the village.[82] Cota "was beginning to feel like 'a little Napoleon'" when colleagues telephoned "their congratulations," but these were premature. Just as Cota began the operation two days earlier, German Army commanders and staff officers with responsibility for defending this region met to conduct a map exercise with the task of defending against another U.S. attack in the Hürtgen Forest![83]

There was nothing Cota could do about that bad luck, but he could have practiced a more inquisitive style of leadership. Instead, Dutch Cota led from his command post and sent other officers forward instead of investigating the status of the battle himself.[84] As the Germans unleashed their November 4 counterattack, no one at Cota's headquarters knew what was happening to the 3rd Battalion; consequently Lieutenant Colonel Peterson and later Brigadier General Davis, the assistant division commander, began to make their way toward the front.[85] If Cota had surveyed the action more closely himself, he could have gained a more precise understanding of the condition of his regiments. As a result, Cota was unaware when his subordinates provided him with inaccurate reports, which may have encouraged him to set unrealistic objectives. For example, the 112th's regimental diary repeatedly stated: "Combat efficiency of our command: Excellent."[86]

Cota fumed after 3rd Battalion lost Schmidt on the 4th and insisted on its recapture: "It is imperative that the town of Schmidt be secured at once. . . . Schmidt, when captured, will be held at all costs." He singled out the 112th's 3rd Battalion for scorn after panzers routed them and was adamant that its soldiers not withdraw from places they captured.[87] To retake Schmidt Cota formed "Task Force Ripple" from portions of units that had been gutted by the fighting.[88] A fresh battalion with the advantage of surprise had been unable to hold the village; why would a battle-worn battalion be able to do any better?[89]

Cota obstinately urged further action, and ill-timed luck exacerbated his lack of awareness of the hollowness of his forces. On the afternoon of the 7th, he spent half an hour with the 112th Infantry. Not a single shell fell on it for the first time in nearly a week, which misled Cota into thinking conditions were not so bad.[90] This was the first and last time he visited the front line.[91] The division's experience demonstrated the peril of a commander spending the bulk of his time in his command post in an effort to maintain a big-picture awareness of the condition of his forces. His CP seemed to be a nexus of communication and reporting, but constant shelling kept cutting telephone lines. Therefore, it was difficult for Cota to know what was happening without personally visiting the battalions.[92]

The stress seemed to unsettle Cota's nerves. Lieutenant Colonel Peterson, claiming that he had received an order to report to the division HQ, was in such bad shape when he arrived that Cota fainted, according to General James Gavin, commander of the 82nd Airborne Division. Shell splinters had wounded Peterson in the head and legs, and he had to drag himself through the woods until some combat engineers heard his shouts for help and took him to the commanding general at his behest. After gathering himself, Cota accused Peterson of abandoning his post, but then he later admitted that someone from the CP might have sent him an order to report.[93]

Under continued pressure from Hodges to retake Schmidt, Cota formed "Task Force Davis" on November 7th under General Davis's command, with "the mission of capturing Schmidt, defending that position, blocking all roads from Southwest-Southeast-Northeast."[94] Cota insisted that "[t]errain once taken MUST be held."[95] Hardly more than the 109th's 1st Battalion, Task Force Davis had to change its mission to covering the withdrawal of forces from the area around Kommerscheidt after Davis realized that German infantry had seized so much of the Kall River gorge that he could not stage an attack.[96] Acceding that efforts to hold Kommerscheidt were futile, Cota ordered its evacuation at noon. He finally realized that Schmidt was unattainable.[97]

When Hodges, Gerow, and Collins discussed the battle with Cota on November 5, Dutch found out that VII Corps was not going to provide any relief by attacking the Germans on its front. Weather compelled a delay in Collins's offensive.[98] During the battle Cota had no good options because Hodges demanded continued assaults. Hodges complained that all the 28th could do "was lose ground," and he refused to countenance a withdrawal. Gerow, however, deferred to Cota's appeals just before midnight of the 7th and told him, "Pull those people back tonight or as soon as you can tomorrow."[99] Cota quickly ordered the wreckage of the 112th Infantry to retreat and reassemble in a safer zone.[100] The division would now concentrate on mopping-up operations and straightening defensive lines. In the midst of the withdrawal, Gerow ordered Cota to hold Vossenack ridge at all costs.[101]

The division's plight finally received attention from the highest authorities when Eisenhower, Bradley, Hodges, and Gerow all paid Cota a visit on the 8th.[102] Skirting his own responsibility for the debacle, "Hodges stingingly rebuked Cota in Gerow's presence," and Gerow did nothing to support his division commander. Hodges still could not comprehend the relationship between terrain and the battle's results, so he ripped into Cota for the catastrophe and even considering relieving him.[103] Eisenhower's message to General Marshall was stunningly uninformed: "Morale is surprisingly high and the men have succeeded in making themselves rather comfortable. There are no signs of [combat] exhaustion and the sick rate is not nearly as high as we would have a reasonable right to expect."[104]

The First Army commander should have recognized that seizing Schmidt was going to do nothing more than put infantry and a couple of tanks in an indefensible, overextended situation, vulnerable to counterattack. Topography made the success of the German counterattack inevitable. By November 9 Cota and Gerow were able to give up trying to capture Schmidt and to focus on just holding the areas around Hürtgen and Vossenack.[105]

These results have attracted wide-ranging criticism over the years. Gerow failed to comprehend the speed at which the 28th ID solders were being killed. He should have perceived the difficulties of fighting in heavily wooded hills after wrecking the 9th Infantry Division on the same ground. General George S. Patton considered Gerow "the poorest corps commander in France" and believed that the only reason he commanded a corps was his friendship with Eisenhower.[106] General Gavin later wrote that forces should have attacked Schmidt along the ridge northeast "from Lammersdorf." He also blamed senior leaders for a complete unawareness of hopeless conditions at the front.[107] All should have realized that the German troops in the woods posed no great danger to VII Corps's flanks. U.S. ground and air forces would have crushed any German attempt to come out of the forest and fight in the open because combat on exposed terrain played into the Americans' advantages of armor and air power.[108]

The Hürtgen Forest was another failure for Courtney Hodges. It has already been explained how he blew an opportunity during September to pierce the Siegfried Line before the Germans coalesced behind it. Hodges lost confidence himself during the fall, retreated into his command post, and relied too heavily on his strong-willed chief of staff, Major General William B. Kean. David W. Hogan notes that "he kept a close watch over operations," but "he spent hours at the situation map in his command post with his inner circle. . . . At first, he made daily trips to corps, division, and occasionally lower-level headquarters, but such visits declined over time."[109]

Cota visited the regiments on November 10th. Unfazed, he ordered "vigorous" patrols.[110] Amazingly, he deemed the "combat efficiency" of his exhausted division to be "excellent."[111] On November 13 Brigadier General Davis walked among the rifle companies and, after seeing the carnage, ordered Colonel Jesse L. Gibney to pull 1st Battalion of the 109th back.[112] They were too tired and frozen to attack anyway.[113] By the 13th, the 110th Regiment could no longer organize the soldiers who still remained into platoons or companies. When General Davis visited the 110th's front line, he recognized that it had been shattered and terminated its operations. Cota still failed to comprehend the toll on the men. Regarding many as malingerers, he had his military police scour medics' tents for men to throw back into combat. He ordered them to keep a list of these soldiers' names. Fortunately Gerow recognized the needless harm continued fighting was having on the division and canceled its next attack just before midnight.[114]

Captain John S. Howe, who conducted most of the combat interviews, concluded that the duration and nature of the fighting permanently damaged the officers of the 110th Infantry. A number of officers asserted that "many of the small number of officer and non coms to survive that action in the Hürtgen forest were never up to par again. They had lost their inner stamina. They, like a violin string had been stretched too far, and too long."[115]

Cota did not realize that, for he once again reported on November 14 that his division's combat efficiency was "excellent." The patrol report for the 109th Infantry, November 13, 1944, had the annotation, "Note: Co. Comdr. failed to give name of patrol leader in time for this report. This condition will be corrected at once." His staff was more concerned with minutiae than with casualties.[116] Hodges had also learned nothing. On the 14th, the 8th Infantry Division began to relieve the Bloody Bucket, and five days later launched an offensive to take the towns of Hürtgen and Kleinhau.[117]

German Reliance on Firepower

The German counterattacks belied a common picture of the place of firepower in the doctrine of the respective armies. The Germans relied on firepower in order to take advantage of the terrain's defensible features and because many of their formations were not adequate for aggressive fire and maneuver tactics. After the Americans took Vossenack, German artillery systematically pounded the village. In sinister fashion panzers shot tank rounds directly at the individual foxholes placed on the eastern slope of the village.[118]

> The Germans then adopted the tactic of standing off out of bazooka range with their tanks and deliberately firing point-blank into the men's foxholes. They would fire repeatedly on one hole until it was knocked out, and then shift to another one,

systematically eradicating each man. This was hell on the men and, after seeing a number of nearby holes shot up, some of them took off and others followed. They streamed back toward the rear.[119]

Such tactics may surprise today's reader, given the common refrain that it was Americans who won solely with superior firepower and mass.[120]

Unrelenting, the Germans launched another counterattack on November 5, which gained momentum as the day wore on. Incessant German artillery seemed to come "from all directions." The 272nd Division relied on its mortars and artillery.[121] Lieutenant Clyde Johnson called the November 5 bombardment "the heaviest artillery barrage I have ever seen." If a soldier left his foxhole, German observers concentrated the shelling on him alone.[122] German artillery progressed in accuracy to the point that anyone who stood up felt that an entire battery was trying to kill him.[123] It pounded the Americans in Vossenack on the 6th, and by three-fifteen the 2nd Battalion warned, "Impossible to hold without immediate help" because the shelling was "unbearable."[124] When the Germans attacked Vossenack on the 6th it was not with overwhelming force—only three hundred infantry participated—but tanks and artillery supported them.[125] On the 7th, Generalmajor Walter Bruns led his division and the tanks of the 16th Panzer Regiment against the remaining U.S. forces in Kommerscheidt.[126] Subsequent attacks on that village relied on artillery fire that numbered up to fifty explosions in ninety seconds, which severely punished the Americans.[127]

U.S. Armored Forces

During the course of the battle, accusations of cowardice were leveled at the division's armored forces. Just past midnight on the 7th, Lieutenant Colonel Peterson raged at General Cota, accusing the 893rd Tank Destroyer Battalion of avoiding direct contact with German armor. Peterson knew that the only weapon that stood a fair chance against the panzers, especially the Mark Vs, was the M10 tank destroyers' 3-inch cannon, and the platoon attached to his regiment refused to fight: "Plan failed because TD refused to advance, disobedience of CO; instead platoon withdrew to cover; their cowardice before the enemy imperiled both Inf. and the success of the operation."[128]

Peterson ordered 1st Lieutenant Raymond E. Fleig's tanks and 1st Lieutenant Turney W. Leonard's TDs to take the fight to the enemy on the afternoon of the 6th. Fleig decided to attract the attention of the panzers firing from Schmidt, thus giving Leonard the opportunity to maneuver and fire. Despite heroic efforts by one TD lieutenant, the tank destroyers of 1st Platoon, Company C refused to advance.

> Lt Leonard dismounted from his vehicle in the face of direct enemy fire from an enemy pillbox . . . and tried to lead his platoon into position. They did not move. I saw him return to his vehicle and from his gestures assumed that he was ordering his gun commanders to follow him. He again walked forward, still under direct small arms fire from this pillbox, and motioned his TDs to come forward. They still did not come. That was the last I saw Lt. Leonard.[129]

Fleig watched as Leonard lashed "a tank destroyer that was bellied up [on a tree stump] with a riding crop. His left arm looked like it had been mangled by artillery, and his uniform was covered in blood." Lieutenant Leonard later died from his wounds and received the Medal of Honor.[130]

Throughout the day of November 7, the 112th Infantry's 1st and 3rd Battalions begged for armored support. At four in the morning it had already warned the division that "situation indicates failure until we have sufficient Med tanks and TD to attack enemy tanks and until supply and evac route is kept open."[131] Following a fierce artillery barrage, approximately eighteen tanks and two battalions of German soldiers closed on Kommerscheidt, and fighting commenced at point-blank range. GIs destroyed two tanks with bazookas, while TDs disabled five more. Panzers quickly wrecked three TDs. By 8:30, GIs were starting to make their way north.[132] Peterson pleaded with the division command post, "situation still very serious need tank destroyers and tanks." But when the 3rd Platoon of TDs arrived in Vossenack, the infantry tried to run them off because they feared their presence would bring an even worse artillery bombardment! Sure enough, shelling increased a few hours later, and the TDs left.[133]

More often, however, Shermans and tank destroyers sought out the enemy. On the 4th the tanks Fleig commanded killed three Mark IVs in short order, then engaged a Panther in a tense shoot-out. He struck it with two HE rounds—which are not armor piercing (AP)—and while the crew evacuated the Panther, Fleig retrieved some AP rounds from within his tank's turret. Realizing what the American was doing and that their tank still functioned, the German troops jumped back in their Mark V and started shooting again. Flieg exclaimed, "By that time we had our AP. We opened fire. We scored four hits. The first one cut the barrel of his gun. The other three tore open the entire left side of the hull of the German tank and set it afire. None of that crew escaped."[134]

After a panzer knocked out Sergeant Tony Kudiak's Sherman, he jumped into a TD and shot at the panzers until they wrecked his new mount.[135] Joseph Perll observed that "[o]ur tanks and TDs were taking a beating. Some of them—three—were burning and every few minutes another house in Kommerscheidt would flame."[136]

Some of Cota's forces used combined arms tactics effectively. As Generalmajor Bruns assaulted U.S. troops in Kommerscheidt, engineers of the 146th Battalion consulted with a company of six tanks about how to take back the eastern half of Vossenack.[137] They decided that engineer troops would direct the Shermans' fire. After fifteen minutes of artillery, the Shermans methodically fired rounds into houses to root out German infantry so that the engineers, who were functioning as infantry that morning, could round them up.[138] By one-thirty, they had completed their sweep all the way to the eastern edge of Vossenack, capturing more than four hundred German soldiers and "mowing down" a few who tried to escape that afternoon.[139]

On the seventh, a Sherman scored a direct hit on a Mark IV, which forced the crew to evacuate the panzer, while another hit turned a Mark V into a flaming wreck. Then four TDs finished off a Panther after disabling it. The broken terrain segregated the fighting into individual contests. One immobilized tank continued firing, and tank soldiers scoured damaged tanks for ammunition so as to keep shooting.[140]

Division artillery was not to be left out; it fired so fiercely that a gunner from the 229th FA wrote, "Our own artillery fired TOTs [time on target] and missions until at least one of the gun tubes exploded." That battalion alone "fired 2,149 rounds."[141] Artillerymen of the 229th and 108th FA found themselves in a direct fire shoot-out with six panzers, which they won.[142] Air power played its part; a squadron of P-47s aided the division by destroying at least three tanks.[143] Altogether, American firepower destroyed nineteen German tanks, five of which were believed to be Mark VIs.[144]

Tree Bursts and Trench Foot

The soldiers of the other two regiments endured a more static battle of cold rain, artillery shells, and isolation. Combat in the Hürtgen Forest was lonely and frightening. One replacement in the 110th Infantry wrote, "I was scared as hell. I hardly knew a soul. It was in the middle of the night and we were told to dig in (to rock), and artillery was constant." A few days into the battle, anyone who was still alive after a week was a veteran and "was too scared to layout the welcome mat" to replacements.[145] After his first night on the line, the replacement Alexander Hadden found the survivors in his new outfit, Company B of the 112th, "filthy, disheveled, exhausted, and despondent. None of them was happy to see us because the clear message of our arrival was that the company would soon be ready to be sent back into the line. Few of them were willing even to speak with us or answer our questions, saying, 'You don't really want to know.'" He had been sent into the line in the middle of the night and was told to stand guard at a foxhole he knew not where, by someone whose name he did not know. "I felt stupid and was scared silly, and it seemed impossible I would survive the night."[146] Replacements were supposed to be eased into combat, but on November 11, a hundred were formed "into a provisional company" for an assault.[147] One platoon sergeant commented, "Replacement lieutenants didn't have a chance to get oriented. One who joined us didn't leave his hole for 11 days even to take a crap. He just did in a ration box and threw it out of his foxhole. I never did know what happened to him."[148]

Forest combat isolated packets of soldiers from their leaders. Much of the communication was via telephone lines strung through the forest, and artillery and mortar shells could easily cut them. For that reason, battalion commanders often did not know what was happening to their soldiers, which made it more difficult for them to make decisions.[149] German small arms fire became so intense that soldiers could seldom bring food and ammunition to those on the front lines.[150] Many got lost in the surrounding woods, and German patrols captured some of them.[151] Maps were inaccurate. Major Robert Ford commented, "If anyone, from a private right on up to myself, said that he knew where he was at any one time, he was a damned liar."[152] The 109th's 3rd Battalion was supposed to set up a defensive position on the afternoon of the 7th, for example, but got lost and found itself hundreds of yards to the west, behind the 110th Infantry.[153]

There were plenty of reasons to be scared. German troops saturated the woods with automatic weapons fire.[154] Those who had survived the hedgerows all agreed that "nothing they encountered there could begin to compare in ferocity and intensity of artillery fire with what happened in the Hurtgen forest." "The artillery and mortar came in so heavy that you no longer could make out individual bursts—it was one long, continuous, bursting earth shaking blast that would last for 10 minutes—there would be an accidental pause, as though the heavens were drawing in a deep breath, and then the hellish 10 minute roar would begin again."[155] German defenders seeded the ground with hundreds of antipersonnel mines and booby traps and placed some antitank mines so deep that they were "undetectable."[156] During one attack, Private Leroy T. Carson tripped a booby trap that went off, causing him to step on a mine, which blew off his leg. When his friend Private William Blatner jumped up to rescue him, an enemy soldier shot him through the head.[157] Often when a soldier tripped one mine, his outstretched arms exploded another when he fell to the ground.[158] After they cut American telephone lines strung through the woods, German soldiers laced the wires with booby traps to greet signals troops trying to repair the cut in the wire.[159]

German gunners set their fuses so that the shells would explode in the tree tops—showering the troops below with wooden shrapnel. Lieutenant Charles Potter said that the "[t]ree bursts were the worst thing we had to contend with. The trees in this place were so thick that it was impossible to see more than thirty yards in any one direction. In many places they were not over four feet apart. The artillery had been knocking the tops out of them and these were piling up and making it more difficult to move or to see any distance from the positions." Burrowing into the ground offered little protection, but if a GI stood up and pressed himself against a tree, he might have a better chance of surviving a tree burst.[160] When a soldier ran forward to escape a mortar barrage, he often ran into a machine gun's field of fire.[161] No place was safe from the artillery shelling. On the 7th, for instance, air bursts were making life terrible for the men of some tank destroyers (the M10 had an open turret), so one tanker sought shelter underneath his armored vehicle. A ground burst killed him.[162] Maneuver in the open areas was suicidal, because the Germans had such good observation of the area that they could bring shells or sniper fire down on anyone who moved.[163]

Ruthlessness was a virtue in the forest. American machine gunners among the trees waited until the last minute before opening fire at approaching patrols. During one attack the dead piled up so high in front of Charles Potter's .30 caliber that he had to shove them out of the way of his field of fire.[164] Among the trees soldiers often found that hand grenades "were more effective than rifle fire." Nevertheless, a platoon ambushed forty Germans marching down a trail with machine gun fire, killing all but one. "Each MG fired a full belt and each BAR fired a full clip." Fed up with a sniper, GIs had a tank destroyer obliterate him with its antitank gun.[165] During their defense of Kommerscheidt, Staff Sergeant Nathaniel Quentin and his squad shot a squad of Germans that passed in front of their position. "They ran, but we shot them anyway. About two got away." When armored troops saw a squad of German soldiers run for cover and then wave a white flag, they ceased fire for three minutes to give them a chance to come out and surrender. When they did not emerge, they burned down the dwelling into which they had escaped by setting its thatched roof on fire with tracers.[166]

The density of the trees and the pervasive small arms fire and shelling isolated individual soldiers into solitary battles against the elements and enemy firepower. Company B of the 109th had to fight without relief for over a week. By November 14 it was nearly surrounded, without food or water, and with only the ammunition each individual possessed. From a ridge above Hürtgen, artillery pummeled these men for days. In addition to enemy fire, the soldiers' inability to help their wounded brethren affected them as well. Frostbite was epidemic because the men were often without coats or blankets. GIs could not always get adequate medical care for their wounded, so "they literally had to 'watch them die.'" The best that the unscathed could do was to put the injured into the soaking wet foxholes, which just hastened their death.[167]

No one could withstand the heavy bombardments out in the trenches for long. James Condon soon realized that "any man we left in an area for a day unfailingly was dead or a combat exhaustion case by night."[168] Lieutenant Melvin J. Barrilleaux inspected the soldiers of his company out in the foxholes on the night of the fifth, and "found most of the men so affected by the battering they had been taking that I felt they all should have been evacuated. They were so badly [sic] off that the platoon leaders practically had to order them to eat. The men could scarcely move in their holes." Following the German counterattack that took Schmidt, over one hundred GIs spent the next two days or more living in their own excrement, with "no rations or water . . . each one lived out his personal hell within himself."[169] Trench foot was so bad that the men could not stand on their feet. Instead, they propped themselves up on their knees to shoot.[170] The snow—as much as a half-foot fell on the 8th—was the worst kind for exposure and hypothermia, "wet and slushy." It filled up foxholes and trenches.

The strain broke even the best. Second Lieutenant Edward Matheny, "a damned good officer," was returned to the line after a severe bout of combat exhaustion. An hour later, he ran back with what was left of his platoon, "almost hysterical." Private Albert W. Dogan witnessed this on his first day of combat after surviving "a heavy artillery attack cuddled up to a dead cow in the middle of the road." When he and the rest of Company C crested a hill, they stared down at "four dead U.S. litter bearers carrying a previously wounded soldier who were crunched in a heap, frozen in place." Lawrence Hall of the 229th kept his men going with alcohol. He had found a truck full of French liquor the Germans had hoped to consume. "When some section showed some signs of weakening & slowing up, I would give them four or five more bottles." They polished off more than one thousand bottles in less than a week.[171]

Although both sides were trying to kill each other at every turn, soldiers still retained an element of mercy toward the wounded lying among the torn pines. On the 9th some agreed to a cease-fire of four hours to find and gather injured soldiers.[172] One of the 112th's aid stations was surrounded in the midst of the fighting, whereupon the regimental surgeon, Major Albert L. Berndt, got permission from Cota to see if the Germans would consider a temporary truce after one of the GIs made his way back to the American lines and reported that the German doctor in charge of the American wounded expressed the hope that the Americans could come and retrieve their wounded. On the 9th snowfall provided him enough cover to make it through. The enemy soldiers had made every effort to help the wounded Americans. When it rained and snowed, the Germans covered the GIs with their own coats and blankets. They offered food, water, and medications to the Americans and even promised to protect the evacuation with their own guns. A captured American chaplain verified that his captors had been "extremely courteous." Not above self-interest, the Germans retained the two captured medical officers and chaplains because wounded Americans were going to need them and besides, there was a shortage of doctors and chaplains among the Germans.[173]

When Private Harold P. Sheffer waved a white piece of cloth at his opponents, they ceased firing so he could drag wounded men to safety. "During this temporary truce, the German soldiers stood up from their bunkers and foxholes holding their rifles at port arms." Lieutenant Kelly and Sergeant Hunter observed that whenever German troops saw a red cross symbol on a vehicle, they would not shoot at it.[174]

Even though the 109th Infantry played a supporting role throughout most of the battle, it emerged as a shell of its former self. Its main task was to guard the division's northeast flank near the village of Hürtgen. Because of mines, barbed wire, and machine gun fire, it advanced only five hundred yards on November 2. After defeating an attack on the 3rd, its efforts unraveled the next day. Pressing toward Hürtgen, the soldiers suffered debilitating losses while trying to cross a minefield covered by German machine gun fire. One "platoon as such was lost." So many German machine guns covered the approaches that attacking was futile. American forces did not help their cause by being so predictable. They launched their assaults on the hour: 0900, 0700, 0700, 0900 on four successive days, to no good end. Chewed up, the regiment was relieved by elements of the 12th Infantry Regiment.[175]

The 110th cleared the woods south of Germeter of remaining German patrols. On the 10th, G Company attacked a group of German foxholes without using artillery or even firing a shot. The Germans were all sleeping as the Americans poked them with their bayonets and persuaded them to surrender quietly.[176] Seeley's regiment had been totally stalemated. Individual companies tried to make their way through the woods, but machine guns firing from "dug in positions" stymied their efforts, as did counterattacks by nothing more than a platoon. He issued orders for another assault on the 10th, but the executive officer of the 1st Battalion doubted that more than a few of the men even left their foxholes. "The men had been on the go for over a week, under constant fire, with no rest, no opportunity to dry out, relax. In addition most of the company officers and key non-coms had been wounded, killed or captured. There was just nothing that resembled an efficient fighting machine." Half of those still fighting were replacements who had joined the battalion since September.[177]

On November 11, 1st Battalion received orders from a command structure out of touch with the condition of its soldiers. Captain Burns had to order C Company to attack again. Lieutenant Francis P. Diamond recounted that the company was down to twenty-four men—just over 10 percent of its original size. "They were exhausted . . . attempting to eat their first meal in two days. Capt. Burns said that the most difficult order he had ever issued was . . . to these men, ordering them to attack around the left flank of A Co. He said that in spite of their terrible fatigue, hunger, and painful feet, not one of the men offered any bitches or complaints." Company B had no officers, and C had but one.[178] Still slamming his depleted regiment into enemy defenses, Colonel Seeley insisted on the 11th that "[g]round captured will be held at all costs,"[179] but the successive attacks and bad weather had used up the riflemen. Company F of the 110th was down to about thirty-five "effectives" by the end of November 10, and over half had bad cases of trench foot.[180]

A composite platoon in the 110th showed the fallacy of throwing half-trained replacements into battle. Cut to pieces, it was "left with 17 odd privates, leaderless, scared and hugging their foxholes . . . most of the men were so disgusted, tired, dispirited, and weak that they didn't give a damn about moving," but Colonel Seeley promised Cota "that he is going to keep on punching until they punch their way through."[181] First Battalion started to fray at the edges, and there were rumors that A and C Companies had surrendered. Lieutenant Francis Diamond decided to form a mass of replacements into another "provisional company" to fill the gaps in the line, but he regretted doing so. These new soldiers did not know each other, nor were the tactics necessary to fight and survive second nature to them. Shelling immobilized them when it was safer to keep moving. "Some would hide behind trees thinking they were safe there. It was necessary to force them forward. They just didn't know what it was all about."[182]

High casualties ravaged the rifle companies, especially those of the 112th Infantry, which was now a wreck. Captain John D. Pruden of 2nd Battalion reported that he did "not feel the Bn will function other than as a mob. No leaders developed yet since replacements received." He feared that the results would be "disgraceful."[183] The regiment suffered losses of 2,093, with 167 of those killed.[184] The fighting nearly obliterated Company L. It left Schmidt with eleven men.[185]

Following the battle, the 110th's 1st Battalion was low on soldiers, tired, cold, and bereft of leaders.[186] Losses reduced Company A of the 109th Infantry to 62 GIs in just five days, while Company B was down to 73 soldiers by November 10. In the case of 3rd Battalion, 112th Infantry, "A full battalion of men went into action on the 3rd of November . . . on the 7th of November, a company of men withdrew."[187] Fighting in the Hürtgen Forest cost the 28th losses "of 241 officers and 5,445 enlisted men, casualties from all causes."[188] Its capture of 1,040 enemy soldiers brought them little comfort.[189]

The pain was distributed unevenly throughout the division. The 107th FA, who provided fire support for the Old Grey Mare, wrote, "Combat experience gained by all personnel as a whole, with only moderate casualties occurring, indicates the combat efficiency to be excellent. Missions accomplished despite stiff resistance encountered." It lost only four men killed and one missing. The 229th FA considered its losses "heavy . . . two officers and five EM were killed."[190] By comparison, Company G of the 112th *left* the fighting at Vossenack with a single officer and twenty-nine riflemen.[191] Neither A nor B Companies even had any officers left.[192]

When one looks at the division's total losses, one has to remember that the rifle companies, which comprised one-third of the division's strength, suffered about 90 percent of those losses. The 110th Infantry bore 1,204 battle casualties, and 890 "non-battle casualties." Seven of ten of the latter were trench foot cases; the rest suffered from combat exhaustion and sickness.[193] Sixty-five were killed and 287 were missing. Two-thirds of the regiment was some kind of a casualty, and it was all for nothing. Daniel Strickler wrote that his regiment "contained the enemy on a 3,000 yard front and gained 3,000 square yards of enemy territory," quite literally the same distance as if each soldier lay down in a line and stretched his arms out in front.[194] When withdrawn from the front on November 13, 1st Battalion had 57 fit for duty; a battalion is supposed to have 871. Captain Burns said, "We left a hell of a lot of our best men up there on that hill. Some of them may have been captured. We don't know."[195] The Old Grey Mare had to receive 1,346 replacements, for German firepower killed 112 and wounded 801, not to mention the nonbattle casualties.[196] The 112th suffered the most, 2,093 casualties, with 167 of those being KIA. For good measure it captured 357 Germans.[197] Cota found solace in the fact that the division fought well when not overmatched: "he felt it had proven its ability by the mere fact that there were three organizations still capable of being relieved. If it were not a good outfit there might well have been merely a disorganized mob"—an inauspicious metric. The division also estimated that the Germans lost 3–5,000.[198] The fighting decimated the 707th Tank Battalion, which lost thirty out of forty-eight tanks by November 10. Its soldiers fared better, with but 5 killed and 16 wounded.[199] Bradley and Eisenhower were pleased that they seemed to be killing twice as many Germans as their own forces were losing. By the end of the month, the American advances had actually threatened the looming Ardennes offensive, but they did not realize that. Had the Americans made it across the Roer River, nearby German forces would have had to react instead of marshaling for the Battle of the Bulge.[200]

The folks back home had no idea how terrible the battle had been. In the main they read of worn-out German soldiers surrendering, others who wanted to but could not because of the Gestapo, that "American casualties are comparatively light," and that after panzers drove the GIs out of Schmidt, artillery shells and bombs from P-47s reduced it to a smoking ruin. A couple of days later the reporting conformed more with reality, admitting that "American losses had not been light" and that the Germans boasted that they had "annihilated" the GIs in Schmidt. Many families grieved as death notifications began to arrive.[201] Cota was ordered to take the Bloody Bucket to a "quiet sector," from where the 8th ID had just traveled, a line along the Luxembourg border with Germany. It came under the control of Troy Middleton's VIII Corps on the 20th of November.[202]

Veterans remembered the Hürtgen Forest as hell on earth. John G. Maher of Connecticut considered it a "debacle." Benajah Bruner commented that "words can never express" what they endured. "It was terrible," Sergeant Robert Toner said. "I wouldn't want to go through it again for any price. Those bastards seemed able to spot a single man and keep shooting at him with their tanks until he was blown to pieces. That's hell."[203] General Rudolf von Gersdorff, a veteran of combat on the Western and Russian fronts, said the fighting was "the heaviest I have ever witnessed."[204] The men of the Bloody Bucket were about to see even worse.

12

Battle of the Bulge

STUBBORNNESS AND FLEXIBILITY

December 16 saw the outbreak of the U.S. Army's fiercest battle since Gettysburg: the Battle of the Bulge. The 28th Infantry Division was in the middle of the action from the beginning, and its performance highlighted two noteworthy traits of the Army: the flexibility of its organization and command structure, and the fighting skill, leadership, and tenacity of the American soldier.

For decades critics from both sides of the Atlantic have derided the GI's use of firepower, maneuver, and ingenuity. In the middle of the war, for example, the British General Sir Harold Alexander denigrated the American Army: "They simply do not know their job as soldiers and this is the case from the highest to the lowest, from the general to the private soldier. Perhaps the weakest link of all is the junior leader, who just does not lead, with the result that their men don't really fight."[1] On the eve of the offensive "the Wehrmacht felt it was far superior to the Allied officers and headquarters staff in terms of the tactical and operational leadership of units."[2] Shortly after the war the American author S. L. A. Marshall astonished the public with assertions that only one in four GIs had the gumption to even fire his weapon in the heat of battle.[3] In 1959 John Toland wrote, "[M]ost Germans think he was a bumbling enemy. They still firmly believed that what beat them were overwhelming numbers of bombs and shells, a mass of machines and materiel. Many Germans still resentfully insist that is was a slovenly, cowardly, expensive way to fight."[4] An examination of American combat during the Battle of the Bulge brings these assertions into question.

Setup for the Battle

After wrecking the 28th ID in the Battle of the Hürtgen Forest, First Army moved it to a 25-mile-wide ridgeline that stretched from Lützkampen, Germany, to Bollendorf, Luxembourg, along the Our River. This sector seemed to be a good place for Cota's men to rest, incorporate an infusion of new soldiers, and practice small-unit tactics. The division had received 3,400 replacements. Colonel Gustin M. Nelson, the new commander of the 112th Infantry, found the morale of his new men to be "high," commenting that "no one could ask for better material to work with."[5]

On Nelson's right flank, the 110th Infantry Regiment placed its headquarters in Clerveaux, Luxembourg. Hoping for some time to train replacements as well, they had no way of knowing that General Hasso-Eckard von Manteuffel coveted the town's roads. He needed to take them in order to capture the strategically important crossroads of Bastogne, Belgium. If Manteuffel's panzers could get through it, they would have open country all the way to Bastogne.[6]

An opportunity for a German breakthrough existed because the division's overall line of resistance was inadequately manned for defensive operations. Only one road, which the Americans called "Skyline Drive," provided lateral mutual support for the battalions. Because of the ratio of troops to frontage, they actually manned a series of isolated outposts. Their commanders positioned their troops to defend river crossings, turning the villages they held into strong fighting positions.[7] The regiment with the widest front, Colonel Hurley E. Fuller's 110th, had only two battalions because Cota took the 2nd as the division's reserve.[8] VIII Corps was responsible for making the 28th ID defend a front three times greater than U.S. Army doctrine recommended.[9] In the opinion of at least one battalion commander, this insufficient ratio of troops to frontage was "the principle [sic] reason for the success of the enemy penetration of December 16–17."[10] GIs knew their front was too wide for one division to defend, "impossible to cover...with a solid defensive line."[11]

Hitler intended to win a victory against the Allied forces in the West by cutting their armies in half with a thrust that seized the port of Antwerp, Belgium. He believed a successful offensive would instigate enough bickering between the American and British high commands to rupture the Grand Alliance. His generals, however, analyzed the operational challenges of such a large mechanized campaign through the rugged Ardennes Forest and were not

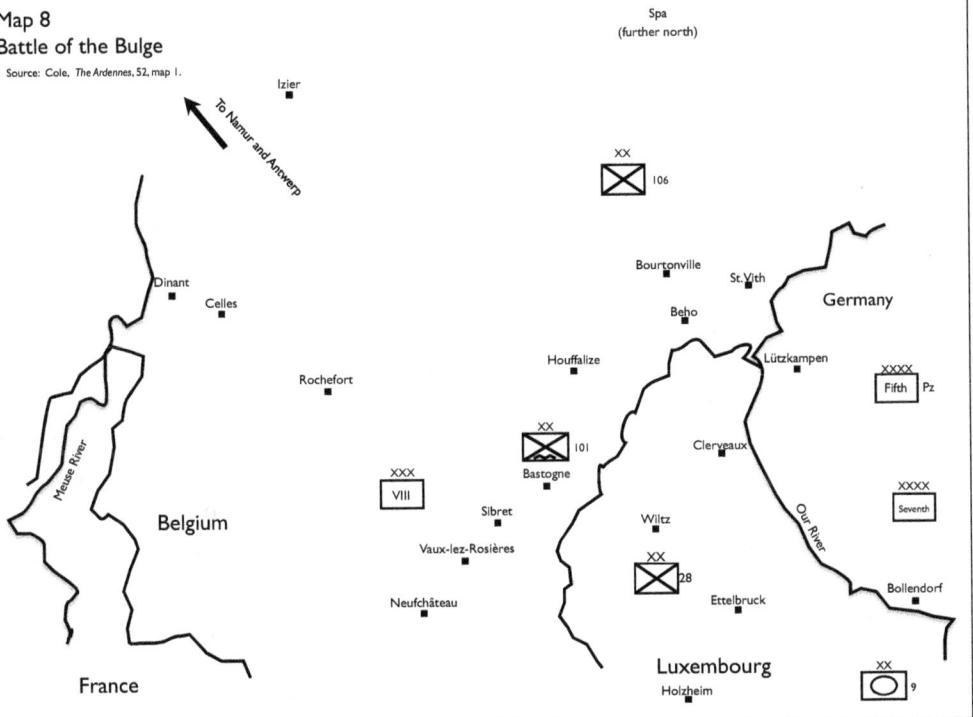

Map 8
Battle of the Bulge
Source: Cole, *The Ardennes*, 52, map 1.

convinced that "Wacht am Rhein" would be a successful operation.[12] General-oberst Alfred Jodl, the operations chief at OKW, believed the German Army no longer had the capabilities necessary to carry out such an ambitious offensive.[13] Field Marshal Gerd von Rundstedt, "Commander in Chief West," had mixed feelings: "all, absolutely all conditions for the possible success of such an offensive were lacking," but he later commented, "The operational idea as such can almost be called a stroke of genius." General Walter Model, a favorite of Hitler, exclaimed that it "hasn't got a damned leg to stand on." Model predicted the eventual outcome: if they reached no farther than the Meuse River, German forces would merely make "a bulge in the line."[14]

The very characteristics—rugged terrain and poor, narrow roads—that later contributed to the slowing of the German offensive also lulled Allied forces into complacency. Why would anyone attack over country cut with hills and ravines? That made it easier for the Germans to deceive the Allies. Furthermore, they moved their forces forward under the cover of darkness, and ingeniously used low-flying aircraft to muffle the sound of approaching vehicles. Even though the Allies had long since cracked the Enigma code, the fact that Germany itself was the stepping-off point for the offensive meant that for coordinating movements, instead of radio they relied on telephone communications, which of course the Allies could not intercept.[15] In addition to attacking in a place the Allies would not expect, the Germans were going to assault a division it considered "battle-worn." General Baptist Kniess assessed the 28th ID to be "a mediocre division with no reputation as a great fighting unit."[16]

Manteuffel intended to force his way through Cota's division to the Meuse River, turn north, and form the southern half of a double envelopment, cutting off Allied forces east of the river.[17] General Walter Krüger's LVIII Panzer Corps was to drive west and "create a bridgehead over the Meuse River in the neighborhood of Namur and Andenne." Manteuffel intended for his other corps, the XLVII Panzer Corps under General Heinrich von Lüttwitz, to take the crossroads at Bastogne, then spearhead the drive to Namur, Belgium.[18] One of the Germans' guiding principles was to "bypass strong points," but that was easier said than done, because the strong points dominated the roads they needed.[19] Manteuffel was supposed to destroy opposing forces as soon as possible, and General von Lüttwitz's XLVII Corps had to fight quickly and move on without getting bogged down by American forces, relying on speed of movement to protect his flanks. He too did not anticipate much trouble from the Keystone Division, since he knew it was recovering from the mauling it had received in the Hürtgen Forest. Besides, his forces outnumbered Cota's "roughly ten to one."[20]

The Allies were not anticipating a major offensive. Only Patton's G-2, Colonel Oscar W. Koch, thought that the Germans still retained a dangerous level of striking power.[21] The Army Air Forces flew 113 reconnaissance missions over "the Cologne plain area opposite the First Army" during the first sixteen days of December, and only reached the vague conclusion that a panzer army was in that area.[22] Bradley believed that the geography of the Ardennes was too rugged to support a swift or sustainable German offensive, so he decided that there was little chance of a major German operation there.[23]

As mid-December approached, soldiers of the 110th Infantry began to notice changes in German behavior on the other side of the front, but bad weather prevented aerial reconnaissance, so the Americans were not sure what lurked to the east.[24] GIs observed that their German counterparts were patrolling more aggressively, often in clean uniforms, and were more "military" in their behavior.[25] Late in the evening of December 15, the division got

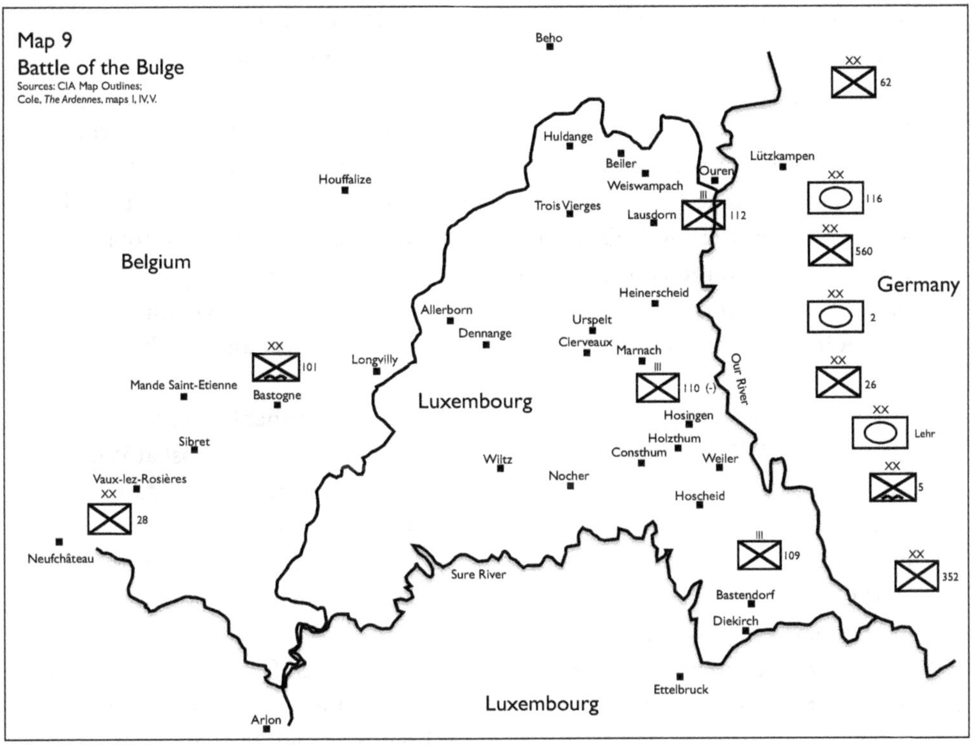

Map 9
Battle of the Bulge
Sources: CIA Map Outlines;
Cole, *The Ardennes*, maps I, IV, V.

word that the Germans in their sector were behaving with more urgency and formality than usual. They were now wearing overcoats, and guards rushed from place to place.[26] Cota's staff dismissed Fuller's concerns, as did General Troy H. Middleton, the VIII Corps commander.[27] Later that night the Germans illuminated the ground by reflecting searchlight beams off low-lying clouds, puzzling the GIs.[28] The artificial light helped German soldiers infiltrate between American posts during the night. When the division sent urgent reports to VIII Corps concerning the enemy troop movements, Middleton's staff disregarded these messages as those generated by a nervous and demoralized unit.[29]

The Battle Erupts

Just before daybreak on the morning of the 16th, German artillery began shelling the 3rd Battalion of the 110th Infantry Regiment. It reported to the division command post that they had never heard "anything like it before," with the shells falling "at a far greater rate than Div had experienced, even in Normandy or Hürtgen Forest." So fierce was the bombardment that it cut all of the telephone lines to the 110th Infantry.[30] These communication disruptions kept Cota and Middleton from building an accurate picture of what was happening at the front, contributing to the slow reaction of the American high command.[31] German tanks were soon crossing the Our River and were on top of the 109th FA's batteries.[32] Seven German divisions, totaling 110,000 troops, targeted the Bloody Bucket.[33] They fought through the gaps in Fuller's line and crushed or scattered its outposts in three days, and forced the regiments on Fuller's flank to retreat to the northwest and southwest in order to survive.

For the rest of the morning General Cota pieced together the reports from his forces and directed local counterattacks from his command post at Wiltz, Luxembourg. The 110th Infantry Regiment bore the brunt of the assault, and Cota ordered it "to hold and fight it out at all costs," which it did, killing dozens of troops who attacked across open fields.[34] That afternoon, Cota informed VIII Corps that "[t]he situation for the division is well in hand," but his forces were actually in grave danger.[35]

Since poor weather grounded Allied tactical aircraft, the foot soldiers were on their own.[36] The Germans welcomed the low overcast because the Allied air forces were "enemy no. 1," according to Model. He hated the way fighter-bombers blunted mechanized offensives and prevented movement during daylight. The Ninth Tactical Air Force was not able to fly much during these first few days, and "[b]ad weather prevented effective ground cooperation from 19 to 22 December."[37] Until the skies cleared this was going to be a rifleman's battle. One of Bradley's aides commented, "The German appears to have picked his time for a strike carefully and once again weather is fighting on his side."[38]

Strategy

The Americans' strategy for defeating the initial German onslaught consisted of a combination of determined fighting, delaying actions, and a careful withdrawal in anticipation of staging a counterattack. Early on, American forces realized that the Germans were after St. Vith, the "Ridge Road" (Skyline Drive) that ran through the 28th's sector, and perhaps Liège and Namur. Since so many divisions were involved, the Germans had to control the road system in order to move with any speed. U.S. forces in Middleton's sector therefore implemented their strategy of delaying by defending the roads at St. Vith, Houffalize, Bastogne, and Luxembourg's capital city (Luxembourg).[39] Bastogne in particular contained road junctions that the Germans had to seize and utilize if they wished to have any success with their offensive. Likewise, the Americans had to hold on to the town if they wished to execute their own counteroffensive.[40] "The enemy is capable of driving straight to the west with Bastogne as an objective," stated one G-2 report. GIs had even captured "a map showing the grand strategic plan of the German drive," including the seizure of Bastogne.[41] To contribute, the division needed to slow down and distract the forces attacking it so as to give this delaying strategy a chance to succeed.

Major General Middleton wanted the forces of VIII Corps to fight hard, but he initially asked them to do too much. He told his division commanders on the 16th, "Troops will be withdrawn from present positions only if positions become completely untenable. In no event will enemy be allowed to penetrate west of line Holzheim . . . Mertert which will be held at all costs."[42] The Keystone Division did not receive this order until the following morning, but they were following Middleton's intent already.[43] He also told his forces to use as much of their artillery ammunition as they wanted. If anyone exceeded their allotments, just let him know.[44] Another witness to the magnitude of the danger was the Army's authorization of the use of proximity-fused antiaircraft artillery shells against ground targets. This kind of shell exploded when it passed close to an object such as an airplane. Used against infantry, it proved to be a devastating antipersonnel weapon.[45]

Some accounts of the battle assert that American gasoline stockpiles were a key German objective, and therefore preventing the Germans from capturing them was a major aspect of Allied strategy.[46] Actually, German troops brought their own gasoline from Germany; their challenge was transporting it to the vehicles farthest out in front.[47] In the event, U.S. commanders realized that it was in their interest to prevent the Germans from capturing American supplies, and the Germans remained unaware of the massive stockpile of fuel near Spa, Belgium, until a resourceful officer set part of it on fire as a barrier.[48] Nevertheless, on December 20th Middleton telephoned Cota and demanded: **"<u>NO GASOLINE WILL BE ALLOWED TO FALL INTO ENEMY HANDS</u>"** [Bold type and underlining in original].[49]

German planners had expected to "encounter little resistance until they reached the Meuse," but American soldiers surprised them with their tenacity.[50] The Americans' actions placed the Germans on the horns of a dilemma. Because U.S. infantry stood their ground and because of the rough terrain, the

Germans faced two choices, both of which would slow them down: either take the time to wipe out American strong points, or leave the roadways to bypass them off-road.

Fight, Retreat, Fight Again

Over the next few days the German assault tore the 28th Infantry Division to pieces and drove it back several miles. During the battle the Army stated "that three divisions figured prominently in stemming the German rush": the 1st ID, the 7th Armored, and the 82nd Airborne. The former PNG division received little attention from the press.[51] S. L. A. Marshall wrote shortly after the war that the division suffered "a complete disintegration of regimental defenses," and years later Charles Whiting stated that the "28th had melted away."[52] Their words mischaracterize what took place.

The soldiers of the 28th Infantry Division realized that the Germans were waging a major offensive that threatened to prolong the war—a far different situation from that in the Hürtgen Forest the previous month. Because they recognized the strategic danger, they fought stubbornly and at great cost to themselves. An examination of the behavior of the men of the 28th Infantry Division during the third week of December 1944 suggests that the American Army had developed the capability and will to inflict severe losses on what has been regarded the best army in the world. A comparison with the Hürtgen Forest battle also suggests a direct relationship between the significance of a campaign and soldiers' willingness to fight.[53] This battle mattered, and the GIs knew it.

Time and again the GIs stood their ground and fought doggedly to delay and wear down the enemy. There was, for example, no discussion of wholesale withdrawal as dusk approached on the first day.[54] Instead, American soldiers routinely demonstrated profound courage before deciding to retreat. Near Fuller's CP at Clerveaux, Luxembourg, for example, Staff Sergeant Neil L. Harbaugh grabbed a bazooka and lay in wait for an approaching panzer. His first shot set one on fire. Not satisfied with that, Harbaugh fired three more rounds at another panzer before falling back to supervise the retreat of his men. Soldiers like him acted of their own volition; no officer was standing behind them ordering them to risk their lives.[55] Groups of soldiers executed most of the acts of resistance. A tank crew just east of Clerveaux, for example, "took an 88 mm shell through its hull, continued to fight and knocked out a Mark VI with three (3) rounds from its 76 mm gun."[56]

Individual companies beat back repeated German assaults, and some concentrated on the fight in front of them so narrowly that enemy forces had time to cut off their escape routes. One of the 112th's mortar sections stood its ground with a machine gun and forced the Germans to kill all of them.[57] Third Battalion (110th Inf.) fended off five attacks against a position near Consthum, forcing the enemy to take cover in the forest.[58] Its CP telephoned from Consthum the afternoon of the second day, "Will hold out as long as possible." Its commander, Major Harold F. Milton, later telephoned, "We are making them pay—house to house. We are still in there but don't know for how long."[59] Company K of the 110th Infantry found itself surrounded after fighting at close quarters in Hosingen.[60] Unable to comply with withdrawal orders, Captain Frederick Feiker cried, "We can't get out, but these Krauts are going to pay a stiff price if they try to get in." He later radioed that he had only a few grenades left: "I don't mind dying and I don't mind taking a beating, but I'll be damned if we give up to these bastards."[61] Not until the company's surviving officers looked at the firepower they had left—a single smoke round for their last mortar, and precious little small arms ammunition—did they decide to surrender on the morning of the 18th. After they smashed their own weapons and equipment, they tallied the dead: only seven, plus ten wounded. "The ranking German officer, a regimental staff colonel, expressed surprise that such a small unit had put up such a good fight, and had suffered as few casualties while inflicting considerable losses on the Germans."[62] The seizure of Marnach and Hosingen was particularly costly for the Germans. Some of the captured GIs had to bury the German dead there, "and there were hundreds of them." Indeed, American prisoners dug graves for "between 2,000 and 2,100 Germans, who were killed in the sector of the 110th Infantry."[63]

Infantry companies were not the only units in the thick of the fighting. At times artillerymen had to fight as infantry, prompting an artillery officer to ask, "Do we have any bayonets for these howitzers?"[64] The 229th FA, some tank destroyers, and the 112th beat back repeated panzer-infantry assaults near Ouren, some of which nearly overran the howitzer batteries. Fortunately for the gunners, a company of antiaircraft machine guns had been assigned for their protection. Their quadruple .50 caliber pieces, designed for use against aircraft, shredded attacking infantry.[65] C Battery of the 109th FA fought off three enemy assaults, killing and capturing many enemy troops. Germans momentarily seized one of the battery's howitzers, but the gunners rallied and took it back with the help of some tanks. The artillerymen stalled the Germans near Maraguerite for thirty-six hours until panzers forced them to move.

Members of A Battery had to fight "as infantry holding up the enemy advance." Although Nazi troops overran it, the artillerymen retaliated with their carbines and took back their howitzers. The Americans then depressed the gun tubes, and unleashed "direct fire with such a short fuse cutting that parts of the shell were blowing back on" their own positions.[66]

Twelve panzers along Skyline Drive lined up themselves nicely for the 112th's cannon company on December 17. Lowering their howitzers to point straight at the tanks, the gunners destroyed the lead tank. For the next hour four howitzers and eleven panzers blasted away at each other. The Americans turned their howitzers into antitank guns by loading a big charge "normally used at several thousand yards range," which "gave the shells a terrific muzzle velocity and a very flat trajectory." Because gunners stood their ground, German small arms and tank fire had time to "decimate" them. The Americans resorted to shooting smoke rounds after using up the rest of their ammunition.[67]

Company F (112th Inf.) defeated repeated attacks by tanks and infantry who got behind them.[68] Well positioned for frontal and enfilading fire, GIs made good use of their rifles and machine guns to slaughter German soldiers who marched out of Lützkampen in columns.[69] The 112th and the 229th FA even captured 250 prisoners.[70] Moving west from the Our River, the 112th and the 630th TD Battalion wrecked fifteen panzers, made prisoners of 186 soldiers, and killed as many as 800.[71] Outnumbered and outgunned, but on eminently defensible ground, the 112th fought well enough to help put Manteuffel a day behind schedule, even though the German attack had pierced the regiment's defenses.[72] But eventually everyone had to retreat. Since the regiment had no more motor transportation, the GIs chose to leave behind the wounded men who could not walk on their own. "We hoped the Germans would provide the medical care we could not."[73]

On the second day of the battle the 109th Infantry's 3rd Battalion inflicted "heavy casualties."[74] Its antitank platoons resisted panzer attacks, scoring "a great many hits," but could not destroy any tanks. As near as the GIs could tell, they were inflicting far greater losses on the attacking Germans than they were taking, but the Germans infiltrated so many infantry among the American units that the 107th and 108th Field Artillery Battalions had to spend all of their efforts in self-defense, also lowering their barrels for direct fire against the enemy onslaught. Although the 107th's A Battery captured 45 Germans and may have killed 150 more, it had to "evacuate" west.[75]

The weight of the German offensive forced everyone to take up arms; even clerks and cooks grabbed weapons and functioned as riflemen.[76] The

103rd Engineers' commander told his staff, "Forget you are a Hq and fight."[77] Indeed, the entire battalion "acted as infantry fighting successive delaying actions. No engineer work accomplished."[78] In the 110th's sector, "A defense point with the aid of Hqrs. personnel, kitchen help, clerks, staff, artillerymen, remnants of Co. L, some from Co. M, and a few miscellaneous troops" held on at Consthum on the 17th.[79] A chronicler in the 112th Infantry noticed repeated instances of "isolated headquarters company men being caught in the battles of other units and behaving well in emergency." Elsewhere, a "squad composed of cooks and drivers" opened fire on a small convoy of German vehicles with enough effect that they fled.[80] Near Wiltz, a provisional battalion of lawyers, mailmen, military police, clerks, and logisticians returned fire against their attackers.[81] After choosing to destroy their guns so as to escape the German wave, two companies of the 109th FA eventually made their way to Neufchâteau, where most of its soldiers fought as infantry.[82]

The men in the division's HQ had to fight, as well. Even though the division relocated its CP three times during the battle, enemy forces kept catching up. First they abandoned Wiltz on December 19. Then a panzer-infantry attack struck the CP at Sibret at 3 AM on December 21. After five hours of fighting, Cota determined "to stay here and fight it out," but German forces attacked again and seized a strongly built building, and shelling by the 771st FA could not dislodge them. The command post evacuated to Vaux-lez-Rosières.[83]

This remnant of the division was not defenseless when the Germans struck with several companies of tanks and infantry. When a panzer carelessly rumbled into a TD's field of fire, the gun crew destroyed it. The GIs defeated German assaults for several hours.[84] By December 22, however, troops manning the few remaining artillery pieces were understandably jittery. Brigadier General Davis, the assistant division commander, gave orders "to take drastic measures with any men who leave their positions without orders,"[85] but his GIs never panicked. Even though they had gone without hot food or dry clothing for days and had been fighting or marching the entire time, "morale was good." They fought hard, and did not move until told to at dusk. This hodgepodge of GIs, however, did not possess the skills or firepower necessary for a firm delaying action, and exhaustion threatened to overcome them. When three enemy companies, including a panzer company, got to within 850 yards of Cota's CP on the 22nd, Cota moved it once again, to Neufchâteau. It and various headquarters and artillery troops fortified the town for the next three days. Cota resolved that they would not retreat again.[86] One of the gunners remained undaunted:

"Division reorganized and gathered in Neufchâteau area and started back toward Berlin."[87]

German forces confronted another stubborn force to the north in Bastogne: the 101st Airborne Division, augmented by soldiers from numerous units, such as those of the 110th Infantry, who had been scattered by the initial waves of panzers and infantry.[88] The men besieged at Bastogne were not about to give in. When General von Lüttwitz demanded a surrender of the town, the Screaming Eagles' acting commander, Brigadier General Anthony C. McAuliffe, reacted with dismissive contempt. After McAuliffe's acting chief of staff, Lieutenant Colonel Ned Moore, read him the terms of surrender, McAuliffe glanced "carelessly at the papers, laughed and said, 'Aw, nuts.' He let the two papers fall to the floor and drove out to personally congratulate some men who had just wiped out a German roadblock." Colonel Joseph Harper handed McAuliffe's reply—"Nuts!"—to the German messengers and explained to the nonplused officers, "[I]n plain English it's the same as 'Go to Hell.' And I'll tell you something else. If you continue to attack we'll kill every godam [*sic*] German that tries to break into this city!"[89]

Meanwhile at Neufchâteau the Bloody Bucket remnants prepared its defenses in case the Germans returned: "All troops and weapons will fight in place. If the enemy penetrates into the town then *fighting* will take place *from house to house*" [emphasis in original].[90] The immediate threat subsided somewhat as the Germans devoted most of their attention to American troops at Bastogne. Then a "wet, sticky snow" began to fall, making "everybody miserable as hell."[91] That the troops defending the division CP consisted of "men from fifteen different divisions and separate outfits" bore witness to the shattering effects of the German offensive.[92]

By Christmas Day Cota had scraped together about six thousand troops, two tanks, fourteen tank destroyers, nine antitank guns, and a 105mm howitzer.[93] The soldiers spent Christmas manning the perimeter in twelve-hour shifts in temperatures nearing zero degrees.[94] There was now little for the rump 28th ID to do except patrol its perimeter. Slowly more and more of its soldiers who had filtered through German lines reunited with the division. The German offensive had crested by Christmas; they would never again reach as far west into U.S. lines as on that day.[95]

Even though the GIs had to retreat, the Americans discovered from prisoners "and captured documents [that] the Germans did not attain any objectives on the schedule they had anticipated."[96] American resistance eroded the tightly wound German timetable to such an extent that these tactical defeats

Cota's division suffered functioned as operational and strategic victories for Bradley's army. It was best that the GIs were not too fluid in their defense, for they would have been backing up toward the west more quickly, which is where the Germans wanted to go. A completely rigid defense would have resulted in more prisoners for the German army, leaving even less between them and their objective, as happened with some of the companies in Fuller's regiment.[97]

The division's soldiers frequently recognized the difference between holding fast and suicide, and often chose to disengage to try to reform a few miles to the west in order to renew their defense.[98] As night approached on the first day, for example, clusters of Fuller's GIs were running low on ammunition as they fought off Germans from every direction. Germans surrounded Company I at Weiler and offered the GIs a chance to surrender. They refused. Later the company's commander, Captain Lloyd K. McCutchan, rejected the pleas of his men that surrender was their only hope for survival and led them west toward friendly troops under the cover of darkness.[99] As the assaults progressed on the 17th, Cota ordered the 109th and 112th to "move all unnecessary vehicles to the rear areas" in anticipation of a withdrawal.[100] That afternoon he issued orders for the antitank company defending Hoscheid to evacuate, but the defenders had already succumbed to the enemy.[101]

Although soldiers needed to remain in their strong points in order to frustrate the German plan, doing so for too long meant death or capture. Some officers managed to disengage just in the knick of time. Captain LeVoe Rinehart of Company A ordered his men to abandon Heinerscheid for points west when the Germans aimed more panzers at them.[102] In Holzthum, Shermans managed to disable a Mark VI, but they too had to make their way west.[103] As evening approached on the 17th, tanks began to retreat toward Wiltz with small groups of infantrymen.[104] Many companies were in dire straits on the 18th, being "overrun," "enveloped," and "either destroyed or captured." Colonel Sieg's 103rd Engineers were down to about one hundred soldiers, so the division HQ told him that evening that if communications were cut, they should just make their way west to the "vicinity of VIII Corps." Middleton suggested that Cota move his command to the southwest when panzers rumbled just a couple of kilometers from the division CP in Wiltz.[105]

The defense of the 110th's CP was a case of a formation fighting until forced to retreat for survival. On the morning of the 17th about ten panzers and a battalion of infantry attacked; Colonel Fuller replied with eight tanks of his own.[106] The tanks decimated each other, but by midmorning Germans had him surrounded. Fuller telephoned the division CP, "They just kept coming. . . . Enemy now 200 yards from me, all I have is some MPs."[107] The 110th Infantry's command post could function as a roadblock for only so long. During the evening of the 17th panzers blasted away at its CP in the hotel Claravallis from fifty yards away, then infantry stormed the first floor. When a tank stuck its cannon barrel into the hotel lobby and fired, Colonel Fuller decided that it was time to go. Fuller and his staff escaped by crawling across a ladder "to an adjacent cliff" from a third-story window, scrambled up a hill a quarter mile away, dug in, and shot at the enemy until they ran low on ammunition. Only then did he order them to skulk their way west in small teams.[108]

Colonel Theodore A. Seeley, whom Cota put in command of the 110th after German troops chased Fuller out of Clerveaux, believed that they would "have to pull out very shortly." Seeley was correct, but he also tarried. Later that day fog reduced visibility so much that German soldiers with a captured Sherman surprised Seeley and his CP at Allerborn. Then eleven Mark IVs followed, and the house was surrounded. "Suddenly, one of them turned his flashlight right on us and we were caught." Seeley managed to escape a few miles down the road, but the fog was so thick that night that he literally walked right into a halftrack and was again taken prisoner.[109]

The American delaying tactics, though effective, had devastating consequences for the 110th Infantry. Manteuffel's army had destroyed the regiment as a cohesive unit by the time December 17 drew to a close. As the evening wore on, the division assistant chief of staff (G-3), Major Carl W. Plitt, discussed the possibility of Strickler standing his ground at Consthum, but then suggested that he "think about moving and to see if they could infiltrate out."[110] Much of 3rd Battalion, 110th Infantry, was surrounded in Consthum and by dusk on the 17th had nothing but hand grenades left: "hand-grenade fighting from building to building."[111] American antitank gunners had to wreck their weapons and retreat.[112] The Germans captured most of 1st Battalion's companies, and obliterated the cannon and antitank companies.[113] Major Milton ordered Company K "to try and infiltrate through the German lines," but its radioman replied that "was impossible. Too much heavy stuff around." When the company made its final radio report on the morning of the 18th, they stated "that they thought they had accomplished their mission." After leaving Consthum, Milton halted his forces a short distance from the town in order to reorganize as a cohesive unit.[114]

Other troops defending Consthum did not decide to evacuate until the 18th. When German panzers attacked yet again, Lieutenant Colonel Strickler ordered a tank to charge the enemy forces to buy time, while GIs defended against German infantry probing from the north and south. That night his troops set up a defensive post at Nocher and further delayed the Germans. Not surprisingly, Strickler informed the division, "Men are terribly exhausted and have had no food or water." He also reported that his detachment of the 707th was "finished." Together they destroyed seven panzers that day.[115]

Strickler ordered the residents out of the village so that they might avoid being killed when the Germans struck once again, but they protested so visibly that they attracted the attention of the German troops who shot at them, killing many. "It was a literal hell during the night of the 17th." Strickler knew that his battalion was the only thing left between German forces and Cota's CP, so he stood fast, sending out two tanks that night, one of which the Germans blew up.[116]

Gunners of the 229th FA were conducting a redeployment as much as a retreat because they managed to deliver supporting fires to the 112th Infantry from two of its three batteries at all times during the withdrawal.[117] But soon this formation also had to concern itself more with survival than with supporting other soldiers. Units that "crack" and run pell-mell abandon their equipment; the 229th FA did not lose any of its artillery even after the Germans threatened to overrun them. The 229th's commander, Lieutenant Colonel John C. Fairchild, later wrote, "My men refused to be rattled by the circumstances and the alarming advance of the enemy almost to their positions, and calmly and methodically went about their individual tasks in fire missions and preparations for withdrawal."[118]

Successive commanders decided that they had fought hard enough to excuse a displacement west. Seeley refused to let members of the regiment try to rescue surrounded comrades because the enemy was too strong.[119] Similarly, Lieutenant Colonel James R. Hughes, the executive officer of 2nd Battalion fighting between Clerveaux and Urspelt, realized that holding fast was futile. As German artillery fired at them from three directions, he ordered his men to infiltrate west in squad-sized groups in hope of uniting with larger U.S. formations.[120]

Cota put Daniel Strickler in charge of defending the division's command post on the 19th so that he could again function as a division commander and lead the headquarters' retreat to Sibret.[121] On the 19th Lieutenant Colonels Thomas Hoban and Strickler organized another delaying action at Wiltz with leftovers from the 3rd Battalion, but Strickler realized that evening "that the mission at Wiltz was finished, and it was best to salvage as many troops and as much equipment as possible." They had to fight their way out that night. During the evacuation, "There was no histeria [*sic*], no commotion. With grim faces everyone went about his business of getting loose from the enemy at Wiltz."[122] Strickler ordered everyone to "break up in small groups" and try to get to Sibret. That was the only way they could evade capture and reach other American forces. Everyone was gone by eleven. Colonel Thomas Briggs later recalled, "This was the last of the active stand[s] by the Div., as such."[123]

Strickler, his jeep driver Bob Martin, and Major Plitt were among the last to leave Wiltz. Enemy fire soon forced them to abandon their jeep and crawl through the woods.[124] With several other soldiers they commenced an odyssey to find their way toward the American lines, evading Germans and encountering civilians who were also on the run. "For hours we plowed our way through [pine brush], having our eyes almost scratched out. It seemed almost hopeless. The boys were getting delirious, famished, fatigued, and disgruntled. We had not seen a house all night." Eventually they broke into a field and then found a farmstead. The farmer invited them in and informed them that the American lines were about three miles to the west. Then "he fed us coffee, bread, butter, and jam. Boy was it good. After an hour's visit we were on our way going straight down the road to the West." American sentries outside of the town of Vaux-lez-Rosières took them to their headquarters—that of the 28th ID, no less. Strickler had been thought dead and "was greeted like a ghost come to life."[125]

Improvised Combat Teams

The soldiers who were driven from their outposts along Skyline Drive often formed ad hoc combat teams under the command of leaders they did not know with soldiers from many units. For the most part the soldiers did not malinger, hide, or panic, although some formations collapsed when their leaders were killed. For example, Captain Gerald A. Harwell of the 110th Infantry telephoned the division and told it that he was trying to form stragglers into a combat team near Dennange. Other stragglers along a road established a defensive line.[126] Groups regained their composure in all the confusion, as when an ammunition train composed of various units, who had "either got scared or lost and are milling about here," formed an ad hoc unit.[127] Soldiers of the 447th AAA Battalion stopped retreating, turned around, and made their way to help with the defense of Wiltz.[128]

Not everyone stood and fought so eagerly. On the 18th, seven halftracks of the 707th passed through Wiltz, and they kept going until military police halted them fifteen miles west of the town. The MPs ordered them to return to Wiltz.[129] Members of Company B 103rd Medical Battalion "all rushed to the rear every time the ambulances left with wounded," Colonel Fuller later wrote, adding, "The conduct of Company B, 103rd Medical Battalion, was disgraceful throughout this operation."[130] A carload of soldiers drove all the way from Weiswampach to Spa, where they availed themselves of the recently abandoned chateau that Courtney Hodges himself had been using. Many soldiers just wanted away from the fighting. Some pushed their way toward Bastogne, thinking that was a means of escaping the onslaught. Private Donald Burgett remembered, "They shambled along in shock and fear, blocking the road completely, eyes staring straight ahead, mumbling to themselves. I had never before—or since—seen such resolute terror in men." A captain in charge of a truck convoy was determined to keep moving west, even though it was preventing the men of the 101st Airborne from getting into Bastogne. Just west of the town at Mande Saint-Etienne, a general had to threaten to kill the captain in order to persuade him to move his vehicles off the road.[131] A replacement soldier, William Gillett, resented the accusations of cowardice he heard, and a half-century later he wrote, "The division was a stand up unit. WE DID NOT RUN!"[132]

Instead, a great many of the GIs confronted the enemy. Artillerymen stood and fought of their own volition, and riflemen joined them when asked to help. The 58th Armored Field Artillery, along with the 109th FA, set up their field pieces near Longvilly, Belgium, and gathered in retreating GIs to help with the improvised roadblock.[133] When two captains began to re-form the 110th's 2nd Battalion near Allerborn, Colonel Seeley coordinated their defense with an adjoining company from the 9th Armored Division. A steady stream of men from the 1st and 2nd Battalions reinforced their effort.[134] Infantry from the armored units were at first reluctant to stay engaged, but they responded to Seeley's leadership.[135]

The soldiers Strickler led during the delay at Wiltz were remnants of engineer, armor, artillery, antiaircraft, and infantry units. Even though the soldiers on hand "were mostly inexperienced men not trained to combat and the remainder were our own infantry and tank men, very battle weary but full of determination," they still were able—cold, tired, and under fire—to set up a good defensive position on some commanding ground to the southeast of

Wiltz.[136] Cota sent Lieutenant Colonel Benjamin Trapani with a "straggler force" to reinforce Strickler. "Stragglers from 707 Tk Bn will act as point." Together they defeated repeated panzer attacks until they left the town on the 19th.[137]

About six hundred stragglers from the 110th Infantry joined with the remnants of the 9th AD's Combat Command Reserve (CCR) to form "Team Snafu" under the command of Colonel William Roberts (Combat Command B, 10th Armored Division). Brigadier General Davis gathered three hundred of the 110th that had streamed into Bastogne and proceeded to take them back to the rest of the division. Most of the 109th FA remained in Bastogne.[138] The remaining troops of the 110th—mainly from the 1st and 2nd Battalions—coalesced into Task Force Caraway for the defense of Sibret. The guns of the 109th and 687th FA supported the task force, and also aimed north, firing in support of the 101st Airborne Division.[139]

Nearly four hundred of the headquarters defenders were stragglers, mostly men from the 110th who had been scattered by the German assault. Virtually all showed up to Sibret with their rifles; these soldiers had not abandoned their weapons in order to flee. Moreover, "The personnel collected, contrary to what might be expected, had good morale . . . most of this [sic] personnel was of good quality, being among the best soldiers in the regiment." Colonel Jesse L. Gibney, the division chief of staff, concluded that the reason for that was "that only the best soldiers were able to filter back through the German lines after the original defensive positions had been over run. During the fight at Sibret in the early morning of December 21st, these men gave a good account of themselves and retired in reasonably good order upon command in the face of enemy infantry and armor."[140] Their fighting spirit impressed hardened riflemen, who noted that "the fact that this group of clerks and other Hq personnel were willing and able to put up a fight was indicated by the fact that a few were killed by small arms fire."[141] Officers gave orders to form defensive lines only to find that soldiers had already done so.[142]

At the division's final CP at Neufchâteau, "over 1,200 stragglers" from at least a dozen different units soon accumulated for its defense. They too were in better condition and higher spirits than expected. Although two shot themselves in order to avoid being put back into a picket line, Colonel Gibney observed that "[t]here were very few personnel collected who were not of high caliber," and he judged that no "more than two or three percent were deliberately straggling from their units."[143] A handful even staggered into camp "with 100% of their fighting equipment."[144] Courtney Hodges considered having the division going "over to the offensive on Army order" along with the rest of VIII Corps, but Middleton preferred that Cota just defend the roadblock he now possessed.[145]

Fighting Mad

GIs fought against their adversary with a staunchness fueled by fury during the Battle of the Bulge. An ad hoc formation, for instance, beat back five attacks against the 3rd Battalion command post at Consthum, even dropping the tubes of their artillery pieces to shoot right at approaching infantry as if they were fighting at Antietam: "The enemy was being slaughtered, but still they came."[146] J. J. Kuhn directed some of the guns of the 109th FA near Marnach and saw the same thing. "The German infantry just kept coming out of the woods, spread out across the whole field, and we kept killing them with our artillery. . . . It was one of the saddest things I'd ever experienced in my life."[147] Down the road, some GIs manning a quad .50 caliber antiaircraft halftrack convinced some enemy troops that they themselves were Germans with a captured piece of American equipment. The GIs beckoned them forward through the fog, then mowed down nearly a hundred at close range.[148] When German infantry used a self-propelled gun to pound a house from which some Americans were shooting, the GIs "must have collected themselves pretty quickly, because they waited until the enemy infantry were within 15 or 20 ft of the windows and then grenaded the hell out of them. They piled 6 to 8 up dead right outside the house."[149]

During the Battle of the Bulge American soldiers often fought without pity. Spotting some of the enemy walking along a ridge, one officer commented, "It was too damn far to do any good, but we fired on them anyway—hell of a lot of fun." GIs in the 112th were not kind to the inexperienced troopers attacking them on first day. "My men gave them a hell of a beating," Major Walden Woodward beamed, and added that the Germans "never had any support from their own artillery."[150] One German action in particular—the massacre of captured Americans at Malmédy on December 17—so enraged the GIs that from then on many set aside acts of mercy.[151] "A German officer was pedaling furiously down the road on a bicycle when he came into view of the roadblock. 10 seconds later, 1 dead heinie [*sic*] lay sprawled across the road, riddled like a sieve. The entire platoon had seen him and they opened fire together."[152] One of the 109th Infantry's cooks shot and wounded a German soldier on the first day. His buddy suggested that they "put him out of his misery," but the shooter wanted to wait until someone else came to help the screaming soldier so as to kill them both, which is what happened. One veteran of the actions, Clarence Blakeslee, could not believe what he was seeing, but soon "felt a deep hatred that I didn't think myself capable of."[153]

The War's Best Soldiers?

American soldiers compared well with their German counterparts in terms of fighting skill. After capturing the regimental commander, Colonel Theodore Seeley, interrogators of the 2nd Panzer Division complimented him for the Bloody Bucket's fighting prowess. When the commander of LXVI Corps, General Walter Lucht, questioned him, the general "was most complementary [*sic*] of the fighting ability of the 28th. He said that he had fought the 28th in Normandy as well as in Luxembourg and that it was the hardest fighting American outfit he had been against." An intelligence officer later flattered Seeley on how difficult it was to gain useful information from 28th ID soldiers, and mentioned that the 110th's "front-line units held very well and were difficult to clean out." He also left Seeley with "the impression" that the 110th had so mauled the infantrymen of the attack that the armored formations had to press on without enough accompanying infantry.[154]

In contrast to these examples of GI ferocity, many of the attacking Germans fought incompetently. German tanks and infantry, for instance, did not support each other correctly when they attacked the 112th's positions. Panzers outran their infantry, and GIs killed off both separately—the tanks once they penetrated their lines, and the infantry who followed, exposed.[155] One company of German soldiers in particular displayed a dearth of tactical expertise when it crested the top of a hill one night. The glow of the searchlights silhouetted "them [as] perfect targets. The slaughter was immense."[156] In a similar example of poor field tactics that the 109th Infantry exploited, German forces "marched at least 2 Bns [battalions] of infantry and one of artillery across our front. The artillery had a field day. We stacked them in piles along that road from Ettelbruck, going north." The Germans paraded "in broad daylight," apparently under the impression that the 109th regiment had withdrawn in greater haste than it had.[157]

Soldiers of the 112th Infantry ambushed one German patrol that strayed onto open ground and failed to see the lurking GIs, who killed half as they attempted to reach a bridge. Private William L. Young remembered, "Suddenly, one man came running out of the wood. The fool came out a few yards and began firing his burp gun. He just swept it across our front as if a million of us were in plain sight, and he were mowing us down like wheat. . . . I got a bead and drilled him. I tell you, these jerries were crazy." He later watched as others attacked a field kitchen, "They even tossed grenades into the ovens."[158]

German attacks against the defenders around Ouren did not go according to schedule. Six German assaults in two days failed to gain a much-needed bridgehead at Ouren—more "friction" for the enemy to overcome.[159] The 112th drove its 2nd Battalion into the enemy's flank that first day, killing more than four hundred. German tactics eased Colonel Nelson's task, since they approached in "almost a close order column formation. As a result, they were easily wiped out by machine gun fire from our dug-in positions."[160] Seeing a group of Germans crossing a bridge, the members of the regiment's cannon company thought they might be prisoners, but seeing their weapons, they opened up on the bunched-up Germans with small arms and machine guns; "they were literally 'mowed down.'"[161] These mistakes were more a reflection of the personnel who had been culled for the offensive than of the German tactical system of fighting. The German infantry who attacked the 112th's cannon company appeared to be "young kids."[162] When gunners of the 107th FA captured a German soldier, they found that he was just "19 years old and very scared," especially of American artillery.[163] He also had reason to be scared of his own. After some of Captain McCutchan's men shot and captured a small German patrol, a "wounded German started to scream in pain. The uninjured German immediately proceeded to drive the bayonet on his rifle into the wounded man and killed him." GIs shot that soldier when he tried to escape.[164]

By December 1944 the German Army was still a formidable force, but the tactical mistakes their small units made, combined with the greater difficulties the American forces caused for the attacking forces, demonstrate that the differences in fighting skill between the two armies had closed. The new divisions the Germans had outfitted and sent into battle were not cut from the same cloth as the German Army of 1940 that gained such a reputation of skill and competence. Not only were the troops of inferior quality, they had not received the months of training that were so beneficial to the soldiers who preceded them in earlier campaigns.[165]

Flexible, Adaptive Leadership

The battle illustrated the flexibility in the American command system, in its officers, and in the structure of the Army. General Middleton, General Cota, and their subordinates maximized the abilities of their fighting forces in order to achieve the intent of the strategy of delay, retreat, and fight. They did so by conferring authority on their subordinates and listening to them. Commanders also concerned themselves with units besides their own.

In a sense there was no such thing as an American infantry "division," if by that one means a hard-and-fast *indivisible* entity. Instead, the basic units were the infantry companies, battalions, and regiments, the artillery battalions, and attached armored battalions.[166] During the Bulge, two of the 28th ID's regiments were successfully transferred to two other divisions and fought effectively even though combat action had "shattered" their parent division. As already noted, groups of soldiers also formed themselves into fighting groups to do what they could. The broken pieces did not need to be put back together in their original order in order to contribute.

Ironically, General Cota used the same leadership method—commanding from his headquarters—that he had used so inappropriately a month earlier, but this time to good effect. During this battle, however, he sought out information from his commanders and delegated decision-making authority to them when their tactical awareness exceeded his. On the first day, Cota sent the division reserve to Fuller and allowed him to decide how to use it. Fuller received the same authority over a company of Shermans from the 9th AD.[167] What led to Cota's growth as a general in just five weeks is unclear. It is nevertheless reasonable to conclude that he pondered the results of the methods he used during the Battle of the Hürtgen Forest and decided to delegate more authority to his subordinates and also to trust their judgment more than he had.

Cota repeatedly ordered his commanders not to concede an inch during the first couple of days of the battle, but he never enforced those instructions, nor did he punish commanders for retreating. Whenever one of his commanders explained that he needed to pull back his forces in order to avoid destruction or capture, Cota eventually relented and accepted his subordinate's judgment. For example, as one company after another reported "situation critical and can't last much longer" on December 17, Fuller and Cota were frank with each other in their noon telephone conversation. Cota closed with, "Remember your orders. Hold at all costs. No retreat. Nobody comes back."[168] Fuller complied, but kept the division HQ apprised of the growing peril to his CP until he gained permission to relocate. Colonel Jesse L. Gibney was less flexible than Cota. When Hurley Fuller spoke with him on the telephone on December 17, Fuller declared, "It's hopeless here. I want to pull back everything I can along the high ground west of the town." Gibney would hear none of it. When

Fuller demanded to speak to Cota, Gobney informed him, "The General's at dinner and can't be reached by phone," to which Fuller replied, "It's going to be the Alamo all over again!"[169] Fuller kept his head and did not evacuate until Colonel Gibney delegated that authority to him: at 6:25 PM Gibney relented and "advised that he was in command there and it was up to him to do whatever he thought was right."[170]

General Middleton exhibited trust in Cota and accepted his advice regarding tactical movements of the 28th ID's formations. Furthermore, a discussion between Generals Middleton and Cota illustrated how a subordinate could contribute to his superior's management of forces in battle. Middleton wanted to use the 112th to plug some of the gaps left by the 110th's destruction, but Cota talked him out of that because Nelson's regiment had endured more punishment than Middleton realized. Cota also warned against too precipitous a withdrawal: "If they pull back it would expose everything."[171]

Colonel Gibney, in contrast to Middleton, communicated poorly with the regiments when Cota was managing other tasks. For example, Major Plitt told him, "Situation is now deemed critical" at Wiltz, but the colonel assured him that Strickler's outpost had "sufficient strength to repel atk [*sic*]," an assertion without foundation because his gunners were in a shoot-out with panzers and infantry. Gibney often painted a one-sided picture to his superiors, informing VIII Corps "that everything is moving along pretty well."[172] In reality, German tanks and infantry had Wiltz encircled, attacked from every direction, and held the escape route to Bastogne.[173] Fortunately for these GIs, Manteuffel did not consider Wiltz to be a critical road junction. Indeed, the paratroopers of the 5th Parachute Division were supposed to skirt the town on their way west. By the evening of the 19th Wiltz was a pile of burning rubble, as were most of the U.S. tanks and TDs.[174]

When the German offensive split the division like a surgeon's spreaders, it separated the 112th Infantry from the rest of the 28th ID. While this happened Cota coordinated with Colonel Nelson and did not dogmatically issue orders. After suggesting at 2 PM on the 17th that they retreat if their situation became "untenable," Cota ordered the regiment to take up new "defensive positions west of the Our River, specifically around Trois Vierges."[175] He soon chose to defer to Nelson because communications were so intermittent and because he trusted the colonel's judgment as the on-the-scene commander. After Cota ordered him to "fight a stiff delaying action" at Trois Vierges, Nelson redirected his men toward Huldange when he discovered that a large force of panzers and infantry already held Trois Vierges.[176] Worried about being cut off, Nelson asked Cota twice in two hours for guidance. Cota subsequently ordered Nelson to "fight it out" and block the Lausdorn–Weiswampach–Beiler road, but then at noon Cota could no longer count on reaching Nelson via radio or telephone.[177]

Nelson's superiors had become so preoccupied with their own crises that he had to exercise leadership and intuitive judgment on his own in order to avoid capture. Nelson's men got to stay in one place for the next two days before moving again on December 20.[178] Subsequently he had to either ask for direction or decide on his own where his regiment would fight. Since he had better communications with the remnants of the 106th Infantry Division to his north, he asked to be placed under the temporary command of Major General Alan W. Jones.[179]

Transferring regiments among divisions was one way for Cota to comply with the intent of Middleton's plan. Another was to delegate decision making to his regimental commanders. He therefore handed off not only the 112th Infantry, but also the 109th (with their respective artillery battalions) to the 106th ID and the 9th Armored Division.[180] When Nelson discussed this arrangement with Jones, he replied, "You are now attached to me and I will assume full responsibility."[181] From then on, the regiment assisted the defense of St. Vith as a part of XVIII Airborne Corps.[182] Nelson's regiment now functioned as an independent combat team covering the withdrawal of other units without being left behind in the process.[183]

Cota worked with the new commander of the 109th Infantry, Lieutenant Colonel James E. Rudder, in a similar manner. On December 18 he listened while Rudder explained the realities of his situation and his options. Cota wanted Rudder to withdraw toward Bastogne, but deferred to the regimental commander's on-the-scene judgment that that was too dangerous, and let Rudder take his regiment to Ettelbruck.[184] Rudder's companies had become strung out, unable to support each other. He started pulling his forces west just in time, for five Tiger tanks with supporting infantry obliterated six anti-tank guns near Bastendorf and then tore through a roadblock. Toward dusk Cota ordered Rudder to "fight a stiff delaying action along Diekirch-Ettelbruck toward Bastogne. Do not uncover left flank of 9th Armd Div."[185] Lieutenant Colonel Rudder was of a like mind. Cota told him to coordinate "with them and protect that flank and keep on plugging." At the same time the CG of the 9th, Major General John W. Leonard, believed that the 109th was too exposed and at risk. He wanted Cota to give him control of the regiment so he could prevent its destruction.[186]

Although senior leaders recognized the opportunity the German offensive gave them to really hurt Hitler's forces with a counterattack, they felt the need to admonish their men two days into the battle because so many at the front were still reeling from the onslaught. Hodges sent this message on the 19th:

It is imperative that every subordinate commander and every soldier be instructed that the enemy is making one final desperate bid for victory and that now is the time for every officer and every soldier to hold high ground and throw the enemy back. Our position is not critical. Reinforcements are constantly arriving. Our position improves each day. We must act with aggressiveness and inflict a crushing defeat on the enemy which in the end will shorten the war considerably.[187]

Middleton was sanguine one minute and concerned the next on the 19th. He had told his soldiers that this offensive was the Germans' "final and desperate bid for victory, and he is throwing everything he has at us in a reckless manner. . . . Our situation is far from critical." U.S. reinforcements were pouring in, while the Germans grew "weaker each day." "This is the Germans' last gasp. Let's take them apart now."[188] True as it was, this was cold comfort to shot-up riflemen covered in snow. Middleton added, "There will be no withdrawal. Units whose front lines are now west of the line will regain lost ground." Like Cota, Middleton did not enforce his dramatic admonitions. On the 17th, for example, he had "advised that the half-tracks and towed TDs should be pulled back to block the roads." Cota had already issued the orders. Middleton "did not want to give up anything but under the circumstances it was very necessary and the situation demanded it."[189]

The division chief of staff, however, did not communicate frankly with the regimental commanders. On the evening of December 19, Colonel Gibney failed to pass on everything he knew to Rudder. CCB of the 10th Armored Division, backing its way into Bastogne, had warned Gibney that German forces might be flanking and thus threatening the 109th Infantry, but all Gibney did was vaguely warn Rudder that he was "liable to be hit hard tomorrow." Use your bazookas, he glibly suggested. Rudder realized that he needed much more than a few antitank rockets; he needed a comprehensive resupply. Gibney assured him a few minutes later that "the big stuff was on its way down." Rudder then told Gibney that he was going to order his regiment to Colmar to maintain contact with the 9th Armored Division.[190]

Soon thereafter Cota telephoned Rudder and discovered the danger in which Rudder had been left. Rudder told the general that German forces were between him and the 9th Armored, which had already made the decision to move to the southwest. He had to do the same if he was going to follow Cota's intent of covering the 9th's left flank. "Position occupied today is untenable." Germans were "infiltrating." We "are whittled down to about 50%." Cota agreed and warned Rudder to pull back west to the Alzette River, lest he leave a gap in the line.

Cota then got on the phone and informed Middleton of the threat to the 109th Infantry Regiment and recommended options. Middleton was on top of the problem and intended to borrow some forces from the 80th ID (from Patton's Third Army) to plug the gap.[191] In rapid succession, Cota spoke with Rudder and General Leonard. Cota informed the general of the 109th's situation and intentions, as well as the instructions he had passed to Rudder. Cota told Rudder to stay put as long as possible, and then to retreat to the river: "He will have to act according to the situation," because no one knew what was going to happen next. As with Colonel Nelson, Cota deferred to the on-scene commander.[192] This was prescient, for by midmorning of December 19, Cota no longer had contact with any of his rifle regiments.[193]

Gustin Nelson took action four days later when his regiment's situation became perilous. In the wee hours of the morning, the regiment was transferred to the 7th Armored Division, which gave it the task of covering the withdrawal of the 106th ID, the 7th and 9th ADs, and Task Force Jones by setting up defensive points from Beho to Bourtonville. The 7th's commander, Brigadier General Robert Hasbrouck, intended to tell Colonel Nelson when to pack up and pull back himself, so the men of the 112th waited. Meanwhile, they heard that German airborne forces had parachuted around the bridges of Vielsalm and Salmchâteau, which were to the regiment's rear, and over which Nelson planned to make his retreat. Then Nelson spent the day at Rogery watching foot soldiers, tanks, and trucks move past him, escaping the German onslaught.[194] By one in the afternoon the American forces faded into the distance and the road was quiet. This Nelson reported to the 7th AD by radio, but he never received a withdrawal order. The regiment was alone, forgotten, and exposed. Then seven panzers with infantry attacked, withdrawing momentarily after towed AT guns punctured two.[195] At three in the afternoon, Nelson decided on his own to pull back to the northwest lest panzers overrun them, but German forces were using so many of the roads that the regiment had to proceed cross-country. Some of Nelson's men were captured, but the 112th made it to territory held by the 82nd Airborne Division at two in the morning on Christmas Eve near Izier, Belgium, largely intact. Individuals who had become separated staggered in throughout the rest of the day.[196] The regiment completed this eighteen-mile march through the night, through snow and bitter cold: "Rations low, morale low. The weather was very cold and the men were tired and hungry."[197] It is no wonder that the medic Robert L. Smith referred to his unit as "a bastard regiment, left to its own devices for survival."[198] Credit Nelson's steadfastness, ability to make decisions, and ability to manage a withdrawal while fighting for saving his regiment from obliteration or, at best, capture.

American soldiers possessed several qualities that made it possible for them to carry out this delaying action. As has been demonstrated, much of their training had been as battalions and regiments, not as a division. The geography of the Ardennes ensured that this battle degenerated into a boggling number of combats waged by small units, sometimes as ad hoc formations of riflemen, tankers, engineers, and artillerymen thrown together to meet the needs of the moment. The GIs knew combined arms warfare, knew how to exploit terrain, and knew how to use their weapons. They were adaptable, brave, and not a little angry. They often knew when to retreat a mile or so before they stopped, turned, and continued their killing of the relentless enemy. It seemed to require a great amount of firepower delivered over several days to break the spirit of the GIs. Even when they were trapped and escape was no longer possible, the GIs often fought on. Because commanders gave the men of the Bloody Bucket the latitude to fall back when they had no other choice, they had the hope of survival—something denied them at the Hürtgen Forest.

Delays

The German offensive fell progressively behind schedule because of the Americans' efforts. Manteuffel hoped to capture St. Vith on December 17, but GI steadfastness prevented him from doing so.[199] To the south, portions of the 110th AT company and some tanks from the 707th at Hoscheid delayed the 5th Parachute Division an entire day. Essentially two battalions of infantry and two medium tank companies ruined the Germans' timetables for December 16.[200] General Jodl later reminisced that "Reconnaissance units" were supposed to "reach the Meuse on the first day," but failed to even come close to that objective in time.[201] Fuller's regiment prevented Colonel Heinz Kokott, the commander of the 26th Volksgrenadier Division (VGD), from reaching his goals in accordance with his timeline. Kokott's division was supposed to be eight to ten kilometers west of the Our River by nightfall, but it did not even complete its crossing until after dark, suffering significant losses in the process.[202] The 352nd VGD was unable to concentrate south of the Sauer River, and did not go on the offensive again for another two days. Indeed, German forces were now "moving spasmodically from traffic jam to traffic jam."[203] Tactically defeated, the 110th had with its "gallant action" ensured that the 2nd Panzer Division never seized Bastogne. Two days into the campaign German generals began to conclude they would never see Antwerp and probably not even the Meuse. By December 20, the best they hoped for was to cross the river, turn in the direction of Aachen, and capture the U.S. forces below Liège in a kill zone.[204] The GIs believed their persistence had persuaded the enemy to turn toward Bastogne on the 19th, but the crossroads was of the highest priority for the XLVII Panzer Corps.[205]

The Tide Turns

Eisenhower coordinated with Patton on December 19 for the Allied counteroffensive to begin against the Germans' southern flank by the 24th, while the Bloody Bucket would watch from the sidelines.[206] Tired as they were, the GIs managed their violence systematically as they switched from wholesale retreat, to stopping and fighting, to counterattack. Gone was the worried tone, the fear, the anxiety. Although the 28th's CP suffered "light casualties" from German bombers on the 26th, it was no longer in the forefront of the fighting.[207]

The Allies were finally able to unleash tactical air power against the German attackers when the weather cleared on the 23rd. News of Allied air strikes heartened Cota's CP: "101st AB Div reports they are having a field day with their Air and Arty."[208] The Screaming Eagles repulsed a German attack on Christmas Day, which "was disastrous for the enemy." After that, the defenders of Bastogne "mopped up" the German infantry.[209] The day after Christmas the 4th Armored's CCR made contact with the Americans holed up in Bastogne, breaking the siege.[210] Thereupon the commander of the 26th Volksgrenadier Division, Colonel Kokott, "knew it was all over."[211]

The German advance reached its deepest point northwest of Bastogne, petering out just as the 2nd Armored Division, along with some attacking P-47s and Typhoons, pushed back the 2nd Panzer Division a few kilometers short of the Meuse. By the 26th Colonel Meinrad von Lauchert was leading his men in a retreat from Celles to Rochefort. He was ordered to "destroy their vehicles, leave their wounded, and get out on foot."[212]

From December 27 through January 3, both sides engaged in a slugfest around Bastogne. The Germans continued to send forces west into the salient, slamming into the U.S. forces that grew stronger by the day.[213] When the Luftwaffe attempted a bold strike against Allied airfields on January 1st, Commonwealth and American forces either killed or captured 214 pilots, losses from which Germany could not recover.[214] The German Army also suffered serious damage. VIII Corps, for example, estimated that the 21st Panzer Division was down to 4,000 soldiers and just 30 tanks.[215] A panzer division was supposed to contain 14,727 soldiers and 168 tanks.[216] The Bastogne salient had drawn the Germans into an attrition battle—never a wise choice for an army with fewer resources.[217]

The limited goals of the Allies' counteroffensive disappointed many of its generals. Montgomery decided that in support of Third Army's attack, the Allies were going to have to be satisfied with trying to cut off a smaller portion of the enemy army farther west of the base of the bulge. Eisenhower had not given Montgomery binding guidance, so he had to accept it when Monty delayed his attack from the north until the 3rd of January.[218] According to the German official history of the war, "the Germans managed to avoid being encircled and . . . to channel most of their troops through to the east" because of Monty's foot-dragging.[219] Indeed, because of Montgomery's disdain for the command abilities of Eisenhower and Bradley, the Allied high command was almost ruptured—one of Hitler's original goals. Following another round of Montgomery's belittling condescension and demand for control of Bradley's 12th Army Group in addition to his own, Eisenhower nearly requested his relief as the new year began. In the end, the Allies simply pushed the Germans back to where they came from in a bloody, grinding fight. When VII and VIII Corps met in Houffalize on January 16 the battle had come full circle, and the German Army was now incapable of offensive action that could do anything more than delay the Allied advance.[220]

The Toll

In its own estimation, the division's strategy of fighting then withdrawing at the last minute with the intention of setting up a delaying defensive position down the road "gave the higher command four (4) days to bring forces to the vicinity of Bastogne and organize its defenses. The Division's efforts provided the time necessary to regroup forces to save the cities of Bastogne, Arlon, and Luxembourg for the Allies." Bloody Bucket soldiers even managed to apprehend 1,054 prisoners, but at great cost. The division's report written on January 15 did not account for all of those killed, listing only 41 men KIA; the figure of 3,509 missing in action was more compelling. Total losses amounted to 4,147, plus 574 nonbattle casualties. Attached units lost 316 soldiers.[221] Even though the division's efforts contributed greatly to the American victory, particularly in buying time for the defense of Bastogne, they were not without their tactical failures. Several companies either waited too long to give way to the onslaught in order to set up defenses farther west, or evacuated too quickly.

As a result, the rifle regiments suffered the worst losses. The 109th Infantry lost 5 KIA out of 145 officers, and 93 out of 2,817 enlisted soldiers, with 19 officers and 294 GIs wounded in action. Germans made prisoners of 9 officers and 341 soldiers. The regiment started with 145 officers, 5 warrant officers, and 2,817 enlisted troops, and ended December with 111, 5, and 1,976 respectively. Total losses—killed, wounded, captured, missing, and nonbattle casualties— numbered 875 for a loss rate of 29 percent.[222] As a tax for blunting the German offensive, the 110th Infantry paid with 139 killed, 333 wounded, 846 captured, and 1,302 missing. The massive losses of all kinds reduced the regiment to a strength of 587.[223] The full strength of a regiment was 3,256 officers and men.

Those in the supporting field artillery battalions fared much better. During the Battle of the Bulge, the 108th Field Artillery Battalion lost 4 GIs killed in action out of 481 effectives, and only 10 missing.[224] The 109th Field Artillery suffered more with 70 battle casualties.[225] The 229th FA suffered no KIA, and only 29 MIA.[226] Not so in the tank battalion. The 707th accumulated losses of 54 tanks, 6 assault guns, and 286 soldiers missing, with an indeterminate number killed.[227]

The records do not specify how many of these casualties were the result of combat exhaustion, but it seems that they were lower than one would expect given the disparity of forces. Reports from earlier battles annotated cases of soldiers and officers breaking down to a far greater degree than did those from the Bulge. Indeed, commanders remarked more than once during this battle about the steadfastness of the troops.

Conclusion

The great differences between the Battle of the Bulge and the division's battles along the German frontier and in the Hürtgen Forest were the allowance for maneuver during the Bulge and the absence of the same during the stationary battles. Furthermore, no strategically significant peril was present in the earlier battles—Hitler's army was not about to threaten the Allied cause with a campaign along the Siegfried Line or in the Hürtgen Forest—which resulted in a proportionately greater level of meaninglessness for those combats. The mud-caked private holding an M1 Garand was quite aware of the strategic significance (or lack thereof) of the battles he was in, and steeled himself accordingly by tapping levels of endurance that rose to the occasion when he recognized that the fighting was worthwhile. This battle-worn division fought well because its men realized the importance of doing so, because their officers allowed them to fall back, and because their commanders were not going to get them killed just to put forth a pretense of determined resolve.

The division assistant chief of staff for operations and General Cota himself later asserted that neither the characteristics of the area's road network nor the relative strengths of the regiments contributed to the tearing apart of the division. The weight of the Germans' attack and General Middleton's concept for delaying their advance were the cause. Middleton ordered the 28th ID to fight hard and retreat slowly in order to gain time for the rest of the corps, with the purpose of delaying the German assault in the center of his sector. According to Plitt, it "stood and fought . . . until bypassed and surrounded by the enemy armor. This isolated our combat teams, negated our defensive capabilities." Nowhere in the interview did Cota blame Middleton for sacrificing the 28th ID to buy a couple of days for the forces in his sector so as to better defend the road junctions.[228] Middleton credited VIII Corps's stand with providing "sufficient time for the Allies to redistribute their forces and contain the thrust." He later asserted that if the 110th Infantry had not fought so stubbornly, "the Germans would have been in Bastogne long before the 101st Airborne reached that town."[229] Third Army also recognized the accomplishments of one of the regiments: "Combat Team 109, by its aggressive defense in successive delaying positions during the period 16 December to 26 December 1944, completely exposed the left flank of the German drive at its base by almost destroying the entire 915th and 916th VG Regiments, and a major part of the 914th VG Regiment of the 352nd VG Division."[230]

The American victory was not a result of the blunt application of firepower. The Americans instead displayed professional skill in executing a retreat well enough to measurably hurt and slow their enemy. Ironically, the Germans won their initial tactical victories with mass, something for which U.S. forces have been frequently criticized. General Montgomery, who had often disparaged the American Army, soon argued that "[t]he battle of the Ardennes was won primarily by the staunch fighting qualities of the American soldier . . . the fighting showed [that the German Army was] no match for the splendidly steady American troops."[231] Omar Bradley wrote after the war, "In valor, however, neither [the 7th Armored Division nor the 4th Infantry Division] had outshone the broken and bruised 28th. . . . For three sleepless days and nights the embattled troops of that division backed grudgingly toward Bastogne buying time for the reinforcement" of the southern shoulder.[232] Strickler plainly asserted that "the 110th was responsible for stopping the enemy long enough for the 101st Airborne Division to get into Bastogne to make its stand until help came from the North and South." Furthermore, "Units and personnel distinguished themselves in a very critical situation. In many instances they literally held at all costs, to the point that there were no survivors."[233] Rudder wrote his wife after the battle that he missed his Rangers, but "the unit I now command is a true American fighting outfit and their manner of performance in the recent crisis was something to behold."[234]

Be that as it may, the 28th ID badly needed several weeks to rest and train replacements, but the infantry division shortage meant that was not going to happen. The division instead performed less-demanding combat missions over the next three months, culminating in occupation duty in the areas around Koblenz and the Saarland.

13

Winter Battles

Following the relief of Bastogne, the division was kept out of major combat operations for a month. The 112th Infantry functioned as part of XVIII Airborne Corps's reserve through the end of December, with only the 2nd Battalion carrying out an attack as an attachment to the 75th Infantry Division. Through much of January its men manned a position between Givet and Verdun.[1] Nelson's regiment was in the best condition of any and conducted some substantial patrolling during the first couple of weeks of the month. It captured, for instance, "200 prisoners . . . in Spineaux" on the 7th.[2] The 112th did not return to Cota's command until January 13.[3]

One of the Bloody Bucket's main tasks throughout January was reconstituting itself and incorporating replacements. The rifle regiments absorbed "droves" of green troops and trained diligently, with the 110th functioning as the division's reserve formation.[4] When the 28th moved to Charleville, a town about seventy miles east of Paris, it began to put its rifle regiments back together more systematically. Refitting the 109th and 112th Regiments was relatively easy because both were "in general, in excellent shape." Only Company E of the Old Gray Mare had taken severe losses. Nelson's regiment needed seven hundred replacements, but he had received enough so that his companies were in good order. Even after a month of combat, the 112th evinced good morale. Rebuilding the 110th was another matter. Headquarters Company and 2nd Battalion had enough of a cadre left so that they were manned first, and any straggler or troop returning from the hospital who was a member of those formations rejoined them. The division rebuilt the 1st and 3rd Battalions almost from scratch, however, establishing "Company X," which formed cadres to reconstitute them. Replacements, 4,168 of them, a testament to the severity of the fighting during December, then brought the units up to strength. By January 25, over 3,000 soldiers once again populated each rifle regiment, and the division was at full strength.[5] Such were the recuperative powers of the American forces that every division save the 106th Infantry had been replenished within a month of Wacht am Rhein.[6]

As a part of this reconstitution, Lieutenant Colonel Rudder trained the junior officers and NCOs in the 109th Infantry and ensured that they practiced small-unit tactics. He recognized that the patrols near Verdun helped his new officers gain needed experience. He also forced his sergeants to learn how to lead by depriving them of constant supervision. Consequently the NCOs gained more responsibility and had to ensure that the men were fed and were keeping their equipment in good condition. As a result, the soldiers respected their sergeants more.[7] Because replacements had filled the 110th's ranks, Daniel Strickler graded his regiment as "FAIR," the best he could grade it given the prevalence of greenhorns. The 110th had to carry out only one minor mission that month, capturing the hamlet of LeNorment, France, on January 28. Losses of only four killed, sixty-three wounded, and none missing or captured made clear that it was a slow month for the regiment.[8]

These GIs would not receive months of time to train together and learn their craft the way the division had a year prior. The German Army was reeling, and there was no time to waste in keeping up the pursuit. Beginning on January 17, the men who did not have to drive the division's vehicles stuffed themselves into boxcars for a move to Ste.-Marie-aux-Mines. They were transferred temporarily to the French II Corps on the 20th before coming under the XXI U.S. Corps's command (15th Army, 6th Army Group) on the 28th.[9] For over two days the men huddled in boxcars, warming themselves around charcoal fires in small buckets.[10]

The journey from the railhead to the front reintroduced them to the random unfairness of the combat zone. A truck full of two dozen soldiers struck a mine, which exploded its fuel tank. The men who were wearing rain ponchos were lucky, for they were able to save themselves by throwing them off their bodies. A couple who were wearing just jackets suffered third-degree burns. "Their bodies were masses of charred flesh, seared together with their clothing by the heat of the burning gas. They looked as if they had been roasted over an open fire. We tried everything we could think of to separate the clothing from the burned men without pealing [sic] the skin off in large pieces, but without much success."[11] Once they arrived at Ste.-Marie-aux-Mines, the Keystone soldiers carried out patrols and raids, but did not have to participate in an operation of the magnitude of the Ardennes. Only eleven were killed in action during January. For one two-week span its artillery did not even shoot, nor was there any contact with enemy troops. By January 29, however, the division entered into more serious action as a part of the Colmar Campaign.[12]

Colmar Campaign

As February approached the outcome of the war was certain. The Allies had launched their counteroffensive to eliminate the Ardennes Bulge on January 3–4, 1945, while to their south, Germany's Operation Nordwind against Allied forces in Alsace was a forlorn diversion. Continued resistance only delayed the day of Germany's surrender.

A two-thrust offensive comprised Eisenhower's strategy for achieving victory. Montgomery's forces were to wage the primary effort to cross the Rhine and envelop the Ruhr industrial region from the north because the geography in that part of Germany was conducive to the fast, mechanized warfare at which the Allies excelled. Geographical considerations also influenced Ike's decision to have 12th Army Group thrust toward Frankfurt. Up to this time the Allies had targeted the German Army for destruction, but capturing the Ruhr would cut off Germany from its source of munitions production. "Taking Berlin and all other objectives then would be but a matter of time."[13]

Farther south and to the west of the Rhine River, German forces maintained a front of 130 miles around the Alsatian town of Colmar. They were a burr in 6th Army Group's side. Reducing the length of this long front would mean that fewer American and French forces would be required to defend it and more would be available for the offensive into Germany. The frozen ground was going to melt before March, turn to mud, and stagnate the Army's efforts. For that reason, General Jacob Devers, commander of the 6th Army Group, knew that he had to finish this operation quickly.[14] A reduction of the Colmar Pocket would be an "unambiguous defeat" for the Nazis, and Eisenhower wanted it "crushed without delay."[15] Devers had no trouble persuading Eisenhower to reinforce him, and he received the 10th AD and the 28th ID for the operation. Devers's staff prepared "Operation Cheerful," a double-envelopment in which French forces would attack from Mulhouse toward the Rhine bridge that lay east of Colmar. Ideally, this would attract German reserves. Then American and French forces would attack from the northwest.[16]

Eisenhower and Devers deemed Cota's division too weak to spearhead this attack, so it played a supporting role, covering the front to the right of

Major General John E. O'Daniel's 3rd Infantry Division and following its attacks. Their adversaries, the Nineteenth Army under Lieutenant General Siegfried Rasp, "were under-strength, under-trained, and under-equipped." His army possessed "perhaps sixty-five operational tanks and assault guns" and insufficient artillery shells. Rasp commanded only 22,500 troops, most of whom lacked experience and sufficient training. A number of factors, however, worked in their favor: interior lines, rugged, defensible ground, telephone communications, plenty of mines, and ammunition for small arms. They had to defend the bridges that were his lifeline to Germany, first at Breisach and also at Neuenburg.[17]

"Cheerful" commenced on January 20 with the I French Corps attack. As planned, it attracted Rasp's reserve formations, but the French "attack remained stalled for the rest of the month," due in part to bad, snowy weather that piled on top of snowfall that varied from one to six feet. To the north, the 3rd Infantry Division stepped off a day later.[18] The Bloody Bucket reentered combat in earnest on the 29th when it drove east to cover the flank of the attacking 3rd ID. The 109th and 110th Regiments seized their objectives and prepared for the next task.[19] Their operations were modest. On the night of January 29, the 109th's 1st Battalion moved its lines one thousand yards forward, while 3rd Battalion captured a portion of the north-south road that went through Colmar.[20] "Meeting little resistance," the 110th took over a mountaintop that overlooked the town of Orbey. Lieutenant Colonel Rudder found his opponents unimpressive. They were well-trained and fit, but since they were Austrians they had little enthusiasm for Hitler's war. "They have a tendency to desert and give up in groups. Morale of prisoners is fair to poor." The Americans found that German forces were vulnerable to attacks at night because they believed that the Yanks "never attack at night." Whenever Rudder's men conducted a night operation, they found success and lost few men. Even though the regiment was back at the front for less than a week, it captured seventy-one prisoners and suffered only a single man killed.[21] Not only did the ease of this operation hearten the men, but just being close to the Rhine River brought the men the hope of crossing it and achieving the final victory.[22]

After the initial effort against the Colmar Pocket failed to produce decisive results, Devers had Major General Frank W. Milburn attack again on February 1. This time the French 5th Armored Division accompanied the 3rd ID as the spearhead, while the 28th and 75th IDs covered the flanks. At the same time, Army Group G concluded that the soldiers inside the Pocket were more valuable than the ground itself and should be preserved, but Hitler refused to

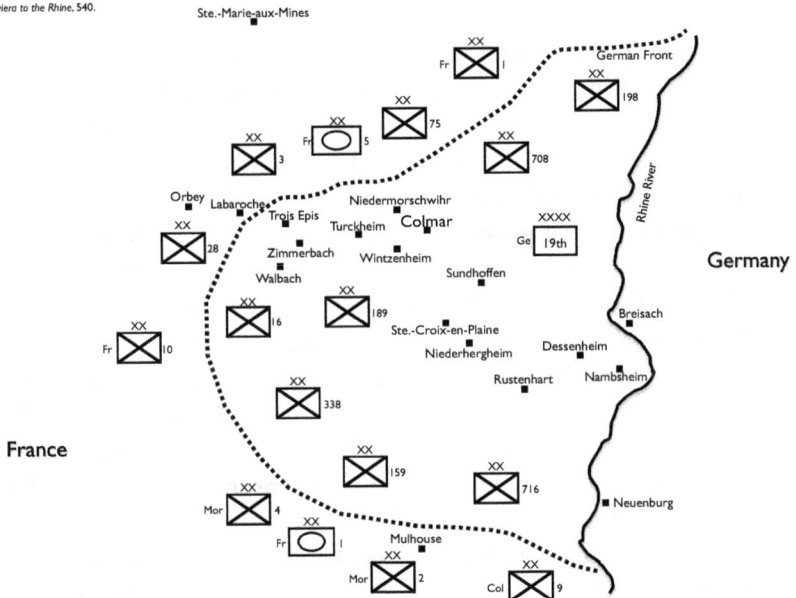

Map 10
The Colmar Campaign in Alsace
January 20-February 5, 1945

Derived from Clarke & Smith, *Riviera to the Rhine*, 540.

allow a withdrawal. Rasp had no reserves available to contest O'Daniel's newest assault. Consequently he began to transfer some troops to the east bank of the Rhine in anticipation that tactical realities would overrule Hitler's stubbornness, but by the time Hitler changed his mind it was too late to save even half of the army. Rasp had still managed to evacuate about 40 percent of his forces to Germany.[23] They did not exert fierce resistance. For example, when Company I of the 109th Infantry charged some trenches, it found them empty. A machine gun crew readily surrendered when a Sherman confronted them; more were going to exploit the fighting as an opportunity for surrender. When the 109th's mortar company searched for a new place to set up its mortars, it "found seventeen enemy soldiers just waiting to surrender."[24]

The Bloody Bucket was not going to have to throw itself against determined German defenders this time. The French Army would do the dirty work of seizing the city, with GIs combing the ground behind them for any enemy the French had missed. This was no repeat of the Aachen campaign; Colmar was in Allied hands by the night of February 2.[25] In spite of enemy action, the Americans did what they wanted with "speed and surprise." The Allies captured several thousand German soldiers and peppered those who tried to cross the Rhine with artillery and firepower from the Army Air Forces during the first week of February.[26]

The Keystone Division did not engage in any severe fighting as it confronted portions of the "16th and 189th Volksgrenadier Divisions, the 338th Division, 2nd Mountain Division, and the 708th Volksgrenadier Division." Nelson's soldiers moved south and east to take the villages of Turckheim, Trois Epis, Labaroche, Wintzenheim, Zimmerbach, and Niedermorschwihr, "mopping up," "clearing," and "cleaning up." First Battalion came under an attack and artillery barrage it did not expect, but merely sidestepped the resistance. Third Battalion reached as far south as Walbach. By the 6th of February, portions of the division were settling along the western edge of Colmar itself, awaiting the next task. Even during these modest operations, the 112th regiment suffered 220 combat casualties, and 38 of those died.[27] When German artillery began to pound Strickler's men, they withdrew to Rustenhart and let the division's howitzers retaliate. For the coup de grace the 109th Infantry surrounded the city on the eastern, southern, and western sides while French troops took it. The Old Gray Mare could have added the liberation of Colmar to its battle honors, but "it stood aside to let the 5ème Blindée do the honors and receive the 'delirious enthusiasm' of the populace."[28] Not until February 5th did Rudder's forces attack. The 1st Battalion took Sundhoffen that evening, bagging "over one hundred (100) prisoners of war with a loss of only two men." As a result, Rudder commented that because of the Colmar Plains' more gentle terrain, night operations were preferable because it was easier to surprise the enemy and to minimize casualties. Because there were no ravines to subdivide the area he did not find command and control at night to be that difficult.

The Old Gray Mare expanded the ground it controlled the next day by occupying Ste.-Croix-en-Plaine, Niederhergheim, and Dessenheim.[29] Before that, however, the 109th Infantry represented the United States in a victory parade through Colmar on the 8th since it had been the first to break through the city's defenses. "To the veterans present who remembered the victory parade in Paris, it was a 'little Paris' repeated. French and American generals were everywhere. The citizens of Colmar were [as] ecstatic as had been those of Paris on 29 August 1944."[30] Afterward XXI Corps continued to spare Strickler's regiment from heavy combat. It served as corps reserve for a couple of days and then began to capture villages around Colmar in conjunction with other forces.

When its 3rd Battalion came under heavy shelling on February 6, the infantry pulled back to Rustenhart so that American artillery could have a free hand. On the 8th, encountering no enemy troops en route, GIs reached Nambsheim and then the Rhine River.[31]

The fighting to drive the Germans across the Rhine was nevertheless worse than what the often-sterile after-action reports conveyed. The weather was just as cold as it had been in the Ardennes, but ice covered the roads, snowdrifts piled as high as six feet, and the snow kept falling. Movement in the mountains was often painfully slow and necessitated tire chains for the vehicles, and the offensive would have ground to a halt without French pack mules for moving supplies forward. Even though the German troops they fought were well-supplied and -equipped, there was not as much fight left in them as in December. Jerry's morale was low, especially in the 2nd Mountain Division. The men had served in Finland for three years and were expecting to spend time with their families, but they had to fight in the Colmar Pocket.[32]

Although German troops were wearing down, GIs had become more steadfast and disciplined by this point in the war. A German battalion commander from the 760th Regiment whom the 110th Infantry captured was impressed with the extent to which American prisoners refused to divulge information. Once again German artillery subjected the soldiers to tree bursts. GIs had to relearn the lessons of the Hürtgen Forest—hugging trees instead of diving to the ground to try to avoid the splinters. Robert L. Smith found that this use of artillery produced wounds that were worse than those from rifle rounds.[33]

Even when temperatures rose, a "rapid thaw" turned the roads into slop.[34] At times men and mules slid off the narrow trails at night, falling "over cliff-like terrain" to their deaths. A snowplow uncovered a German machine gunner frozen solid just as he was when he fired his last shots. In a macabre adaptation to the stress of combat, "the snowplow crew, themselves machine-gunners, hoisted the rigid corpse onto their jeep behind a pedestal-mounted machine gun and paraded it through the local village."[35]

The Army's preoccupation with the Colmar Pocket resembled that of Hürtgen Forest. Like the previous debacle, the forces defending Colmar did not have the firepower to threaten the flank of 6th Army Group, but the ground they controlled was ideal for defensive fighting. Bernard Law Montgomery has been criticized for his preoccupation with having a "tidy" front line, but apparently some of this rubbed off onto Dwight Eisenhower. Devers had tried to convince Eisenhower that those German forces were not a danger and that French forces were adequate for containing them, but Eisenhower worried that if the Germans reinforced their army there, Devers would have to pull back in order to prevent a rupture in his lines. That scenario would imperil Strasbourg, which would have resulted in a pyroclastic reaction by General Charles de Gaulle.[36] French politics demanded that German troops be expelled from French soil.

Following the seizure of the Colmar Pocket the division redeployed by truck to the vicinity of Toul for three days of training. Rudder wanted more time to train his inexperienced replacements, rest his veterans, and provide them with adequate deep-snow equipment, such as snowshoes, but that was not going to happen. From there the Keystoners moved via truck and railcar to the location of the 2nd Infantry Division southeast of Monschau and west of Schleiden, only about forty kilometers from the Hürtgen Forest. There it relieved the "Indianhead" Division and took responsibility for defending the area on February 24.[37]

To the Rhine

As March approached, the Allied advance had become inexorable, and the German forces that were still west of the Rhine constituted "a rear guard" that faced "inevitable destruction by the Anglo-American forces if they failed to cross the river."[38] By this time German propaganda efforts were futile. In the vicinity of Harperscheid, German artillery peppered the 110th Infantry with propaganda leaflets in an effort to intimidate the GIs. Calling the 28th ID the "Bloody Butchers" because of their "inhuman offensive," they warned that they would no longer take prisoners from 28th ID units. The relentless nature of the American entry into Germany left soldiers of the Reich infuriated. GIs were able to sit on a hill overlooking their counterparts and direct shell fire their way. The Americans were living in the bunkers the Germans had meticulously constructed, while German soldiers—"cold, hungry, and miserable"—could not dare to make fires to warm themselves, lest more artillery fall on their heads. The Americans used loudspeakers to call for German soldiers to surrender.[39] Farther afield, more and more Germans were giving up, and GIs began capturing larger units, including "whole headquarters."[40]

The 28th ID commenced its final operation at the beginning of March. It formed but one part of a larger effort west of Koblenz to comprise the northern half of a double envelopment to correspond with General Patton's forces closing from the south.[41] When Major General Clarence R. Huebner, the V Corps commander, met with Cota to make sure he understood the intent of his plan,

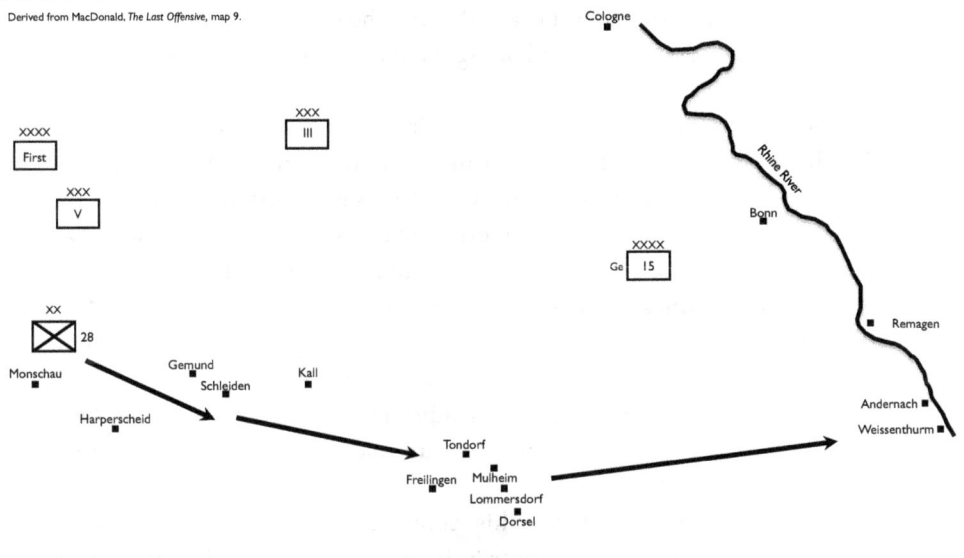

Map 11
The Approach to the Rhine
March 1945

Derived from MacDonald, *The Last Offensive*, map 9.

he explained that the Keystone Division was to support the maneuvers of the 2nd ID to the north. He wanted the 28th to keep the Germans in front of them busy so that they could not turn more of their attention to the 2nd Division.

> Huebner said that his attack would be a series of "pinwheels," with the main thrusts in the 2nd Division area, by cutting units out and down behind the enemy. Each thrust would gouge a chunk out of the German position by moving from north to south axially along the line, putting the attacking troops in a position to enfilade the defenders. He said he did not want any frontal or direct flanking attacks and, while he wanted to maintain contact in front of the 28th Division, he did not want to lose too many men by placing them out on the high ground to its front. In short, in the scheme of maneuver, the 28th Division initially was to be the base of fire and the 2nd Division the moving force, hitting the enemy from his right rear.

More specifically, the 112th Infantry was to attack south from the Gemund bridge across the Olef River while the 109th Infantry supported with fire from the west of Schleiden. The 110th was to be ready to exploit opportunities in the zone of either regiment. The operation, however, did not take place this way.[42]

As Cota briefed the plan to his officers on the morning of March 3, Huebner abruptly telephoned and abrogated the orders he had just issued to Cota.

German forces were now withdrawing east due to the success of the Allied offensive. Because of the German movement Huebner told Dutch to rush forces east to try to cut off their escape. These efforts to maintain contact with the enemy continued throughout the next day, but the Germans were determined to pull back and seldom initiated firefights. Escape, not inflicting casualties, was their goal.[43]

Huebner issued additional orders on March 4th and 5th. First, he had the 28th relieve the 2nd Infantry Division and then turn south. Nelson's regiment was to expel German soldiers from the Olef River's east bank and then seize the town of Schleiden and the dominant terrain to the south of the Schleiden–Kall road. They also had to be ready for further action.[44] Along the way the 112th encountered the mines and booby traps the defenders had left in their wake, avoided them, and advanced. On the 6th it cleared out pillboxes near Gemund and then turned east the next day. It swept clean the towns of Schleiden, Freilingen, Dorsel, and Lommersdorf, losing only one soldier to enemy action. After the 11th the only contact it had with German soldiers was the 232 prisoners it placed into custody.[45]

Similarly, Strickler was to take his regiment through Gemund, attack the village of Kall, and also be ready to strike to the southeast. Rudder and his men functioned as the "holding and following force and, throughout the rest of the action, never took a prominent part."[46] Nevertheless, seventeen men lost their lives as the regiment endured a rain of artillery shells and mortar fire during the first week of March.

Operating around Schleiden, the 109th Infantry encountered "the most extensive enemy mines both AT and AP which it had ever experienced in combat." Retreating soldiers booby-trapped houses and mined roads, which forced the Americans to slow their advance so as to first clear the mines.[47] They used equipment such as "primer cord," a rope-like explosive that is draped over a minefield using the grenade-launching capability of three M1 rifles. Detonating the cords detonated nearby mines. Company I of the Old Gray Mare found this to be no easy task on the night of February 25. Although Company I blew a path through the minefield that was in their way, German machine gunners overlooked the minefield and drove back the GIs.[48]

Not for long. When an explosive charge destroyed the bridge at Gemund early on the morning of March 6, it took only thirty minutes for the men of the 103rd Engineers to erect a new one. While German fire was light, they had left the ridge north of Schleiden covered with mines and booby traps. These slowed the American pursuit but momentarily. Soon they were past the mines, and the 110th "met no opposition and encountered no mines. Its advance was swift." The 109th had the same experience of finding the town devoid of soldiers, but full of mines: "In one house, seventy wired explosives were found and disarmed!"[49] Pouring rain and ubiquitous mud could not stop the GIs who took one town after another, avoiding or crushing what little resistance they crossed. Strickler's men captured several hundred prisoners and plenty of vehicles.[50] After following the lead of other American units, his regiment struck with such speed that the Germans "fled in confusion in an attempt to cross to the east bank of the Rhine River." They also "offered only light resistance, and generally surrendered after a brief exchange of small arms fire." Only four men under Strickler's command lost their lives that month.[51] By midnight the men were in the village of Zingaheim. On the afternoon of the 6th, V Corps gave the division "the green light" to press to the Ahr River. The only concern now was placing a new bridge over the river at Schleiden in the dead of night.

The next day Strickler's regiment moved with such speed that the signals troops could barely string telephone lines quickly enough for him to maintain contact with Cota. By midday they were in Tondorf, and then they captured LXVI Corps's chief of staff, a Lieutenant Colonel Moll, who had shut down the command post and was about to flee in a car. They reached the Ahr River on the morning of the 8th, as did the 112th, after picking their way through yet another minefield. Neither regiment moved fast enough to keep their enemy within range of small arms fire. That night Nelson's men captured forty-five more prisoners, who surrendered quickly. The 110th's speed, "thirty-five miles in two days," was a testament as much to the magnitude of the Germans' flight as to the capabilities of the regiment.[52] Not every soldier escaped: the regiment captured 632. Amidst the German collapse, there was less and less actual combat. The 229th FA, for example, fired its last shells of the war on March 26.[53]

This action constituted the 28th Infantry Division's final combat operation. For the rest of March, its soldiers shuttled from location to location, practiced tactical drills, and transitioned into an occupying force. Destroying captured munitions was about as exciting as life got.[54] American forces crossed the Rhine over the Remagen Bridge on March 9th, and portions of the Bloody Bucket reached the river by the 18th, taking positions at Andernach and Weissenthurm. Four days later a few men from the 110th rowed across the river, captured a hapless German soldier, and brought him back to their lines for questioning. Division records claim that it crossed the river at Honningen on March 29.[55] Both the 110th and the 112th Regiments claimed to have been first with the latter crossing on the northern outskirts of Koblenz.[56]

Occupation

Cota's soldiers now busied themselves with occupation duty: establishing checkpoints and combing the woods for Germans, especially for Nazi Party officials. With the passing of winter, "[t]he weather, which had begun to clear late in March, had turned warm, and the scent of growing things was in the air. Germany, which had been a nightmare of rains, sleet and snow, was changing her dress and her mood. Flowers poked tentative, inquiring heads from between inchoative blades of grass and the deep valleys and rambling hills which comprised the Reich grew greener and brighter daily."[57]

The scale of the German defeat by springtime was staggering. Losses in the Western Theater totaled 2,889,452 since D-Day, with just over 2 million of those being captured.[58] Civilian refugees, liberated slaves, and dying concentration camp inmates clogged the roadways. Troops that surrendered by the multitude during the last days of the war literally covered square miles of ground. When the American First and Ninth Armies joined hands at Lippstadt, they had encircled over 300,000 men, who gave their captors surprisingly little trouble.[59]

With a sigh of relief, the Bloody Bucket was transferred to XXIII Corps of 15th Army. During the last week of April, the 110th began occupation duty in the Saarland, and Strickler received a new title, "Military Governor of the Saarland." The Americans had German workers busy themselves with coal mining, and local magistrates keep order among civilians. GIs stood ready to put down riots, should they occur, and to enforce laws against more serious crimes. The occupiers found that the American commitment to impartial justice perplexed freed Russian and Polish workers, who "were the worst violators of law and order. Murder, rape, robbery, and looting were common offenses. . . . Indeed, the Russians and Poles could not be persuaded to believe that any act committed against a German could be a crime, and were invariably puzzled and hurt when their American friends arrested one of the D.P. [displaced persons] group who, in spite of continued warnings, insisted on plundering German homes."[60]

German civilians were less troublesome, mainly refusing to stay put.[61] In order to better manage them, GIs conducted a local census to register the residents with the help of German civilians. It was a huge task, as 300,000 people lived within the area (Koblenz) of the 109th Infantry alone. American forces put them to work removing debris and rubble from their villages and towns. Even though individuals still committed crimes, the fact that Rudder's regiment, for example, expended no ammunition during April suggested that German civilians recognized their new condition as a defeated people.[62]

Whatever their feelings about the strictness of the American occupation laws, the American practice of holding local *Burgomeisters* "directly responsible for the actions of all persons in his town" resulted in cooperation by civilians and greater law and order.[63] The American policy was successful in the aggregate, for the Army had but a "brief impact" on civilian life.[64]

However "brief" the effect might have been, the occupying American and Commonwealth armies were at times pretty rough on the defeated as they swept over the German heartland. Feeling empowered and possibly entitled, many Allied soldiers ransacked and looted German houses and buildings haphazardly. Civilians of one village returned to find their possessions pilfered, while the neighboring village escaped the attention of the passing victors. One GI might steal everything he could in a house, while others searched a home with respect and took nothing.[65]

Many GIs recognized the wisdom of the policy that prohibited them from socializing with Germans, but the German people found it insulting. Not a few Keystone soldiers violated the policy; sixty fraternization cases were pending by June. One of its officers commented that GIs were going to socialize with German women no matter what the rules were.[66] The nonfraternization policy was in place for several reasons. Commanders wished to prevent their troops from looting (or worse), sought to convince the population that Germany and its people were defeated, and did not want the GIs to catch or spread venereal disease.[67]

The Army made efforts to prosecute soldiers who had committed rape. Complete enforcement of occupation laws should have protected civilians from the worst sort in the Army, but that was not the case. One evening a soldier who had been spending time with a 12-year-old Polish girl returned to his buddies boasting "about what a wonderful whore the child was." Robert Smith was not the only one who realized what had happened: "I was called by the head man at the dormitory where she was housed. The girl, still in hysterics, had been brutally raped." The Army did not charge the rapist. Smith found it amazing that soldiers could see the suffering and pain of war and still be so callous as to harm without pity an innocent person whose only mistake was "being friendly to a stranger and being in the wrong place at the wrong time. The villains were not all on the other side of the war."[68] Four hundred eighty-seven soldiers stood trial for rape in March and April 1945, but "the conviction rate was relatively low," primarily because of difficulties in proving the guilt of the accused. Severe consequences threatened those who were convicted. Seventh Army, for instance, sentenced eleven to death, seven more to life in prison, and "several" up to twenty years of incarceration. Recent scholarship places the number of convictions from January to September 1945 at 284. Although 100 soldiers were executed for rape in Britain and 100 more in France, the Army commuted all death sentences for rapes that occurred in Germany.[69] Given that rape is an underreported crime, there were many more rapes than these.[70]

The anguish of war was ending for the Keystone soldiers, who found occupation duty pleasing. There was time for baseball and volleyball, USO events, and movies every night. There remained a vague tension, however, for the actual German surrender was not in clear sight.[71] But happily:

> V/E day came as an anti-climax to the weeks of rumor, false report and wild hope. Even the radio commentators treated the day mildly, remarking its arrival without bombast. No one would have denied the symbolic importance of the event, but it had been prematurely celebrated so frequently that the element of surprise had vanished, and the genuine joy with which the official surrender news was received lacked the hysteria which had marked previous reports. Shortly afterward, however, came news which, while of possibly less importance to the world at large, was tremendously received by the men of the Regiment—the 28th Division was going home; albeit in category IV, which meant redeployment to the Pacific.[72]

Thankfully for the men of the 28th ID the Japanese surrender on September 2 ended that possibility. They would not have to add to their casualty list of 24,840.[73]

14

Conclusion

One obvious question for the end of a book that examines the transformation of a National Guard division into an infantry division of the U.S. Army is this: Which kind of officer was better: National Guard, Regular, or Reserve? The surviving records may not yield a definitive answer, and anecdotal accounts from veterans follow no pattern. The small number of veterans who answered questions about the relative merits of these officers decades later expressed strongly held opinions. Some considered National Guard and Reserve officers to possess skills equal to those of Regulars, while others held West Point graduates in high esteem. George Dane and Anthony J. Geronimo considered NG officers to have been "political commissions," found West Pointers arrogant, but thought well of OCS and battlefield commissioned officers. Howard F. Harvier preferred West Pointers. Roger Lee Farrand wrote, "Some National Guard officers left a lot to be desired." Morris G. Sykes said the same, but about OCS officers. John F. Ritter ranked Guard officers second only to West Pointers. Miner M. Lang's preference was for officers with either National Guard or battlefield commissions, while James T. Bryant observed that National Guard and OCS officers "normally didn't last long." William Mansberry plainly preferred Guardsmen. John F. Forsell and Robert Probach disagreed: "it depended on the individual." Christopher Sotiro preferred the leadership of NCOs to officers. Marion Bedford Davis could not see any pattern of leadership quality among officers based on their source of commissioning. Among veterans' questionnaires examined, only West Point graduates escaped scathing criticism.[1]

In his account of the Battle of the Hürtgen Forest, Cecil B. Currey asked whether "the breakup of Guard units, the system of filler replacements, and the loss of the peacetime National Guard structure with all the local associations of Guardsmen . . . injured the division greatly and helped account for the troubles in the Hürtgen in November 1944."[2] Currey assumes that the soldiers' primary attachments were to other people from their hometowns and to their National

Guard units. Well before the 1940s, however, Americans identified themselves as Americans first. One's hometown and state held second place in terms of one's attachments. National identity was complete, and local identity was but a sentiment. A soldier went to war for the United States—not, to paraphrase one Civil War soldier, "for Virginia." Furthermore, national divisions such as the 88th Infantry Division fought well, even though they were a blending of conscripts from across the country and had no long-term National Guard–like traditions and identity.[3] Once in combat, soldiers fought for each other and in order to end the war so they could go home; political ideals, so important for recruiting, receded during battle. In any event, National Guard soldiers had become a tiny minority by 1944, when a member of the 112th Infantry wrote, "Of course only a few of the original men are left that were mobilized on the 17th of Feb. 1941."[4] Throughout the Army they comprised only 1.7 percent of rifle companies on D-Day and just 0.5 percent prior to the Bulge.[5]

The breakup of Guard units was not entirely the result of Army and federal action. As chapter 8 demonstrated, thousands of PNG soldiers took action as individuals, seeking opportunities in the Army Air Forces or branches other than the infantry. In that way the soldiers largely dissolved the state character of the division themselves. What is more, the division reached a peak of efficiency in late 1942 through early 1943, after General Bradley broke up the cliques. His time with the division demonstrated the conclusive influence of leadership on the combat capability and morale of a military unit, which surpassed local attachments. If the division was going to exhibit "troubles" resulting from its transformation from a state to a national division, it would have done so during the first weeks of fighting. Here again it fought reasonably well when led well, and it helped to chase the German Army across northern France. Bradley's and Hodges's poor strategy and Cota's choice to lead from his command post without personally scouting what was happening to his men were the causes of the division's problems at Hürtgen Forest. Ascribing the Bloody Bucket's combat difficulties in November 1944 to its transformation from a National Guard to a U.S. Army division does not make sense in light of its solid performance during the Battle of the Bulge. If it was a unit without the proper essence for maintaining cohesion and fighting power during November 1944, why was it able to fight comparatively well with numerous replacements against greater forces?

The United States Army completely assimilated the Pennsylvania National Guard into itself. References to Pennsylvania were gone from the written records by 1943. According to Peter Mansoor, "By the end of the war, there were no appreciable differences in the personnel composition of the sixty-seven standard American infantry divisions."[6] The amalgamation of National Guard units such as the 28th ID into the Army was another step in the trends of nationalization, consolidation, and rationalization that had so altered the order and management of American society. The absence of resistance to these trends among the troops demonstrates that these changes had already occurred within the country. That this took place in a country so imbued with individuality, movement, and mobility should not come as a surprise.

The Keystone soldiers of December 1944 benefited from a cadre of experienced leaders who had survived the Hürtgen Forest. Important to their commendable performance, given the odds, was the character of the Battle of the Bulge. This was the great battle of the Western Front in World War II, and the GIs took its strategic importance personally. Unlike the situation in the Hürtgen Forest, the soldiers along Skyline Drive had choices. Some chose to run, more chose to stay and fight to the end, and many took advantage of the ability to maneuver to escape one near-catastrophe in order to continue to fight a couple of miles to the west. The soldiers in the Hürtgen Forest were ordered to move forward against hopeless odds, or to stay put against hopeless odds, but those in the Ardennes were allowed to move to improve their chances of surviving and of hurting the enemy. One reason American soldiers engaged in combat was to support and defend their buddies, but in the Hürtgen Forest the character of the fighting often physically isolated men from each other. Soldiers also fought on when leaders guided them in battle, a condition that was more common during the Battle of the Bulge.[7]

The behavior of men under fire during the Battle of the Bulge was a testament to the awareness of the American soldier of the nature of the war he was fighting, not just the tactical character of the German onslaught. The fight they put up stands as proof of their awareness as well as their bravery. They chose to fight when it mattered the most.

The soldiers who defended the country during World War II did so as Americans in the United States Army. The ones who were a part of the Pennsylvania National Guard in 1939–41 would have preferred to enlist in a well-equipped army capable of training them in a way that would have prepared them for combat at a faster pace instead of the running in place as they did for what seemed like years. This case study highlights a lack of preparedness for war in the Army and the National Guard that I find difficult to fathom. While the absence of interwar training and procurement may have been somewhat of a national tantrum against the injustices surrounding the First World War, those policy choices of anti-interventionism and unpreparedness did nothing to forestall the onset of the Second World War. One of the most irksome short-comings was the absence of basic infantry training for National Guard recruits. Not until 1958 did federal statutes mandate a six-month basic training course for new NG recruits, the minimum acceptable amount of time according to the Army.[8] At last there was some national standardization and consolidation in fundamental military training that all soldiers need.

Another characteristic this case study has revealed is the volition of individual soldiers. National Guard service was a choice, and for some, a preference over conscription into the Army. Following the Pearl Harbor attack, many chose to leave the infantry for the Army Air Forces. Individual volition manifested itself to the greatest extent during combat. Soldiers judged the merits of tactical actions and considered their own self-interests in deciding what efforts they were going to exert. Their awareness of the true importance of battles—Hürtgen Forest versus the Bulge—manifested itself in the persistence of their fighting: fighting bitterly against greater odds for a strategically important campaign, fighting and fleeing to survive a smaller onslaught for ground that was not critical to the war's outcome. They knew that the German attack of December 16 was a major and threatening offensive that put at risk their personal goals of winning the war so they could return to civilian life. Not a few GIs fled, but more realized that they could help turn the tide of the war by fighting.

These soldiers and officers embraced the need for a professional approach to combat, not in terms of commissioning source, but in terms of recognizing the multitude and difficulty of skills inherent in modern infantry warfare and in seeking to practice them with competence. Bringing great combat capability to the battlefield, as opposed to learning it on the battlefield, was necessary in order to win battles, campaigns, and wars. The prewar Protective Mobilization Plan exemplified a nineteenth-century rush-to-the-colors mindset, decades behind the realities of mid-twentieth-century warfare. The years the United States military required to grow, expand, and train its Army, and the years of training the 28th Infantry Division required to become combat-ready point to the necessity of maintaining substantial well-trained armed forces, both regular and reserve, during times of peace—before war breaks out. This ongoing effort, prior to the eruption of an international military crisis, is a necessary tax for the national security of a people and their state—one that must be paid either through peacetime training or through greater battlefield casualties during wartime.

Appendix 1

The Execution of Private Slovik

One soldier in particular did not survive to see the Allies win the war. Private Edward Slovik, Company G of the 109th Infantry Regiment, died in front of a firing squad on January 31.[1] Following the execution, one of General Cota's bodyguards, Corporal Michael Fedoro, watched as Dutch "cried like a young kid." Harry M. Kemp, who published a history of the 109th Infantry in 1990, discussed the execution with a number of Keystone veterans. "To a man, they did not understand why Slovik was shot and other deserters were not. To a man, they did not believe Slovik's death changed their combat duty performance or that of any other soldiers around them."[2] Out of 40,000 deserters, Slovik was the one man of forty-nine condemned to die whose sentence was not commuted.[3]

Bad luck had hounded Slovik most of his life. He had been to reform school and accumulated a record of petty crime. His introduction to the combat zone was about as bad as could be arranged. He and other replacements passed through the wreckage of the German forces that had been pounded at the Falaise Pocket. For miles they gawked at mutilated horses and burned-up men. He joined Company G of the 109th Infantry on August 25, 1944. By his own admission, Slovik deserted the next day because the perils of the front line scared him that badly. The confession he wrote on October 9th even read, "I'LL RUN AWAY AGAIN IF I HAVE TO GO OUT THEIR [sic]." From late August through early October he avoided rejoining his unit by staying with Canadian Army forces, cooking for them and doing odd jobs. He finally caught up to the regiment on his own initiative, but then tried to persuade Lieutenant Colonel Ross Henbest not to send him to the front again, lest he run away. Prosecutors later deduced that Slovik sought out prison as a way of surviving the war and avoiding the horrors of combat. Indeed, Slovik refused the offer of the division judge advocate, Lieutenant Colonel Henry J. Sommer, to throw out the desertion charges if he would just enter combat with the rest of his unit. "No, I've made up my mind," he said. "I'll take my court-martial."[4]

The trial lasted less than two hours. Slovik's attorney, Captain Edward P. Woods, made little effort to defend his client. Five witnesses testified, and Woods never cross-examined any of them. Slovik elected to not testify. Slovik's admission that he had deserted and promised to do so again sealed the deal. The jury found him guilty and recommended execution.[5] Colonel Guy M. Williams, the presiding officer for the court-martial, later said that no one thought Slovik would really face a firing squad: "I thought that not long after the war ended—two or three years maybe—Slovik would be a free man." A couple of factors convinced General Cota to recommend that the Army carry out the sentence: Slovik's written confession, which was unique among desertion cases, and his pre-Army record of petty crime, for which he was not on trial. Cota was also sick of the problem of soldiers leaving their posts during the Battle of Hürtgen Forest.[6]

Eisenhower confirmed the sentence on December 23. Army regulations required a review of the case, so the execution did not follow immediately. Seven lawyers scrutinized the case over the next month. Unlike the jury, they found out about Slovik's past record. That knowledge influenced them to not press Eisenhower to grant Slovik clemency. Brigadier General E. C. McNeil stated as much, writing, "His unfavorable civilian record indicates that he is not a worthy subject of clemency."[7]

Eddie Slovik was selfish and was a deserter. He tried to exploit the Army penal system to escape combat duty and trade short-term incarceration for eventual long-term freedom. Slovik did not desert, for instance, after a week of incessant shelling, but instead made his choice quickly after deliberating the merits. His determination to run away from the terrors of infantry combat, however, was not his worst crime. It never seemed to occur to him that his desertion forced another man to take his place in combat and face all the perils therein. Demanding that another person suffer the misery of fighting because front-line duty makes you uncomfortable personifies selfishness—a demand for self-preservation that requires others to be put at risk so that you may avoid discomfort.

Given the frequency of desertion in the U.S. Army—with all the varying manifestations of that behavior—it was unfair that Slovik was the one man who was executed. Nor was it right for his past record to influence his fate. This writer is no expert in jurisprudence, but the negligence of Slovik's lawyer adds to the scandal. There was plenty of blame to go around, as well. Cota blamed the replacement system for sending men into combat zones without a sufficient emotional support system. He later concluded, "To thrust an individual, no matter how well trained an individual he may be, into battle as a member of a strange unit is in my opinion expecting more than many men are capable of giving."[8]

Appendix 2

The Reestablishment of the Pennsylvania National Guard

There were those in the Army who opposed the reestablishment of the National Guard after World War II, but General Marshall was not one of them. Guardsmen under the leadership of Minnesota's Ellard A. Walsh, the former commander of the 34th Division, began planning and lobbying for a postwar National Guard in 1943. Marshall welcomed Walsh's advice as well as that of John McAuley Palmer, a longtime advocate of a citizen army. In September 1944, General Marshall informed the secretary of war of his support for the National Guard's reestablishment as "an integral part and a first line reserve component of the post-war military establishment." A War Department directive issued in October 1945 confirmed that the Guard would be renewed as the Army's primary reserve, with a dual state and federal character. Growth was rapid in 1946: 97,526 men staffed 2,615 units by year's end, and the Guard was authorized almost 655,000 soldiers. On November 11, 1946, a ceremony of considerable substance took place: "the Army returned to the States the guidons and battle flags of the National Guard units that had fought in World War II." Furthermore, the War Department reestablished the eighteen divisions.[1] Pennsylvania's 28th Infantry Division was the first that received authorization to organize. Its adjutant general, Brigadier General Robert M. Vail, was going to oversee a force numbering "approximately 30,000 troops."[2] Many of these were veterans, giving "the postwar Guard a dedicated, hard core of officer leadership."[3] This latest manifestation of the National Guard was certainly off to a better start than what it had experienced after the last war. Because of the planning of Marshall, Walsh, and Palmer, the foundation was laid for what would become a key component of the "total force" of active duty, Guard, and Reserve forces, working together for the defense of the United States.

Notes

1. Introduction

1. Bernard Bailyn, *The Ideological Origins of the American Revolution* (Cambridge, Mass.: Belknap Press of Harvard University Press, 1967), 116. John Shy, *Toward Lexington: The Role of the British Army in the Coming of the American Revolution* (Princeton, N.J.: Princeton University Press, 1965), 376.

2. John Resch, *Suffering Soldiers: Revolutionary War Veterans, Moral Sentiment, and Political Culture of the Early Republic* (Amherst: University of Massachusetts Press, 1999), 3–5, 65, 69–71. Charles Royster, *A Revolutionary People at War: The Continental Army and American Character, 1775–1783* (New York: W. W. Norton, 1979), 327–30, 333. John Shy, *A People Numerous and Armed: Reflections on the Military Struggle for Independence* (Ann Arbor: University of Michigan Press, 1990), 263. Russell F. Weigley, *Towards an American Army: Military Thought from Washington to Marshall* (New York: Columbia University Press, 1962), 18.

3. Lawrence Delbert Cress, *Citizens in Arms: The Army and the Militia in American Society to the War of 1812* (Chapel Hill: University of North Carolina Press, 1982), 143–44.

4. Don Higginbotham, *The War of American Independence: Military Attitudes, Policies, and Practice, 1763–1789* (New York: Macmillan, 1971), 457.

5. C. Edward Skeen, *Citizen Soldiers in the War of 1812* (Lexington: University Press of Kentucky, 1999), 121. Russell F. Weigley, *The American Way of War: A History of United States Military Strategy and Policy* (New York: Macmillan, 1973), 55.

6. Robert V. Remini, *The Battle of New Orleans* (New York: Viking, 1999), 192. Weigley, *Towards an American Army*, 29. Richard Bruce Winders, *Mr. Polk's Army: The American Military Experience in the Mexican War* (College Station: Texas A&M University Press, 1997), 4. Weigley, *The American Way of War*, 54–55.

7. Roger J. Spiller, "Calhoun's Expansible Army: The History of a Military Idea," *South Atlantic Quarterly* 79, no. 2 (Spring 1980): 189–209. Weigley, *Towards an American Army*, 31–33.

8. Edward M. Coffman, "The Duality of the American Military Tradition: A Commentary," *Journal of Military History* 64, no. 4 (October 2000): 972.

9. William B. Skelton, *An American Profession of Arms: The Army Officer Corps, 1784–1861* (Lawrence: University Press of Kansas, 1992), 210–12. Winders, *Polk's Army*, 196–98.

10. Winders, *Polk's Army*, 12–13, 73–78.

11. Coffman, "Duality," 975–76.

12. David F. Trask, *The War with Spain in 1898* (New York: Macmillan, 1981), 155.

13. Jerry Cooper, *The Rise of the National Guard: The Evolution of the American Militia, 1865–1920* (Lincoln: University of Nebraska Press, 1997), xv, 46–52, 61, 54–55, 70–77, 81, 100–101.

14. Russell F. Weigley, *History of the United States Army* (New York: Macmillan, 1967), 320–22. Cooper, *Rise of the National Guard,* 108–109, 122.

15. Cooper, *Rise of the National Guard,* 110–12, 123–25.

16. Ibid., 130, 140–42, 145.

17. Ibid., 151–52.

18. Ibid., 155–60.

19. Ibid., 163.

20. Ibid., 153–54.

21. Michael D. Doubler, *Civilian in Peace, Soldier in War: The Army National Guard, 1636–2000* (Lawrence: University Press of Kansas, 2003), 173, 179–80. Cooper, *Rise of the National Guard,* 169–70. Barry M. Stentiford, "The Meaning of a Name: The Rise of the National Guard and the End of a Town Militia," *Journal of Military History* 72, no. 3 (July 2009): 744–45.

22. John K. Mahon, *History of the Militia and the National Guard,* Macmillan Wars of the United States, general ed. Louis Morton (New York: Macmillan, 1983), 162–64. Jim Dan Hill, *The Minute Man in Peace and War: A History of the National Guard* (Harrisburg, Pa.: Stackpole, 1964), 296–97.

23. Coffman, "Duality," 977.

24. Cooper, *Rise of the National Guard,* 171–73.

25. Weigley, *History,* 399–400. John B. Wilson, *Maneuver and Firepower: The Evolution of Divisions and Separate Brigades,* Army Lineage Series (Washington, D.C.: Center of Military History, United States Army, 1998), 87. This "Army of the United States" was an amalgamation of the peacetime regular army (the United States Army), the National Guard "while in the service of the United States," and "the Organized Reserves." The latter comprised reservists who were officers in the Officers' Reserve Corps, or ORC. During wartime, these officers were to fill out "nine Reserve Divisions . . . and train conscripts during national emergencies." Doubler, *Civilian in Peace,* 188.

26. Cooper, *Rise of the National Guard,* 174–77.

27. William H. Riker, *Soldiers of the States: The Role of the National Guard in American Democracy* (Washington, D.C.: Public Affairs Press, 1957), 95.

28. The Army fielded nine divisional formations. The 1st, 2nd, and 3rd Divisions each possessed between 8,500 and 10,000 soldiers. The other six "divisions" averaged about 3,500 each. Marvin A. Kreidberg and Merton G. Henry, *History of Military Mobilization in the United States Army, 1775–1945,* Department of the Army Pamphlet No. 20–212 (Washington, D.C.: Department of the Army, 1955), 549–50.

29. Additional units included the 213th Coast Artillery Regiment (Anti-aircraft), 166th Field Artillery, 22nd Cavalry Division, 103rd Cavalry, 104th Cavalry, 101st Radio Intelligence Company, Troop C 122nd Medical Squadron, and 176th Field Artillery, which was attached to the 29th Division. *Directory: Pennsylvania National Guard* (Harrisburg, Pa.: January 1, 1940), RG-19, Slot 14-2201, Box 3, Folder 3–16. Pennsylvania State Archives, Harrisburg, Pa. (hereafter referred to as PSA).

30. Robert H. Wiebe, *The Search for Order, 1877–1920* (New York: Hill and Wang, 1967).

31. John Sloan Brown, *Draftee Division: The 88th Infantry Division in World War II* (Lexington: University Press of Kentucky, 1986).

32. Michael D. Doubler, *Closing with the Enemy: How GIs Fought the War in Europe, 1944–1945* (Lawrence: University Press of Kansas, 1994).

33. See, for example, Robert E. Humphrey, *Once Upon a Time in War: The 99th Division in World War II* (Norman: University of Oklahoma Press, 2008). James Campbell, *Ghost Mountain Boys, Their Epic March and the Terrifying Battle for New Guinea* (New York: Crown, 2008); Tony LeTissier, *Patton's Pawns: The 94th Infantry Division at the Siegfried Line* (Tuscaloosa: University of Alabama Press, 2007).

2. Relations with the Army and State Identity

1. Wiebe, *The Search for Order, 1877–1920,* passim.

2. George C. Marshall to Major General Milton A. Reckord, August 30, 1939, plus footnotes 2 and 3. George C. Marshall, *The Papers of George Catlett Marshall*, vol. 2: "*We Cannot Delay*": July 1, 1939–December 6, 1941, ed. Larry I. Bland, Sharon R. Ritenour, and Clarence E. Wunderlin Jr. (Baltimore, Md.: Johns Hopkins University Press, 1986), 41–42 (hereafter referred to as *MP 2*). The "Army of the United States" comprised the Regular Army, the Organized Reserves, and the National Guard together. In 1940 the term expanded to include "units that had not been a part of the mobilization plans during the interwar years," such as the 25th Infantry Division. Wilson, *Maneuver and Firepower,* 156.

3. War Department, *Army Regulations 130–10, National Guard Induction into the Service of the United States (March 27, 1940).*

4. Marshall to Reckord, August 30, 1939.

5. "Regular Insignia for National Guard," *The Pennsylvania Guardsman,* December 1940, 19 (hereafter referred to as *TPG*). *TPG* was published in magazine form, but since officers of the Pennsylvania National Guard wrote nearly all of the articles, the magazine was really an ongoing published diary of the PNG's activities.

6. Adjutant General's Office to Commanding Generals of all Corps Areas and Departments, September 6, 1940, "Induction of the National Guard of the United States," RG-168, File 325.452, National Archives and Records Administration, College Park, Md. (hereafter referred to as NARA).

7. George C. Marshall to Brigadier General Edmund L. Daley, July 20, 1939, *MP 2*, 17–18.

8. "General Edward Martin Outlines Division Policies," *TPG*, July 1939, 32.

9. "Quote," *TPG*, February 1939, 21.

10. Herbert E. Smith, "Parrish of the Alabam's," *TPG*, November 1939, 3–4. "More Attention to National Guard Training Days," *TPG*, June 1939, 14.

11. "War Trained Leaders Passing On," *TPG*, September 1939, 23.

12. Marshall to Brigadier General Ralph M. Immell, September 14, 1939, *MP 2*, 55–58. Marshall to Brigadier General Charles H. Cole, September 26, 1939, ibid., 67. Brigadier General George V. Srong, Memo for the Chief of Staff, September 20, 1939, RG-165, File War Plans Division General Correspondence, 1920–42, NARA. Edward Martin joined the PNG in 1899. Following action along the Mexican border in 1917, he served as commander of the 110th Infantry Regiment in the 28th Division during World War I, fighting on the Western Front. He was promoted to brigadier general in command of the PNG's 55th Brigade in 1922. He went to work as a banker in 1921. His political career began when he was auditor general of Pennsylvania in 1925–29. Before the decade was out Martin was state chairman for the Republican Party, and then moved on to be the state treasurer from 1929 to 1933. He never lost one of the fifteen elections for which he campaigned. Martin anticipated another world

war and left electoral politics in 1934 to devote himself to the Pennsylvania National Guard. In January 1939 he became the state's adjutant general and took command of the division on June 26. Martin also served as an elder of the First Presbyterian Church in Washington, Pennsylvania, and was a 33rd Degree Mason. Edward Martin, *Always Be On Time: An Autobiography* (Harrisburg, Pa.: Telegraph Press, 1959), 34, 52, 54–56, 75–81, 106–109. "Edward Martin's Service Record," *TPG*, February 1939, 3.

13. Martin, *Always Be On Time*, 106, 109.

14. "Open Forum Discussions Conducted by Major General Edward Martin at the Twenty-first Annual Convention of the National Guard Association of Pennsylvania, October 12–14, 1939," MG-156, Slot 0934, Box 1, PSA. "Martin Urges Guard Boosted to 435,000," *Harrisburg Telegraph*, October 13, 1939, 1.

15. Major J. E. Raymond, Memorandum for the Chief of Staff, GHQ (no date) Visit to 28th Division, RG-337, File 333.1, NARA. In Army nomenclature G-1 stands for personnel, G-2 intelligence, G-3 operations, and G-4 logistics.

16. Lt. Col. Lloyd D. Brown, Memorandum for General McNair, February 5, 1941, RG-337, File 333.1, NARA.

17. Report of Meeting of the General Council in the Chief of Staff's Office, September 15, 1939. Marshall Papers, Reel 20, Item 7639. George C. Marshall Research Library, Virginia Military Institute, Lexington, Virginia (hereafter referred to as GCMRL).

18. Wiebe, *Search for Order*, 12, 14, 23–24, 53–58, 70, 84, 113, 174, 181–87. Wiebe notes that "[t]he more intricate such fields as the law and the sciences became, the greater the need for men with highly developed skills," and that in such conditions, "big businessmen leaned more and more on expert assistants" (ibid., 174, 181).

19. "Open Forum Discussions." "Resolutions by National Guard Association," *TPG*, November 1939, 21.

20. Edward Martin to George C. Marshall, December 6, 1939. Box 75, Folder 28, GCMRL.

21. George C. Marshall to Major General John F. Williams, June 8, 1940, *MP* 2.

22. Lt. Col. Charles E. Dissinger, "Chronological Report of Actions Taken by the National Guard Bureau," 48–50, RG-168, File 325.452, NDA Sect 127A, NARA (hereafter referred to as "Chronological Report").

23. Marshall, Memorandum for the Chief, National Guard Bureau [Williams], "Exemptions and Relief Measures," August 6, 1940. *MP* 2, 284.

24. Brigadier General Frank M. Andrews, Memorandum for the Chief of Staff, April 1, 1940, RG-168, File 325, 455, NARA.

25. Colonel Eric Fisher Wood, "Pennsylvania National Guard Policy Relative to Organization," in "Open Forum Discussions." A triangular division consisted of three regiments and no brigades, instead of four regiments divided between two brigades in the prewar "square" division. Thus streamlined, the command structure contained one less level. Kenneth Finlayson, *An Uncertain Trumpet: The Evolution of U.S. Army Infantry Doctrine, 1919–1941* (Westport, Conn.: Greenwood, 2001), 127.

26. George C. Marshall to Edward Martin, July 30, 1941. Box 75, Folder 31, GCMRL.

27. Capt. Frederick H. Weston, Memorandum for Lt. Col. M. M. Montgomery, Office of the Chief of the Morale Branch, September 8, 1941, RG-337, File GHQ USA Third Army File, NARA. Regulars had criticized NG and militia favoritism for their own for over a century. Ricardo Adolfo Herrera, "Guarantors of Liberty and the Republic: The American Citizen Soldier and the Military Ethos of Republicanism, 1775–1861" (Ph.D. diss., Marquette University, 1998; UMI Number 9901729), 123. Skeen, *Citizen Soldiers*, 1999, 56.

28. Marshall to Martin, July 30, 1941.

29. Edward Martin to George C. Marshall, September 8, 1941. Box 75, Folder 31, GCMRL.

30. *Philadelphia Inquirer*, May 14, 1940, 1–5. "Hitler May Risk All at Once," "Germans Conquer Holland," ibid., May 15, 1940. *Harrisburg Telegraph*, May 13, 1940, 1.

31. Wayne S. Cole, *Roosevelt and the Isolationists, 1932–45* (Lincoln: University of Nebraska Press, 1983), 367.

32. No. 83, March 19, 1941, *Laws of the General Assembly of the Commonwealth of Pennsylvania* (Harrisburg, 1941), 6–8.

33. *Journal of the House of Representatives, Extraordinary Session of the Commonwealth of Pennsylvania for the Session Begun at Harrisburg on the Sixth Day of May, 1940*, 136–41. "Governor James Formally Calls Special Session," *Allentown Morning Call*, April 30, 1940, 1.

34. "Report of the Joint Legislative Committee on Aerial Defense of Pennsylvania," July 10, 1940, 13–16, 19, 24, 26, RG-7.31, Committee Hearing Transcripts, Slot 14/4621, Carton 14, Folder "July 10, 1940." PSA.

35. Mayor Dick M. Reeser, to Representative Robert G. Allen, May 21, 1940, RG-168, File 325.4, Box 723, Folder 325.4 C. Art'y Penna, NARA. "Ring of 23 Airports Urged for Defense Here," *Pittsburgh Sun Telegraph*, July 14, 1940, 1. "This City's Safety Vital to Defense," editorial, *Philadelphia Inquirer*, July 13, 1940, 6.

36. Mark Skinner Watson, *United States Army in World War II. The War Department, Chief of Staff: Prewar Plans and Preparations* (Washington, D.C.: Historical Division, Department of the Army, 1950), 151. John Richard Smith and Antony L. Kay, *German Aircraft of the Second World War*, with drawings by E. J. Creek (London: Putnam, 1972), 200–207.

37. No. 3, March 19, 1941, *Laws of the General Assembly of the Commonwealth of Pennsylvania* (Harrisburg, 1941), 6–8.

38. U.S. Congress, Senate Committee on Military Affairs, *Compulsory Military Training and Service, Hearings before the Committee on Military Affairs, United States Senate*, 76th Cong. 3rd sess., July 12, 1940, 329–32.

39. "Martin Declares U.S. Should Have 500,000 Well-Trained Troops," *Allentown Morning Call*, April 4, 1940, 1.

40. "Conscription without Strings to It," *Allentown Morning Call*, July 6, 1940, 6.

41. U.S. Congress, Senate, Committee on Military Affairs, *Hearings on Compulsory Military Training and Service*, 76th Cong, 3rd sess., 12 July 1940, 334.

42. J. Garry Clifford and Samuel R. Spencer Jr., *The First Peacetime Draft* (Lawrence: University Press of Kansas, 1986), 105.

43. Senate, *Hearings*, 12 July 1940, 353–54.

44. "'Laziness Perils U.S. Freedom,' Martin Says," *Pittsburgh Sun Telegraph*, July 26, 1940, 5. "Local Units May Be Affected by Orders," *Canonsburg Daily Notes*, July 13, 1940, Scrapbook No. 23, Papers of Edward Martin, MG-156, Scrapbooks, 1894–1963, Box 5, PSA.

45. Senate, *Hearings*, 12 July 1940, 350.

46. Ibid., 59, 334.

47. "'We'll be Goats,' Say Guardsmen Here of Mobilization Call," *Pittsburgh Sun-Telegraph*, July 14, 1940, 1.

48. Major General Roy D. Keehn to General George C. Marshall, July 12, 1940. Pentagon Office 1938–51 Correspondence, Selected, Box 72, Folder 23, GCMRL. "National Guard Demoralization Feared in Row," *International News Service*, May 6, 1941, Martin Scrapbook 23.

49. Lieutenant H. R. Graham to Franklin D. Roosevelt, June 22, 1940, RG-407, File 353, NARA. U.S. Congress, House, Extension of Remarks of Representative Ben F. Johnson of

Iowa, "Letter from an Officer in the National Guard of Iowa," 76th Cong. 3rd sess., *Congressional Record* (12 June 1940), vol. 86, appendix pt. 16, 3795. Roosevelt declared a national emergency on May 27, 1941. Justus D. Doenecke, *Storm on the Horizon: The Challenge to American Intervention, 1939–1941* (Lanham, Md.: Rowman and Littlefield, 2000), 188.

50. "National Guard Lacks Answer to Future Service," *Easton* [Pennsylvania] *Express,* July 30, 1940, Martin Scrapbook 23.

51. "P.N.G. Set for Duty, Gen. Martin Says," *Philadelphia Inquirer,* July 13, 1940, 3.

52. "'Just Plain Talk,' by Willie Live," *TPG,* August 1940, 19.

53. Colonel Eric Fisher Wood, C.O. 107th Field Artillery, "Let's Get Together," *TPG,* October 1940, 26. There were nine "corps areas" in the United States. They "were administrative organizations that focused almost solely on mobilization." William O. Odom, *After the Trenches: The Transformation of U.S. Army Doctrine, 1918–1939* (College Station: Texas A&M University Press, 1999), 113–14. According to an in-depth study of military mobilization, "the corps area commanders . . . were responsible for preparing plans for the defense of their areas, and . . . their primary mission was the organization, administration, training, and mobilization of troops." Kreidberg and Henry, *Military Mobilization,* 395.

54. "Conscription without Strings to It," *Allentown Morning Call,* July 6, 1940, 6.

55. Sixty-sixth Congress, 2nd sess., *Statutes at Large,* 41, sec. 49, 784 (1920). Lt. Col. F. W. Boye, to the Adjutant General, September 27, 1940, RG-168, File 325.452, NARA.

56. Skeen, *Citizen Soldiers,* 11, 12, 39, 68; Winders, *Mr. Polk's Army,* 200, 252; Doubler, *Civilian in Peace,* 101.

57. Robert Bruce Sligh, *The National Guard and National Defense: The Mobilization of the Guard in World War II,* with a foreword by Roger Beaumont (New York: Praeger, 1992), 83.

58. Conference in General Marshall's Office, October 15, 1941. GMM-Chief of Staff—Conferences, Verifax 100 Folder, GCMRL.

59. Adjutant General's Office to Commanding Generals, September 6, 1940, RG-168, File 325.452, NARA.

60. "Army Determined to Place No Square Pegs in Round Holes," *TPG,* December 1940, 15.

61. William W. Dick, Adj. Gen. Office, to CNGB, November 2, 1940, Officers of the National Guard Ordered to Active Duty as Individuals, RG-168, Box 343, NARA.

62. Brigadier General Harry L. Twaddle, Memo for the Chief of Staff, "Preservation of Identity of National Guard Units While in Active Federal Service," October 7, 1941, 16810-346, RG-165, Entry 12, NARA.

63. Major General John F. Williams to Adjutant Generals of All States, "Enlistments and Reenlistments in National Guard Units in Active Service," November 1, 1941, RG-168, File 325.452, NARA. MG Lesley J. McNair to LTG Hugh A. Drum, April 4, 1941, RG-337, File 333.1, NARA.

64. Colonel S. G. Brown, Memorandum for the Public Relations Branch, Deputy Chief of Staff: "Status of National Guard Units Called into the Service of the United States . . . ," November 12, 1940, RG-168, File 325.452, NARA.

65. Lt. Col. F. W. Boye to the Adjutant General, September 27, 1940, ibid.

66. "Army Passes One Million Mark," *TPG,* March 22, 1941, 8. *TPG,* June 21, 1941, 1.

67. Major General Emory S. Adams, to Commanding Generals All Armies, June 5, 1941, "Officer Strength for NG," RG-168, File 325.452, NARA.

68. War Department, War Department Circular No. 191 (September 12, 1941). BG Wade H. Haislip, Memo for the Chief of Staff, "Reclassification of Officers," June 9, 1941. Reel 276, Item 430, GCMRL.

69. "National Guard Association in Three-Day Business Session," *TPG*, December 1940, 7–8. "Digest of Resolutions Adopted at the Annual Convention of the N.G. Assn. of the U.S. in Washington, D.C.," ibid., 11–12.

70. Major General John F. Williams to Commanding Generals . . . and All State Adjutants General, May 15, 1940, RG-168, File 325.452, NARA. "What Do You Know About Mobilization? Questions Based on New Army Regulation 130–10," *TPG*, June 1940, 9.

71. Franklin Delano Roosevelt, *The Public Paper and Addresses of Franklin Delano Roosevelt* with a special introduction and explanatory notes by President Roosevelt, 1940 vol.: *War—and Aid to Democracies* (New York: Macmillan, 1941), 252.

72. George C. Marshall to Representative Walter G. Andrews, May 16, 1940, *MP 2*, 216. BG George V. Strong, Memorandum for the Chief of Staff, "Premobilization Objective for the Regular Army," June 13, 1940, RG-165, War Plans Division General Correspondence, 1920–42, Box 143, Folder 3674-28 to 2674-42, NARA.

73. *MP 2*, 232. Watson, *Prewar Plans*, 211.

74. Sligh, *The National Guard and National Defense*, 76–79, 96.

75. Major V. A. Winton, to the Adjutant General of Pennsylvania, June 16, 1940, RG-168, File 325.4, NARA.

76. Major Lloyd D. Brown, Measures Toward a Possible Induction of the National Guard, June 18, 1940, RG-168, File 342.452, NARA.

77. "Chronological Report," 63.

78. "News of the 107th Field Artillery," *TPG*, November 1940, 28.

79. U.S. War Department, *Annual Report, 1941*, 18. "U.S. to Permit Married Men to Quit Guard," *Pittsburgh Sun Telegraph*, July 15, 1940, 8. Seventy-sixth Congress, 3rd sess., *Statutes at Large*, 54, ch. 689, sec. 3, 860 (1940).

80. Major General Emory S. Adams, to Commanding Generals, All Corps Areas and Departments, October 1, 1940, RG-168, File 325.452, NARA.

81. Colonel Charles A. Curtis, "Induction of the 213th Coast Artillery," *TPG*, November 1940, 10–11.

82. "112th Infantry," *TPG*, December 1940, 28. "Today's Selectee Is Much Bigger, Healthier Than His 1917 Buddy," *TPG*, February 1941, 27.

83. Watson, *Prewar Plans*, 191.

84. Brigadier General Frank N. Andrews, Memorandum for the Chief of Staff, July 22, 1940, RG-165, File OCS 16810–126, NARA. "Chronological Report," 60, 62.

85. Clifford and Spencer, *The First Peacetime Draft*, 171, 179, 194–96, 221, 223. Roosevelt, *War—and Aid to Democracies*, 314–15.

86. Roosevelt, *War—and Aid to Democracies*, 357.

87. Robert Dallek, *Franklin D. Roosevelt and American Foreign Policy, 1932–1945*, with a new afterword (New York: Oxford University Press, 1995), 70–71. Cole, *Roosevelt*, 298. Doenecke, *Storm on the Horizon*, 185.

88. "Old Grey Mare of the 109th Infantry," *TPG*, March 1941, 27.

89. "First Selectee for 28th Division," *TPG*, April 12, 1941, 1. "Troops from Indiantown Take Part in Induction of Selective Service Trainees," *TPG*, March 22, 1941, 1. "Cavalry Selectees Interested and Interesting," *TPG*, June 28, 1941, 7.

90. "Selectees this Month," *TPG*, June 7, 1941, 1. "Trained Replacements for 28th Division," *TPG*, March 29, 1941, 1. "Replacements Arriving Daily," *TPG*, July 12, 1941, 1. "112th Infantry," *TPG*, July 12, 1941, 6. "109th Infantry," *TPG*, August 9, 1941, 4. "109th FA," *TPG*, July 19, 1941, 7. Illustrative of the country's changed attitude, troops of the Second Rhode Island Cavalry bristled at General Benjamin Butler's order in 1863 to merge with the First Louisiana Cavalry (U.S.). Rhode Island Governor James Y. Smith complained that his soldiers would "lose all their identity with their native state." Richard Nelson Current, *Lincoln's Loyalists: Union Soldiers from the Confederacy* (New York: Oxford University Press, 1992), 149–50.

91. Lieutenant General Henry K. Fluck, interview by Dr. James W. Williams, 1989, Project 1989-S, Senior Officer Oral History Program, transcript, 27–28, U.S. Army War College/U.S. Army Military History Institute, Carlisle Barracks, Pa. (hereafter referred to as MHI).

92. "109th Infantry," *TPG*, July 26, 1941, 4.

93. "103rd Quartermaster Regiment," *TPG*, July 12, 1941, 5.

94. Marshall to Edward Martin, September 4, 1941, Slot 0830, Box 3, Martin Papers, PSA.

95. *MP 2*, 483.

96. The Chief of Staff, Memorandum for the Secretary of War, February 14, 1941, RG-107, Entry 100, NARA. Reports from several schools attached to the memo documented the high prestige of ROTC on several campuses.

97. Undersecretary of War, July 5, 1941, Memorandum for the Secretary of War: "Officers' Training Camps for Enlisted Men," RG-107, Entry 143, NARA.

98. Colonel Howard R. Smalley, Final Report of Officer in Charge of National Guard Affairs, III Corps Phase First Army Maneuvers, vol. 1, sec. 2, pt. 17, 2, U.S. Army Military History Institute, Carlisle Barracks, Pa.

99. First Lieutenant Le Roy V. Greene, "We're in the Same Army: Reserve Officers Comment on Training with Pennsylvania National Guard," *TPG*, January 1940, 9.

100. "The Chief Reports," *Time*, July 14, 1941, 34.

101. Marshall to Martin, May 17, 1941, Box 75, Folder 31, GCMRL.

102. Martin to Marshall, May 19, 1941, Box 75, Folder 31, GCMRL. Morale seemed to be good within the PNG, but that is not easy to assess because of Martin's aversion to bad news. His actions and statements suggest that he took measures to keep morale high because he was more aware of the threats to morale than were many of his fellow generals.

103. Marshall, Memorandum for the Secretary of War, June 20, 1941, RG-165, File OCS 16810-293, NARA.

104. "Fort Dix Units Attack Proposal to Extend Service Beyond Year," *New York Times*, July 18, 1941, 1, 11 (hereafter referred to as *NYT*). Senator Wheeler was a prominent isolationist and was FDR's staunchest critic on foreign policy in the Senate. Cole, *Isolationists*, 468.

105. Major General Emory S. Adams, to Chief of Staff, GHQ, Commanding Generals of All Armies . . . , November 24, 1941, RG-168, File 325.452, NARA.

106. "Roosevelt to Ask Service Extension," *NYT*, July 19, 1941, 28.

107. Memorandum for Lt. Col. Montgomery.

108. Elbridge Colby, *The National Guard of the United States: A Half Century of Progress* (Manhattan: Kansas State University Press, 1977), X 12. (The page numbering of this book is nonstandard.) This source does not state which division cheered.

109. Theodore A. Huntley, "Penna. Guard Scheduled to Serve for Duration," *Pittsburgh Sun-Telegraph*, June 24, 1941, Martin Scrapbook 1941–42, Slot GM 0934, MG-156, Box 5, PSA.

110. Martin to Marshall, September 8, 1941.

111. Stephen D. Wesbrook, "The Railey Report and Army Morale, 1941: Anatomy of a Crisis," *Military Review* 60, no. 6 (June 1980): 19–20. Sulzberger sent a copy straight to President Roosevelt, ibid. Lee Kennett, *GI: The American Soldier in World War II* (New York: Charles Scribner's Sons, 1987), 69.

112. Robert Patterson, Undersecretary of War, Memorandum, July 17, 1941, RG-107, File 322.15-334, NARA.

113. *MP 2*, 565.

114. Roosevelt, *The Call to Battle Stations*, 276.

115. Doenecke, *Storm on the Horizon*, 231.

116. U.S. War Department, *Annual Report of the Chief of the National Guard Bureau, 1942* (Washington, D.C.: War Department, 1941), 15. This was Public Law 213, 77th Congress, "Service Extension Act of 1941." Weigley, *History*, 434. Doenecke, *Storm on the Horizon*, 235.

117. Frederick R. Barkley, "Vote Is 203 to 202: Speaker Declares Army Bill Adopted after Recapitulation," *NYT*, August 13, 1941, 1.

118. Roosevelt, *The Call to Battle Stations*, 277. *MP 2*, 629. "The Draft: Lift for Morale," *Time*, September 1, 1941, 30. Exempted from the extension were "those past 28 years old, those whose dependents would suffer unduly and those who could be spared": "President Extends Army Service to 18 Months of Amended Law," *NYT*, 6.

3. Readiness and Training

1. Maurice Matloff and Edwin M. Snell, *United States Army in World War II. The War Department: Strategic Planning for Coalition Warfare, 1941–1942* (Washington, D.C.: Center of Military History, United States Army, 1990), 5. U.S. War Department, *Mobilization Regulations No. 1–5 (October 1, 1940) Procurement and Reception of Volunteers during Mobilization* (Washington, D.C.: War Department, 1940), 1. "National Guard Troops Available for M-Day," *TPG*, July 1939, 34–35.

2. Brigadier General Edward Martin to the Commanding General, Third Corps Area, January 27, 1939, RG-168, File 325.4 State Staff, NARA.

3. Kreidberg and Henry, *Military Mobilization*, 484–88.

4. Major General Emory S. Adams, Adjutant General to Commanding Generals of the Four Armies . . . December 28, 1938, War Department Training Directive for 1939–40, RG-168, File 353, NARA.

5. Brigadier General George V. Strong, September 20, 1939, Memorandum for the Chief of Staff, RG-165, File 3674-20, NARA. The authorized peacetime strength for an infantry division was 8,953 officers and men. "Chart 1: Infantry Division (Peace)," MG-156, Slot GM0934, Box 1, PSA.

6. U.S. War Department, *Annual Report of the Chief of the National Guard Bureau 1939*, by Major General Albert J. Blanding, 1, 28. (Washington, D.C.: National Guard Bureau, June 30, 1939).

7. U.S. Congress, Senate, Committee on Military Affairs, *National Defense: Hearing before the Committee on Military Affairs, Statement of General Marshall*, 76th Cong., 2nd sess., February 21, 1939, 287.

8. George C. Marshall, Letter to Lieutenant General Hugh A. Drum, April 26, 1941, *MP 2*, 486.

9. RG-19.124, Records of Pa Guardsmen Mustered into World War II, 1940–41, PSA.

10. Final Report of Ordnance Activities First Army Maneuvers (Plattsburg Area), to Commanding General, First Army, September 11, 1939, RG-338, File HQ First U.S. Army, Reports of Maneuvers and C.P. Exercises, NARA.

11. "Drum Reveals Arms Shortage in War Games," *Harrisburg Telegraph*, August 16, 1939, 16.

12. U.S. Congress, House, Subcommittee of the Committee on Appropriations, *Military Establishment Appropriations Bill for 1941: Hearing before the Subcommittee of the Committee on Appropriations*, 76th Cong., 3rd sess., March 13, 1940, 702. Ibid., February 23, 1940, 20.

13. Major General Nicholas P. Kafkalas, interview by Lt. Col. John F. Harkins, 1982, Project 82-B, transcript, Senior Officer Oral History Program, MHI.

14. Lieutenant Henry C. Smith, 104th Cavalry, "With the Black Army," *TPG*, September 1939, 17. (No author), *TPG*, January, 1939, 6.

15. Constance McLaughlin Green, Harry C. Thomson, Peter C. Roots, *United States Army in World War II, The Technical Services. The Ordnance Department: Planning Munitions for War* (Washington, D.C.: Office of the Chief of Military History, Department of the Army, 1955), 41, 47, 53, 55–58.

16. Harry C. Thomson and Lida Mayo, *United States Army in World War II, The Technical Services. The Ordnance Department: Procurement and Supply* (Washington, D.C.: Office of the Chief of Military History, Department of the Army, 1960), 161–62.

17. Green, Thomson, and Roots, *Ordnance Department*, 177.

18. Thomson and Mayo, *Procurement and Supply*, 163–67.

19. Green, Thomson, and Roots, *Ordnance Department*, 178, 182–88.

20. Marion N. Fisher, Major, CAC-Va.-NG to Chief, Militia Bureau, Washington, D.C., January 25, 1924, RG-168, File 330.1, NARA. Kreidberg and Henry, *Military Mobilization*, 569.

21. Capt. Louis B. Ely, Report of Special Inspection for Federal Recognition, June 13, 1939, Headquarters Battalion, 2nd Battalion, 166th Field Artillery. Major George P. Seneff, to Chief of the National Guard Bureau, July 22, 1940, RG-168, File 325.4, NARA. WDGS, Memorandum for the Adjutant General, April 28, 1939, "Special Subjects . . . in General Inspections Made during Fiscal Year 1939," RG-407, File 333.1 Archives I, Washington, D.C., NARA. MS 78092, West Chester Organizations, National Guard Company I, "Headquarters 111th Infantry Memos," Chester County Historical Society, West Chester, Pennsylvania.

22. "Open Forum Discussions." "Guard Advised Able Defense in U.S. Need," *Harrisburg Telegraph*, October 14, 1939, 13.

23. David E. Johnson, *Fast Tanks and Heavy Bombers: Innovation in the U.S. Army, 1917–1945* (Ithaca, N.Y.: Cornell University Press, 1998), 112–15.

24. "The Inspector Says," *TPG*, January 1939, 20. Capt. Nathaniel Nathanson, "The Rampant Lion," *TPG*, March 1939, 22. "The Inspector Says," ibid., 23. "Activities: 103d Quartermaster Regiment," ibid., 24–25. Cartoon, *TPG*, December 1939, 22. Cartoon, *TPG*, May 1939, 7.

25. "Secretary of War Proposed Rigid Physical Examination of Officers," *TPG*, June 1939, 8. "Guard to Meet New U.S. Ruling," *Harrisburg Telegraph*, May 23, 1939, 1.

26. "The Pill Box, 103d Medical Regiment," *TPG*, March 1940, 24.

27. "Recoils from the 176th Field Artillery, *TPG*, April 1939, 26–27. Capt. Nathaniel Nathanson, "The Rampant Lion," *TPG*, December 1939, 26–27. "Tanbark Topics, 107th F.A. by Hardleigh Wright," *TPG*, January 1939, 27.

28. "Trigger Squeezes: 110th Infantry," *TPG*, February 1939, 30.

29. "The Passing Gates of the 103rd Cavalry," *TPG*, February 1939, 36. Equestrianism had seen a revival in the Army at large during the interwar period. Johnson, *Fast Tanks*, 125.

30. First Sergeant George G. Ley, "103d Engineers Punch Press, *TPG*, June 1939, 25. Roland Vermont, "Soldier's Soliloquy," *TPG*, March 1940, 29.

31. Hill, *Minute Man*, 398. Fully equating local National Guard units with fraternal organizations is a stretch. The PNG, for one, had too much turnover in its membership, identity formation was not the NG's primary mission, and ultimately the state and federal governments had "proprietorship" over the members. Mary Ann Clawson, *Constructing Brotherhood: Class, Gender, and Fraternalism* (Princeton, N.J.: Princeton University Press, 1989), 243–44.

32. Clawson, *Constructing Brotherhood*, 15, 101, 177, 264. Vincent Paul McNally Jr., "A Most Dangerous and Noble Calling: The Development, Organization, and Operation of the American Volunteer Fire Service," 2 vols. (Ph.D. diss., Temple University, 1979; UMI Order Number AAT7924008), 438–519.

33. David L. Porter, *The Seventy-Sixth Congress and World War II* (Columbia: University of Missouri Press, 1979), 55–58.

34. "Old Grey Mare of the 109th Infantry," *TPG*, June 1940, 24.

35. Ibid., 23.

36. Seventy-sixth Congress, 3rd sess. *Military Establishment Appropriations Act, Statutes at Large*, 54, sec. 343, (1940), 371. "Chronological Report," 40.

37. Herbert E. Smith, "Parrish of the Alabam's," *TPG*, November 1939, 6.

38. "Are N.G. Shock Troops?" *Army and Navy Register*, June 3, 1939, 6.

39. Clarence P. Childers, *Training Schedule for the Rifle Company, National Guard* (Colorado National Guard, 1929), 2, MHI.

40. *Statutes at Large* 41, sess. 2, Ch. 227, 784 (1919–21).

41. Major General Albert J. Blanding to Commanding General __ Corps Area, January 15, 1938, RG-168, File 353-gen 107, NARA.

42. Commanding General 29th Division, *Final Report, III Corps Phase First Army Maneuvers, Manassas, Virginia, August 5–19, 1939* (Carlisle Barracks, Pa.: U.S. Army Military History Institute) (hereafter referred to as Manassas Report).

43. Major General Edward Martin, Final Report, Commanding General 28th Division, First Army Maneuvers, III Corps Phase, August 25, 1939, 1–2. Manassas Report, MHI.

44. Steven L. Ossad and Don R. Marsh, with a foreword by Martin Blumenson, *Major General Maurice Rose: World War II's Greatest Forgotten Commander* (Lanham, Md.: Taylor Trade Pub., 2003), 113.

45. "National Guard Instructors," *Army and Navy Register*, April 13, 1940, 6. Memorandum for the Assistant Chief of Staff, G-3 from the Chief of Staff, September 26, 1939, *MP 2*, 65. The Command and General Staff School provided important military education for mid-career officers of the rank of major. It taught advanced war fighting and operational planning. Timothy K. Nenninger, "Leavenworth and Its Critics: The U.S. Army Command and General Staff School, 1920–1940," *Journal of Military History* 58, no. 2 (April 1994): 199–232.

46. "The Senior Instructor's Column," *TPG*, February 1939, 25.

47. George C. Marshall, Memorandum for Colonel [Omar N.] Bradley, March 30, 1940, *MP 2*, 182. George C. Marshall to Brigadier General Lesley McNair, April 9, 1940. ibid., 191.

48. Major General Edward Martin, Final Report, Commanding General 28th Division, First Army Maneuvers, III Corps Phase, August 25, 1939, 4, MHI.

49. George C. Marshall to Brigadier General Charles H. Cole, September 26, 1939, *MP 2*, 67.

50. *War Department Bulletin No. 18,* September 12, 1939, Executive Order No. 8244, "Increase in the Strength of the Army." Watson, *Prewar Plans,* 158.

51. Memorandum for the Secretary of War, September 7, 1939, *MP 2,* 52–53.

52. Colonel Robert Morris, Chief of Staff, 28th Division, "Pennsylvania's Winter Field Training," *TPG,* January 1940, 6.

53. "New Inspection Plan for P.N.G.," *TPG,* November 1939, 17.

54. "111th Infantry Invades New Jersey," *TPG,* January 1940, 10.

55. "Field Training Schedule," "Baby Regiment First to Winter Camp," *TPG,* December 1939, 10–11.

56. "109th Reports from Tobyahanna," *TPG,* December 1939, 11.

57. "112th Infantry," *TPG,* January 1940, 22–23.

58. "Altoona Infantry Units Profit by Field Exercise at Juniata Gap," *TPG,* January 1940, 14–15. "103d Cavalry Trains at Clearfield," ibid., 16–17. "The Pill Box, 103d Medical Regiment," ibid., 34. "New Type Training for Commanders and Staffs at Winter Training," ibid., 20–21, 35–36. "Trigger Squeezes 110th Infantry," ibid., 32.

59. "112th Infantry," *TPG,* January 1940, 23.

60. Morris, "Winter Field Training," 7, 35. "Duds from the 109th Field Artillery," *TPG,* January 1940, 23.

61. Major General Roy D. Keehn to Marshall, November 20, 1939, telegram. Papers of George C. Marshall, Pentagon Office 1938–52 Correspondence, Selected, Box 72, Folder 20, GCMRL. Memorandum from G-3 to General Keehn, December 7, 1939, "Reasons for Increased Effectiveness," RG-407, File 353, NARA.

62. Colonel Charles Haffner to George C. Marshall, December 7, 1939, RG-407, File 353, NARA.

63. U.S. Congress, Senate, Appropriations Committee, *Emergency Supplemental Appropriation Bill for 1940, Hearing before a Subcommittee of the Senate Committee on Appropriations,* 76th Congress, 3rd sess., November 27, 1939, 52. Ibid., November 30, 1939, 140. Sligh, *The National Guard and National Defense,* 51. Memorandum from G-3 to General Keehn.

64. "Extra Training Nearly Over for Guardsmen," *Allentown Morning Call,* January 5, 1940, 18.

65. "The Commanding General's Message," *TPG,* December 1939, 2. "Baby Regiment," ibid., 11.

66. War Department General Staff, G-3, Memorandum for the Chief of Staff, January 11, 1940, RG-407, File 353, NARA.

67. "The Commanding General's Message," *TPG,* February 1940, 8. "Indiantown Gap Terrain Exercise for Headquarters Units," *TPG,* May 1940, 19. The 22nd Cavalry Division was a short-lived formation that consisted mainly of PNG units, namely the 103rd and 104th Cavalry Regiments, and the 166th Field Artillery Battalion. Edward Martin, Commonwealth of Pennsylvania, Department of Military Affairs, General Orders No. 6, April 20, 1939, RG-19.116, Slot 14-0254, Box 1, PSA. There were still high-ranking advocates who insisted that horse cavalry had a place on the mid-twentieth-century battlefield. The chief of cavalry in 1938 was a major general, John K. Herr. He believed "that the cavalry should constitute 15 to 25 percent of the active Army." Johnson, *Fast Tanks,* 136–37.

68. "Commanding General Presents Important Facts at Training Conference," *TPG,* May 1940, 3–4.

69. William R. Keast, "Service Schools of the Army Ground Forces," in Robert R. Palmer, Bell I. Wiley, and William R. Keast, *United States Army in World War II. The Army Ground*

Forces: The Procurement and Training of Ground Combat Troops (Washington, D.C.: Historical Division, Department of the Army, 1948), 260–61.

70. "Staff Schools for NG Officers," *TPG,* January 1940, 3. "Pennsylvania Guardsmen to Service Schools," *TPG,* February 1940, 23. Each Army branch—infantry, artillery, signal, etc.—had a service school for advanced training.

71. U.S. War Department, *Annual Report, 1939,* 12, 26, 27.

72. "General Martin Throws Spotlight on Department on Department of Military Affairs," *TPG,* March 1939, 10."

73. Kent Roberts Greenfield and Robert R. Palmer, "Origins of the Army Ground Forces: General Headquarters United States Army, 1940–42," in Kent Roberts Greenfield, Robert R. Palmer, and Bell I. Wiley, *United States Army in World War II. The Army Ground Forces: The Organization of Ground Combat Troops* (Washington, D.C.: Historical Division, Department of the Army, 1947), 11.

74. "Chronological Report," 35–37. U.S. War Department (Albert J. Blanding), *Annual Report of the Chief of the National Guard Bureau, 1940* (Washington, D.C.: War Department, June 30, 1940), 15.

75. George C. Marshall, Memorandum for Colonel Bradley, March 30, 1940, *MP 2,* 181–83. MG Emory S. Adams, "War Department Training Directive," March 2, 1940, RG-168, File 353, NARA.

76. U.S. War Department, *Annual Report, 1939,* 27. Lt. Col. E. C. Hanford, National Guard Bureau, Memorandum for the Chief, November 1, 1938, RG-168, File 325.52, NARA.

77. "Announcement of Army Extension courses, 1939–40," RG-168, File 325.52, NARA. Men in the Reserve Officers Corps had received training and commissions through ROTC during their undergraduate educations.

78. "General Martin Throws Spotlight."

79. Colonel B. M. Bailey, National Guard Bureau to Major E. R. Block, Field Artillery, December 19, 1939, RG-168, File 325.54, NARA.

80. Major General Emory S. Adams, "Instructions for Corps Area and Department Extension Schools," June 27, 1939, RG-168, File 325.52, NARA.

81. U.S. War Department, *Annual Report, 1940,* 26.

82. Major General Emory S. Adams, "Attending Command and General Staff Course," April 26, 1939, RG-168, File 325.52, NARA.

83. Marshall to Brigadier General Lesley J. McNair, August 16, 1939, *MP 2,* 36–37.

84. Hanford, November 1, 1938. U.S. War Department, *Annual Report, 1939,* 8–9. Weigley, *History,* 401–402. Mahon, *History of the Militia,* 174. U.S. War Department, *Annual Report, 1940,* 10–11. War Department, *Army Regulations No. 130–15, National Guard, National Guard of the United States, (November 1, 1934)* (Washington, D.C.: War Department, 1934), 5–6.

85. War Department, *Army Regulations No. 130–15, National Guard: National Guard of the United States Changes No. 2 (September 2, 1939)* (Washington, D.C.: War Department, 1939), 2.

86. RG-19.124, Slot 14-2162, Carton 6, Folder 8, PSA.

87. Brigadier General Harry L. Twaddle, Memorandum for the Chief of Staff, "Training of Junior Officers of the National Guard at Replacement Training Centers," October 6, 1941, RG-165, Entry 12, OCS 16810-344, NARA.

88. RG-19.124, PSA.

89. "Data Covering Induction of National Guard Officers" in Major General John F. Williams to Major General Edward J. Stackpole Jr., November 19, 1940, RG-168, File 325.452, NARA.

90. Major J. H. Dailey, to Adjutant General of Pennsylvania, State Recognition, 22nd Cavalry Division, November 21, 1939, RG-19, Slot 14-255, Box 2, PSA.

91. Major General Emory S. Adams, "Measures Toward a Possible Induction of the National Guard," June 7, 1940, RG-168, File 425.452, NARA.

92. War Department, *Bulletin No. 1, Act of Congress—Emergency Supplemental Appropriation Act, 1940* (Washington, D.C.: March 14, 1940), 5. *Military Establishment Appropriations Bill 1941, Statutes at Large,* 54 part 1, ch. 343, 371 (1940).

93. U.S. War Department, *Annual Report, 1940,* 25.

94. "Chronological Report," 46–47. "Origins of the Army Ground Forces," 36. A division chief of staff had at this time four assistants: G-1 personnel, G-2 intelligence, G-3 operations, G-4 logistics.

95. "Service School Courses Announced," *TPG,* June 1940, 15.

96. Edward Martin to George C. Marshall, December 15, 1940. Edward Martin to George C. Marshall, February 3, 1941. Box 75, Folder 29, GCMRL.

97. *Military Establishment Appropriation Bill for 1941, Hearings,* 23 February 1940, 2, 12–13.

98. U.S. War Department, *Annual Report, 1940,* 14.

99. "Trigger Squeezes 110th Infantry," *TPG,* January 1941, 46. Kafkalas interview.

100. "News of the 107th Field Artillery," 50. Colonel Charles A. Curtis, "Induction of the 213th Coast Artillery," *TPG,* November 1940, 10–11.

101. "Chronological Report," 108–14.

102. "Commanding General's Message," *TPG,* January 1941, 7. "Generals Martin and Aiken Home," *Washington Observer,* December 26, 1940, Martin Scrapbook No. 24, Slot GM 0934, Box 5, Martin Papers, PSA. Stackpole was also the *Harrisburg Telegraph*'s editor. One might expect that he would have used the newspaper as a bully pulpit for the interests of the PNG, but only one editorial on NG policy appeared between January 1939 and May 1940—"Aid National Defense" on November 10, 1939, 8. The newspaper gave the PNG only occasional passing attention. Most of the editorials addressed international politics and repeatedly tore apart Nazism and German policy.

103. "75 Guard Officers Going to School," *Philadelphia Evening Bulletin,* January 21, 1941, Martin Scrapbook 24.

104. "Officer's Course at Valley Forge," *TPG,* February 1941, 15. "The Commanding General's Message," ibid., 7. "112th Infantry," *TPG,* March 1941, 30. Marshall to Martin, February 13, 1941; Martin to Marshall, February 27, 1941; Colonel Harry L. Twaddle, G-3, WDGS Memo for the Chief of Staff, March 29, 1941, Box 75, Folder 30, GCMRL.

105. Adams, December 28, 1938.

106. Bell I. Wiley, "The Building and Training of Infantry Divisions," in Palmer, Wiley, and Keast, *The Procurement and Training of Ground Combat Troops,* 442.

107. Major General Lesley J. McNair to Major General Edward Martin, January 23, 1941, RG-337, File 333.1, NARA. Memo for General McNair, February 5, 1941, Subject: Visit to 28th Division, ibid.

108. Major Thomas E. Lewis, Memo for the Chief of Staff, GHQ, February 5, 1941, ibid.

109. Major General Lesley J. McNair to MG Henry C. Pratt, HQ II Corps, February 6, 1941, ibid.

110. Lt. Col. Jerry V. Matejka, Memorandum for the Chief of Staff, GHQ, February 5, 1941; Visit to the 28th Division HQ, February 4, 1941, RG-337, File 333.1, NARA.

111. Major J. C. Christiansen, Memorandum for the Chief of Staff, GHQ, February 4, 1941, ibid., Folder 28th Division 333.1.

112. McNair to Pratt, February 6, 1941. Marshall to Westbrook Peglar, March 22, 1941, *MP 2*, 451.

113. "General Martin Takes Press on Tour of Camp," *Lebanon Daily News*, February 22, 1941, Martin Scrapbook 24.

114. Greenfield and Palmer, "Origins of the Army Ground Forces," 36.

115. "Training Program Gets Good Start," *TPG*, March 15, 1941, 3. "111th Infantry," *TPG*, March 22, 1941, 5. "107th Field Artillery," *TPG*, March 29, 1941, 4. "Sick in Hospital," *TPG*, April 5, 1941, 4. Warrant Officer John E. McDonald, *109th Infantry Regiment, Regimental History, 28th Division*, MHI.

116. Robert P. Patterson to W. Sterling Cole, May 7, 1941, RG-107, Box 55, Folder 327.5, "Drafted Men," NARA. Marshall, Memorandum for General Richardson, May 19, 1941, *MP 2*, 516.

117. Brigadier General Francis B. Wilby, Headquarters First Army, Training Memorandum No. 1, January 11, 1941, RG-338, File Beginning 1st Army Man. Area through Training Memoranda, 1st Army, NARA.

118. "111th Infantry," *TPG*, April 26, 1941, 6. "Evacuation of Casualties Demonstration by Medicos Wins Praise of Observers," ibid., 1. "Demonstrations Prove Quick and Effective Method of Instruction," *TPG*, April 12, 1941, 4.

119. Marshall, Speech at Trinity College, Hartford, Connecticut, June 15, 1941, *MP 2*, 537.

120. Brigadier General Howard McC. Snyder, Memorandum for the Chief of Staff, "Special Inspection at Indiantown Gap Military Reservation, Pennsylvania," March 10, 1941; Lt. Col. Clarkson, IGD, Memorandum to be Filed with Report on 28th Division, March 13, 1941, RG-159, File 333.1, NARA.

121. "General Drum Pleased with Inspection and Progress of Training," *TPG*, April 5, 1941, 1.

122. Lt. Col. Frank A. McKenry, IGD, to Commanding General First Army, through Commanding General 28th Division and Commanding General II Army Corps, June 7, 1941, RG-159, File 333.1, NARA.

123. Kreidberg and Henry, *History of Military Mobilization*, 604–605.

124. Brigadier General Francis B. Wilby, HQ First Army, Training Memorandum No. 15, May 15, 1941, RG-338, File Beginning 1st Army Man. Area through Training Memoranda 1st Army, NARA.

125. "112th Infantry," *TPG*, May 3, 1941, 6. "111th Infantry," *TPG*, May 10, 1941, 6.

126. "Instruction at Chemical Warfare School Interesting as Well as Important," *TPG*, May 3, 1941, 5. "In the Field of Sports," *TPG*, May 24, 1941, 3. "108th Field Artillery Fires Combat Problem Under Simulated Gas Attack," *TPG*, June 28, 1941, 1. One is left questioning the veracity of these claims of walking through clouds of mustard gas because that agent attacks exposed skin.

127. "112th Infantry," *TPG*, May 24, 1941, 6. "56th Infantry Brigade: Headquarters Company," *TPG*, June 7, 1941, 5.

128. "Soldiers Learn to Work in the Dark," *TPG*, May 24, 1941, 7. "112th Infantry," *TPG*, July 12, 1941, 6.

129. "109th Field Artillery," *TPG*, May 30, 1941, 5. "103rd Engineers," *TPG*, June 7, 1941.

130. "Vehicle Loading Demonstration at Lickdale Railhead," *TPG*, June 14, 1941, 1. BG Francis B. Wilby, Headquarters First Army, Training Memorandum No. 12, April 12, 1941, RG-338, NARA.

131. "Infantry Brigade Qualifications," *TPG*, June 14, 1941, 8.

132. "110th Infantry," *TPG*, June 21, 1941, 4. "112th Infantry," *TPG*, June 28, 1941, 5.

133. "Army Injects Realism into Field Training," *TPG*, June 7, 1941, 3.

134. "28th Division Infantry Regiments Receive New Air-Cooled Light Machine Guns," *TPG*, March 15, 1941, 3. "55th Infantry Brigade," *TPG*, March 22, 1941, 4.

135. "Shortages in Equipment in Forthcoming Maneuvers," *TPG*, June 7, 1941, 1. Matloff and Snell, *Strategic Planning, 1941–1942*, 48–49.

136. "Special Troops," *TPG*, August 16, 1941, 4. "Simulated Weapons Have Important Training Function," *TPG*, August 2, 1941, 2.

137. "Antitank Battalion, 28th Division, Ready for Virginia Maneuvers," *TPG*, August 1941, 2. Kafkalas interview, 17.

138. Lieutenant General Charles A. Corcoran, interview by Lt. Col. Joseph A. Langer Jr., February 13, 1975, transcript, Senior Officer Oral History Program, MHI, 12, 15.

139. Ibid., 16.

140. Ibid., 22.

141. "New Training Program Announced," *TPG*, June 21, 1941, 1. Donald St. John, "28th Division Team Training is Postponed," *Wilkes-Barre Record*, June 24, 1941, Martin Scrapbook 1941–42.

142. "To the Commanding General, First Army," Radio, Confidential, June 26, 1941, *MP* 2, 548–49.

143. "111th Infantry," *TPG*, July 12, 1941, 6. Robert Patterson, Undersecretary of War, Memorandum, July 17, 1941, RG-107, File 322.15–334, NARA.

144. "News in Brief," *TPG*, July 26, 1941, 1. "Command Post Exercise for Division and Brigade Headquarters Units," *TPG*, August 2, 1941, 1. "Non-Coms Replace Officers for Division Command Post Exercise," *TPG*, August 9, 1941, 1.

4. Peacetime Maneuvers

1. Odom, *After the Trenches*, 114.

2. Wilson, *Evolution of Divisions*, 94, 95, 110, 111. Other records show 8,953 officers and men. MG-156, Slot GM 0934, Box 1, PSA.

3. "Trigger Squeezes 110th Infantry," *TPG*, July 1939, 74.

4. "112th Infantry," *TPG*, August 1939, 29.

5. Final Report, III Corps Phase First Army Maneuvers, Manassas Report, MHI.

6. "Final Report of the Commanding General, III Corps," Manassas Report, 1–2, MHI. Nationwide, 53,000 NG troops participated. U.S. War Department, *Annual Report, 1940*, 15. "Section IV. Final Report of the Division Commander (Black), Part II, Narrative of Events," Manassas Maneuvers, 3, MHI (hereafter referred to as "Manassas Maneuvers").

7. Vol. 1, sec. 1, pt. 1: Final Report of the Director. Manassas Maneuvers, 1. Sec. 6, pt. 1: Directives for the Maneuver Plan for Supply and Administration. Training sec. 3, "Instruction for Troop Concentration with Umpires," Manassas Maneuvers. Final Report of the Commanding General, III Corps, 2. "Observations of an Umpire," *TPG*, September 1939, 14.

8. "Some Statistics on Pay, Rations, and Transportation," *TPG*, September 1939, 28. "Local Units of Guard Start Virginia Trek," *Harrisburg Telegraph*, 1. "Final Report of the Director," Manassas Maneuvers, 10.

9. "The Third Battle of Bull's Run by Willie Live," *TPG*, September 1939, 5.

10. George C. Marshall to William R. Mathews, August 31, 1939, *MP* 2, 43.

11. "Sec. 2, pt. 2. Final Report of Assistant Chief of Staff, G-2, Enclosure No. 3 List of Visitors; Publicity and Public Relations," Manassas Maneuvers. "Third Battle," 5.

12. "Drum Reveals Arms Shortage in War Games," *Harrisburg Telegraph,* August 6, 1939, 16.

13. "Third Battle," 5.

14. Final Report of the Commanding General, III Corps, 3. Brigadier General Maxwell Murray was the Black Force commander.

15. "Operations Journal, Headquarters 28th Division," *TPG,* September 1939, 3. Capt. Joseph A. Lee, "The Flying Battalion," ibid., 10. Philip Carlton Cockrell, "Brown Shoes and Mortar Board: U.S. Army Officer Professional Education at the Command and General Staff School, Fort Leavenworth, Kansas, 1919–1940" (Ph.D. diss., University of South Carolina, 1991; UMI Order Number DA 9200799), 247–48, 264.

16. Information Bulletin #3, Noon, 14 August 1939. Section IV, Final Report of the Provisional Division Commander (Black), Part II. Narrative of Events. Manassas Maneuvers, 3.

17. Final Report of the Commanding General, III Corps, 3. "Operations Journal 28th Division," 3. "Flying Battalion," 10. "The Cavalry at Manassas," *TPG,* September 1939, 20. Robert Smith, "Notes on the Maneuvers, In *The Manassas Journal* of August 17, 1939," reprinted in ibid., 26.

18. Final Report of the Commanding General, III Corps, 3. "Operations Journal Headquarters 28th Division," 3. "Flying Battalion," 10.

19. "Flying Battalion," 10.

20. Final Report of the Commanding General, III Corps, 3. "Operations Journal Headquarters 28th Division," 3.

21. Colonel S. D. Smith, Chief of Staff, Headquarters III Corps, Field Order No. 2, 14 August 1939, 6:00 PM. "Operations Journal Headquarters 28th Division," 3.

22. Information Bulletin #4, 12 Noon, 15 August 1939. Final Report of the Commanding General, III Corps, 3. Final Report of Provisional Division Commander (Black), 4. "Speed Thrusts Defense in War Games," *Harrisburg Telegraph,* August 15, 1939, 1.

23. Information Bulletin # 5, 12 Noon, 16 August 1939, Manassas Maneuvers.

24. Order to be Telephoned at 5:45 AM 16 August to Commanding Generals 28th and 29th Divisions, in "Operations Journal Headquarters, 28th Division," 3.

25. Colonel S. D. Smith, Field Order No. 3, August 16, 1939, 3:00 PM. Final Report of Provisional Division Commander, 5. Manassas Maneuvers.

26. "With the Black Army," *TPG,* September 1939, 31. Major General Edward Martin, Message 17, 3/45 PM August 16, 1939. Manassas Maneuvers.

27. Final Report of the Commanding General, III Corps, 3–4. "Operations Journal 28th Division," 3. "Drum Reveals Arms Shortage." Assistant Chief of Staff G-3 George W. Phillips, Message #20, Headquarters 28th Division, 7:20 PM, August 16, 1939. Manassas Maneuvers.

28. Message #20.

29. Final Report of the Commanding General, III Corps, 4. "Operations Journal 28th Division," 3.

30. "The Flying Battalion," 12.

31. General Orders No. 5, August 18, 1939, reprinted in *TPG,* September 1939, 23.

32. Final Report 28th Division, 2–7. "Operations Journal."

33. Odom, *After the Trenches,* 134. This is surprising, since in 1937 the Army Command and General Staff School looked forward to a fully mechanized division with the ability to penetrate deeply behind enemy lines. Cockrell, "Professional Education," 264.

34. Final Report of the Commanding General 29th Division, sec. IV. Final Report Manassas Maneuvers.

35. "The Flying Battalion," 12

36. "Old Grey Mare of the 109th Infantry," *TPG*, October 1939, 29.

37. Colonel Howard R. Smalley, Final Report of the Officer in Charge of National Guard Affairs, vol. 1, sec. 2, pt. 17, 2. Manassas Maneuvers. Final Report of the Commanding General, III Corps, 2. "Third Battle," 5.

38. "Third Battle," 4–6.

39. Final Report, 28th Division, 6.

40. "The Cavalry at Manassas," *TPG*, September 1939, 20.

41. James F. Danser, "Maneuver Mirthmakers," *TPG*, November 1939, 15.

42. Final Report III Corps Phase, First Army Maneuvers, sec. 5, pt. 3, Final Report of the Senior Umpire, Black, 3–4.

43. "Marshall Finds Troops Require Field Training," *Harrisburg Telegraph*, August 10, 1939, 1.

44. War Department letter December 26, 1939, cited in RG-338, Records of U.S. Army Commands, Entry 1st Army, Box 7, First Army Maneuvers 1940, Final Report, February 15, 1941 (hereafter referred to as "1940 Final Report"). MG Emory S. Adams, War Department Training Directive, 1940–41, March 2, 1940, RG-168, File 353, NARA. "The Commanding General's Message," *TPG*, June 1940, 4.

45. "Training Orders No. 1, HQ 28th Division, May 9, 1940," *TPG*, June 1940, 7.

46. HQ, Director First Army Maneuvers, February 14, 1940, First Army Maneuvers Preliminary Plans, to the Commanding General Second Corps Area. Station List No. 20, August 21, 1940, RG-338, Entry 1st Army, Box 7.

47. First Army Maneuvers: Opening Conference by Lieutenant General Hugh A. Drum, August 7, 1940. 1940 Final Report, 2–4.

48. Remarks by Brigadier General Irving J. Phillipson, at the Critique, Canton, N.Y., August 22, 1940. 1940 Final Report.

49. Opening Conference, 3–4.

50. Final Report, 2. Opening Conference by Lieutenant General Hugh A. Drum, August 7, 1940. 1940 Maneuvers, Final Report, 5. Section I "General" November 4, 1940, 1940 Final Report, 4.

51. Guy V. Miller, "107th Field Artillery Makes Fine Record," *TPG*, October 1940, 27. "108th Artillery Tries Nazi System," *Philadelphia Inquirer*, August 4, 1940, 3.

52. Henry A. Reninger and Le Roy V. Greene, "The History of the 28th in New York," *TPG*, October 1940, 9. Miller, "107th," ibid., 27. "109th Infantry," ibid., 40. "The 110th Infantry," ibid., 45. B. C. Jones, "Maneuvers of the 22nd Cavalry Division," ibid., 16.

53. Lee E. Isreall, "The 213th C.A. in First Army Maneuvers," ibid., 24.

54. "110th Infantry," ibid., 45. "109th Field Artillery," ibid., 54.

55. "The 110th Infantry," ibid., 46.

56. "103rd Cavalry Activities," ibid., 20. Jones, "Maneuvers of the 22nd Cavalry Division," ibid., 17.

57. Major General Walter Short, Final Report of the Commanding General II Corps, First Army Maneuvers, 1940, RG-338, Entry 1st Army, Box 8, NARA.

58. "Citations for Meritorious and Outstanding Services," *TPG*, October 1940, 79.

59. 1940 Maneuvers Final Report. Colonel Eric Fisher Wood, C.O. 107th Field Artillery, "Let's Get Together," *TPG*, October 1940, 26. Short, Final Report II Corps, 8.

60. Colonel Monroe A. Means, "The 112th Infantry: High Standards Established in Field Training," *TPG*, October 1940, 33.

61. "The 109th Infantry: The Fighting 109th in the First Army Maneuvers," ibid., 40.

62. Final Report, First Army Maneuvers, sec. 2, 3. Reninger and Greene, "History of the 28th in New York," 9.

63. Address by General Drum at the Critique, Canton, N.Y., August 22, 1940.

64. February 14, 1940, Preliminary Plans.

65. Message to Commanding General Blue Army, August 18, 1940, 10:45 AM. Note: all messages and field orders are a part of the "Final Report."

66. Sec. 3, Blue Operations in the Two-Sided Army Exercise, 3–4. Change 1, Field Orders No. 1, HQ First Army, August 17, 1940, 10 AM. The DMF consisted of an infantry regiment, a battalion of 75mm field artillery, a company of engineers, all from the 27th Division, one troop from the 21st Reconnaissance Squadron, a provisional battalion of tanks composed of the 27th and 29th Tank Companies, and two truck companies for moving the foot soldiers. The order did not designate the infantry, artillery, or engineer units. First Army records emphasize the actions of corps and rarely refer to any divisions.

67. Field Order No. 2, August 18, 1940, 7:15 PM HQ First Army. First Army Blue Operations Map, August 18, 1940, Annex 1 and 2 to F.O. 2.

68. Remarks by Colonel Waldo C. Potter, Chief Umpire, Critique, August 22, 1940.

69. Sec. 3, Blue Operations, 4.

70. "The Fighting 109th," 40. Guy V. Miller, "107th Field Artillery Makes Fine Record," *TPG,* October 1940, 27.

71. "The 110th Infantry," 46.

72. Jones, "22nd Cavalry Division," 18–19.

73. Field Order N. 3, August 19, 1940, 6:15 PM HQ First Army. Jones, "22nd Cavalry Division," 18–19.

74. Jones, "22nd Cavalry Division," 19. "103rd Cavalry Activities," *TPG,* October 1940, 20.

75. Sec. 3, Blue Operations, 4–5. Potter, August 22, 1940. Map, Situation am-20. Drum address, August 22, 1940.

76. Miller, "107th," 28.

77. "109th Infantry," *TPG,* October 1940, 46, 54.

78. "The Roving Guns of the 166th Field Artillery," *TPG,* October 1940, 72.

79. Field Order No. 4, August 20, 1940, 5:44 PM HQ First Army. "110th Infantry," 46.

80. Annex No. 2 to Field Order No. 4.

81. Sec. 3, Blue Operations, 5. Potter, 22 August 1940. Means, "High Standards," 33.

82. "109th Infantry," 40. Means, "High Standards," 33.

83. Potter, August 22, 1940. Sec. 3, Blue Operations, 5.

84. "Comments by the Director," sec. 1, November 4, 1940, Final Report, 12.

85. Lt. Col. John C. Davis, Final Report of G-3 Section, First Army, August 23, 1940.

86. Remarks by Colonel Francis B. Wilby, Chief of Staff First Army, 22 August 1940. 1940 Final Report. Lt. Col. C. L. Clark, G-2, First Army Maneuvers, Final Report.

87. Address by General Drum.

88. Wilby remarks. Remarks by Brigadier General Irving J. Phillipson, Deputy Directory First Army Maneuvers. Final Report. Colonel A. J. Cooper, Final Report, Office of the Chief of Artillery. Final Report.

89. "103rd Engineers Perform Varied Tasks," *TPG,* October 1940, 29. Sec. 4, Comments, Final Report.

90. Address by General Drum.

91. "Roving Guns."

92. Lt. Col. William J. Mangino, Report of National Guard Liaison Officer with First Army Quartermaster, September 1, 1940, RG-338, Entry 1st Army, Box 7, NARA.

93. Lt. Maxwell M. Kahn, "The 103rd Observation Squadron Reports," *TPG*, October 1940, 30–31.

94. "Extracts of Interest from the 28th Division Maneuver Report," ibid., 42.

95. Wilby remarks.

96. "Tank Company Scores on Maneuvers," *TPG*, October 1940, 56. The article does not give the date of the action.

97. Address by General Drum.

98. First Army Maneuvers Final Report, 13.

99. Final Report of G-3 Section, August 23, 1940.

100. First Army Maneuvers Final Report, 13.

101. Lt. Col. Don C. Faith, Memorandum for Colonel Buchanan, October 28, 1940, RG-337, File 333.1, NARA.

102. Colonel James G. Ord, U.S.A. Senior Instructor, P.N.G., "Impressions of the Maneuvers," *TPG*, October 1940, 25.

103. "Extracts of Interest from the 28th Division Maneuver Report," 42–43.

104. Final Report of G-3 Section, August 23, 1940.

105. "A Message from Lieutenant General Hugh A. Drum, U.S. Army to Pennsylvania Guardsmen," *TPG*, January 1941, 3. Sec. 5, "Recommendations," February 15, 1941. 1940 Final Report.

106. "28th Division to March on Monday," *TPG*, August 23, 1941, 1. "The Commanding General Says," *TPG*, August 39, 1941, 1.

107. "Virginia Maneuvers Put Troops in Fine Condition for First Army Exercise," *TPG*, September 13, 1941, 1.

108. "112th Infantry," 5. "110th Infantry," 4. "112th Infantry," *TPG*, September 20, 1941, 5. Official records and the *Pennsylvania Guardsman* provide little information on the Virginia Maneuvers. They would have been big news in 1939, but the maneuvers that followed overshadowed them.

109. Christopher R. Gabel, *The U.S. Army GHQ Maneuvers of 1941* (Washington, D.C.: Center of Military History, United States Army, 1992), 44–68.

110. "Commercial Busses to Augment Army Vehicles in Moving 28th Division to Maneuvers," *TPG*, September 20, 1941, 1. "First Army to Oppose IV Army Corps in Final GHQ-Directed Maneuver of 1941," *TPG*, October 25, 1941, 1.

111. "111th Infantry," *TPG*, October 25, 1941, 5. "55th Infantry Brigade," ibid., 4.

112. Director Headquarters, First Army Maneuvers, Opening Conference, Friday, October 3, 1941, Address by the Deputy Director, Brigadier General Henry Terrell Jr., "Reports of Maneuvers and Command Post Exercises," RG-338, Entry 1st Army, Box 10, NARA.

113. Director Headquarters, First Army Maneuvers, Critique, Field Maneuver No. 1, October 24, 1941. Discussion by the Deputy Director Brigadier General Henry Terrell Jr., RG-338, "Reports of Maneuvers and Command Post Exercises," NARA.

114. Lieutenant General Hugh A. Drum to General Marshall, December 6, 1941, Box 66, Folder 26, GCMRL.

115. "Corps Maneuver, Training Exercise No. 1—One Day to be Played Monday, 6 October 1941," Headquarters II Army Corps, October 1, 1941, RG-338, File 354.23/321 A-2, NARA. "Corps Maneuvers, Exercise No. 2, Date 6–8 October," ibid.

116. "Corps Maneuvers Training Exercise No. 3—Two Days to be Played Thursday and Friday, 9–10 October 1941," Headquarters II Army Corps, October 2, 1941, ibid.

117. "Corps Exercise No. 4 (Two-sided Free Maneuvers);" Headquarters II Army Corps, 9 October, 1941, Headquarters II Army Corps, 2 October 1941, File 354.23/, NARA.

118. "Corps Maneuvers Training Exercise No. 5—Two Days to be Played 15–17 October," October 9, 1941, ibid.

119. Lt. Col. H. E. Watkins, Assistant Director, Cavalry, 104th Cavalry, Horse Mcz, October 23, 1941. Lt. Col. Norbert E. Manley, "Notes on Army Corps Maneuvers: 28th Division Field Artillery," October 17, 1941, RG-338, Entry 1st Army, NARA.

120. Brigadier General Henry Terrell Jr., October 1, 1941, Field Maneuver No. 1, First Army 19–25 October 1941, Reports of Maneuvers and Command Post Exercises. Address by the Deputy Director, Brigadier General Henry Terrell Jr., ibid. Address by the Deputy Director, October 3, 1941.

121. Message No. 4, October 20, 1941, 3:30 AM Field Maneuver No. 1. Reports of Maneuvers and Command Post Exercises. Red Force consisted of I Corps: 8th, 9th, and 30th Divisions.

122. Director, Headquarters First Army Maneuvers, Critique Field Maneuvers No. 1, Friday, October 24, 1941, RG-338, Entry 1st Army, NARA. First Army Maneuvers. Reports of Maneuvers and Command Post Exercises. E. H. Freeland, Liaison Officer, 28th Infantry Division, Director's Headquarters, First Army Maneuvers, Liaison Officers' and First Army Observer's Report. Memorandum to the Chief of Staff, First Army, through G-3, Detailed Comments of First Army Observers, FM #1, RG-338, Entry 1st Army, NARA.

123. Critique Field Maneuver No. 1, Friday, October 24, 1941, Discussion by the Deputy Director. Lieutenant Harold E. Gentile, Umpire, Headquarters 2nd Bn 110th Infantry, RG-338, Entry 1st Army, NARA.

124. Unsigned, handwritten evaluations notes, ibid.

125. Lt. Col. L. S. Partridge, Memorandum for the Director, F.M. #2, "Observations on Artillery Fire Marking," October 30, 1941, ibid.

126. Memorandum to the Chief of Staff, First Army, through G-3, Detailed Comments of First Army Observers, FM #1, ibid.

127. Lt. Col. Norbert E. Manley (no date), a handwritten comment sheet, ibid.

128. "110th Infantry," *TPG*, November 1, 1941, 4.

129. Director Headquarters First Army Maneuvers, Comments on FM No. 1, First Corps vs. Second Corps Maneuvers, RG-338, Entry 1st Army, NARA.

130. Memorandum to the Chief of Staff, First Army, through G-3, Detailed Comments.

131. Lt. Col. E. H. Freeland, Liaison Observers' Report, to Directors Headquarters First Army Maneuvers (no date), ibid.

132. "Here and There," *TPG*, October 25, 1941, 1.

133. Discussion by the Deputy Director, Brigadier General Henry Terrell Jr., Reports of Maneuvers and Command Post Exercises. Director Headquarters First Army Maneuvers, 1941, Field Maneuver No. 2, First Army, October 26–November 1, 1941, RG-338, Entry 1st Army, NARA.

134. Lloyd H. Seiler, "The Crossing of the 'Rocky River' by the 1st Bn. 112th Infantry," *TPG*, November 29, 1941, 3.

135. Liaison Officers' and First Army Observers' Report, 2nd FM, Lt. Col. E. H. Freeland, File "Field Maneuvers through Liaison Reports," RG-338, Entry 1st Army, NARA.

136. Director Headquarters, First Army Maneuvers, Critique Field Maneuver No. 2, October 31, 1941. Discussion by the Deputy Director, Brigadier General Henry Terrell Jr., ibid.

137. Liaison Officers' and First Army Observers' Report, 2nd FM, Lt. Col. E. H. Freeland, File "Field Maneuvers through Liaison Reports," ibid.

138. Major Montgomery C. Jackson, Umpire Report, October 30, 1941, Team No. 10, ibid.

139. Director Headquarters, First Army Maneuvers, October 30, 1941, Comments of FM No. 2, II Army Corps v. VI Army Corps Maneuvers, ibid.

140. Critique Field Maneuver No. 2, October 31, 1941. Discussion by the Deputy Director, Brigadier General Henry Terrell Jr., ibid.

141. Lieutenant General Lesley J. McNair, November 8, 1941, to Commanding General First Army, "Field Maneuvers 1 and 2, First Army," ibid.

142. Director Headquarters First Army Maneuvers, Critique Field Maneuver No. 3, Monday, November 10, 1941, Discussion by the Deputy Director, Brigadier General Henry Terrell Jr., "Reports of Maneuvers and Command Post Exercises." G-3 Periodic Report No. 17, ibid.

143. "28th Division Rolls on in High Gear," TPG, November 8, 1941, 3. "112th Infantry," 5.

144. Critique Field Maneuver No. 3, November 10.

145. Comments by the Director, Lieutenant General Hugh A. Drum, RG-338, Entry 1st Army, NARA.

146. Critique Field Maneuver No. 3, November 10.

147. Lt. Col. Burton Lucas, G-3 Periodic Report No. 18, RG-338, Entry 1st Army, NARA.

148. Director Headquarters First Army Maneuvers, November 7, 1941, Comments on FM No. 3, RG-338, Entry 1st Army, NARA.

149. Memorandum to the Chief of Staff, First Army, FM #1, October 20–23, 1941.

150. Lt. Col. Thacher Nelson, Special Report on Matters Noted in a Number of Units Visited (no date), RG-338, Entry 1st Army.

151. "Carolina Maneuvers Approaching Final Stages with 28th in Top Form," TPG, November 3, 1941, 1.

152. Gabel, Maneuvers, 134–47.

153. Lt. Col. W. C. McMahon, II Corps Chief of Staff, Plans of CG. II Army Corps for First Phase of GHQ Maneuvers, II Army Corps in the Field, 15 Nov. 41 10:35 AM, RG-338, Entry 1st Army, NARA.

154. "28th Division Battering Its Way to Glorious Victory as Maneuvers Approach Finale," TPG, November 22, 1941, 1. Field Order No. 20, II Army Corps in the Field 17 Nov. 41, "G-3 Maneuver Reports." Field Order No. 21, II Army Corps in the Field 18 Nov. 41 10:00 PM, ibid.

155. G-3 Periodic Report No. 11, ibid.

156. G-3 Periodic Report No. 14, ibid. Gabel, Maneuvers, 144.

157. Field Order No. 23, II Army Corps in the Field 20 Nov. 41, 10:30 PM, G-3 Maneuver Reports. Gabel, Maneuvers, 148.

158. Gabel, Maneuvers, 155.

159. "The 28th's Battle for Lynches River," TPG, December 6, 1941, 1.

160. Field Order No. 25, II Army Corps in the Field, Nov. 24, 1941, 5:00 PM, G-3 Periodic Report No. 18, II Army Corps in the Field 26 Nov. 41. G-3 Maneuver Reports.

161. "28th Division Glorious Record," 28.

162. "Battle for Lynches River," 1.

163. Field Order No. 26, II Army Corps in the Field, Nov. 25, 1941, 10:30 PM. Field Order No. 27, II Army Corps in the Field, Nov. 26, 1941, 10:00 AM. G-3 Maneuver Reports.

164. Gabel, *Maneuvers*, 161.

165. G-3 Periodic Report No. 19, 26 Nov. 41. G-3 Maneuver Reports. "Battle for Lynches River," 8. G-3 Periodic Report No. 20, 27 Nov. 41. G-3 Maneuver Reports.

166. Field Order No. 28, II Army Corps in the Field, 26 Nov. 41. G-3 Periodic Report No. 21, 27 Nov. 41. G-3 Periodic Report No. 22, 28 Nov. 41. G-3 Maneuver Reports.

167. "Historic Record of the 28th."

168. Gabel, *Maneuvers*, 162.

169. G-3 Periodic Report No. 24, 28 Nov. 41. G-3 Maneuver Reports. "Historic Record of the 28th."

170. Gabel, *Maneuvers*, 165.

171. Lieutenant General Lesley J. McNair, Critique of Second Phase of GHQ-Directed Maneuvers, Carolina Area, November 25th to 28th, 1941. Field Maneuvers 1 and 2 First Army, Nov. 1941.

172. Ibid.

173. War Department, Memorandum for the Secretary, Notes on Conference Re: Maneuvers, December 4, 1941, RG-107, Entry 100, Box 6, NARA.

174. Major General Edward Martin, Headquarters 28th Infantry Division, December 15, 1941, Commander's Report, 28th Infantry Division, to the Commanding General, First Army, RG-338, Entry 1st Army, File 354.23/321, NARA. General Orders No. 24, 28th Infantry Division, November 30, 1941, RG-407, File 328-1.6 to 328-1.9, NARA. "Maneuver Casualties Eulogized at Review," *TPG*, December 20, 1941, 1.

175. Fluck interview, 35–36.

5. The Pennsylvania National Guard and American Society

1. U.S. Bureau of the Census, *Historical Statistics of the United States, Colonial Times to 1970*, 2 vols. (Washington, D.C.: Bureau of the Census, 1975), 1:135; 2:1104, 1114. Portions of this chapter first appeared in my article "The Volunteers of 1941: The Pennsylvania National Guard and Continuity in American Military Policy," *Pennsylvania History* 72, no. 3 (Summer 2005): 347–68. Reproduced with permission.

2. Vol. 2, sec. 3, pt. 1: Final Report of the Commanding General, 28th Division, Manassas Maneuvers Final Report, 1–2, MHI.

3. "The Pill Box: 103d Medical Regiment," *TPG*, November 1939, 23.

4. "Governor's Statement to Employers," *TPG*, December 1939, 12. Documents from the Records of the Governor are not helpful because Governor James kept no records beyond lists of some military commissions and several thousand notary publics, RG-26, Records of the Department of State, PSA.

5. RG-19.124, Department of Military and Veteran's Affairs, Records of Pa. Guardsmen Mustered into WWII, 1940–41, PSA. "Aid National Defense," *Harrisburg Telegraph*, November 10, 1939, 8.

6. "Aid National Defense."

7. "Baby Regiment First to Winter Camp," *TPG*, December 1939, 11. Nathaniel Nathanson, "The Rampant Lion," ibid., 26. "Old Grey Mare of the 109th Infantry," ibid., 23.

8. "Old Grey Mare of the 109th," *TPG*, November 1939, 27.

9. "The Commanding General's Message," *TPG*, December 1939, 2. "Martin Praises Pittsburgh Guardsmen," *Harrisburg Telegraph*, November 13, 1939, Martin Scrapbook 22, 106, MG-156, PSA.

10. "Martin Lauds Spirit Shown by Guard Units," *Harrisburg Telegraph,* December 2, 1939, 13.

11. Colonel Robert Morris, "Pennsylvania's Winter Field Training," *TPG,* January 1940, 7. "112th Infantry," ibid., 22–23. "Duds from the 109th Field Artillery," ibid., 24.

12. *MP* 2, 116n.

13. George C. Marshall to Brigadier General Charles H. Cole, September 26, 1939, *MP* 2, 67.

14. George C. Marshall, "Speech to the National Guard Association of Pennsylvania," October 13, 1939, Washington, Pa., *MP* 2, 88.

15. "Turn out the Guard!" *TPG,* March 1940, 31.

16. George C. Marshall, Memorandum for General Blanding, December 20, 1939, *MP* 2, 121.

17. Memorandum for Assistant Chief of Staff, G-3, "Training of Reserve Officers at Training Schools (G-3/41500)," October 6, 1939, *MP* 2, 75.

18. "112th Infantry," *TPG,* January, 1940, 23.

19. "112th Infantry, *TPG,* May 1940, 22. "103d Engineers Punch Press," *TPG,* July 1939, 73. "The Flying Squirrel 103d Observation Squadron," ibid., 76. "111th Rifles Pass in Review," *TPG,* September 1939, 30.

20. Edward Martin to John F. Williams, February 21, 1940, RG-168, File 353, NARA. Brigadier General Herbert R. Dean, Adj. Gen. of Rhode Island, to BG John F. Williams March 1, 1940, ibid. Major General Charles Haffner to George C. Marshall, December 7, 1939; War Department General Staff G-3, Memorandum for the Chief of Staff, January 11, 1940, RG-407, File 353 (1-1-40) to (2-29-40), NARA. The Adjutant General Office, Record of Communication Received, April 22, 1940, RG-407, File 353 (3-1-40) to (4-24-40), NARA. Edward Martin to George C. Marshall, February 28, 1940. Box 75, Folder 28, GCMRL.

21. Brigadier General Raymond S. McClain, 70th Field Artillery Brigade to John F. Williams, March 28, 1940, RG-168, File 353, NARA.

22. E. H. Kent to Representative J. Harold Flannery, May 10, 1940, RG-407, File 353, NARA.

23. Reports of Conference Held in the Chief of Staff's Office, February 16, 1940. GCM-Chief of Staff Conferences, Verifax 100 Folder, GCMRL.

24. "'I See by the Newspapers That . . .' Editorial Opinion Urges Employers to Cooperate with National Guard in Permitting Men to Attend Camps," *TPG,* June 1940, 16.

25. Ibid.

26. "Martin Asks Training Time," *Harrisburg Telegraph,* April 10, 1940, 12. "National Guard to Take Part in War Games," *Harrisburg Telegraph,* April 11, 1940, 1.

27. Howard Coonley to Major General Emory S. Adams, May 18, 1940, RG-407, File 353, NARA.

28. "Chronological Report," 38.

29. "Martin Appeals for Three Weeks Off for Guards," *Easton Express,* May 22, 1940, 9. "Martin Reveals Task Facing State Guard," *Pittsburgh Post-Gazette,* June 13, 1940, Martin Scrapbook 23.

30. "Well Deserved," *Altoona Mirror,* July 22, 1940, Martin Scrapbook 23.

31. "Pay, Vacations Assured Guard Members Here," *Pittsburgh Sun-Telegraph,* July 21, 1940, 4.

32. "Militia May Get Leave with Pay," *Philadelphia Inquirer,* July 15, 1940, 3.

33. "'We'll be Goats,' Say Guardsmen Here of Mobilization Call," *Pittsburgh Sun-Telegraph*, July 14, 1940, 1. *Congressional Record*, 1940, vol. 86, 3795.

34. Christiansen, Memorandum for the Chief of Staff, GHQ, February 4, 1941.

35. "National Guard Association Busy in 1940 Convention," *TPG*, November 1940, 12.

36. *Joint Resolution 286, Statutes at Large*, 54, ch. 689, sec. 3, 859–60 (1940). Richard L. Harkness, "Senators Vote Job Safeguard into Draft Bill," *Philadelphia Inquirer*, July 26, 1940, 1.

37. War Department Circular No. 131, November 12, 1940.

38. "111th Rifles Pass in Review," *TPG*, March 1939, 22.

39. Private Frank Solominsky, Carnegie, Pennsylvania, to the War Department, February 28, 1939, RG-168, File 325.4, NARA. The governors of West Virginia, California, and Ohio, among others, had used National Guard troops to break strikes in 1921, 1932, 1934, and 1936. Mahon, *History of the Militia*, 176–77.

40. "Activities: 103d Quartermaster Regiment," *TPG*, June 1939, 25.

41. "Hometown Honors General Shannon with 'Shannon Day' and Exercises," *TPG*, August 1939, 13.

42. "National Guard Plans Display," *Harrisburg Telegraph*, April 4, 1940, 1. "112th Infantry," *TPG*, July 1940, 23.

43. "Forward Observations, 109th Field Artillery," *TPG*, July 1940, 28.

44. "112th Infantry," ibid., 22.

45. "Trigger Squeezes 110th Infantry," *TPG*, October 1939, 23. The Grand Army of the Republic was an organization that honored Civil War veterans.

46. *TPG*, July 1939, 74. *TPG*, August 1939, 29.

47. "112th Infantry," *TPG*, August 1939, 29–30.

48. "112th Infantry," *TPG*, November 1939, 24.

49. "103d Cavalry Trains at Clearfield, *TPG*, January 1940, 16.

50. "Old Grey Mare of the 109th Infantry," *TPG*, December 1939, 23.

51. "111th Infantry Invades New Jersey," *TPG*, January 1940, 11.

52. "Duds from the 109th Field Artillery," 24.

53. "Trigger Squeezes 110th Infantry," *TPG*, May 1940, 23. "Trigger Squeezes 110th Infantry," *TPG*, June 1940, 28.

54. "The Rampant Lion," 28.

55. Major James H. Dailey to the Adjutant General of Pennsylvania, "State Recognition—HQ Troop, 22nd Cav. Division," November 21, 1939, RG-19, Slot 14-255, Box 2, PSA.

56. "104th Cavalry," *TPG*, May 3, 1941, 5. "104th Cavalry," *TPG*, May 17, 1941, 5. "104th Cavalry," *TPG*, June 7, 1941, 5.

57. "Trigger Squeezes 110th Infantry," *TPG*, May 1940, 23.

58. "Old Grey Mare of the 109th Infantry," *TPG*, March 1940, 26.

59. "111th Rifles Pass in Review," *TPG*, June 1940, 24.

60. Kafkalas interview, 7.

61. "112th Infantry," *TPG*, July 1940, 22.

62. "Regimental Day of the 213th Planned Sunday, April 21," *Allentown Morning Call*, March 22, 1940, 5.

63. Ibid.; "213th Coast Artillery's Record Lauded on Regimental Day," *TPG*, June 1940, 17.

64. Three decades earlier French soldiers had mutinied when serving in their home regions. David B. Ralston, *The Army of the Republic: The Place of the Military in the Political*

Evolution in France, 1871–1914 (Cambridge, Mass.: M.I.T. Press, 1967), 284–85. Brian Bond, *War and Society in Europe, 1870–1970* (New York: Oxford University Press, 1986), 37, 66.

65. "Open Forum Discussions."

66. Wiebe, *Search for Order*, 68, 74. Such community spirit had ebbed and flowed in the militia and National Guard for generations. Cooper, *Rise of the National Guard*, 6, 82–83.

67. "The Commanding General's Message," *TPG*, December 1939, 2. "Baby Regiment," ibid., 11.

68. Paul F. Potter to Representative Albert G. Rutherford, U.S. Congress, September 13, 1939, RG-168, File 325.4, NARA.

69. "'Laziness Perils U.S. Freedom,' Martin Says," *Pittsburgh Sun-Telegraph*, July 26, 1940, 5.

70. *Carlisle Sentinel*, October 13, 1939, clipping, Slot GM-0934, Box 1, Folder Adj. Gen. PNG Association Convention, Oct. 12–14, 1939, PSA.

71. "Memorial Day Service for World War Dead and Review of Troops Feature Memorial Day," *TPG*, June 7, 1941, 1.

72. "Open Forum Discussions."

73. "The National Guard and Its Place in National Defense," *TPG*, March 1940, 9–10, 23.

74. "The National Guard," *Army and Navy Register*, February 15, 1941, 8.

75. Hill, *Minute Man*, 290.

76. Ibid., 383.

77. "Honor Roll of Units Recruited to Authorized Strength," *TPG*, December 1939, 11, 19.

78. "Old Grey Mare of the 109th Infantry," *TPG*, November 1939, 26–27.

79. "112th Infantry," ibid., 25.

80. "Recoils from the 176th Infantry, ibid., 27.

81. "A Message to Mothers," *TPG*, January 1941, 41.

82. "MP's On the Air," *TPG*, June 1940, 17.

83. "111th Rifles Pass in Review," *TPG*, December 1940, 23.

84. "Forward Observations 109th Field Artillery," ibid., 26. "Forward Observations 109th Field Artillery," *TPG*, February 1941, 31.

85. "Old Grey Mare of the 109th Infantry," *TPG*, November 1939, 26–27.

86. Ibid.

87. "Chronological Report," 11. This was an old problem that dated back as far as the War of 1812. Skeen, *Citizen Soldiers*, 63.

88. "111th Rifles Pass in Review," *TPG*, November 1939, 30.

89. "Recoils from the 176th Field Artillery," *TPG*, February 1940, 28.

90. U.S. War Department, *Army Regulations No. 600–750, Personnel Recruiting for the Regular Army and Regular Army Reserve* (April 10, 1939) (Washington, D.C.: 1939), 13.

91. "Old Grey Mare of the 109th Infantry, *TPG*, February 1940, 23.

92. *TPG*, March 1940, 26.

93. "Trigger Squeezes 110th Infantry," *TPG*, December 1939, 30. Commonwealth of Pennsylvania, Department of Military Affairs, General Orders No. 14 (September 26, 1939), RG-19.116, Slot 14-0254, Box 1, PSA.

94. "Old Grey Mare of the 109th Infantry," *TPG*, December 1939, 23.

95. "112th Infantry," *TPG*, August 1940, 27.

96. "Flashes in Brief," *TPG*, July 3, 1941, 1.

97. "109th Infantry," *TPG*, August 23, 1941, 4.

98. "Flashes in Brief," *TPG*, July 3, 1941, 1.

99. Colonel Robert Morris, Memorandum for the Inspector General, August 14, 1941, RG-159, File 333.1, NARA.

100. "Old Grey Mare of the 109th Infantry," *TPG*, December 1939, 23. "Biggest Job Rise in 4 Years Brings State Relief Slash," *Philadelphia Inquirer*, November 6, 1939, 1.

101. "Trigger Squeezes 110th Infantry," *TPG*, February 1940, 28–31.

102. "Old Grey Mare of the 109th Infantry," *TPG*, December 1940, 28.

103. "Recruiting Responsibility," *TPG*, January 1940, 25. "Trigger Squeezes 110th Infantry," *TPG*, February 1940, 31.

104. "112th Infantry," *TPG*, January 1940, 28.

105. "Trigger Squeezes 110th Infantry," *TPG*, June 1940, 28.

106. "A Message to Mothers."

107. "News of the 107th Field Artillery," *TPG*, November 1940, 28. "News of the 107th Field Artillery," *TPG*, December 1940, 24. "Old Grey Mare of the 109th Infantry," *TPG*, January 1941, 46.

108. "News of the 107th Field Artillery," *TPG*, December 1940, 24. "Old Grey Mare of the 109th Infantry," ibid., 28. "Old Grey Mare of the 109th Infantry," *TPG*, January 1941, 46; "Keep in Scranton's Own," *Scranton Times*, December [date not readable], 1940; Martin Scrapbook 24, 55.

109. Doubler, *Civilian in Peace*, 198. Sligh, *The National Guard*, 119. "A Message to Mothers," 41. "Keep in Scranton's Own."

110. Roland Vermont, "Soldier's Soliloquy," *TPG*, March 1940, 29. Colonel Oswald W. McNeese, "The National Guard and its Place in National Defense," ibid., 10. "The Pill Box, 103d Medical Regiment," ibid., 24. "The Passing Gates of the 103d Cavalry," *TPG*, February 1939, 36. "Trigger Squeezes: 110th Infantry," ibid., 30.

111. Jay Cook, "As in 1776, Oldest Regiment Issues Call for Volunteers," *Harrisburg Patriot*, January 2, 1941, Martin Scrapbook 24, 68. "Old Grey Mare," December 1940. Lt. Col. F. H. Kohloss, Planning Branch, Memorandum for the Secretary of War, April 30, 1941, RG-107, File 327.5, NARA.

112. "News of the 107th Field Artillery," *TPG*, December 1940, 24.

113. "Old Grey Mare of the 109th Infantry," ibid., 28.

114. "News of the 107th," ibid., 24.

115. "Keep in Scranton's Own."

116. "Join the National Guard," *Canonsburg Daily*, January 23, 1941; Martin Scrapbook 24, 67.

117. Cook, "Oldest Regiment," 68.

118. "Final Report of Assistant Chief of Staff, G-4," Manassas Maneuvers Final Report, 1, 7, MHI.

119. "The Flying Battalion," *TPG*, September 1939, 10.

120. "The Pill Box: 103d Medical Regiment," *TPG*, October 1939, 27.

121. W. F. Kennedy, "Excerpts from a Soldier's Diary," *TPG*, September 1939, 25.

122. "Diary Didoes," *TPG*, September 1939, 6.

123. Final Report, 28th Division, Manassas Maneuvers Final Report, 8. "The Third Battle of Bull's Run by Willie Live, Author and Photographer," *TPG*, September 1939, 4.

124. "110th Infantry," *TPG*, October 1940, 45.

125. "The Commanding General's Message," *TPG*, August 1940, 6.

126. Reninger and Greene, "History of the 28th in New York," ibid., 9.

127. "103d Cavalry Activities," ibid., 20.

128. "111th Infantry," ibid., 52.

129. "103rd Quartermaster Regiment," *TPG*, October 1940, 92.

130. "109th Infantry," ibid., 40. Reninger and Greene, "History of the 28th in New York."

131. "108th Field Artillery," *TPG*, September 6, 1941, 6.

132. "Special Troops," ibid., 5.

133. "With the Blitz Busters," *TPG*, August 9, 1941, 1.

134. "104th Cavalry," *TPG*, August 30, 1941, 7. "'28th Division Man Thanks Fredericksburg,' from the *Fredericksburg Free-Lance Star*," September 20, 1941, 1.

135. "Fredericksburg Serving the 28th Division with True Southern Hospitality," *TPG*, September 6, 1941, 8.

136. George C. Marshall, "NBC Radio Address on the Progress of National Defense," November 29, 1940, *MP* 2, 357–58. George C. Marshall, Memorandum for General Bryden, November 22, 1940, ibid., 354.

137. "Army Morale: It Must be Kept High to Turn Soldiers into Good Fighters," *Life*, December 23, 1940, 57. The War Department never endorsed prostitution; "Draft of a Possible Statement by the Secretary of War," December 26, 1940, *MP* 2, 373–74.

138. "28th Division Antitank Battalion Is Proud of Their Progress to Date," *TPG*, August 30, 1941, 4.

139. "108th FA," *TPG,*, October 4, 1941, 6. Corcoran interview, 11.

140. *TPG*, September 6, 1941, 4.

141. "111th Infantry," *TPG*, October 4, 1941, 6. "Southern Hospitality Accorded 28th," ibid., 1.

142. "Carolina Houses Open to Soldiers," *NYT*, October 13, 1941, 19.

143. "Here and There," *TPG*, October 11, 1941, 1. "In the Field of Sports," *TPG*, October 25, 1941, 3.

144. "112th Infantry," *TPG*, October 4, 1941, 5.

145. "General Martin Praises Greensboro," *TPG*, October 11, 1941, 1.

146. "108th Field Artillery Regiment," *TPG*, October 25, 1941, 6.

147. "Division Surgeon Says," *TPG*, October 11, 1941, 7.

148. "This Is What the Soldiers Complain About," *Life*, August 18, 1941, 18.

149. Lee Kennett, *For the Duration . . . The United States Goes to War: Pearl Harbor—1942* (New York: Charles Scribner's Sons, 1985), 92. As soldiers overwhelmed the South in 1942, since that was where the majority of the training camps were, civilians again turned a cold shoulder to them. Ibid.

150. "53rd Field Artillery Brigade," *TPG*, December 13, 1941, 6.

151. "108th Field Artillery," *TPG*, December 20, 1941, 6.

152. Letter to the Editor, "Southern Praise for Northern Men," *NYT*, October 18, 1941, 18.

153. Corcoran interview, 11. Fluck interview, 23–24. Guardsmen who were 28 years old prior to July 2, 1941 originally did not have to complete the full term of duty. Major General Allen W. Gullion, Judge Advocate General, Memorandum for the Chief of Staff, G-1, May 13, 1941, RG-168, File 325.452, NARA.

154. "28th Division to be Granted Furloughs if Present Plans Are Followed," *TPG*, December 13, 1941, 1.

155. "Training Program Continues Despite Furloughs," *TPG*, December 20, 1941, 2. "111th Infantry," ibid., 5. Kafkalas interview, 14.

156. "Three Full Scholarships Offered 213d Regt. Enlisted Men," *TPG*, August 1940, 27.

157. "Forward Observations 109th Field Artillery," *TPG*, January 1941, 51.

158. "112th Infantry," *TPG*, March 1941, 30–31.

159. "Public Views 109th Artillery Parade and Presentation," newspaper unknown, Martin Scrapbook 24.

160. Kafkalas interview, 9–10.

161. "In the Field of Sports," *TPG*, April 5, 1941, 3. "In the Field of Sports," *TPG*, August 2, 1941, 3.

162. "109th FA," *TPG*, August 23, 1941, 6.

163. "107th FA," ibid.

164. Kafkalas interview, 9–10.

165. "The Commanding General's Message," *TPG*, February 1941, 7.

166. Headquarters 28th Division, General Orders No. 9, February 27, 1941, RG-407, File 328-1.13, NARA.

167. Thomas E. Lewis, "General Martin Has Human Side, Indiantown Gap Troops Find," *Philadelphia Evening Bulletin*, March 1941, Martin Scrapbook 1941–42. "General Martin Takes Press on Tour of Camp," *Lebanon Daily News*, February 22, 1941, Martin Scrapbook 24.

168. "Training of Troops and Road Parade Witnessed by Veterans on Army Day," *TPG*, April 12, 1941, 1.

169. Edward Martin to George C. Marshall, February 14, 1941, Pentagon Office Selected 1938–51, Box 75, Folder 30, GCMRL.

170. "111th Infantry Sponsors Radio Broadcast over Station WCAU," *TPG*, May 24, 1941, 1.

171. "Camp Hostesses and Librarian Report for Duty at Indiantown Gap," *TPG*, April 26, 1941, 1.

172. "Commanding General's Message," *TPG*, April 5, 1941, 2.

173. "Pennsylvania's Leaders in Education and Religion Confer with Division Commander," *TPG*, April 19, 1941, 1. "Hospitality of City's Homes and Churches Sought for Army Boys of Indiantown," *Harrisburg Evening News*, January 8, 1941, Martin Scrapbook 24. "Morale Program Has Many Angles," *TPG*, April 26, 1941, 8.

174. "To the Folks Back Home," *TPG*, August 9, 1941, 2.

175. Edward Martin to George C. Marshall, September 8, 1941, Box 75, Folder 31, GCMRL.

176. Kennett, *GI*, 32.

177. "109th Infantry," *TPG*, July 3, 1941, 4.

178. "111th Infantry," *TPG*, August 16, 1941, 5; July 3, 1941, 6.

179. "109th Infantry," *TPG*, April 26, 1941, 4. "55th Infantry Brigade," *TPG*, March 22, 1941, 4. "109th Field Artillery," *TPG*, March 22, 1941, 7. "111th Infantry," *TPG*, March 15, 1941.

180. "109th Field Artillery," *TPG*, May 24, 1941, 5.

181. Martin to Marshall, September 8, 1941.

182. Keith E. Eiler, *Mobilizing America: Robert P. Patterson and the War Effort, 1940–1945* (Ithaca, N.Y.: Cornell University Press, 1997), 106.

183. "Commanding General's Message," *TPG*, August 2, 1941, 2. "109th Infantry, ibid., 4.

184. "110th Infantry, *TPG*, August 9, 1941, 4.

185. "State School Authorities to Cooperate in Continued Education of Guardsmen," *TPG*, March 29, 1941, 1.

186. Headquarters 28th Division, General Orders No. 2, February 17, 1941, RG-407, File 328-1.13, NARA.

187. "State School Authorities."

188. "Night Vocational Schools Concluded," *TPG*, August 23, 1941, 1.

189. "Voluntary Evening Classes Available," *TPG*, May 30, 1941, 1, 4. "Unexpected Enrollment for Evening Classes," *TPG*, June 7, 1941, 1. "Evening Schools," *TPG*, July 12, 1941, 8.

190. "Night Vocational Schools."

191. *National Defense Act of 1916, Statutes at Large*, 39, ch. 134, 186 (1916). This use of military service as a "school for the nation" had also found success in Germany. Eliot A. Cohen, *Citizens and Soldiers: The Dilemmas of Military Service* (Ithaca, N.Y.: Cornell University Press, 1985), 129.

192. Cohen, *Citizens and Soldiers*, 130. Dallek, *Roosevelt and American Foreign Policy*, 256–57. Waldo Heinrichs, *Threshold of War: Franklin D. Roosevelt and American Entry into World War II* (New York: Oxford University Press, 1988), 85. Doenecke, *Storm on the Horizon*, 269.

193. "In the Field of Sports," *TPG*, April 19, 1941, 3.

194. Jack Conlin, "In the Field of Sports," *TPG*, March 8, 1941, 3. "In the Field of Sports," *TPG*, June 7, 1941, 3.

195. "In the Field of Sports," *TPG*, April 19, 1941, 3.

196. "In the Field of Sports," *TPG*, June 21, 1941, 3. "In the Field of Sports," *TPG*, July 3, 1941, 3. "108th Field Artillery," *TPG*, June 28, 1941, 6.

197. "104th Cavalry," *TPG*, April 19, 1941, 8. "Cavalry Horse Show," *TPG*, May 24, 1941, 6.

198. "Commanding General's Message," *TPG*, May 3, 1941, 2. "In the Field of Sports," *TPG*, April 19, 1941, 3.

6. Social Class, Recruiting, and Ideology

1. RG-19.124, Department of Military and Veteran's Affairs, Records of Pa. Guardsmen Mustered into WWII, 1940–41, PSA. Because of privacy laws, the author could not write down the names of individual volunteers. That is inconsequential for this study, since it is an analysis not of individuals, but of groups of soldiers. The enlistment records of the 111th Infantry Regiment are not held in the PSA, so Chester, Delaware, and Philadelphia counties are underrepresented in this study. Surveying 1,988 soldiers, the size of the collection comprises 17 percent of the size of the division, which was 11,709 officers and men when it was federalized on February 17, 1941. This sample size compares favorably with another study of enlisted troops, John Robertson's analysis of western Pennsylvania soldiers during the Civil War, which employs a sample of 1,355 men from four regiments and fifteen companies. John Robertson, "Re-enlistment Patterns of Civil War Soldiers," *Journal of Interdisciplinary History* 32 (2001): 21. Much of this chapter was published as "The Volunteers of 1941: The Pennsylvania National Guard and Continuity in American Military Policy," *Pennsylvania History* 72, no. 3 (Summer 2005): 347–68. Reproduced with permission.

2. Clifford and Spencer, *First Peacetime Draft*, 221–23.

3. Weigley, *History*, 208–10, 435.

4. RG-19.124, Records of Pa. Guardsmen Mustered into WWII, 1940–41. "All Penna. Guards Ordered Mobilized," *Philadelphia Inquirer*, October 20, 1940, Martin Scrapbook 23, 134.

5. United States Department of Commerce, Bureau of the Census, *Sixteenth Census of the United States: 1940. Population*, vol. 3: *The Labor Force*, part 5: Pennsylvania-Wyoming (Washington, D.C.: Government Printing Office, 1943), table 11, 26–27. The categories "craftsmen, foremen, and kindred workers," and "operatives and kindred workers" have been combined to roughly constitute "skilled labor."

6. Ibid., table 10, 23.

7. RG-19.124. *The Labor Force,* part 5, table 10, 23.

8. Jack Barbash, *The Practice of Unionism* (New York: Harper and Bros., 1956), 170, 276; Richard P. Clevenger, "Apprenticeship in Great Britain and the United States," (M.A. thesis, University of Oklahoma, 1964), 69–70.

9. RG 19.124.

10. United States Department of Commerce, Bureau of the Census, *Sixteenth Census of the United States: 1940. Population,* vol. 2: *Characteristics of the Population,* part 6: Pennsylvania-Texas (Washington, D.C.: Government Printing Office, 1943), table 16, 32.

11. "Biggest Job Rise in 4 Years Brings State Relief Slash," *Philadelphia Inquirer,* November 6, 1939, 1.

12. Weigley, *History,* 58. Robertson, "Re-enlistment Patterns," 16.

13. Memorandum of the Chief of the National Guard Bureau [no date, c. 1940], "Chronological Report," 98, 100.

14. *Sixteenth Census of the United States: 1940. Population, Vol. 3, The Labor Force,* Part 5, Pennsylvania-Wyoming, table 15, 74.

15. Sue E. Berryman, *Who Serves: The Persistent Myth of the Underclass Army* (Boulder, Colo.: Westview, 1988), 40.

16. *Sixteenth Census of the United States: 1940. Population, Vol. 3, The Labor Force,* Part 5, Pennsylvania-Wyoming, table 13, 29.

17. George Q. Flynn, *The Draft, 1940–1973* (Lawrence: University Press of Kansas, 1993), 234.

18. Samuel A. Souffer et al., eds., *The American Soldier: Adjustment during Army Life* (Princeton, N.J.: Princeton University Press, 1949; reprint, New York: John Wiley and Sons, 1965), 57 (page references are to reprint edition).

19. RG-19.124, Slot 14-0259, Box 4, Folder 8, PSA. Troop A never saw combat. The War Department separated it from the 28th Infantry Division on April 6, 1942, and restricted it to guard duty in Philadelphia and later in Oregon. It arrived in England on February 17, 1945, and conducted "police and outpost service" in Belgium. First Troop Philadelphia City Cavalry, *History of the First Troop Philadelphia City Cavalry, 1948–119, Together with an Introductory Chapter Summarizing Its Earlier History and the Rolls Complete from 1774* (Philadelphia: First Troop City Cavalry, 1991), 32–33.

20. "Blueblood Units," *Time,* February 10, 1941, 20.

21. RG-19.124.

22. U.S. War Department, *Table of Organization No. 7, Infantry Division (Square),* (Washington, D.C.: Department of the Army, 1940), 2.

23. "General Martin Takes Press on Tour of Camp."

24. Except where noted, these data come from the *Official National Guard Register for 1943.* Published by authority of the Secretary of War (Washington, D.C.: United States Government Printing Office, National Guard Bureau, March 1, 1943).

25. Edward P. O'Connor to the Chief of the National Guard Bureau, October 17, 1938, RG-168, File 353-gen 107, NARA.

26. RG-19.124.

27. *Register for 1943.*

28. "Airport Manager," *TPG,* May 1940, 18.

29. "Leaders of the 109th Infantry Honored," *TPG,* March 1940, 7.

30. "Letter by Edward Martin," *TPG,* July 1939, 12.

31. Athenaeum of Philadelphia, *Philadelphia Architects and Buildings*, http://www.phila delphiabuildings.org/pab/app/ar_display.cfm/ww511?&printable=1.

32. Major James H. Dailey, to the Adjutant General of Pennsylvania, November 21, 1939, RG-19, Slot 14-255, Box 2, PSA.

33. RG-19.124, Slot 14-0260, Carton 5, Folder 13, PSA.

34. Ibid., Slot 14-2162, Carton 6, Folder 5.

35. "U.S. to Permit Married Men to Quit Guard," *Pittsburgh Sun-Telegraph*, July 15, 1940, 8. Lt. Col. Lloyd D. Brown to Chief, National Guard Bureau, June 18, 1940, RG-168, File 325.452, NARA. Adjutant General's Office, August 22, 1941, to Commanding Generals . . . Release of Enlisted Men During the Remainder of the Calendar Year 1941, ibid.

36. RG-19.124, Slot 14-0258, Carton 3, Folder 22, PSA.

37. Ibid., Slot 14-2162, Carton 6, Folder 5.

38. "Penna. Guardsmen Balk at Quitting Despite Right," *Pittsburgh Sun-Telegraph*, September 6, 1940, Martin Scrapbook 23, 100.

39. RG-19.124, Slot 14-2162, Carton 6, Folder 13. Slot 14-0260, Carton 5, Folder 10.

40. "Penna. Guard Balk at Quitting."

41. RG-19.124, Slot 14-2162, Carton 6, Folder 13.

42. Nancy Gentile Ford, *Americans All! Foreign-Born Soldiers in World War I* (College Station: Texas A&M University Press, 2001), 3.

43. Berryman, *Who Serves*, 33, 81. Gregory T. Knouff, *The Soldiers' Revolution: Pennsylvanians in Arms and the Forging of Early American Identity* (University Park: Pennsylvania State University Press, 2004), 39, 50–52, 205. Flynn, *The Draft*, 27.

44. Cress, *Citizens in Arms*, 54–55. Steven Rosswurm, "The Philadelphia Militia, 1775–1783: Active Duty and Active Radicalism," in *Arms and Independence: The Military Character of the American Revolution*, ed. Ronald Hoffman and Peter J. Albert (Charlottesville: Published for the United States Capitol Historical Society by the University Press of Virginia, 1984), 90, 104. Mark Edward Lender, "The Social Structure of the New Jersey Brigade," in *The Military in America, from the Colonial Era to the Present*, ed. Peter Karsten (New York: Free Press, 1980), 27. Royster, *A Revolutionary People at War*, 374–78.

45. Skeen, *Citizen Soldiers*, 44.

46. James M. McPherson, *Battle Cry of Freedom: The Civil War Era* (New York: Oxford University Press, 1988), 606–608. Robertson, "Re-enlistment Patterns," 16, 30.

47. Weigley, *History*, 357.

48. Edward M. Coffman, *The Regulars: The American Army, 1898–1941* (Cambridge, Mass.: Belknap Press of Harvard University Press, 2004), 288.

49. Nathaniel R. Helms, "Falling Morale Hurts Guard Retention," http://www.military .com/NewContent/0,13190,Defensewatch_112404_Helms,00.html; Erika N. Cotton, "NGB Chief: Army Guard Stressed," *National Guard Association of the United States*, February 3, 2005, http://www.ngaus.org/newsroom/armyguardstressed020305.asp.

50. Howard G. Young, "The United States and the Nazi Menace," *TPG*, January 1939, 3–4. Recent scholarship confirms this assessment. Bernd Stegemann, "Politics, and Warfare in the First Phase of the German Offensive," in Klaus A. Maier, Horst Rohde, Bernd Stegemann, and Hans Ubreit, *Germany's Initial Conquests in Europe*, trans. Dean S. McMurray and Eward Osers, vol. 2 of *Germany and the Second World War*, Militargeschichtliches Forschungsamt (Research Institute for Military History), Freiburg im Breisgau, Germany (Oxford: Clarendon Press, 1991), 7. Norman J. W. Goda, *Tomorrow the World: Hitler, Northwest Africa, and the Path toward America* (College Station: Texas A&M University Press, 1998).

51. *TPG,* March 1939, 30.

52. W. R. Cunningham, "Food for Thought: Making the Grade," *TPG,* July 1939, 36.

53. Ibid., 13. W. R. Cunningham, "Preparedness," *TPG,* January 1939, 8.

54. "Minding Our Own Business," *TPG,* May 1940, 17–18.

55. W. R. Cunningham, "Our National Defense," *TPG,* March 1941, 18–19.

56. "We Thank You!" *TPG,* February 1939, 19. Coffman, *Regulars,* 245–47.

57. "Allentown Armory Dedicated as 'Peace Memorial,'" *TPG,* May 1939, 9.

58. "Cavalryitis by Willie Live," *TPG,* August 1939, 6.

59. "Old Grey Mare of the 109th Infantry," *TPG,* July 1940, 23. The officer's information was old by four months, as Congress appropriated additional money for drills in March 1940, $5,469,962. U.S. War Department, *Bulletin No. 1, Act of Congress—Emergency Supplemental Appropriation Act, 1940* (Washington, D.C.: March 14, 1940), 5. In June, Congress appropriated $19,309,100.00 for NG armory drills alone for FY1941. *Military Establishment Appropriations Bill 1941, Statutes at Large,* 54, part 1, ch. 343, 371 (1940).

60. "A Message for Mothers," *TPG,* January 1941, 41.

61. "Americanism," *TPG,* April 1939, 12.

62. W. R. Cunningham, "Food for Thought: Propaganda," *TPG,* June 1939, 18.

63. Fred G. Hyde, "P.N.G. Sifts Bund Ties of Officers," *Philadelphia Inquirer,* September 9, 1939, 3. Commonwealth of Pennsylvania, Department of Military Affairs, Adjutant General's Office, *Directory: Pennsylvania National Guard,* January 1, 1940 (Harrisburg, Pa.: Department of Military Affairs, 1940), 46, RG-19, Slot 14–2201, Box 3, Folder 3-16, PSA.

64. Nathaniel Nathanson, "The Rampant Lion," *TPG,* April 1939, 21. "111th Rifles Pass in Review," *TPG,* June 1939, 23.

65. "111th Rifles Pass in Review, *TPG,* May 1939, 23. Once the United States entered the war, fifteen thousand communists joined the U.S. military, not as subversives, but as enemies of Germany, out of loyalty to the Soviet Union. Fraser Ottanelli, *The Communist Party of the United States: From the Depression to World War II* (New Brunswick, N.J.: Rutgers University Press, 1991), 206. The Supreme Court supported loyalty oaths in April 1940 in the case *Minersville School District v. Gobitis.* Richard W. Steele, *Free Speech in the Good War* (New York: St. Martin's, 1999), 73–78.

66. "Pennsylvania Guard Officers Urge Rapid Defense in Memorial Day Addresses," *TPG,* July 1940, 8. In the November 1940 elections, the Communist Party presidential candidate, Earl Browder, received 4,519 votes in Pennsylvania. Brown Focht, ed. *The Pennsylvania Manual,* vol. 85: *1941,* Published by the Commonwealth of Pennsylvania, Arthur H. James, Governor (Harrisburg: Bureau of Publications, 1942), 152.

67. "Mark Sullivan Says," *Harrisburg Telegraph,* August 24, 1939, 6.

68. "Pennsylvania Guard Officers Urge Rapid Defense."

69. "Allentown Armory Dedicated as 'Peace Memorial,'" *TPG,* May 1939, 9. Americanism was often discussed in the military press. See for example, "Definition of Americanism," *Army and Navy Register,* May 6, 1939, 6, and "Away with Hate," *Army and Navy Register,* May 20, 1939, 6.

70. W. R. Cunningham, "Food for Thought," *TPG,* May 1939, 12. Compare to Robert B. Westbrook, *Why We Fought: Forging American Obligations in World War II* (Washington, D.C.: Smithsonian Books, 2004), 17, 28.

71. W. R. Cunningham, "Rats in the Pantry," *TPG,* July 1940, 10.

72. Philip Jenkins, "'It Can't Happen Here:' Fascism and Right-Wing Extremism in Pennsylvania, 1933–1942," *Pennsylvania History* 62, no. 1 (Winter 1995): 31–32.

73. Ibid., 33–37, 41–43.

74. Ibid., 50.

75. "Plot to Blow Up GOP Convention Revealed," *Pittsburgh Sun-Telegraph*, July 11, 1940, 1. "Bomb Plot to Kill James at GOP Convention Bared," *Philadelphia Inquirer*, July 12, 1940, 1.

76. "111th Rifles Pass in Review," *TPG*, February 1940, 26, 28.

77. "Food for Thought," *TPG*, May 1939, 12.

78. W. R. Cunningham, "Racial Differences," *TPG*, March 1940, 14. Here the PNG was in step with national ideology on race during the war. Combat units were ordinarily, and proudly, portrayed as multiethnic in this manner. Benjamin Alpers, "This Is the Army: Imagining a Democratic Military in World War II," *Journal of American History* 85, no. 1 (June 1998), 143–44. Robert Westbrook has argued that after Pearl Harbor American identity narrowed down to "an ethnocultural understanding of American citizenship." Westbrook, *Why We Fought*, 36.

79. "Quartermaster Regiment in Folk Festival," *TPG*, May 17, 1941, 1.

80. Bo Brown, unnamed cartoon, *TPG*, March 1940, 14. Unnamed cartoon, *TPG*, November 1939, 11; unnamed cartoons, *TPG*, March 1942, 8, 25.

81. Herbert E. Smith, "What's in an Army Name," *TPG*, March 1940, 3–4.

82. "Open Forum Discussions."

83. Hazel Threadgold, "'Fishin' Ain't Always Jes' Fishin' . . . A Short Story Completed on This Page," *TPG*, May 1940, 3. The roles and imagery in the story bear a resemblance to romantic notions of the loyal and faithful slave, and may have reflected paternalism rather than equality. George M. Fredrickson, *The Black Image in the White Mind: The Debate on Afro-American Character and Destiny, 1817–1914* (New York: Harper and Row, 1971), 102–25, 207, 289–91.

84. RG-19.124, PSA. John B. Kirby, *Black Americans in the Roosevelt Era: Liberalism and Race* (Knoxville: University of Tennessee Press, 1980), 18–31.

85. "Color Line in Armed Forces Condemned in Resolution to Legion," *Philadelphia Tribune*, September 26, 1940, 3.

86. Pennsylvania Assembly, *Journal of the House of Representatives of the Commonwealth of Pennsylvania for the Session Begun at Harrisburg on the Third Day of January, 1939*, pt. 1, H.R. 22, February 28, 1939, 277; C. H. Westbrook, ed., *The Pennsylvania Manual*, vol. 84: *1939* (Harrisburg: Commonwealth of Pennsylvania, 1940), 785.

87. Pennsylvania Assembly, *Journal, 1939*, pt. 3, May 24, 1939, 2821–22.

88. Pennsylvania Assembly, *Journal, 1939*, pt. 1, March 20, 1939, 476. Thompson was a veteran private first class who had served on the Western Front. He held a degree from Meharry Dental College in Nashville and belonged to the American Legion. Westbrook, *Pennsylvania Manual*, 794–95.

89. Pennsylvania Assembly, *Journal, 1939*, pt. 1, March 29, 1939, 662, 676, 775.

90. Pennsylvania Assembly, *Journal, 1939*, pt. 3, 3736–37. The list of bills acted upon went from HB 559 to HB 567, so it would seem that the house let HB 562 die through inaction. Ibid.

91. U.S. Congress, House, *Resolution for Two Colored Battalions in Pennsylvania National Guard*, 76th Cong., 1st sess., R.R. 6046, *Congressional Record*, vol. 84 (April 27, 1939), H4902; U.S. Congress, House, *Bill for Colored Regiment, Pennsylvania National Guard*, 76th Cong., 1st sess., H.R. 6467, *Congressional Record*, vol. 84 (April 27, 1939), H6467, H6038. (H4902, H6467, and H6038 are page numbers, as listed in the *Congressional Record*).

92. "Veterans Organizations Unite," *Philadelphia Tribune,* June 13, 1940, 3. Hinkson was an African American physician who practiced in a hospital in France during the Great War. Terry Radtke, *The History of the Pennsylvania American Legion* (Mechanicsburg, Pa.: Stackpole Books, 1993), 58.

93. "Negro Guardsmen for Penna. Backed," *Philadelphia Inquirer,* September 8, 1940, Martin Scrapbook 23, 101. "Legion Confab Urges Negroes for N. Guard," *Philadelphia Tribune,* August 22, 1940, 1.

94. Radtke, *Legion,* 58.

95. "Negroes Protest Military Ruling," *United Press,* September 13, 1940, Martin Scrapbook 23, 102.

96. General George C. Marshall, "Memorandum for General Shedd," September 14, 1940, *MP* 2, 306.

97. Charles Johnson Jr., *African American Soldiers in the National Guard: Recruitment and Deployment during Peacetime and War,* Contributions in Afro-American and African Studies, no. 149 (Westport, Conn.: Greenwood, 1992), 142–45.

98. Flynn, *The Draft,* 44.

99. Brigadier General F. M. Andrews, Memorandum for the Chief of Staff, July 30, 1940, RG-168, File 325.452, NARA.

7. The October Purge

1. Mahon, *Militia,* 43, 77, 162–63. Weigley, *Towards an American Army,* 129–35. Skelton, *An American Profession of Arms,* 211.

2. Mahon, *Militia,* 162–63.

3. "Chronological Report," 77–80.

4. Major General Emory S. Adams, "Re-Ordering of National Guard Officers to Active Duty," October 16, 1940, RG-168, File 325.452, NARA.

5. Marshall to Major General Roy D. Keehn, November 19, 1940, *MP* 2, 351–52.

6. Colonel Charles A. Curtis, "Induction of the 213th Coast Artillery," *TPG,* November 1940, 10–11.

7. Charles Hurd, "Shifts 20 Generals to Vitalize Army," *NYT,* July 17, 1941, 8.

8. Greenfield and Palmer, "Origins of the Army Ground Forces," 50.

9. Inspector General, Major General Virgil I. Peterson, Memorandum for the Chief of Staff, Officer Personnel-Reclassification, July 23, 1941, Reel 14, Item 442, GCMRL.

10. Memorandum for the Chief of Staff from Brigadier General Wade H. Haislip, G-1/16172-626, August 29, 1941, Reel 14, Item 442, GCMRL.

11. Mahon, *Militia,* 162–63.

12. Brigadier General Wade H. Haislip, Memo for the Chief of Staff, September 17, 1941, "Report of Reclassification and Removal Proceeding of all Components of the Army," G-1/3615-35, Reel 21, Item 780, GCMRL. McNair to Marshall, October 7, 1941, GCMRL. Forrest C. Pogue, *George C. Marshall: Ordeal and Hope, 1939–1942,* with a foreword by General Omar N. Bradley (New York: Viking, 1965), 101.

13. Brigadier General Wade H. Haislip, Memo for the Chief of Staff, "Personnel Policies Effecting the National Guard of the United States," July 31, 1941, 168–307, RG-165, Entry 12, Records of the Office of the Chief of Staff, Security-Classified General Correspondence, 1920–42, NARA.

14. *Public Law 190, Statutes at Large* 55, ch. 326, 606 (1941).

15. U.S. War Department, *Army Regulation 605–230, Reclassification of Commissioned Officers* (August 25, 1941), 1, 3, 8.

16. George C. Marshall to Colonel Hjalmar Erickson, October 6, 1941, *MP 2*, 630.

17. *MP 2, 629.*

18. George C. Marshall, "Interview Notes, September 28, 1956," interview by Forrest C. Pogue, *George C. Marshall Interviews and Reminiscences for Forrest Pogue,* rev. ed. with an introduction by Dr. Pogue, ed. Larry I. Bland, Joellen K. Bland, Sharon Ritenour Stevens (Lexington, Va.: George C. Marshall Research Foundation, 1991), 578.

19. Major General Virgil I. Peterson, Memorandum for the Chief of Staff, July 17, 1941, Reel 14, Item 442, GCMRL.

20. Pogue, *Ordeal and Hope,* 97.

21. Officers of the National Guard of the United States: Promotion List (no date), Reel 14, Item 442, GCMRL.

22. Lesley J. McNair, Memorandum for General Marshall, Subject: High Commanders, October 7, 1941, Box 76, Folder 31, GCMRL.

23. Lesley J. McNair, Memorandum for General Marshall, September 10, 1941, Box 76, Folder 31, GCMRL.

24. Brigadier General Wade H. Haislip, Memo for the Chief of Staff, Reclassification of Officers, June 9, 1941, Reel 276, Item 4300, GCMRL.

25. Report of Conference Held in Chief of Staff's Office at 8:30 AM August 15, 1940, GCM—Chief of Staff—Conferences, Verifax 100 Folder, GCMRL.

26. George C. Marshall to Major General Roy D. Keehn, June 11, 1942. George C. Marshall, *The Papers of George Catlett Marshall,* vol. 3: *"The Right Man for the Job": December 7, 1941–May 31, 1943,* ed. Larry I. Bland and Sharon Ritenour Stevens (Baltimore, Md.: Johns Hopkins University Press, 1991), 235–36 (hereafter referred to as *MP 3*).

27. George C. Marshall to Major General John F. Williams, June 8, 1941, *MP 2*, 529.

28. Lesley J. McNair, Memorandum for General Marshall, October 24, 1941, "Cases in Connection with High Command," Reel 28, Item 1161, GCMRL.

29. Lesley J. McNair, October 7, 1941, Memorandum for the Chief of Staff, "High Commanders," Pentagon Office 1938–51 Selected, Box 76, Folder 31, GCMRL.

30. Henry D. Russell, *The Purge of the Thirtieth Division* (Macon, Ga.: Lyon, Marshall, and Brooks, n.d., 1949 at the latest), 96–99, 104, 106.

31. Hill, *Minute Man,* 410–14. MG Wade H. Haislip, Memorandum for the Chief of Staff, July 9, 1941. G-1/13615–12. Reel 276, Item 4300, GCMRL.

32. Watson, *Prewar Plans,* 260.

33. *MP 2,* 481.

34. Weigley, *Towards an American Army,* 129–31. Logan was a volunteer soldier who rose to command the Army of the Tennessee in 1864.

35. Ibid., 130, 129.

36. Russell, *Purge,* 49.

37. Ronald M. Pavalko, *Sociology of Occupations and Professions,* 2nd ed. (Itasca, Ill.: F. E. Peacock Publishers, 1988), 22–25.

38. Major General John F. Williams, Memorandum for the Chief of Staff, July 31, 1941, OCS 16810-306, Larry I. Bland Personal Manuscript Collection (Xerox), Folder National Guard and Reserves, 1939–41, GCMRL.

39. *Official National Guard Register for 1943,* passim. These figures are extrapolations. The *Register* lists officers who were National Guardsmen when the Guard was federalized in

1940–41 and were still on active duty in early 1943, so those discharged for age or incompetence were not in the register. As noted in chapter 2, the general was Charles C. Curtis. The colonels were Laurence C. Atwood and Walter A. Hardie, ibid., 44, 282, 506.

40. Theodore A. Huntley, "Draft Army," *Pittsburgh Sun-Telegraph*, August 6, 1941, Martin Scrapbook 1941–41.

41. "Army Inefficiency," *Williamsport News*, October 11, 1941, Martin Scrapbook 1941–42.

42. "Housecleaning," *Time*, September 22, 1941, 32.

43. On September 15, *Time* devoted only one-half of a column to the announcement of the age-in-grade policy. "Tired Old Men," September 15, 1941, 34. The *New York Times* reported the policy as one directed at regulars, guardsmen, and reservists alike, Hanson W. Baldwin, "Army's Shake-up Underway," *NYT*, September 14, 1941, 36.

44. U.S. War Department, Office of the Chief of Staff, September 4, 1941, to Edward Martin, MG-156, Box 3, Folder General Correspondence 1941–42, PSA.

45. Chief of Staff to Martin, September 4. Wade H. Haislip, Memo for the Adjutant General, Subject: Officer Personnel—Reclassification, G-1/3615-13, Reel 14, Item 442, GCMRL.

46. Chief of Staff to Martin, September 4.

47. War Department: Adjutant General's Office, September 5, 1941, to Commanding General of Each Army . . . Subject: Service with Troop Units—Maximum Age of Commissioned Officers, Folder General Correspondence 1941–42, PSA.

48. George C. Marshall to Hugh A. Drum, October 17, 1941, Pentagon Office 1938–51 Selected, Box 66, Folder 26, GCMRL.

49. Edward Martin to George C. Marshall, September 16, 1941, Folder General Correspondence 1941–42, PSA.

50. Edward Martin to George C. Marshall, October 13, 1941, ibid.

51. Brigadier General Wade H. Haislip, Memo for the Chief of Staff, "Relief of Officers from Active Duty," October 10, 1941, Reel 14, Item 442, GCMRL.

52. *MP 2*, 637n, 649n. George C. Marshall to Lieutenant General Walter Krueger, October 30, 1941, *MP 2*, 655–56.

53. H. L. Stimson Diary 35: 66–67, September 15, 1941, cited in *MP 2*, 637–38n.

54. George C. Marshall to Lieutenant General Walter Krueger, October 11, 1941, *MP 2*, 637.

55. "General Lear Accused by Senator Clark of Making General Truman Army 'Goat'," *NYT*, October 16, 1941, 11.

56. *MP 3*, 169n.

57. "Retirement Asked by General Aiken," *Washington Observer*, October 6, 1941, Martin Scrapbook 1941–42.

58. U.S. War Department, Office of the Chief of Staff, to Edward Martin, September 20, 1941, Folder General Correspondence 1941–42, PSA.

59. Brigadier General Wade H. Haislip, Memorandum for the Chief of Staff, September 13, 1941, Subject: Letter from Major General Edward Martin, RG-165, File OCS 16810-310, NARA.

60. "The General Martins," *Scranton Times*, November 13, 1941, Martin Scrapbook 1941–42.

61. H. L. Stimson Diary 34: 165–66, October 27, 1941, cited in *MP 2*, 656–57n.

62. Martin to Marshall, October 13, 1941.

63. Ibid. Chief of Staff, to Edward Martin, October 9, 1941. Stackpole's military education consisted only of the Cavalry School's National Guard Officer course in 1928. *1943 Register*.

64. Marshall to Martin, October 9, 1941. Martin to Marshall, October 13, 1941. George C. Marshall to Edward Martin, December 12, 1942, Box 75, Folder 32, GCMRL.

65. Edward Martin to Major General William Bryden, Office of the Chief of Staff, December 23, 1941, Folder General Correspondence 1941–42, PSA.

66. Edward Martin to Major General William Bryden, December 24, 1941, ibid.

67. Edward Martin to George C. Marshall, January 21, 1942, ibid.

68. Colonel Louis Roberts, 38th Division, Testifying as a Witness in an Open Hearing before a Reclassification Board, n.d., ibid. Martin and MG John F. Williams considered Roberts's case to be representative. Williams forwarded Roberts's statement to Martin, who said it was "excellent." Edward Martin to John F. Williams, January 27, 1942, ibid. Units from Indiana, Kentucky, and West Virginia formed the 38th Division.

69. Colonel Louis Roberts, 38th Division, Testifying.

70. Watson, *Prewar Plans,* 244–46. Mahon, *Militia,* 184. In the fall of 1941 there were approximately 14,000 Regular, 20,000 NG, and 55,000 Officers' Reserve Corps officers. Chief of Staff, United States Army, Biennial Report of the Chief of Staff of the United States Army, July 1, 1939 to June 30, 1941, to the Secretary of War (Washington, D.C.: United States Government Printing Office, 1941), 24–29.

71. "40 Officers in 28th Division Shifted to Air Corps Duty," *TPG,* November 8, 1941, 4.

72. Watson, *Prewar Plans,* 246.

73. Edward Martin, Matters for General Fredendall, December 16, 1941, Headquarters 28th Division, Memorandum on Command Assignments, December 15, 1941, Folder General Correspondence 1941–42, PSA. John Kennedy Ohl, *Minuteman: The Military Career of General Robert S. Beightler* (Boulder, Colo.: Lynne Rienner, 2000), 91.

74. Telegram, Edward Martin to Major General Lloyd Fredendall, HQ II Corps, December 13, 1941, Folder General Correspondence 1941–42, PSA.

75. Edward Martin to Lloyd Fredendall, HQ II Corps, December 19, 1941, ibid.

76. Martin to Bryden, December 24, 1941.

77. Edward Martin to George C. Marshall, September 8, 1941, Box 75, Folder 31, GCMRL.

78. Telegram to General Fredendall, December 13, 1941.

79. Martin to Marshall, September 8, 1941.

80. Matters for General Fredendall.

81. *National Guard Register.* Matters for General Fredendall.

82. Edward Martin to G. Mason Owlett, Pennsylvania Manufacturing Association, January 16, 1942. Edward Martin to Mr. and Mrs. Worthington Scranton, February 4, 1942. Mr. and Mrs. Worthington Scranton to Edward Martin, February 7, 1942. Folder General Correspondence 1941–42, PSA.

83. Joseph R. Miller, "Gen. Martin Pushed by Mellon Forces for Governor in '42," *Philadelphia Inquirer,* May 1, 1941. Martin Scrapbook No. 43.

84. Edward Martin to George C. Marshall, January 21, 1942. Mr. and Mrs. Worthington Scranton to Edward Martin, January 28, 1942. HQ Third Corps Area, Major General Henry C. Pratt to Commanding Officers All Posts, Camps, and Stations within Third Corps Area, September 29, 1941. Folder General Correspondence 1941–42, PSA.

85. War Department, Office of the Chief of Staff, March 9, 1942, to Edward Martin, HQ Fifth Corps Area. Edward Martin, Headquarters Fifth Corps Area, March 14, 1942, to George C. Marshall. War Department, Office of the Chief of Staff, March 23, 1942, to Edward Martin. Ibid.

86. Robert Grant Crist, ed., *The First Century: A History of the 28th Infantry Division,* Prepared under the Direction of Colonel Uzal W. Ent (Harrisburg: 28th Infantry Division, 1979), 159.

87. Martin, *Always Be On Time,* 143.

88. Fluck interview, 40–41.

89. McDonald, *Unit History 109th Infantry Regiment,* January 1942 entry.

90. "Men of 28th Sad at Retirement of Gen. Martin," *Pittsburgh Sun-Telegraph,* November 12, 1941, Martin Scrapbook 1941–42.

91. Major General John F. Williams to Edward Martin, December 5, 1941, MG-156, Slot 0934, Box 1, PSA.

92. Martin, *Always Be On Time,* 96.

93. Fluck interview, 8.

94. Robert L. Daugherty, *Weathering the Peace: The Ohio National Guard in the Interwar Years, 1919–1940* (Lanham, Md.: Wright State University Press, 1992), 193.

95. Fluck interview, 30–32. Kafkalas interview, 16.

8. Stateside Training

1. Robert R. Palmer, "Mobilization of the Ground Army," in Greenfield, Palmer, and Wiley, *The Organization of Ground Combat Troops,* 203. Weigley, *History,* 435–40. The entire Army was 8.3 million, but 2.3 were the Army Air Forces, with the remainder in the Army Service Forces. Ibid.

2. Peter R. Mansoor, *The GI Offensive in Europe: The Triumph of American Infantry Divisions, 1941–1945* (Lawrence: University Press of Kansas, 1999), 73.

3. Wiley, "The Building and Training of Infantry Divisions," 435–36.

4. U.S. Congress, Senate Committee on Military Affairs, *Compulsory Military Training and Service, Hearings before the Committee on Military Affairs, United States Senate,* 76th Cong. 3rd sess., July 12, 1940, 330–31.

5. Major George A. Cockfair, March Memorandum, January 8, 1942, File 328-3.9, NARA.

6. Edward Martin to John F. Williams, January 16, 1942, MG-156, Slot GM 0830, Box 3, PSA.

7. Major General John F. Williams to CC 28th Division Camp Beauregard, Louisiana, January 27, 1942, RG-168, File 325.4. MG John F. Williams to Adjutant General of Pennsylvania, March 7, 1942, RG-168, File 325.4. Commander's Report, 28th Division, December 15, 1941, to the Commanding General, First Army, RG-338, File 354.23/321, NARA. The 111th Infantry was at first set aside for the GHQ Reserve, and later saw action on Kwajalein Atoll on January 31, 1944. Major General John F. Williams to the Adjutant General of Pennsylvania, March 7, 1941, RG-168, File 325.4, NARA. Shelby L. Stanton, *Order of Battle, U.S. Army, World War II* (Novato, Calif.: Presidio Press, 1984), 217. Stanton does not indicate which, if any, division the 111th was transferred to.

8. General Orders No. 9, 28th Infantry Division, February 16, 1942, RG-407, File 28th ID 328-1.13, NARA. This change dissolved the 53rd Artillery Brigade and the 55th and 56th Infantry Brigades, and the 107th Field Artillery Battalion spawned the 229th Field Artillery Battalion. Ibid. Wilson, *Evolution of Divisions,* 159.

9. Finlayson, *Uncertain Trumpet,* 136–37, 154

10. Wilson, *Evolution of Divisions,* 161–62.

11. General Orders No. 3, HQ 28th Infantry Division, Camp Beauregard, Louisiana, January 28, 1942, RG-407, File 328-1.13, NARA.

12. "History of the Third Army," Study No. 17, RG-407, File 103-0, NARA.

13. Capt. Louis Duenweg to CG Third Army, February 14, 1942, RG-337, Files 341 to 354.2, NARA.

14. James Garesche Ord, letter to mother, February 7, 1942, Ord Family Papers, Box 14, Folder 22. Ord Family Papers Part 2, Special Collections Division, Lauinger Library, Georgetown University.

15. "History of the Third Army," Study No. 17, 25. Bell I. Wiley, "The Training of Nondivisional Units," in Palmer, Wiley, and Keast, *Procurement and Training of Ground Combat Troops*, 435–36.

16. Wiley, "The Training of Nondivisional Units," 501, 503.

17. "History of the Third Army," Study No. 17, 26.

18. Corcoran interview, 15.

19. 28th Infantry Division Special Orders 1942: No. 3, January 3; No. 5, January 5; No. 6, January 6; No. 11, January 20, No. 14, January 23; No. 20, January 30; No. 21, January 31, RG-19.87, Slot 14–2169, Carton 4, Folder 35, PSA.

20. 28th Infantry Division Special Orders 1942: No. 23, February 3; No. 26, February 6; No. 31, February 11; No. 32, February 12; No. 35, February 16; No. 37, February 18, RG-19.87, PSA.

21. 28th Infantry Division Special Orders 1942: No. 47, March 1; No. 48, March 2; No. 59, March 14; No. 61, March 16, No. 84 March 11, RG-19.87, PSA.

22. Major General Virgil I. Peterson, Memo for the Deputy Chief of Staff, Major General William Bryden, February 3, 1942 [OCS 17633/62], Reel 14, Item 497, GCMRL.

23. 28th Infantry Division Special Orders 1942: No. 92, April 21; No. 94, April 23; No. 95, April 23; No. 108, May 8; No. 132, June 6; No. 135, June 9; No. 145, June 20, RG-19.87, PSA.

24. General Orders No. 18, 28th Infantry Division, April 13, 1942, RG-407, File 28th ID 328-1.6 to 328-1.19, Folder 328-1.13, NARA.

25. HQ IV Corps, Training Memorandum No. 9, Annex 4, March 6, 1941; Training Memorandum No. 9, February 27, 1942, RG-338, Box 91, NARA.

26. Joseph Balkoski, *Beyond the Beachhead: The 29th Infantry Division in Normandy* (Harrisburg, Pa.: Stackpole Books, 1989), 28. Mansoor, *GI Offensive*, 69.

27. "Southward Ho!" *TPG*, April 1942, 15. Tom Brislin, "U.S.O. Keeps Army Wives Busy, or, How to Trump Partner's Ace," *TPG*, June 1942, 6. "103rd Quartermaster Battalion," *TPG*, July 1942, 21.

28. "229th Field Artillery Battalion," *TPG*, May 1942, 24. "109th Infantry," *TPG*, June 1942, 14. "109th Infantry," *TPG*, August 1942, 13.

29. "Large Scale Athletic Program for 1942," *TPG*, January 3, 1942, 3. Dave Zinkoff, "In the Field of Sports," ibid., 3.

30. "New U.S.O. Building Is Open to Soldiers," *TPG*, March 1942, 11.

31. "Dancing Classes," ibid., 19.

32. "Backstage with the 28th," *TPG*, April 1942, 15. "Alexandria Booms," ibid., 30.

33. "28th Division Granted Furloughs," ibid., 15.

34. Biographical Sketches of Commissioned Personnel, 28th Infantry Division, RG-407, File 328-1.19, NARA. "Greetings," *TPG*, March 1942, 17.

35. Edward Martin to J. Garesche Ord, October 30, 1940. Edward Martin, Memo to the Adjutant General, U.S. Army, "Services of Brigadier General James G. Ord," October 31, 1940, Ord Papers. Edward Martin to George C. Marshall, October 13, 1941.

36. George C. Marshall, Memorandum for General McNair, (Confidential), April 25, 1942, *MP 3*, 171–72, 172n. M.T.D Memorandum for the Chief of Staff, Inspection Reports of General Peterson, April 24, 1942, Xerox 1886, GCMRL. Hugh A. Drum to George C. Marshall, October 31, 1941, *MP 2*, 663n.

37. Lieutenant General Hugh A. Drum to George C. Marshall, October 31, 1941, *MP 2*, 663n.

38. "Bayonet Drills Inject Realism into Training Program," *TPG*, April 1942, 7.

39. "112th Infantry," *TPG*, May 1942, 19.

40. Major Wilbar Halbert, "Addresses and Telephone Numbers of Commanding General and Division Staff Officers Living Off Post," February 26, 1942, RG-19, Slot 14-2202, Box 3, PSA.

41. James Garesche Ord, February 7, 1942, Ord Papers.

42. James Garesche Ord, Letter to Sister, March 18, 1942, Ord Papers.

43. VI General Training Policies (IV Army Corps), RG-407, File IV Corps 204-0 to 204-0.1, NARA.

44. "History of the Third Army," Study No. 17, 29–31.

45. Edward Martin to George C. Marshall, October 13, 1941, Folder General Correspondence 1941–42, PSA. *National Guard Register for 1943*. John F. Williams, Memo for the Chief of Staff, July 31, 1941. OCS 16810-306, GCMRL.

46. Edward Martin to Commanding General II Corps, December 12, 1941, MG-156, Slot 0830, Box 3, PSA. Marshall may have confused Colonel Van Vliet with Admiral Van Vleet, who drank too much. Mansoor, *GI Offensive*, 203.

47. Mansoor, *GI Offensive*, 81. Martin Blumenson, "America's World War II Leaders in Europe: Some Thoughts," *Parameters* 19, no. 4 (December 1989): 5.

48. *MP 3*, 172n.

49. James Garesche Ord, Biographical File, MHI.

50. Fluck interview, 42.

51. Lt. C. B. Hansen, "Maneuver Summary Story," *TPG*, December 1942, 3.

52. Omar N. Bradley and Clay Blair, *A General's Life* (New York: Simon and Schuster, 1983), 108–109.

53. Headquarters 28th Division, February 17, 1941, General Order No. 2, RG-407, File 328-1.6 to 328-1.19, NARA. Headquarters 28th Infantry Division, July 27, 1942, General Orders No. 32, ibid.

54. Bradley and Blair, *A General's Life*, 109–10. Cecil B. Currey has suggested that Bradley's assessment may have been overstated, and blames him for the gutting of the division. In fact, the draining of the division for cadres occurred primarily before his tenure. Cecil B. Currey, *Follow Me and Die: The Destruction of an American Division in World War II* (New York: Military Heritage Press, 1984), 58.

55. "VI General Training Policies" (IV Army Corps), Training Memorandum No. 41, HQ IV Corps, June 3, 1942, RG-338, Entry IV Corps, Box 91, NARA.

56. Bradley and Blair, *A General's Life*, 110.

57. "1st Training Battalion," *TPG*, May 1942, 28.

58. Bradley and Blair, *A General's Life*, 110. One may ask where references to Bradley's personal papers are. His papers are held at the U.S. Army Military History Institute, and were not helpful for the topic at hand.

59. Reynold W. Ross, Veteran's Questionnaire, Box 28th Infantry Division, 110th Infantry Regiment, MHI.

60. Harry M. Kemp, *The Regiment: Let the Citizens Bear Arms! A Narrative History of an American Infantry Regiment in World War II* (Austin, Tex.: Nortex Press, 1990), 29.

61. Ibid., 28.

62. Edward Martin to George C. Marshall, September 8, 1941. Box 75, Folder 31, GCMRL.

63. Capt. Frederick H. Weston, Memorandum for Colonel Montgomery, September 8, 1941, "Report of Observation made at the Third Army Maneuvers for period August 15–16, 1941," RG-337, File 353.8, NARA. Mansoor, *GI Offensive*, 64.

64. Bradley and Blair, *A General's Life*, 110. Ohl, *Beightler*, 83.

65. Headquarters 28th Infantry Division, Officers' Roster Division Headquarters, June 26, 1942, RG-19, Slot 14-2201, Box 3, Folder 3-25, PSA.

66. Headquarters 28th Infantry Division, Officers' Roster Division Headquarters, May 1, 1943, ibid.

67. George C. Marshall to Major General Frank Parker, August 21, 1942, *MP 3*, 313.

68. George C. Marshall to Major General Roy D. Keehn, June 11, 1942, ibid., 235–36.

69. Wiley, "The Building and Training of Infantry Divisions," 460.

70. "VI General Training Policies" (IV Army Corps).

71. "Furloughs Out," *TPG*, July 1942, 7.

72. Bradley and Blair, *A General's Life*, 110–111.

73. Ibid., 111.

74. Edmund Lewis, Veteran's Questionnaire, Box 109th Regiment, MHI.

75. Kemp, *The Regiment*, 32.

76. "103rd Engineers," *TPG*, September 1942, 22.

77. Master Schedule IV Army Corps, June 1–November 8, 1942, 28th Infantry Division, RG-338, Entry IV Army Corps, Box 91, NARA. Bradley and Blair, *A General's Life*, 110–11. McDonald, *109th Infantry Regiment*.

78. "History of the Third Army," Study No. 17. 33.

79. McDonald, *109th Infantry*, September 1942.

80. Hansen, "Maneuver Summary," 2.

81. "108th Field Artillery," *TPG*, October 1942, 24. "The Commanding General's Message," *TPG*, December 1942, 1. McDonald, *109th Infantry*, September 1942.

82. Tactical Situation Documents, Third Army Headquarters, RG-407, File IV Corps 204-0 to 204-0.1, Box 3346, NARA.

83. Comments by Colonel Robinson, Deputy Director, at Critique, Problem C-15, IV Corps Maneuver, October 12, 1942, RG-337, File General Staff, G-3 Section Training Group, Box 93, NARA. A Combat Command was a headquarters formation that allowed "the division commander to build fighting teams as the tactical situation dictated yet still have units in reserve." An armored division normally had three, one of which was a reserve combat command. Wilson, *Maneuver and Firepower*, 163, 185.

84. Part III Camp Beauregard Phase, Pre-Maneuver Training, Louisiana Maneuvers, RG-407, File 2-4-0 to 204-0.1, Box 3346, NARA.

85. "History of the Third Army," Study No. 17, 34, 36.

86. Comments by General Krueger at Critique on C-15, October 12, 1942, RG-337, File General Staff, G-3 Section Training Group, Troop Training Division, Maneuvers, Sp Projects and Ammo Br. Subject Correspondence File Mar. 9, 1942–44, Box 93, NARA.

87. Ibid.

88. Part III Camp Beauregard Phase, Pre-Maneuver Training, Louisiana Maneuvers 1942, Post-Maneuver Training.

89. Lieutenant General Lesley J. McNair to Commanding General, Third Army, Phase C-17 Maneuvers, November 1, 1942, RG-337, File 354.2, NARA.

90. Ibid.

91. Summary of Operations by Colonel Robertson, November 4, 1942, Problem C-9, RG-337, Box 93, NARA.

92. Comments by Major General Oscar W. Griswold, Director, November 4, 1942, Problem C-9, ibid.

93. Ibid.

94. Hansen, "Maneuver Summary Story," 4.

95. Lieutenant General Lesley J. McNair to Commanding General Third Army, November 18, 1942, Phase C-20, IV Corps Maneuvers, November 6–8, 1942, RG-337, File 354.2, NARA.

96. General Orders No. 44, 28th Infantry Division, December 24, 1942, File 28th Infantry Division 328-2.6 to 328-1.19.

97. Lieutenant General Lesley J. McNair to Commanding General Third Army, November 18, 1942, Phase C-20, IV Corps Maneuvers, November 6–8, 1942, RG-337, File 354.2, NARA.

98. Daily History of the 110th Infantry Regiment, Box WWII, 110th Infantry Regiment, Fifth U.S. Army, Strickler Papers, MHI.

99. Robert R. Palmer, "The Procurement of Enlisted Personnel: The Problem of Quality," in Palmer, Wiley, and Keast, *Procurement and Training of Ground Combat Troops*, 3–5, 19–20, 50, 65. The Army had an intelligence ranking system called the Army General Classification Test (AGCT) that rated men in classes I to V, from best to worst.

100. Ibid., 15–17, 29–36.

101. "'Army Cuts Specialized Training Program,' Immediate Release," February 18, 1944, *MP 3*, 309–10.

102. Mansoor, *GI Offensive*, 116.

103. Palmer, "The Procurement of Enlisted Personnel," 69.

104. Wiley, "The Building and Training of Infantry Divisions," 443, 463.

105. "VI General Training Policies" (IV Army Corps). Brown, *Draftee Division*, 72, 84–85. Mansoor, *GI Offensive*, 52.

106. Fact Sheet of the 28th Infantry Division.

107. George C. Marshall to Omar N. Bradley, December 23, 1942, *MP 3*, 491.

108. Omar N. Bradley to George C. Marshall, December 29, 1942, Box 58, Folder 9, GCMRL.

109. Bradley and Blair, *A General's Life*, 111. Journal, Chief of Staff, Army Ground Forces, December 30, 1942, RG-337, Box 1, Chief of Staff Journals, Mar. 30, 1942–Sept. 13, 1945, NARA.

110. "History of the Third Army," Study No. 17, 35.

111. Matloff and Snell, *Strategic Planning for Coalition Warfare, 1941–1942*, 376–77.

112. Supplement No. 4. to Administrative Memo No. 2, January 11, 1943, RG-407, File 328-3.9, NARA. General Orders No. 10, February 20, 1943, 28th Infantry Division, RG-19.87, Slot 14-2169, Carton 4, Folder 36, PSA. Brown graduated number one in his class from the University of Georgia in 1912. The eventual commanding general of the NG 30th Division, Henry D. Russell, criticized him for being "meek in appearance and conduct throughout his stay at the University." He was commissioned in the Army on June 5, 1917, but never saw combat in the Great War. Brown graduated from the Infantry School in 1923, and the Command and General Staff School in 1929. After serving as a NG instructor in Illinois in 1934–38, he held

three posts in the NGB from 1938–40. Prior to commanding the 28th he was assistant division commander of the 102nd Infantry Division from June 1942 to February 1943. Biographical File, MHI. Russell, *Purge of the 30th Division*, 29, 83.

113. J. J. Kuhn, *I Was Baker 2: Memoirs of a World War II Platoon Sergeant* (West Bend, Wis.: DeRaimo, 1994), 127.

114. *Amphibious Training Center, Study No. 22* (Washington, D.C.: Historical Section, Army Ground Forces, 1946), 58. The army established its own Amphibious Training Command because it lost trust in the Navy's ability to train its soldiers in landing operations. A desire to avoid submitting to Navy commanders also factored heavily into this duplication of effort. Adrian Lewis, *Omaha Beach: A Flawed Victory* (Chapel Hill: University of North Carolina Press, 2001), 57, 69–71.

115. Training Memorandum No. 5, January 14, 1943, "Training Schedule for 28th Infantry Division," Amphibious Training Center, RG-337, Box 107, NARA. David J. Coles, "'Hell-by-the-Sea': Florida's Camp Gordon Johnston in World War II," *Florida Historical Quarterly* 74, no. 1 (July 1994): 7.

116. *Amphibious Training Center*, 60.

117. Ibid., 60–61.

118. "Prelude to Invasion: Real Bullets Enforce Lesson at Army Amphibious Training Center," *Newsweek*, March 22, 1943, 22. Kuhn, *Baker 2*, 26.

119. *Amphibious Training Center*, 61. Coles, "Hell-by-the-Sea," 11.

120. "Prelude to Invasion," 23.

121. Field Order 33, Annex 11, HQ 28th Infantry Division, HQ 3rd Engineering Amphibious Brigade, Camp Gordon Johnston, Florida, 1500 February 24, 1943, File 328-3.9, NARA.

122. Field Order 33, Annex 4, HQ 28th Infantry Division, 4 mi. west of Carrabelle, Florida, February 23, 1943, ibid.

123. Field Order 33, Annex 3, Annex 7e Appendix 1, ibid.

124. Lt. Col. Paul M. Kienzle, Adjutant General, Memorandum: Make up of Battalion Landing Teams, July 23, 1943, Camp Pickett, RG-407, File 328-3.12, NARA.

125. "112th Infantry," *TPG*, July 1942, 16.

126. Dorothy Chernitsky, *Voices from the Foxholes: By Men of the 110th Infantry, World War II* (Uniontown, Pa.: By the Author, 1991), 290.

127. "How to Get into Bed," *The Trumpeter, Division's Original Unit Paper, 110th Infantry*, May 30, 1943, 40, RG-407, File 328-23, NARA.

128. "Trading Posts of Northwest Florida," ibid. "'Hell-by-the-Sea,'" 8–11. Actually, the name is a corruption of the Indian word "Lockchoppe," the former name of the waterway in Wakulla County. *My Florida.com*, http://dhr.dos.state.fl.us/facts/reports/names/city3.cfm.

129. "'Hell-by-the-Sea,'" 8–9.

130. Bradley and Blair, *A General's Life*, 112.

131. Training Circular Number 8, March 2, 1943, "Synopsis of Events, 28th Infantry Division Amphibious Exercise March 4–March 6, 1943," RG-337, Box 107, NARA.

132. *Amphibious Training Center*, 67.

133. General Order No. 11, March 8, 1943, 28th Infantry Division, RG-407, File 328-1.13, NARA.

134. Daily History of 110th Infantry Regiment, Strickler Papers.

135. General Orders No. 11, March 8, 1943, 28th Infantry Division, File 328-1, NARA.

136. Brigadier General Frank A. Keating, HQ Amphibious Training Center, to Lieutenant General Lesley J. McNair, March 8, 1943, RG-337, Entry 58a, Box 9, NARA.

137. Kemp, *The Regiment*, 34. Kuhn, *Baker 2*, 27.

138. General Order No. 11, March 8, 1943, 28th Infantry Division.

139. Kemp, *The Regiment*, 37. Kemp's is the only useful account of the division's experiences from April to July 1943. The only other unpublished source that mentions the period is John E. McDonald's narrative of the 109th Infantry, which actually formed the basis of Kemp's account. Apparently the division continued routine training during the spring, but information is lacking. Kemp barely mentions March–May 1943. Ibid., 37–38.

140. McDonald, *109th Infantry*, April, May 1943. Kuhn, *Baker 2*, 39.

141. Colonel Clyde L. Hysong, Memo for the Chief of Staff, April 3, 1943, Reel 122/3046. CCMRL.

142. General Orders No. 17, June 3, 1943, 28th Infantry Division, RG-19.87, Slot 14-2169, Carton 4, Folder 36, PSA.

143. McDonald, *109th Infantry*, June, July 1943.

144. AGF Fact Sheet-28th Infantry Division, RG-407, File 328-0. File 328-INF(112)10-0 to 328-INF(112)10-0.2, NARA. The Company D diary does not annotate the exact dates of the entries.

145. August 8, 1943, History Company M, 3rd Battalion, 112th Infantry Regiment, RG-407, File 328-INF(112)10-0 to 328-INF(112)10-0.2.

146. Daily History of 110th Infantry Regiment, Strickler Papers.

147. Major H. L. Berning, Asst. AG, Director's HQ, West Virginia Maneuver Area to Commanding General XIII Corps, August 30, 1943, RG-337, General Staff G-3 Section File, NARA.

148. Field Order 34, 28th Infantry Division, Camp Pickett, Virginia, 1930, July 21, 1943, File 328-3.9. Lt. Col. P. M. Kienzle, Adjutant General, Memorandum: Amphibious Umpire Instructions, July 22, 1943, Camp Pickett, Virginia, RG-407, File 328-3.12, NARA.

149. Colonel Charles H. Valentine, Training Memorandum No. 26, July 22, 1943, RG-407, File 328-3.13. Col. Charles H. Valentine, Supplement 1 to Administrative Instructions for Amphibious Maneuvers, July 28, 1943, File 328-1.12, NARA.

150. Lt. Col. Adam J. Dreibelbies, HQ Second Battalion, 112th Infantry, August 6, 1943 to Director Headquarters W. Va. Maneuver Area, RG-337, Box 72, NARA.

151. Lt. Col. William S. Houghton, HQ Third Battalion, 112th Infantry, August 13, 1943, to Commanding Officer 112th Infantry, ibid.

152. Lt. Col. Thomas J. Noto, 109th Infantry, Third Battalion, August 22, 1943, to Director, HQ W. V. Maneuver Area, ibid.

153. See also letters by Lt. Col. Daniel Strickler, August 16, 1943; Lt. Col. Roy P. Huff, Commander 107th FA Bn, August 23, 1943; and Lt. Col. Adam J. Dreibelbies, August 22, 1943; ibid.

154. George C. Marshall, Memorandum to General McNair, August 4, 1943, in George C. Marshall, *The Papers of George Catlett Marshall*, vol. 4: *"Aggressive and Determined Leadership," June 1, 1943–December 31, 1944*, ed. Larry I. Bland and Sharon R. Ritenour Stevens (Baltimore, Md.: Johns Hopkins University Press, 1996), 79.

155. Palmer, "The Procurement of Enlisted Personnel," 48–49, 61–69.

156. Mansoor, *GI Offensive*, 116.

157. Bell I. Wiley, "The Preparation of Units for Overseas Movement," in Palmer, Wiley, and Keast, *Procurement and Training of Ground Combat Troops*, 574. September 29, 1943, Monthly Histories, Co. M, Third Battalion, 112th Infantry.

158. October 2, 8, 1943, Monthly Histories, Co. M. Third Battalion, 112th Infantry.

159. Wilson, *Evolution of Divisions*, 180–82. Robert R. Palmer, "Reorganization of Ground Combat Troops for Combat," in Greenfield, Palmer, and Wiley, *The Organization of Ground Combat Troops*, 274, 276–314.

160. Finlayson, *Uncertain Trumpet*, 154. Weigley, *History*, 439.

9. Training in Wales

1. October 10, 1943, Monthly Histories, Co. M, Third Battalion, 112th Infantry.

2. No date, approximately October 1943, Diary of Company H, Second Battalion, 112th Infantry Regiment, RG-407, File 328-INF(112)10-0.2, NARA. Hereafter all documentary sources are from RG-407, NARA, unless noted.

3. October 10–18, 1943, Monthly Histories, Co. M, Third Battalion, 112th Infantry.

4. Kuhn, *Baker 2*, 68.

5. History 229th Field Artillery Battalion, John Fairchild Papers, MHI.

6. Diary Co. H.

7. Thomas Hickman, Raymond J. Ulmer, Box 109th Infantry Regiment; John G. Maher, Horale Osterman, Albert W. Burhardt, Box 110th Infantry Regiment; Veterans' Questionnaires, MHI.

8. Co. D, First Battalion, 112th Infantry Regiment File 328-INF(112)0.1.

9. Kemp, *The Regiment*, 47.

10. David Reynolds, *Rich Relations: The American Occupation of Britain, 1942–1945* (New York: Random House, 1995), 184.

11. Kemp, *The Regiment*, 45.

12. 28th Infantry Division G-3 Journal, October 30, November 3, 10, 1943, File 328-3.2. Hereafter all "G-3 Journal" records are those of the 28th Infantry Division unless otherwise noted. Training at the ATC was to "cover all phases of the landing-assault operation, under realistic conditions, simulating as closely as possible, those to be encountered by combat teams in an invasion of Western Europe." The Center also experimented with and taught new tactics. Lewis, *Omaha Beach*, 108.

13. G-3 Journal, November 24, 1943. Edwin H. J. Cornell, Roger Lee Farrand, Veterans' Questionnaires, 110th Infantry Regiment, MHI.

14. Hickman Questionnaire.

15. October 31, November 6, 14, 1943, Co. M, Third Battalion, 112th Infantry. History of the 108th Field Artillery Battalion, 3, Pennsylvania National Guard Museum, Box 1, Indiantown Gap, Pennsylvania.

16. Diary of Co. D, First Battalion, 112th Infantry.

17. 1st Lt. William E. Hall, Diary of Company C, December 24, 1943, File 328-INF(112)0-0.3.0. Kemp, *The Regiment*, 55.

18. History 109th FA, File 202-109FA, MHI.

19. History 108th FA, 4.

20. Reynolds, *Rich Relations*, 196–97.

21. Dec. 13, 20, 25, 26, 1943, History Co. M, 112th.

22. History of the 28th Infantry Division, June 24, 1944, 7, File 328-0 to 328-0.1.

23. G-3 Journal, Jan. 31, May 14, 1944. Diary Co. M, October 27, 31. Diary Co. D. History of the 108th FA, 4.

24. Reynolds, *Rich Relations*, 186–89.

25. G-3 Journal, Nov. 1, 4, 6, 10, 1943.

26. G-3 Journal, Nov. 22, 1943.

27. G-3 Journal, Nov. 19, 24, Dec. 19 1943; Feb. 21, Mar. 1, 6, May 11, 1944.

28. History Co. M, 112th, Nov. 7, 1943.

29. January 24, 1944, Diary Co. M.

30. Sept. 1 through Dec. 31, 1943, Journal, Inspection General Section, 28th Infantry Division, File 328-24.1. G-3 Journal, Apr. 10, 1944.

31. G-3 Journal, Oct. 27, 30, Nov. 2, 1943, Jan. 27, 1944. Diary Co. M, Apr. 4, May 23, 1944.

32. Ulysses Lee, *United States Army in World War II. Special Studies: The Employment of Negro Troops* (Washington, D.C.: Office of the Chief of Military History, United States Army, 1966), 440.

33. G-3 Journal, Jan. 27, Apr. 10, 1944. Diary Co. M, Oct. 27, Nov. 2, 1943; Apr. 4, May 23, 1944. Graham Smith, *When Jim Crow Met John Bull: Black American Soldiers in World War II Britain* (London: I. B. Tauris, 1987), 150.

34. Smith, *Jim Crow*, 138–39.

35. Lee, *Negro Troops*, 441.

36. Ibid., 625.

37. William R. Keast, "Service Schools of the Army Ground Forces," in Palmer, Wiley, and Keast, *Procurement and Training of Ground Combat Troops*, 246.

38. G-3 Journal, Feb. 5, 7, 9, 1944. Diary Co. D.

39. G-3 Journal, Nov. 6, 1943.

40. Ibid., Nov. 16, 1943.

41. History Co. M, 112th Infantry, Nov. 6, 7, Dec. 2, 1943.

42. Ibid., Dec. 27, 1943.

43. Hall, Diary Company C, November 29, 1943.

44. Ibid., December 20, 1943.

45. Ibid., December 18, 1943, January 20, 25, April 13, 1944.

46. G-3 Journal, Oct. 26, 27, Nov. 1, 1943.

47. Ibid., Nov. 26, 1943.

48. Ibid., Feb. 9 21, 1944.

49. Diary Co. D, File 328-INF(112)0.1.

50. G-3 Journal, November 6, 11, 12, 1943.

51. Ibid., Nov. 12, 1943. Diary Co. D.

52. Oct. 28, Nov. 22, 1943, Diary Co. M.

53. G-3 Journal, Nov. 26, Dec. 2, 1943.

54. Hall, Diary Co. C, March 2, 1944.

55. G-3 Journal, Dec. 8, 15, 1943.

56. Hall, Diary Co. C, Nov. 24. 1943.

57. Diary Co. D. History of the 108th FA, 4.

58. Hall, Diary Co. C, Nov. 25, 1943.

59. The 109th RCT included the 109th Infantry, the 107th FA, the 103rd Engineer and Medical Battalions, the 28th Signal, 28th Quartermaster, and 728th Ordnance Companies.

60. Kemp, *The Regiment*, 51–53. Braunton was one of eight major training sites the Americans used. The ATCs, particularly at Woolcombe, not only provided training, but also engaged in assault experiments and rewrote doctrine. Lewis, *Omaha Beach*, 108.

61. Kemp, *The Regiment*, 54.

62. G-3 Journal, Dec. 29, 31, 1943.

63. G-3 Journal, Nov. 29, Dec. 8, 15, 1943. Feb. 7, 14, 18, May 4, 1944. Diary Co. M, Nov. 17, 1943. Diary Co. D. The only diaries that made it into the National Archives are those from the 112th Infantry. Daniel Strickler's diary of the 110th Infantry, for example, does not provide details of the regiment's stay in Britain.

64. Diary Co. D. The narrative from January on that follows is not comprehensive. The day-to-day tasks were basically the same as in November and December 1943. Exhaustive coverage from the G-3 Journal and the diaries would be redundant.

65. Lewis, *Omaha Beach,* 174.

66. G-3 Journal, Dec. 29, 1943.

67. Ibid., Feb. 2, 9, 23, 1944.

68. Ibid., Jan. 23–25, 28, 30–31; Feb. 2–3, 27, 1944. Diary Co. M. Diary Co. D.

69. Diary Co. M.

70. Diary Co. D.

71. Hall, Diary Co. C, Jan. 29, 1944. Jan. 29, Diary Co. M. History of First Battalion, January 1944, Folder 328-INF(112)0.1.

72. Jan. 22, 1944, Diary Co. M. History of First Battalion, January 1944.

73. Feb. 28, 1944, Diary Co. M.

74. G-3 Journal, no date, logged between February 23 and 24, 1944.

75. Ibid., Mar. 1–3, 1944.

76. History of First Battalion, March 1944, File 328-INF(112)0.1.

77. G-3 Journal, Mar. 14, 1944.

78. Ibid., Mar. 20, 1944.

79. Kemp, *The Regiment,* 64–65. Kemp does not write when Patton spoke. It was probably in April 1944.

80. Diary Co. M, April 1, 1944.

81. Marion B. Davis Jr., M.D. "Frozen Rainbows: The World War II Adventures of a Combat Medical Officer in the ETO," 1994, unpublished manuscript, 118. Veterans' Questionnaires, Box 110th Infantry Regiment, MHI.

82. Robert P. Probach, "Army and POW Experiences," WWII, Veteran's Questionnaire, Box 109th Infantry Regiment, MHI.

83. Kemp, *The Regiment,* 62.

84. G-3 Journal, Apr. 20, 27, 28, 1944. History 1st Battalion, June 1944. Doubler, *Closing with the Enemy,* 250–51.

85. Lt. William E. Hall, History of Company C, From 1 November '43, January 30, 1944, File 328-INF(112)0-0.0.3.0.

86. McDonald, 109th Infantry, February 29, March 4, 1944.

87. G-3 Journal, May 23, 27, 1944.

88. History of the 28th Infantry Division, June 24, 1944, 11. Kemp, *The Regiment,* 71.

89. Mansoor, *GI Offensive,* 94, 161.

90. Johnson, *Fast Tanks,* 215–17.

91. Palmer, "Reorganization," 294–95.

92. Lieutenant General George S. Patton Jr. to Lieutenant General Lesley J. McNair, April 15, 1944, RG-337, Entry 58A, Box 10, Folder P-Q, NARA.

93. Robert R. Palmer, "Organization and Training of New Ground Combat Elements," in Greenfield, Palmer, and Wiley, *The Organization of Ground Combat Troops,* 411–16.

94. Hall, History Company C, May 6.

95. Document SSD 51, Secret, February 4, 1944, "Agenda for Headquarters V Corps Conference for Planning for Operation Overlord," Pre-invasion Files, Box 24310, Folder 219. "Planning Guide, Operation Overlord," February 28, 1944, ibid., Folder 217.

96. Major General Lloyd D. Brown to Commanding General V Corps, January 31, 1944. "Composition and Formation, Assault Infantry Division, Operation Overlord," Pre-invasion Files, Box 24308, Folder 199.

97. Roger Hesketh, *Fortitude: The D-Day Deception Campaign,* with an introduction by Nigel West (Woodstock, N.Y.: Overlook, 2000), xii–xiii, 8–12, 90–91. Mary Kathryn Barbier, *D-Day Deception: Operation Fortitude and the Normandy Invasion* (Westport, Conn.: Praeger Security International, 2007), 13, 21, 40.

98. 2nd Lt. Irwin J. Degnan, HQ V Corps, to Commanding General 28th Infantry Division, March 31, 1944, Security Violation, Pre-invasion Files, Box 24382, Folder 702. The ability to encrypt telephone transmissions did not yet exist.

99. Barbier, *Deception,* 33, 66–67, 75, 99.

100. History of the 28th Infantry Division, June 24, 1944, 9. Hereafter History, 24 June 1944. Martin Blumenson, *United States Army in World War II. The European Theater of Operations: Breakout and Pursuit* (Washington, D.C.: Center of Military History, United States Army, 1989), 187.

101. History, 24 June 1944, 11.

102. Barbier, *Deception,* 118.

103. G-3 Journal, Apr. 17, 1944.

104. "Great Send-off to Uncle Sam's Boys, Impromptu Street Concert and Fond Farewells," clipping from the *Tenby Observer,* April 27, 1944, Box 2, Folder 28th Inf. Div., Newspaper Clippings, Pennsylvania National Guard Museum, Indiantown Gap, Pennsylvania.

105. Kemp, *The Regiment,* 60.

106. History, 24 June 1944, 10.

107. Hall, History Co. C, May 12, 1944.

108. Diary Co. M, 112th, May 5, 12, 13, 19, 22, 30, 1944. History, 24 June 1944, 9.

109. Barbier, *Deception,* 104.

110. 2nd Lt. Howard P. Scherer, 112th Infantry File 328-INF(112) 10-0.2.

111. Diary Co. M, June 5, 1944.

112. History 109th FA. History 108th FA, 6.

113. Blumenson, *Breakout,* 187.

114. 2nd Lt. H. A. Morris, T/4 F. M. Ludden, History XX Corps, Third United States Army, File XX Corps 220–0.2.

115. Blumenson, *Breakout,* 210.

116. History 108th FA, 7.

117. Kemp, *The Regiment,* 68. Blumenson, *Breakout,* 210.

118. Johnson, *Fast Tanks,* 191. Mansoor, *GI Offensive,* 94. David R. Mets, "A Glider in the Propwash of the Royal Air Force?" in *Airpower and Ground Armies: Essays on the Evolution of Anglo-American Air Doctrine, 1940–43,* ed. Daniel R. Mortensen (Maxwell AFB, Ala.: Air University Press, 1998), 80–81.

10. From Normandy to the West Wall

1. History of the 110th Infantry Regiment, 30–39, File 328-INF(110). History of the 28th Infantry Division, ibid., Box 8478.

2. History 110th Infantry, 27.

3. Kemp, *The Regiment*, 69.

4. A massive joint operation utilizing massed bombing and ground force breakthroughs, Cobra resulted in Bradley's 12th Army Group breaking out of the hedgerows into the kind of open country conducive to American mobile warfare. Olivier Wieviorka, *Normandy: The Landings to the Liberation of Paris*, trans. M. B. DeBevoise (Cambridge, Mass.: Belknap Press of Harvard University Press, 2008), 277–92. Russell F. Weigley, *Eisenhower's Lieutenants: The Campaign of France and Germany, 1944–1945* (Bloomington: Indiana University Press, 1981), 144–69. Carlo D'Este, *Decision in Normandy* (New York: E. P. Dutton, 1983), 437–38.

5. Field Order 2, HQ First U.S. Army, July 28, 1944, File 328-3.2. Blumenson, *Breakout*, 301, 302, 449–50, map 8. Over many generations, local farmers had cultivated thick shrubberies and earthen embankments as natural fences. These segmented the farmland into hundreds of imminently defensible sections, each several acres in size, and were called *bocage*, or hedgerows.

6. History 110th Infantry.

7. 28th ID, Unit Report No. 2, September 10, 1944, File 585.028, July 1944–February 1945, U.S. Air Force Historical Research Agency, Maxwell Air Force Base, Ala. (hereafter referred to as AFHRA). This Air Force archive contains a substantial collection of photostat copies of Army Ground Forces documents from World War II. The originals are in NARA.

8. 2nd Lt. Julian W. Farrior, Company G, 112th Infantry, Company History, File 328-INF(112) 9-0.2.

9. 28th ID, Unit Report No. 2.

10. Farrior, Co. G History.

11. 110th Infantry Unit Report No. 2. Unit Report No. 2, 109th Infantry, September 4, 1944, File 328-INF(109)-0.3. Kemp, *The Regiment*, 107.

12. History 110th Infantry.

13. 28th ID, Unit Report No. 1, August 13, 1944, File 585.028, July 1944–February 1945, AFHRA.

14. Weigley, *Eisenhower's Lieutenants*, 370.

15. Interview with Capt. Charles W. Scott, S-2, 109th Infantry Regiment on November 1, 1944, Combat Interviews (hereafter referred to as "CI"). Text-fiche.

16. Blumenson, *Breakout*, 452. 110th Infantry, Unit Report No. 2.

17. 110th Infantry, Unit Report No. 2. Unit Report No. 2, 109th Infantry, September 4, 1944, File 328-INF(109)-0.3. Kemp, *The Regiment*, 80–89.

18. History of the 28th Infantry Division, June 24, 1944.

19. 112th Infantry, Unit Report No. 2, September 13, 1944, File 328-INF(112)-0.3, Aug–Dec 1944.

20. Farrior, Co. G History. 2nd Lt. Charles Fowler, Unit History, 3rd Battalion, 112th Infantry, September 1, 1944. The Infantry—28th Infantry Division Papers, Box 1, MHI. Lawrence Percival Hall Jr., *My Brother's Letters Home: Blutiger Eigmer (28th Division) Field Artillery Officer's Letters Home*, ed. John Milliken Hall (New York: Vantage, 1999), 58.

21. Fowler, 3rd Bn Unit History, September 15, 1944.

22. Ibid., August 2, 1944.

23. Kuhn, *Baker 2*, 106.

24. Fowler, 3rd Bn Unit History, August 14, 1944.

25. Scott interview. Crist, *The First Century*, 164.

26. History 110th Infantry, 10.

27. Kemp, *The Regiment,* 77–78. Strickler was at this time commander of the 109th's 1st Battalion.

28. Bradley, *A General's Life,* 287.

29. 110th Infantry, Unit Report No. 2. The division's wartime history in file 328-0 sheds no additional light on the relief of General Brown.

30. Weigley, *Eisenhower's Lieutenants,* 90. D'Este, *Decision,* 114. This quote has also been attributed to Colonel George A. Taylor of the 16th Infantry Regiment, but Omar Bradley believed that they were Cota's words. Cota was a 1917 West Point graduate, but training assignments kept him from reaching the Western Front and gaining combat experience. In World War II he was the chief of staff for the 1st Infantry Division, and fought with it in Algeria in November 1942. He preceded his assignment to the 29th "Blue and Grey" Division with a stint as an advisor to Admiral Lord Louis Mountbatten, with whom he shared methods of conducting amphibious operations. Trevor N. Dupuy, David L. Bongard, and Richard C. Anderson Jr., *Hitler's Last Gamble: The Battle of the Bulge, December 1944–January 1945* (New York: Harper Collins, 1994), 101–103.

31. Spot G-2 Estimate, HQ XIX Corps, August 18, 1944, File 328-3.2. G-3 Journal, August 18–22, 1944, File 328-3.2. The division was a part of XIX Corps from July 26 to August 27, 1944, under Major General Charles H. Cortlett. On August 28 it was transferred to V Corps. V Corps, G-3 Report of Operations, August 1944, File 585.51, 6 June–December 1944, AFHRA.

32. G-2 Periodic Report, August 19, 1944, File 328-3.2.

33. Fowler, 3rd Bn Unit History, August 19, 1944.

34. G-2 Periodic Report, August 21, 1944, File 328-3.2. G-3 Journal, August 18–22, 1944.

35. History of the 28th Infantry Division, June 24, 1944. Blumenson, *Breakout,* 580.

36. HQ 28th ID, G-3 Periodic Report, August 25, 1944, File 328-3.2. G-3 Journal, August 25–28, 1944.

37. 28th ID, G-3 Periodic Report No. 39, August 26, 1944, File 328-3.2. 109th Infantry, Unit Report No. 2.

38. 28th ID, Field Order 12, August 28, 1944, File 328-3.2.

39. Annex No. 1 to G-2 Report, August 19.

40. Message from S-2, 110th Infantry Regiment, August 21, 1944, File 328-3.2 G-3 Journal, August 25–28, 1944. GIs were merciless toward snipers, and tended to just kill SS troops because they normally refused to surrender. Peter S. Kindsvatter, *American Soldiers: Ground Combat in the World Wars, Korea, and Vietnam,* with a foreword by Russell F. Weigley (Lawrence: University Press of Kansas, 2003), 216. Wieviorka, *Normandy,* 248.

41. 28th ID, G-2 Estimate of the Enemy Situation No. 1, August 28, 1944, File 328-3.2. G-3 Journal, August 25–28, 1944.

42. History of the 28th Infantry Division, June 24, 1944, 4–6.

43. Robert L. Smith, *"Medic": A WWII Combat Medic Remembers* (Berkeley, Calif.: Creative Arts Book Co., 2001), 52.

44. Dwight D. Eisenhower, *Crusade in Europe* (Garden City, N.Y.: Doubleday, 1948), 297–98. Weigley, *Eisenhower's Lieutenants,* 252. Wieviorka, *Normandy,* 350.

45. G-3 Periodic Report No. 43, August 30, 1944. The 110th Infantry's historian noted that the 4th ID "had previously fought its way through many portions of the city." History 110th Infantry, 22.

46. History 110th Infantry, 43.

47. Kemp, *The Regiment,* 99.

48. Hall, *My Brother's Letters*, 60.

49. History 28th ID, 6. Blumenson, *Breakout*, 622, 673, 692.

50. Charles B. MacDonald, *United States Army in World War II. The European Theater of Operations: The Siegfried Line Campaign* (Washington, D.C.: Office of the Chief of Military History, Department of the Army, 1963), 12.

51. 110th Infantry, Unit Report No. 3, October 7, 1944, File 328-INF(110)-0.3. Unit Report No. 1-5.

52. Field Order 25, V Corps After Action Report, October 5, 1944, File 585. 51, AFHRA.

53. 630th Tank Destroyer Battalion, Unit Report No. 3, September 3, 1944, File TDBN-630-0.9.

54. 112th Infantry Regiment, Unit Report No. 3, October 1, 1944, File 328-INF(112)-0.3, Aug-Dec 1944. Lt. Col. Ross C. Henbest took over as regimental commander on September 10. Hodes survived, and rose to four-star general, commanding the U.S. Army in Europe 1956–59. "United States Army, Europe and Seventh Army," http://www.usarmygermany .com/Units/HqUSAREUR/USAREUR_HqUSAREUR%201.htm.

55. Randall B. Patterson, Diary, September 10, 1944, File 328-INF(112)9-0.3.0.

56. MacDonald, *Siegfried*, 14. Gerow had been the CG of the 29th Infantry Division before taking command of V Corps in 1943. He was a 1911 graduate of the Virginia Military Institute; some officers believed he had no peers as an infantry tactician. Mansoor, *GI Offensive*, 60–61. Weigley, *Eisenhower's Lieutenants*, 48. See also, Harold R. Winton, *Corps Commanders of the Bulge: Six American Generals and Victory in the Ardennes*, with a foreword by Dennis Showalter (Lawrence: University Press of Kansas, 2007), 31–35. Hall, *My Brother's Letters Home*, 52.

57. Ronald Andidora, *Home by Christmas: The Illusion of Victory in 1944* (Westport, Conn.: Greenwood, 2002), 120, 146–47.

58. History 110th Infantry, 47–48.

59. History 28th ID, 6. Peter Schrijvers, *The Crash of Ruin: American Combat Soldiers in Europe during World War II* (Washington Square: New York University Press, 1998), 89–90.

60. Interview, Capt. William J. Maroney S-3, 109th Infantry. Interviewer name is illegible on the microfilm, CI. 109th Infantry Unit Report No. 2.

61. 1st Lt. John S. Howe, "28th Inf. Div. Siegfried Line, 11–16 Sep 44," CI. This is an "integrated narrative" that Howe wrote from his interviews and notes. V Corps Logistics Report, October 3, 1944, File 585.51, AFHRA.

62. Howe interview. Cota was now a major general, having been promoted on September 26.

63. History 110th Infantry, 49. V Corps reported that it was "firmly established on German soil." V Corps After Action Report, October 5, 1944.

64. MacDonald, *Siegfried*, 38. Hodges was a plebe at West Point in 1904, but its math courses drove him out of the academy. He then enlisted in the Army as a private, and was commissioned in 1909. He fought along the Mexican border in 1917, then won the Distinguished Service Cross while fighting for the 5th Division on the Western Front. By the time American entered the war in December 1941, Hodges was the chief of infantry. Weigley, *Eisenhower's Lieutenants*, 84.

65. Rudolf Freiherr von Gersdorff, "Questions for Consideration and Reply by General Frhr von Gersdorff by the Siegfried Line," sub-section, Historical Section, November 1945, St. Germain, trans. A. Rosenwald, Foreign Military Studies, Box 3, A-892, MHI.

66. MacDonald, *Siegfried*, 40–41, 56. Allied strategy had relegated First Army to a supporting role for British General Bernard Law Montgomery's bold thrust into Belgium and thence

toward the Rhine. When Montgomery's Operation Market Garden failed, First Army turned its attention to an offensive against Aachen. Montgomery was the commander of the 21st Army Group, consisting of the First Canadian Army and the Second British Army. Ibid., 8–9.

67. Chester Wilmot, *The Struggle for Europe* (New York: Harper and Bros., 1952), 572. Interview of General Alfred Jodl, ETHINT 52, in *World War II German Military Studies: A Collection of 213 Special Reports on the Second World War Prepared by Former Officers of the Wehrmacht for the United States Army*, ed. Donald S. Detwiler, and Charles B. Burdick and Jürgen Rohwer, assoc. eds., vol. 3, pt. 2, European Theater Historical Interrogation Series (New York: Garland, 1979), 2 (hereafter referred to as ETHINT).

68. MacDonald, *Siegfried*, 4.

69. Wieviorka, *Normandy*, 298.

70. Weigley, *Eisenhower's Lieutenants*, 362.

71. 110 Infantry, Unit Report No. 3.

72. Fowler, 3rd Bn Unit History, August 7, 1944.

73. Howe, CI.

74. V Corps, G-2 Historical Report, October 7, 1944, File 585.51, AFHRA.

75. MacDonald, *Siegfried*, 55.

76. V Corps After Action Report, October 5, 1944. MacDonald, *Siegfried*, 42–43.

77. 2nd Lt. Robert F. Flynn, History of 1st Battalion, 112th Infantry, File 328-INF (112)0.1.

78. History 110th Infantry, 49.

79. MacDonald, *Siegfried*, 39.

80. Howe interview. 109th Infantry, Unit Report No. 2.

81. 110th Infantry Regiment, Unit Report No. 3.

82. MacDonald, *Siegfried*, 47–48. Howe interview. A company is normally 193 officers and men. George Forty, *U.S. Army Handbook, 1939–1945* (New York: Charles Scribner's Sons, 1980), 54.

83. Maroney interview.

84. 109th Infantry, Unit Report No. 2.

85. 109th Infantry, interviews with 2nd Lt. Carl G. Murphy, 1st Platoon Leader, 1st Sgt. _____ Mancuso, E Company, and other enlisted members of the Company, September 30, 1944, interviewer's name illegible, CI. Kemp, *The Regiment*, 132.

86. Murphy and Mancuso interviews. Davis made Strickler the regimental commander on September 19. Kemp, *The Regiment*, 132, 327. Homanisch challenged his relief, was reassigned to the 112th Infantry, and fought as the commander of Company I. His three combat wounds more than confirmed his bravery. Ibid. The U.S. Army recognized these collapses as responses to hellish conditions, not as manifestations of cowardice. Wieviorka, *Normandy*, 248–60.

87. 28th ID, Unit Report No. 3, October 7, 1944, File 585.028, AFHRA. 109th Infantry, Unit Report No. 2.

88. Flynn, History.

89. Farrior, Co. G History.

90. MacDonald, *Siegfried*, 62.

91. 28th ID, Unit Report No. 3. This figure clearly does not include those sick, missing, and captured. V Corps tallied the division's losses from August 27 to October 1 at 3,342. V Corps After Action Report, October 3, 1944.

92. Howe interview.

93. V Corps G-2 Historical Report, October 7, 1944, File 585.51, AFHRA. Approximately 25,000 troops opposed V Corps. Interview of Major Herbert Buechs, Luftwaffe aide to General Alfred Jodl, ETHINT 37, 3.

94. Howe interview. MacDonald, *Siegfried,* 55–56.

95. 28th ID, Unit Report No. 3, October 7, 1944. I suspect that this figure includes all kinds of fortifications, not just the massive concrete pillboxes.

96. MacDonald, *Siegfried,* 35.

97. Howe interview.

98. HQ 103 Engineer Combat Battalion, Report of Demolition Tests on Dragon's Teeth, October 31, 1944, File 328-3.2. G-3 Journal, November 1–3, 1944.

99. Major Harold S. Yeager, 110th Infantry S-3, October 7, 1944, "Account of Battalion Commander of the 2nd Bn 110th Inf. in the Capture of a Limited Objective in the Siegfried Line," File 328-3.2. G-3 Journal and File, October 6–10, 1944.

100. Howe interview.

101. Yeager, "Account."

102. 28th ID, G-2 Periodic Report No. 54, September 20, 1944, File 328-3.2.

103. 28th ID, G-3 Periodic Report No. 64, September 20, 1944, ibid.

104. Flynn, History.

105. Howe interview.

106. 110th Infantry Regiment, Unit Report No. 4, November 4, 1944, File 328-INF(110)-0.3. Unit Reports No. 1–5.

107. David W. Hogan Jr., *A Command Post at War: First Army Headquarters in Europe, 1943–1945* (Washington, D.C.: Center of Military History, United States Army, 2000), 160.

108. Nigel Hamilton, *Monty: The Battles of Field Marshall Bernard Montgomery* (New York: Random House, 1994), 381. Weigley, *Eisenhower's Lieutenants,* 291. Richard Overy, *Why the Allies Won* (New York: W. W. Norton and Co., 1995), 167. Max Hastings, *Overlord: D-Day and the Battle for Normandy* (New York: Simon and Schuster, 1984), 222.

109. Weigley, *Eisenhower's Lieutenants,* 282.

110. Seminar Discussion with Russell Weigley, Temple University, 1997.

111. V Corps After Action Report, November 10, 1944, File 585.51, AFHRA.

112. 28th Infantry Division, Unit Report No. 4, November 14, 1944, File 585.028, AFHRA. History 28th ID.

113. 110th Infantry, Unit Report No. 4.

114. Edward G. Miller, *A Dark and Bloody Ground: The Hürtgen Forest and the Roer River Dams, 1944–1945* (College Station: Texas A&M University Press, 1995), 54.

115. G-3 Journal, October 6, 1944. G-2 Periodic Report No. 69, October 7, 1944. G-2 Periodic Report No. 70, October 8, 1944, File 328-3.2.

116. 112th Regimental Combat Team, Field Order 27, October 6, 1944, File 328-3.2. G-3 Journal and File 6–10 October 1944.

117. 28th Infantry Division, Unit Report No. 4, November 14, 1944, File 585.028, AFHRA.

118. V Corps, Letter of Instruction, October 4, 1944, File 328-3.9.

119. History 28th ID.

120. 28th ID, Unit Report No. 4.

121. 112th Infantry Regiment, Unit Report No. 4, November 4 1944, File 328-INF(112)-0.3, Aug–Dec 1944.

122. V Corps, Familiarization Training of Replacement Troops, October 19, 1944, File 585.51, AFHRA.

123. V Corps G-1 Operations Report, November 7, 1944, ibid.

124. Smith, *Medic*, 48–49.

125. Interview with Lt. Thomas H. Whitney, Co. B, 109th Infantry, by 1st Lt. Harry G. Jackson, Diekirch, December 9, 1944, CI.

126. 1st Sgt. Marshall C. Lewis, Veteran's Questionnaire, Box 28th Infantry Division, 110th Infantry Regiment, MHI.

127. Interview of 1st Lt. Francis P. Diamond, Bn S-4, 1st Bn, 110th Infantry, by Capt. John S. Howe, Urspelt, Luxembourg, December 12–14, 1944, CI. Interview of Capt. Lake W. Coleman, CO of Company F, 110th Infantry, 2nd Lt. Edward J. Matheny, 2nd Lt. D. J. King, 1st Sgts. Steve N. Levering, George W. Fetzer, and Warren H. Dunlap, by Capt. John S. Howe, Niederfeulen, Luxembourg, December 3–4, 1944, CI.

128. Fowler, 3rd Bn Unit History, October 16, 1944.

129. MacDonald, *Siegfried*, 35. Capt. James T. Nesbitt, Unit History, 2nd Battalion, 112th Infantry, October 4, 1944, File 328-INF(112) 0.3. Mansoor, *GI Offensive*, 230.

130. Tracey A. Bailey, "Cold Weather Injury Prevention," *Army Medical Department*, http://www.armymedicine.army.mil/hc/healthtips/13/200311coldweather.cfm. See also, Graham A. Cosmas and Albert E. Cowdrey, *United States Army in World War II, Technical Services. The Medical Department: Medical Services in the European Theater of Operations* (Washington, D.C.: Center of Military History, United States Army, 1992), 489.

131. Hogan, *First Army*, 167–68.

132. Omar N. Bradley, *A Soldier's Story* (New York: Henry Holt, 1951), 445.

133. 28th ID Unit Report No. 5, Status of Supply, File 585.028, AFHRA.

134. 112th Infantry Regiment, Unit Report No. 4, November 4, 1944, File 328–INF(112)-0.3, Aug–Dec 1944.

135. V Corps Engineer After Action Report, October 31, 1944, File 585.51, AFHRA.

136. Currey, *Follow Me and Die*, 57.

11. Battle of the Hürtgen Forest

1. Miller, *Dark and Bloody Ground*, 25–45. Miller's account examines the campaign from the perspective of all the divisions that participated.

2. Hogan, *First Army*, 181–82. HQ V Corps, Field Order No. 29, October 21, 1944, File 328-3.9.

3. Gersdorff, "Questions for Consideration," 13.

4. MacDonald, *Siegfried*, 348.

5. Miller, *Dark and Bloody Ground*, 50.

6. Ibid., 52. Gersdorff, "Questions."

7. MacDonald, *Siegfried*, 342. In a 1948 interview, Carl Peterson stated that the dams "never entered the picture." Charles B. MacDonald and Sidney T. Mathews, *United States Army in World War II. Three Battles: Arnaville, Altuzzo, and Schmidt* (Washington, D.C.: Office of the Chief of Military History, Department of the Army, 1952), 252.

8. Interview of Major Richard S. Dana, 112th Infantry S-3, by Capt. William J. Fox, Ouren, Belgium, December 1, 1944, CI. 112th Infantry Unit Report No. 5, December 2, 1944.

9. Interview of 2nd Lt. Richard Tyo, Platoon leader, Co. K, 112th Infantry, by Capt. William J. Fox, near Sevenig, Germany, December 3, 1944, CI.

10. Interview of Lt. Col. Richard W. Ripple, CO of 707th Tank Battalion, by Capt. John S. Howe, Mulartschütte, Germany, November 14, 1944, CI.

322 | *Notes to pages 189–191*

11. Interview of 1st Sgt. Robert C. Toner, I Co. 112th Infantry, by Capt. William J. Fox, December 10, 1944, near Sevenig, Germany, CI. Tyo interview. Ripple interview. Fowler, 3rd Bn Unit History, November 3–6, 1944.

12. MacDonald, *Siegfried,* 355–56. Currey, *Follow Me,* 127–30. Currey's is a book-length account of the battle.

13. 28th ID G-3 Periodic Report No. 110, November 5, 1944, File 328-3.2. Dana interview.

14. Fowler, 3rd Bn Unit History, November 3–5, 1944.

15. Interview of Capt. Jack W. Walker, CO of Company L, 112th Infantry, Ouren, Germany, December 2, 1944 by Capt. William J. Fox, CI. Fox commented, "Walker was a glib-tongued evasive spokesman. Throughout the interview, I had the feeling that he was holding out more than he told, since his own part in the rout was so prominent and personal. He like others always shied away from direct statements which would give a true picture of the men in flight completely demoralized and scared, which was the case." Fox almost never added comments to his interviews. German infantry captured at least 133 of these GIs. MacDonald, *Siegfried,* 361.

16. Interview of Capt. Guy Piercey, CO of Company M, 112th Infantry, Lieler, Belgium, December 10, 1944 by Capt. William J. Fox, CI.

17. Walker interview.

18. Interview of 1st Sgt. Hank Ripperdam, I Company, 112th Infantry, Ouren, Germany, December 2, 1944, by Capt. William J. Fox, CI.

19. Piercey interview.

20. Interview of SSgt. Nathaniel Quentin, 1st Sgt. Harvey Hausman, SSgt. Stephen J. Kertes, Sgt. Travis C. Norton, A Company 112th Infantry, by Capt. William J. Fox, December 7, 1944, CI.

21. Interview of SSgt. Joseph Perll, C Company, 112th Infantry, by Capt. William J. Fox, December 7, 1944, 1st Bn 112th Inf. HQ, CI.

22. Interview of Sgt. Carl E. Stadelbacher, Co. K, 112th Infantry, by Capt. William J. Fox, Sevenig, Germany, December 3, 1944, CI. Diary Co. K, 3rd Bn, 112th Infantry, File 328-INF(112)9-0.3.0.

23. MacDonald and Mathews, *Three Battles,* 335.

24. Johnson interview. Interview with General Major Rudolf von Gersdorff and General Major Siegfried von Waldenburg, "116th Panzer Division in the Hurtgen Forest," ETHINT 56, 2.

25. Interview of 1st Lt. Eldeen Kauffman, CO Co. F, 112th Infantry, by Capt. William J. Fox, Leiler, Belgium, December 8, 1944, CI.

26. Interview of 1st Lt. Melvin J. Barrilleaux, CO of Company E, by Capt. William J. Fox, near Sevenig, Germany, December 1, 1944, CI.

27. Interview of 1st Lt. Clifton W. Beggs, 2nd Platoon, Co. E, 112th Infantry, by Capt. William J. Fox, December 9, 1944, at Leiler, Belgium, CI.

28. Interview of Corporal Joe E. Philpot, Company Clerk, G Company, 112th Infantry, by Capt. William J. Fox, near Lieler, Belgium, December 15, 1944, CI. Charles MacDonald differs, stating that there was no attack before 12:00, but that "fire and the threat of attack" caused the panic. MacDonald, *Siegfried,* 365.

29. Interview of Capt. John D. Pruden, Ex. Officer, 2nd Battalion, 112th Infantry, by Capt. William J. Fox, Leiler, Belgium, December 8, 1944, CI.

30. Kauffman interview.

31. G-3 Journal, November 6, 1944. 28th ID, Unit Report No. 5.

32. Condon interview.

33. Ibid.

34. Interview with SSgt. Charles W. Cascarano, Co. F, 112th Infantry, by Capt. William J. Fox, in Malamuhle, Germany, December 15, 1944, CI.

35. G-3 Journal, November 7, 1944.

36. Condon interview.

37. Ripple interview.

38. Field Order 25, 28th Infantry Division, October 29, 1944, File 328-3.9.

39. V Corps Field Order 29. V Corps, Letter of Instruction, Supplement to Field Order No. 30, October 23, 1944, File 328-3.9. History 28th ID, 11.

40. G-3 Journal, November 3, 1944. Folder G-3 Journal and File, November 1–3, 1944. 110th Infantry Regiment, Unit Report No. 5, December 3, 1944, File 328-INF(110)-0.3. Unit Report No. 1-5. 28th ID G-3 Periodic Report No. 109, November 4, 1944, File 328-3.2. Interview of Major General Norman D. Cota and Brigadier General George A. Davis by Capt. William J. Fox, Wiltz, Luxembourg, December 13, 1944, CI. This interview is a disappointment for those trying to understand Cota's reasoning. Capt. Fox did not ask either of the generals probing questions, and they offered no gems of insight. Fowler, 3rd Bn Unit History, November 5–7. Interview of Lt. Col. Daniel B. Strickler and Maj. William J. Moraney by 1st Lt. Harry G. Jackson, December 8, 1944, near Ettlebruck, CI.

41. Colonel Lewis C. Pattillo, V Corps Engineer After Action Report, December 1, 1944, File 585.51, AFHRA.

42. Cota and Davis interview. MacDonald, *Siegfried,* 345.

43. MacDonald, *Siegfried,* 343. Lieutenant Colonel Peterson took command of the 112th sometime between September 10 and October 31. 112th Infantry Regiment, Unit Report No. 4, October 31, 1944, File 328-INF(112)-0.3, Aug–Dec 1944. Peterson had joined the PNG in 1922. *Directory Pennsylvania National Guard.*

44. Nesbitt, 2nd Bn Unit History.

45. Dana interview.

46. 707th Tank Battalion S-3 Journal, November 3, 1944, File ARBN-707-0.3, Nov.–Dec. 1944.

47. 707th S-3 Journal, November 4, 1944. Ripple interview. 707th Tank Battalion After Action Report, December 3, 1944, File ARBN-707-0.3, Nov.–Dec. 1944.

48. Ripple interview. Interview of 1st Lt. Leon Simon, 112th Infantry, by Capt. William J. Fox, Leiler, Belgium, December 6, 1944, CI.

49. Interview of 1st Lt. Howard S. Rogers, Recon. Platoon Leader, Hq Co., 707th Tank Battalion, by Capt. John S. Howe, Mulartschütte, Germany, November 14, 1944, CI.

50. Interview of Capt. Bruce M. Hastrup, CO of C Company, 707th Tank Battalion, by Capt. John S. Howe, Mulartschütte, Germany November 14, 1944, CI. The bulk of the interviews of the armored troops discuss efforts to move the tanks over the Kall trail.

51. Currey, *Follow Me,* 224.

52. Interview of Capt. William C. Dobbs, 110th Infantry E Company Commander, 1st Lt. Frank J. Deptula, 1st Sgt. Lonnie C. Bland, by Capt. John S. Howe, Niederfeulen, Luxembourg, December 4, 1944, CI.

53. 110th Infantry, Unit Report No. 5.

54. V Corps After Action Report, December 4, 1944, File 585.51.

55. 28th Infantry Division, Unit Report No. 5. MacDonald, *Siegfried,* 35.

56. 1st Lt. William J. Scanlon, Unit History 391st Fighter Squadron, December 7, 1944, SQ-FI-391-HI, November 1944, AFHRA.

57. 28th ID, Unit Report No. 5.

58. Interview of Major Edwin M. Howison, 9th Tactical Air Command, by Capt.s William J. Fox and John S. Howe, Rott, Germany, November 1, 1944, CI.

59. Field Order 25. 28th ID, Unit Report No. 5.

60. Miller, *Dark and Bloody Ground,* 69.

61. 28th ID, Unit Report No. 5. Cota and Davis interview.

62. 28th ID, G-2 Periodic Report No. 93, October 28, 1944, File 328-3.2.

63. 89th Inf. Div.—History and Order of Battle, File 328-3.2. He may have referred to the 116th Panzer Division, which "constituted the principle [sic] enemy force opposing the 28th." V Corps G-2 Historical Record, December 7, 1944, File 585.51, AFHRA.

64. Von Gersdorff, A-891, p. 5. Three months earlier, at least, "most of the officers and NCOs were veterans of the Eastern Front." Terry Copp, *Fields of Fire: The Canadians in Normandy* (Toronto: University of Toronto Press, 2003), 199.

65. 28th ID, Unit Report No. 5. The 272nd's moniker "Volksgrenadier," was "an honorific title selected to appeal to the national and military pride of the German people." MacDonald, *Siegfried,* 15. Currey, *Follow Me,* 76.

66. Douglas E. Nash, *Victory Was beyond Their Grasp: With the 272nd Volks-Grenadier Division from the Hürtgen Forest to the Heart of the Reich* (Bedford, Pa.: Aberjona Press, 2008), 66.

67. 109th Infantry, Annex 1 to Field Order 14, October 30, 1944, CI.

68. MacDonald, *Siegfried,* 346.

69. G-2 Section, Telephone from S-2 Lt. Montgomery, File 328-3.2, November 1–3, 1944.

70. 28th ID G-2 Periodic Report No. 96, November 2, 1944, ibid.

71. 28th ID G-3 WR Journal, November 2, 1944, ibid.

72. Ibid.

73. Received G-2 from Division Artillery, November 4, 1944, File 328-3.2, November 4–5, 1944.

74. 112th Infantry, Unit Report No. 5, December 2, 1944, File 328-INF(112)-0.3.

75. G-3 Journal, November 4, 1944.

76. 112th Infantry Regiment, G-2, "Report of Interrogation of 5 Deserters from 3rd Co. 156 Pz Gr Regt., 116 Pz Div. taken at Vossenack," November 5, 1944, File 328-3.2, November 4–5, 1944. MacDonald and Mathews, *Three Battles,* 342.

77. 2nd Bn, 112th RCT, Field Order 2, October 30, 1944, File 328-3.2.

78. HQ 28th ID to CG V Corps, "Plan of Operation," November 2, 1944. Ibid.

79. Capt. John S. Howe, "The Battle for Vossenack-Kommerscheidt-Schmidt 2–16 November 1944," February 24, 1945, CI. The First Army diary states that Hodges considered the plan "excellent." William C. Sylvan and Francis G. Smith Jr., *Normandy to Victory: The War Diary of General Courtney H. Hodges and the First U.S. Army,* ed. John T. Greenwood (Lexington: University Press of Kentucky, 2008), 161.

80. Cota and Davis interview.

81. MacDonald and Mathews, *Three Battles,* 255.

82. 28th ID G-3 Periodic Report No. 109, November 4, 1944, File 328-3.2. History 3rd Bn, HQ Co., November 5–7, 112th Infantry.

83. MacDonald, *Siegfried,* 352–54.

84. MacDonald, *Three Battles,* 313. Cota and Davis interview.

85. Dana interview.

86. Unit Report Number 5, 112th Infantry. Neither did it list the hundreds of troops missing and captured.

87. Major General Norman D. Cota, November 5, 1944, Message to Commanding Officer, 112th Infantry Regiment. 28th ID G-2 Reports, November 4, 1944, File 328-3.2.

88. 707th S-3 Journal, November 6, 1944. 28th ID, Unit Report No. 5. MacDonald, *Siegfried Line,* 363.

89. Currey, *Follow Me,* 156.

90. Interview of 1st Lt. James A. Condon, Co. E, 112th Infantry, December 14, 1944, in Maluamuhle, Luxembourg, by Capt. William J. Fox, CI. 1st Lt. Robert F. Flynn, HQ and 2nd Bn, 112th Infantry, Unit History for November, December 6, 1944, File 328-INF(112)-0.1 to 328-INF(112)-1.13.

91. Currey, *Follow Me,* 198.

92. Nesbitt, 2nd Bn Unit History.

93. Miller, *Dark and Bloody Ground,* 76–77. Dana interview. Currey, *Follow Me,* 216–17. James M. Gavin, *On to Berlin: Battles of an Airborne Commander, 1943–1946* (New York: Viking, 1978), 268. No other confirmation that Cota fainted has been found.

94. 28th ID, Unit Report No. 5. MacDonald, *Siegfried Line,* 368. BG George Davis, Letter of Instruction, November 8, 1944, File 328-3.2, G-3 Journal, November 8–9, 1944.

95. 28th ID Field Order 26, November 7, 1944, 0830 hours, File 328-3.9.

96. 28th ID, Unit Report No. 5. MacDonald, *Siegfried,* 368. BG George Davis, Letter of Instruction, November 8, 1944, File 328-3.2. G-3 Journal, November 8–9, 1944. Cota and Davis interview. Dana interview. Colonel Gustin M. Nelson to Assistant Division Commander, 28th ID, November 13, 1944, CI.

97. G-3 Journal, November 7, 1944. MacDonald and Mathews, *Three Battles,* 389. G-3 Journal, November 8, 1944.

98. Currey, *Follow Me,* 224.

99. Telephone call, General Gerow to General Cota, 2310 hours, November 7, 1944. G-3 Journal, November 6–7, 1944.

100. G-3 Journal, November 7, 1944. Dana interview.

101. G-3 Journal, November 8, 1944.

102. History 28th ID, 13.

103. Winton, *Corps Commanders,* 373. MacDonald, *Siegfried,* 369.

104. Dwight D. Eisenhower to George C. Marshall, November 11, 1944. Alfred D. Chandler Jr., ed., *The Papers of Dwight David Eisenhower,* vol. 4: *The War Years* (Baltimore, Md.: Johns Hopkins Press, 1970), 2297.

105. CG's Oral Instructions to Comdrs of: 12th Inf, 109th Inf, 110th Inf, 2nd Bn 112th Inf, 1171st Engr C Gp, and Div Arty, November 9, 1944, Folder G-3 Journal November 8–9, 1944.

106. Martin Blumenson, *The Patton Papers, 1940–1945* (Boston: Houghton Mifflin, 1974), 739–40.

107. Gavin, *On to Berlin,* 265–66.

108. Gersdorff, A-892, 13–14.

109. Hogan, *First Army,* 121–22. Weigley, *Eisenhower's Lieutenants,* 84–85, 298, 325.

110. G-3 Journal, November 10–11, 1944.

111. G-3 Periodic Report No. 116, November 10, 1944, File 328-3.2.

112. Interview of 1st Lt. Francis P. Diamond, Bn S-4, 1st Bn, 110th Infantry, by Capt. John S. Howe, Urspelt, Luxembourg, December 12–14, 1944, CI, 76. Gibney had already fought in the Forest as the commander of the 60th Infantry Regiment, 9th ID. Miller, *A Dark and Bloody Ground*, 24. Gibney became the 109th's commander on November 7. He was a 1918 West Point graduate, "of average size, taciturn, quiet mannered, and an experienced leader." Kemp, *The Regiment*, 189, 212–13.

113. Dobbs interview.

114. 110th Infantry, Unit Report No. 5. MacDonald, *Siegfried*, 372. The 13th Infantry Regiment replaced what was left of the 110th in the line. G-3 Journal, November 10, 13, 1944.

115. Howe comment in Cook interview transcript. Interview of SSgt. John B. Cook, Platoon Sgt. 2nd Platoon, Co. B, 707th Tank Battalion, by Capt. John S. Howe, Pintsch, Luxembourg, December 1, 1944, CI.

116. 28th ID G-3 Periodic Report No. 119, File 328–3.2.

117. V Corps After Action Report. One of the 8th Infantry Division's regiments, the 22nd, is the subject of Robert Sterling Rush's excellent *Hell in Hürtgen Forest: The Ordeal and Triumph of an American Infantry Regiment* (Lawrence: University Press of Kansas, 2001).

118. Condon interview.

119. Dana interview.

120. Lt. Col W. Wagner, "Report by SS 'Frundsberg' 10th Panzer Division," captured document in Annex 1 of Periodic Report No. 74, First U.S. Army, File 580.606, July–August 1944, AFHRA. MacDonald, *Siegfried*, 25. John Ellis, *Brute Force: Allied Strategy and Tactics in the Second World War* (New York: Viking, 1990), 422, 429–34. Martin Van Creveld, *Fighting Power: German and U.S. Army Performance, 1939–1945* (Westport, Conn.: Greenwood, 1982), 167. Hastings, *Overlord*, 315–18. John Keegan, "The Making of the American G.I.," *Time*, December 29, 2003, 104.

121. G-3 Journal, November 5, 1944. 28th ID G-2 Reports, November 4, 1944, File 328-3.2. Nash, *Victory*, 70.

122. Interview of 1st Lt. Clyde R. Johnson, G Co. 112th Infantry, by Capt. William J. Fox, near Lieler, Belgium, December 15, 1944, CI.

123. 1st Lt. Benajah H. Bruner, History Company G, 112th Infantry, December 1, 1944, File 328-INF(112)9-0.2.

124. G-3 Journal, November 6, 1944.

125. 28th ID G-2 Periodic Report No. 101, November 7, 1944, File 328-3.2. G-3 Journal, November 6–7, 1944.

126. MacDonald and Mathews, *Three Battles*, 372. MacDonald, *Siegfried*, 368.

127. 28th ID G-2 Periodic Report No. 103, November 9, 1944, File 328-3.2. Dana interview.

128. G-3 Journal, November 7, 1944. A TD's cannon shot rounds with a speed of 2,600 feet per second, while the Sherman's gun fired at 1,800 feet per second. *World War II Vehicles*, http://www.wwiivehicles.com/usa/tank_destroyers/m10_tankdestroyer.html. http://www.wwiivehicles.com/usa/guns.html#3inM7.

129. Fleig interview.

130. Miller, *Dark and Bloody Ground*, 75.

131. G-3 Journal, November 7, 1944.

132. MacDonald and Mathews, *Three Battles*, 374–75.

133. G-3 Journal, November 7, 1944. Gardner interview.

134. Fleig interview. 707th S-3 Journal, November 4, 1944.

135. Interview of 2nd Lt. Richard H. Payne, 3rd Platoon Leader, 707th Tank Battalion, by Capt. John S. Howe, Roetgen, Germany, November 14, 1944, CI.

136. Perll interview.

137. Interview of Capt. George W. Granger by Capt. John S. Howe, December 1, 1944, CI.

138. Cook interview. 707th S-3 Journal, November 7, 1944.

139. Granger interview. 707th S-3 Journal, November 7, 1944. Cook interview.

140. Davis interview. 707th S-3 Journal, November 7, 1944. Perll interview.

141. John C. Fairchild, "History of the 229th Field Artillery Battalion," 21, 62. A time on target is the coordinated firing of all artillery pieces within range of a single aim point at that one target.

142. G-3 Journal, November 8, 1944.

143. History of 390th FS, SQ-FI-390-HI, AFHRA.

144. 28th ID G-2 Periodic Report No. 103, November 9, 1944, File 328-3.2. 893rd Tank Destroyer Battalion, November 8, 1944, CI.

145. Edwin H. J. Cornell, Veteran's Questionnaire, Box 28th Infantry Division, 110th Infantry Regiment, MHI.

146. Alexander H. Hadden, *Not Me! The World War II Memoirs of a Reluctant Rifleman* (Bennington, Vt.: Merriam Press, 1997), 36–37, 40.

147. 110th Infantry, Unit Report No. 5.

148. Kemp, *The Regiment*, 202.

149. Dobbs interview.

150. Bruner, History Company G, 112th Infantry, December 1, 1944. Interview of Lt. Charles E. Potter, 109th Inf., 1st Bn S-2, by Lt. Harry G. Jackson, December 9, 1944, CI.

151. Interview of Private Dorn [no first name given], Co. K, 112th Infantry, by Capt. William J. Fox, Sevenig, Germany, December 3, 1944, CI.

152. Interview with Lt. Thomas H. Whitney, Co. B, 109th Infantry, by 1st Lt. Harry G. Jackson, Diekirch, December 9, 1944, CI.

153. 109th Infantry Regiment, Unit Report No. 5, December 4, 1944, File 328–INF(109)-0.3.

154. 110th Infantry, Unit Report No. 5, December 3, 1944. Strickler Papers.

155. Fowler, 3rd Bn Unit History, November 5–7, 1944.

156. 103rd Engineer Battalion, Unit Report No. 5, November 1944, File 328-ENG-0.3. A/A Report, 103rd Eng. Bn, November 1944.

157. Dobbs interview.

158. Interview of Sgts. Avery Lanning, William M. Pennington, SSgts. Joseph K. Pacz-esna, Abraham Kumuku, Manuel Suarez, Morris G. Sykes, Company G, 110th Infantry, by Capt. John S. Howe, Niederfeulen, Luxembourg, December 6, 1944, CI.

159. Kemp, *The Regiment*, 192.

160. Whitney interview. Kemp, *The Regiment*, 154.

161. Interview of Capt. Lake W. Coleman, CO of Company F, 110th Infantry, 2nd Lt. Edward J. Matheny, 2nd Lts. D.J. King, 1st Sgts. Steve N. Levering, George W. Fetzer, and Warren H. Dunlap, by Capt. John S. Howe, Niederfeulen, Luxembourg, December 3–4, 1944, CI.

162. Interview of Capt. Donald C. Kelly, Headquarters Company CO, 707th Tank Battalion, by Capt. John S. Howe, Mulartschütte, Germany, November 14, 1944, CI. Kelly interview.

163. Interview of 1st Lt. Eldeen Kauffman, CO Co. F, 112th Infantry, by Capt. William J. Fox, Leiler, Belgium, December 8, 1944, CI.

164. Interview of Lt. Charles E. Potter, 109th Inf., 1st Bn S-2, by Lt. Harry G. Jackson, December 9, 1944, CI.

165. Interview of Capt. Max R. Whitetree, CO of A Company, 109th Inf., Lt. Samuel J. Leo, TSgt. Charles E. Frawley, and TSgt. Lee D. Balleger, by 1st Lt. Harry G. Jackson, Diekirch, Germany, December 9, 1944, CI. G-3 Journal, November 12, 1944.

166. Quentin interview. Granger interview.

167. Whitney interview. Perll interview. Tyo interview.

168. Condon interview.

169. Barrilleaux interview. Toner interview.

170. Whitney interview.

171. Coleman interview. Kemp, *The Regiment*, 191. Hall, *My Brother's Letters*, 78.

172. 112th Infantry, Unit Report No. 5.

173. 1st Lt. Loyd Johnson, "Casualty Evacuation Report," no date, Co. C, 103rd Medical Battalion. Major Albert L. Berndt, 112th Infantry Regiment, Report on Medical Evacuation, November 10, 1944, MG-272, Robert H. Henschen Papers, Slot 5-0271, Box 19, Folder Files Relating to Hurtgen Forest, PSA.

174. Coleman interview. Interview of Sgt. Thomas G. Hunter, and 1st Lt. Jack E. Kelly, Co. D, 112th Infantry by Capt. William J. Fox, D Co. CP, December 4, 1944, CI.

175. 28th ID, Unit Report No. 5. 109th Infantry, Unit Report No. 5.

176. 28th ID, Unit Report No. 5. Lanning interview.

177. 110th Infantry, Unit Report No. 5. Burns interview.

178. Diamond interview. G-3 Journal, November 11, 1944.

179. HQ CT 110, Plan of Attack, November 11, 1944, File 328-INF(110)-0.3. Unit Reports No. 1–5.

180. Coleman interview.

181. Ibid. 110th Infantry, Unit Report No. 5. G-3 Journal, November 11, 1944.

182. Interview of Capt. James H. Burns, S-3 of 1st Bn, 110th Infantry. Interviewed by Capt. John S. Howe, Urspelt, Luxembourg, December 12–14, 1944, CI. Diamond interview.

183. G-3 Journal, November 10, 1944.

184. 28th ID, Unit Report No. 5. MacDonald, *Siegfried,* 373–74.

185. Fowler, 3rd Bn Unit History, November 8–13, 1944.

186. 110th Infantry, Unit Report No. 5.

187. Kemp, *The Regiment*, 191–92. Fowler, 3rd Bn Unit History, November 5–7, 1944.

188. 28th ID, Unit Report No. 5, Administrative. Charles MacDonald gives the figure of 6,184 casualties; he probably included more attached units than did the HQ of the 28th ID at the time. MacDonald, *Siegfried,* 374.

189. V Corps After Action Report, G-2 Report, December 7, 1944.

190. 107th FA, Unit Report No. 5, November 1–30, 1944, File 328-FA(107)-0.3. "History of the 229th."

191. Bruner History.

192. 1st Lt. Clarence J. Barwick, Historical Officer, Co. G, 112th Infantry, May 1, 1945, File 328-INF(112)9-0 to 328-INF(112)9-0.2. Interview of Capt. Richard Gooley, S-1, 1st Bn, 112th Infantry, by Capt. William J. Fox, December 4, 1944, probably in Ouren, Belgium, CI. Fowler, 3rd Bn Unit History, November 8–13, 1944.

193. 110th Infantry, Unit Report No. 5. Capt. John S. Howe, 110th Infantry Regiment, 28th Division, Summary of Action, CI.

194. 110th Infantry, Unit Report No. 5.

195. Burns interview.

196. 109th Infantry, Unit Report No. 5.

197. 112th Infantry, Unit Report No. 5. Killed: 167, wounded: 719, MIA: 431, nonbattle casualties: 544, captured by the enemy: 232.

198. History 28th ID, 14. The actual figure was about 2,000, not including prisoners. Mac-Donald, *Siegfried*, 374.

199. HQ 707th Tank Battalion, "Report on Tank Losses," November 10, 1944. HQ 707th Tank Battalion S-3 Journal, File 328–3.2.

200. Eisenhower, *The Great Crusade*, 338. Nash, *Victory*, 82.

201. Ivan H. (Cy) Peterman, "British Span Key Canal," *Philadelphia Inquirer,* November 5, 1944, 1–2. "Threat of Death Stops Nazi Unit's Surrender," *Philadelphia Inquirer,* November 6, 1944, 1, 3. James F. McGlincy, "Patton Drive Cracks Nazi Line Near Metz," *Philadelphia Inquirer,* November 9, 1944, 2. "43 Are Killed from Phila. Area," *Philadelphia Inquirer,* November 14, 1944, 1.

202. History 28th ID.

203. 1st Lt. John G. Maher, Veteran's Questionnaire, Box 28th Infantry Division, 110th Infantry Regiment, MHI. Bruner history. Toner interview.

204. Gersdorff, A-891, 12.

12. Battle of the Bulge

1. Hastings, *Overlord,* 25. Lloyd Clark, *Anzio: Italy and the Battle for Rome—1944* (New York: Atlantic Monthly Press, 2006), 9. Thanks are in order to Harold Winton, Harold Nelson, and Ed Rouse for their comments on this chapter.

2. Horst Boog, Gerhard Krebs, and Detlef Vogel, *Germany and the Second World War: The Strategic Air War in Europe and the War in the West and East Asia 1943–1944/5,* vol. 7 (Oxford: Clarendon Press, 2006), 683.

3. S. L. A. Marshall, *Men against Fire: The Problem of Battle Command in Future War* (New York: William Morrow, 1947), 54. In the late 1980s, Frederic Smoler and Roger Spiller found that Marshall's research was deeply flawed, and that he may have fabricated his statistical research out of nothing. Frederic Smoler, "The Secret of the Soldiers Who Didn't Shoot," *American Heritage,* March 1989, 40–43. Roger J. Spiller, "S.L.A. Marshall and the Ratio of Fire," *RUSI Journal* 133, no. 4 (Winter 1988): 68.

4. John Toland, *Battle: The Story of the Bulge* (New York: Random House, 1959), 380.

5. History of the 28th Infantry Division, June 24, 1944. HQ VIII Corps, Report of VIII Corps After Action against Enemy Forces for the Period 1–31 December, 1944, File 208-0.3. Colonel Daniel B. Strickler, "Action Report of the German Ardennes Breakthrough as I Saw It from 16 Dec. 1944–2 Jan. 1945," 2, File 328-INF(110)-0.1 to 0.3. Colonel Gustin M. Nelson, interviewed by 1st Lt. George M. Tuttle, January 14, 1945, CI. Nelson had previously served in the headquarters of the 5th Armored Division. http://www.5ad.org/10_44.html.

6. Strickler, Action Report, 2. Toland, *Battle,* 79. Hugh M. Cole, *United States Army in World War II, The European Theater of Operations. The Ardennes: Battle of the Bulge* (Washington, D.C.: Center of Military History, United States Army, 1994), 312. Manteuffel commanded the Fifth Panzer Army.

7. Cole, *Ardennes,* 179–81. Strickler, Action Report, 2.

8. HQ 28th Infantry Division, Unit Report No. 6, January 15, 1945, File 585.028, AFHRA. Fuller took command of the regiment on November 21. He had lost his previous command

during Normandy but used his friendship with Major General Troy Middleton to gain a second chance. Charles B. MacDonald, *A Time For Trumpets: The Untold Story of the Battle of the Bulge* (New York: William Morrow and Co., 1985), 134–35.

9. Cole, *Ardennes*, 56, 177.

10. Lt. Col. William H. Allen, interview by 1st Lt. George M. Tuttle, January 16, 1945, 112th Infantry, CI.

11. Henschen Manuscript, 1945, Robert H. Henschen Collection, MG-272, Slot 5-0271, Box 19, Folder Robert Henschen, 28th Div, Files Relating to Hürtgen Forest Operation, Nov. 2–9, 1944; "Bulge" reminiscences, 1945, PSA.

12. Cole, *Ardennes*, 17. MacDonald, *Trumpets*, 19–24, 38. Dupuy, Bongard, and Anderson, *Hitler's Last Gamble*, 9. The name *"Wacht am Rhein,"*—watch on the Rhine—was designed for operational security; anyone who saw the phrase would assume it was for a plan to defend the Rhine River. Cole, *Ardennes*, 21.

13. OKW: Oberkommando der Wehrmacht, "the Armed Forces High Command." Dupuy, *Gamble*, 10.

14. Cole, *Ardennes*, 20, 25, 26, 38. Weigley, *Eisenhower's Lieutenants*, 44.

15. MacDonald, *Trumpets*, 48, 57, 61. Operational History of the Ninth Air Force, Book 1, Battle of the Ardennes: 1 December 1944–31 January 1945, File 533.01-2 Book No. 1, Dec. 1944–Jan. 1945, AFHRA, 31–32.

16. Interview with General Alfred Jodl, July 31, 1945, ETHINT 51, 16. Interview with General Baptist Kniess, ETHINT 40, 2.

17. Interview with General der Panzertruppen Hasso von Manteuffel, June 21, 1945, ETHINT 45, 2.

18. Cole, *Ardennes*, 174.

19. Jodl, ETHINT 51, 17.

20. Cole, *Ardennes*, 175–76. MacDonald, *Trumpets*, 130.

21. MacDonald, *Trumpets*, 52, 94. Hogan, *Command Post*, 207–208. Regarding this intelligence failure, readers should reference pages 62–79 of *A Time for Trumpets*, as well as Dupuy, *Hitler's Last Gamble*, 35–44, and Winton, *Corps Commanders*, 79–84.

22. "Ninth Air Force," 31–32.

23. Weigley, *Eisenhower's Lieutenants*, 463. MacDonald, *Trumpets*, 74.

24. Report of VIII Corps, December 1944. VIII Corps was headquartered in Bastogne. Winton, *Corps Commanders*, 39.

25. Henschen Manuscript.

26. HQ 28th Infantry Division, G-3 Report, December 15, 1944, File 328-3.2.

27. Colonel Hurley S. Fuller, Report of Operations of the 110th Infantry Combat Team, December 16–18, 1944, MG-356, Carton 4, PSA.

28. 1st Lt. Thomas J. Flynn, Executive Officer, Company K, 110th Infantry, interview by Capt William J. Dunkerley, May 1–2, 1945, transcript, CI. 1st Lt. James C. Sharpe, interviewed by Technician 3rd Grade William Henderson, January 20, 1944, CI. Clarence Blakeslee, *A Personal Account of WWII by Draftee #36887149* (Rockford, Mich.: Clarence Blakeslee, 1989), 35.

29. MacDonald, *Trumpets*, 265. Dupuy, *Gamble*, 37.

30. 28th ID G-3 Report, December 16, 1944, File 328-3.2. 108th Field Artillery, Unit Report No. 6, January 1, 1945, File 328-FA(108)-0.3.

31. Cole, *Ardennes*, 331–32. Troy H. Middleton gained an outstanding combat record during WWI and excelled at all of his interwar assignments. He left the Army in 1937 to become the administrative dean at Louisiana State University, but rejoined the Army after the Pearl

Harbor attack. He quickly earned command of the 45th Infantry Division and led it with great skill on Sicily. Eisenhower awarded him with VIII Corps in March of 1944. His seniors considered him a first-rate tactician. Winton, *Corps Commanders*, 36–38. Cole, *Ardennes*, 55.

32. Strickler, Action Report, 3.

33. 28th ID, Unit Report No. 6. 58th Panzer Corps and 47th Panzer Corps. 26th Volksgrenadier Division, 116th Panzer Division, Panzer Lehr, 5th Parachute Division, 325 Volksgrenadier Division, 560 Volksgrenadier Division, 2nd Panzer Division. HQ VIII Corps, G-2 Estimate No. 13, December 29, 1944, File 208-3.9. Cole, *Ardennes*, maps 4, 5. Dupuy, *Gamble*, 106.

34. G-3 Report, December 16, 1944. G-3 Journal, December 16, 1944. "Ardennes Breakthrough, 16 December 1944–15 January 1945," File 328-INF(110)-0.1 to 0.3, 41. Strickler, "Action Report," 3–4.

35. Telephone Message from 28th Infantry Division to VIII Corps, 16 December 1944, File 208-3.2.

36. HQ VIII Corps, G-3 Section, R.C. Embree, G-3 Air, Memorandum to Colonel Evans, December 16, 1944, File 208-3.2.

37. Ninth Air Force, Section II, 5, 23–25. G-3 Journal, December 17, 1944.

38. Winton, *Corps Commanders*, 110.

39. Ibid. Weigley, *Eisenhower's Lieutenants*, 480. American strategy on a greater scale included holding fast at the north and south shoulders of the bulge, delaying at the Amblève River, releasing the strategic reserve to VIII Corps, and preventing the Germans from crossing the Meuse River. Weigley, *Eisenhower's Lieutenants*, 470–82.

40. Cole, *Ardennes*, 176–77, 509.

41. 28th ID G-2 Periodic Report No. 142, December 18, 1944, File 328-3.2, December 9–20, 1944. Strickler, "Action Report," 7.

42. HQ VIII Corps, Letter of Instruction, December 16, 1944, File 208-3.9.

43. G-3 Journal, December 17, 1944.

44. HQ VIII Corps G-3 Section, December 17, 1944, File 328-3.2.

45. VIII Corps G-3 Journal, December 18, 1944, File 208-3.2. Cole, *Ardennes*, 361, 375, 504.

46. Ivan H. (Cy) Peterman, "Nazi Drive Aims at U.S Supplies," *Philadelphia Inquirer*, December 22, 1944, 1–2. Wilmot, *Struggle for Europe*, 584. Currey, *Follow Me*, 63n. *Battle of the Bulge* (Warner Brothers, 1965).

47. Winton, *Corps Commanders*, 91. MacDonald, *Trumpets*, 46.

48. Weigley, *Eisenhower's Lieutenants*, 475, 478. Jodl, ETHINT 51, 16, 19.

49. Troy F. Middleton, Letter of Instruction, December 20, 1944, File 208-3.9. Troy F. Middleton, Letter of Instruction, December 20, 1944, ibid. The commander of the 526th Armored Infantry Battalion, Major Paul J. Solis, had already taken action to keep German forces from stumbling upon the fuel. He used gasoline from the stockpile at Francorchamps to create a burning roadblock at Stavelot. Cole, *Ardennes*, 266.

50. Dupuy, *Gamble*, 109. Boog, *Germany*, vol. VII, 682.

51. Edward Kennedy, "Patton Smashes Sure River Line; 15 Towns Taken, *Philadelphia Inquirer*, December 30, 1944, 1.

52. S. L. A. Marshall, *Bastogne: The Story of the First Eight Days*, assisted by John G. Westover and A. Joseph Webber (Washington, D.C.: Infantry Journal Press, 1946), 7. Charles Whiting, *The Last Assault: The Battle of the Bulge Reassessed* (New York: Sarpedon, 1994), 140.

53. Similarly, Olivier Wieviorka has argued that soldiers who believe they are fighting for something worthwhile suffer combat exhaustion at a lower rate than those who believe they are engaged in meaningless combat. Wieviorka, *Normandy*, 269–70.

54. G-3 Journal, December 16.

55. MacDonald, *Trumpets*, 278–79. Robert H. Phillips, *To Save Bastogne* (New York: Stein and Day Publishers, 1983), 88–89, 136. Phillips has written an excellent book-length account of the division's experience, especially that of the 110th Infantry.

56. After Action Report, 2nd Battalion, Annex 3 to Unit Report No. 6, 110th Infantry Regiment, January 6, 1945, MG-356, Carton 4, PSA.

57. Lt. Col. William H. Allen, interview by 1st Lt. George M. Tuttle, January 16, 1945, 112th Infantry, CI.

58. After Action Report, 3rd Battalion, Annex 4 to Unit Report No. 6, 110th Infantry, MG-356, Carton 3, PSA.

59. G-3 Journal, December 17, 1944.

60. Flynn interview.

61. Phillips, *Bastogne,* 160.

62. Flynn interview.

63. Theodore E. Seeley to Norman D. Cota, May 8, 1945. Col. Hurley E. Fuller, Enclosure No. 2 to accompany citation for WD Distinguished Unit Citation, File 328-INF(110). Strickler, "Ardennes Breakthrough." Fuller, Report of Operations.

64. History, 229th FA, 39, 41.

65. C Company of the 447th AAA Bn, Colonel Gustin M. Nelson, interviewed by 1st Lt. George M. Tuttle, January 14, 1945, CI. 112th Infantry Regiment, Unit Report No. 6, January 16, 1945, File 328-INF(112)-0.3. After Action Report, 229th Field Artillery, December 16, 1944, File 328-FA(229)-3.2. Tec. 3rd Grd William Henderson, interview with Lt. Col. John C. Fairchild and Capt. Neil Fergerson, 229th Field Artillery Battalion, January 21, 1945, CI.

66. 109th FA, Unit Report No. 6, File 328-FA(109)-3.2. Fuller, Report of Operations. This town may actually be spelled Mageret.

67. 1st Lt. Richard V. Purcell, interviewed by Tec 3rd Grd William Henderson, January 23, 1945, CI. G-3 Journal December 17, 1944.

68. 2nd Lt. Edwin B. Cline, interview on January 22, 1945, CI.

69. Hadden, *Not Me,* 56.

70. 1st Lt. Frances G. Smyson, interview, May 4, 1945, CI. Fairchild and Fergerson interview.

71. Nelson interview. 630th TD, Unit Report No. 6, File TDBN-630-0.9.

72. MacDonald, *Trumpets,* 134. 28th ID, Unit Report No. 6.

73. Smith, *"Medic!"* 86.

74. G-3 Journal, December 17, 1944. Verbal Message from 28th Infantry Division to VIII Corps, December 17, 1944. VIII Corps G-3 Journal.

75. 109th Infantry, Unit Report No. 6, January 4, 1945, File 328-INF(109)-0.3, July–Dec. 1944.

76. Strickler, "Ardennes Breakthrough," 41. Strickler, Action Report, 3–4. G-3 Journal, December 16, 1944. Annex 4 to Unit Report No. 6, 110th Infantry.

77. Major W. F. Thomas, S-3 and Executive Officer, 103rd Engineering Battalion, interview, [interviewer name not provided], CI.

78. 103rd Engineer Battalion, Unit Report No. 6, January 7, 1945, File 328-ENG-0.3.

79. G-3 Journal, December 17, 1944. Unit Report No. 6.

80. Fowler, 3rd Bn Unit History, December 17, 20, 1944.

81. 28th ID, Unit Report No. 6.

82. A and C batteries, to be precise. 109th FA, Unit Report No. 6. Telephone message from 28th ID to VIII Corps, 6:25 PM, December 22, 1944. VIII Corps G-3 Journal.

83. G-3 Journal, December 21, 1944. 28th ID, Unit Report No. 6. Cole, *Ardennes,* 324. The paucity of records for December 21 suggests that it was the most harrowing day of the battle for the division headquarters.

84. Report of VIII Corps. 28th ID, Unit Report No. 6. 28th ID G-3 Periodic Reports Nos. 161–64, December 23–26, 1944, File 208-3.2. Cole, *Ardennes,* 327.

85. G-3 Journal, December 22, 1944.

86. 28th ID, Unit Report No. 6. 28th ID G-3 Periodic Reports Nos. 161–64, December 23–26, 1944, File 208-3.2. Cole, *Ardennes,* 327–28. History 28th ID.

87. 108th FA, Unit Report No. 6.

88. Clay Blair, *Ridgway's Paratroopers: The American Airborne in World War II* (Garden City, N.Y.: Dial Press, Doubleday, 1985), 360–67, 381.

89. Toland, *Battle,* 210–11. McAuliffe was in temporary command of the division because Maj. Gen. Maxwell D. Taylor was on his way back from Washington, D.C. He had been ordered to the capital to make the case for additional soldiers for the 101st. MacDonald, *Trumpets,* 263. MacDonald's account states that McAuliffe wrote the reply of "nuts" himself on the paper that replied to the surrender demand. Ibid., 512.

90. 28th Infantry Division Operations Instructions, December 23, 1944, File 328-3.2.

91. 28th ID, Unit Report No. 6. 1st Sergeant George E. Mortimer, "Extracts from First Sergeant's Diary," 112th Infantry, CI.

92. Strickler, Action Report, 21.

93. 28th Infantry Division Troop List No. 1, December 25, 1944, File 208-3.2. 28th ID, Unit Report No. 6. Report of VIII Corps.

94. G-3 Journal, December 25, 1944. Strickler, Action Report, 21–22.

95. G-3 Journal, December 23, 1944. Report of VIII Corps.

96. 110th Infantry, Unit Report No. 6. MG-356, Carton 4, PSA.

97. Report of VIII Corps.

98. G-3 Journal, December 16, 1944.

99. MacDonald, *Trumpets,* 142–43.

100. Annex 4 to Unit Report No. 6.

101. Cole, *Ardennes,* 190–91, 219.

102. John C. McManus, *Alamo in the Ardennes: The Untold Story of the American Soldiers Who Made the Defense of Bastogne Possible* (Hoboken, N.J.: John Wiley and Sons, 2007), 99.

103. G-3 Journal, December 17, 1944. According to Robert F. Phillips, the Germans used no Mk VI "Tigers" against the 110th Infantry, even though GIs often claimed that Tigers were attacking them. Phillips, *Bastogne,* 138. Jeffrey Clark and Robert Smith second this observation: "foot troops tended to identify all as Tigers." Jeffrey J. Clarke and Robert Ross Smith, *United States Army in World War II. The European Theater of Operations: Riviera to the Rhine* (Washington, D.C.: Center of Military History, United States Army, 1993), 554.

104. Maj. R. C. Garner, interviewed by Capt. W. J. Dunkerley, June 12, 1945. CI.

105. G-3 Journal, December 18, 1944.

106. Strickler, "Ardennes Breakthrough," 42. G-3 Journal, December 17, 1944.

107. G-3 Journal, December 17, 1944.

108. Strickler, Action Report, 9–11. G-3 Journal, December 18, 1944. 707th S-3 Journal, December 18, 1944. 28th ID, Unit Report No. 6.

109. Seeley to Cota, May 8, 1945. G-3 Journal, December 18, 1944.

110. Strickler, "Ardennes Breakthrough," 42. G-3 Journal, December 17, 1944.

111. G-3 Journal, December 17, 1944.

112. Flynn interview. G-3 Journal, December 17, 1944.

113. Lt. Col. Thomas E. Briggs, 28th ID G-3, interview, January 1, 1945, CI.

114. Annex 4, Unit Report No. 6, 110th Infantry.

115. Strickler, Action Report, 9–11. G-3 Journal, December 18, 1944. 707th S-3 Journal, December 18, 1944. 28th ID, Unit Report No. 6.

116. Strickler, Action Report, 8–9. Phillips, *Bastogne,* 141.

117. Fairchild and Fergerson interview.

118. Hall, *My Brother's Letters,* 87. Fairchild and Fergerson interview.

119. G-3 Journal, December 18, 1944.

120. Briggs interview.

121. Strickler, Action Report, 12–13. 28th ID G-3 Journal, December 19, 1944.

122. Strickler, "Action Report," 14–15. Annex 4, Unit Report No. 6, 110th Infantry. 28th ID, Unit Report No. 6.

123. "Analysis of 'The German Breakthrough' Material" by 1st Lt. Ralph Larson, 28th ID, CI. Briggs interview.

124. Strickler, Action Report, 14–15.

125. Ibid., 15–20. Once Strickler had recovered, Cota put him in command of what was left of the 110th Infantry. Ibid., 21.

126. G-3 Journal, December 18, 1944. 28th ID G-3 Periodic Report No. 157, December 20, 1944, File 328-3.2.

127. G-3 Journal, December 20, 1944.

128. Phillips, *Bastogne,* 172. G-3 Journal, December 18, 1944.

129. G-3 Journal, December 18, 1944.

130. Fuller, Report of Operations.

131. Hadden, *Not Me,* 60. McManus, *Alamo,* 160–67.

132. Capt. William Allen Gillett, Veteran's Questionnaire, Box 28th Infantry Division, 110th Infantry Regiment, MHI.

133. Strickler, Action Report, 9–11. Phillips, *Bastogne,* 169, 172, 173. G-3 Journal, December 18, 1944.

134. Strickler, "Ardennes Breakthrough," 42. 110th Infantry, Unit Report No. 6. 28th ID, Unit Report No. 6. G-3 Journal, December 18, 1944.

135. Seeley to Cota, May 8, 1945.

136. Strickler, Action Report, 12–13.

137. G-3 Journal, December 19, 1944. Hoban was the division headquarters commandant. 28th ID, Unit Report No. 6.

138. MacDonald, *Trumpets,* 503. George E. Koskimaki, *Battered Bastards of Bastogne: The 101st Airborne in the Battle of the Bulge, December 19, 1944–January 17, 1945* (Haverton, Pa.: Casemate, 2003; New York: Ballantine Books, 2007), 170.

139. G-3 Periodic Report No. 158, December 21, 1944, File 328-3.2.

140. 28th ID, Unit Report No. 6. 28th ID, Unit Report No. 7, February 10, 1945, File 585.028, July 1944–February 1945, AFHRA.

141. History 28th ID.

142. G-3 Journal, December 21, 1944. This kind of initiative in improvising fighting units was not exclusive to the 28th ID during the battle. Cole, *Ardennes,* 111–12.

143. 28th ID, Unit Report No. 7.

144. History 28th ID.

145. First Army Letter of Instruction, December 21, 1944, File 208-3.9. HQ VIII Corps, Letter of Instruction, December 20, 1944, ibid.

146. Cole, *Ardennes*, 181–83. Strickler, Action Report, 5.

147. Kuhn, *Baker 2*, 186.

148. MacDonald, *Trumpets*, 138–39.

149. James C. Sharpe interview.

150. Major Walden F. Woodward, interviewed by William Henderson, January 20, 1945, 112th, CI. Woodward was 3rd Battalion commander.

151. Gerald F. Lindermann. *The World Within War: America's Combat Experience in World War II* (New York: Free Press, 1997), 138–39. Weigley, *Eisenhower's Lieutenants*, 467–68. Schrijvers, *The Crash of Ruin*, 79.

152. Fowler, 3rd Bn Unit History, December 20, 1944.

153. Blakeslee, *Personal Account*, 37.

154. Seeley was appointed the regimental commander when Fuller was driven out of his CP. Seeley to Cota, May 8, 1945.

155. Nelson interview. When infantry do not accompany tanks, foot soldiers can sneak up on the armored vehicles and wreck them with antitank rockets.

156. Interview of Lt. Col. William H. Allen, CO 1st Battalion, 112th Infantry, and 1st Lieutenant Joseph W. Morgan, S-3, 1st Battalion, 112th Infantry, January 16, 1945, CI.

157. Lt. Col James E. Rudder, interview by unnamed historian, January 6, 1945, CI. 109th Infantry, Unit Report No. 6.

158. Fowler, 3rd Bn Unit History, December 16, 1944.

159. MacDonald, *Trumpets*, 131–34.

160. Nelson interview.

161. 1st Sergeant George E. Mortimer, interviewed by Tec 3rd Grd William Henderson, January 23, 1945, CI.

162. Mortimer diary.

163. G-3 Journal, December 17, 1944.

164. Annex 4, Unit Report No. 6.

165. MacDonald, *Trumpets*, 44. Dupuy, *Gamble*, 17.

166. Fairchild and Fergerson interview. Cole, *Ardennes*, 671. In a similar manner the combat commands of the 9th Armored Division fought as separate components. Walter E. Reichelt, *Phantom Nine: The 9th Armored (Remagen) Division, 1942–1945* (Austin, Tex.: Presidial Press, 1987), passim.

167. Fuller, Report of Operations.

168. G-3 Journal, December 17, 1944. Toland, *Battle*, 81.

169. Toland, *Battle*, 89. Some veterans held Gibney in low esteem. He did not provide personal leadership under fire, and once had a tantrum over a soldier who lost a compass during a German artillery bombardment. Kemp, *The Regiment*, 213.

170. G-3 Journal, December 17, 1944. Toland's account differs. Gibney told Fuller to hold fast, the telephone line was cut, and Fuller decided on his own to evacuate when German infantry poured into the hotel. Toland, *Battle*, 90–91. Given Cota's countermanding of Gibney's instructions to Rudder, Cota may have been the source of permission for Fuller to evacuate.

171. G-3 Journal, December 17, 1944.

172. G-3 Journal, December 19, 1944.

173. 28th ID, Unit Report No. 6. G-3 Journal, December 19, 1944. Strickler, Action Report, 13–14.

174. MacDonald, *Trumpets*, 299–301. Miller interview.

175. G-3 Journal, December 17, 1944. 112th Infantry, Unit Report No. 6. Nelson interview. 229th FA After Action Report, December 1944. Fairchild and Fergerson interview. 229th Field Artillery Battalion, January 21, 1945.

176. Nelson interview.

177. G-3 Journal, December 18, 1944. The order went out at 1130. 28th ID G-2 Periodic Report No. 143, December 18, 1944, File 328-3.2.

178. History 3rd Battalion, 112th Infantry, December 18–20, 1944.

179. 28th ID G-3 Periodic Report No. 157, December 20, 1944, File 328-3.2. Two of the 106th's three regiments were captured because its commander misunderstood instructions from Middleton. Toland, *Battle*, 5–6, 36. Cole, *Ardennes*, 157. Dupuy, *Hitler's Last Gamble*, 87, 98–99.

180. G-3 Journal, December 19, 1944. 28th ID G-3 Periodic Report No. 158, December 20, 1944, File 208-3.9.

181. Nelson interview. All the while, the command section of the 106th ID was holed up in St. Vith, surrounded, with tanks raining shells on their heads. 28th ID G-3 Journal, December 18, 1944.

182. Blair, *Ridgway's Paratroopers*, 376–77.

183. 112th Infantry, Unit Report No. 6.

184. G-3 Journal, December 18, 1944. Lt. Col James E. Rudder, interviewer unnamed, January 6, 1945, CI. Rudder took command of the 109th on December 8, replacing Daniel Strickler, who became the executive officer of the 110th Infantry. He had commanded the 2nd Ranger Battalion at Normandy on June 6. A man of enormous courage, he continued to lead his men after he was wounded twice, exhorting the 2nd Ranger Battalion up the cliffs of Point du Hoc overlooking Omaha Beach in one of the more impressive feats of bravery and the soldier's craft in World War II. Harrison, *Cross-Channel Attack*, 322. Douglas Brinkley, *The Boys of Pointe du Hoc: Ronald Reagan, D-Day, and the U.S. Army 2nd Ranger Battalion* (New York: William Morrow, 2005), 63–98. Kemp, *The Regiment*, 212–13. "The Our River," 37, File 328-INF(110)-0.1 to 0.3.

185. G-3 Journal, December 18, 1944. 108th FA, Unit Report No. 6.

186. G-3 Journal, December 19, 1944.

187. Lt. Gen. Courtney H. Hodges, HQ First United States Army, Letter of Instructions, December 19, 1944, File 208-3.2.

188. Troy F. Middleton, to all Commanders and Troops of the VIII Corps, December 19, 1944, File 328-3.2.

189. G-3 Journal, 19 December 1944. Troy F. Middleton, Letter of Instruction, December 19, 1944, File 208-3.9. General Cota to General Middleton, File 328-3.2.

190. G-3 Journal, December 19, 1944.

191. G-3 Journal, December 19, 1944. The division did not know it at the time, but "on or about 19 December," it went over to Third Army along with VIII Corps. "Assignments and Attachments," File 328-INF(110) 0.1 to 0.3.

192. G-3 Journal, December 19, 1944.

193. Telephone Message from 28th Infantry Division to G-3 VIII Corps, 10:15 AM, December 19, 1944, File 208-3.9. Cota later regained intermittent contact.

194. 112th Infantry, Unit Report No. 6. Cole states that the 112th was placed under Hasbrouck's command on December 20. Cole, *Ardennes,* 395. The on-the-scene commander of forces at St. Vith from December 18 was Hasbrouck's subordinate, Brig. Gen. Bruce C. Clarke. MacDonald, *Trumpets,* 327.

195. 112th Infantry, Unit Report No. 6. MacDonald, *Trumpets,* 484.

196. 112th Infantry, Unit Report No. 6. Smith, *Medic,* 92. Cole, *Ardennes,* 421. Hadden, *Not Me,* 64.

197. James T. Nesbitt, History of Headquarters Company, 112th Infantry, December 1944, File 328-INF(112)-0.1 to 328-INF(112)-1.13. Fowler, 3rd Bn Unit History, December 24, 1944. Hugh Cole observed, "It is difficult to determine with surety how much of the 7th Armored Division, CCB, 9th Armored, 424th Infantry, 112th Infantry, and the numerous attached units had been lost during the fight for St. Vith and in the subsequent withdrawal. Many records were destroyed during the final retreat." Cole, *Ardennes,* 422.

198. Smith, *Medic,* 82.

199. Phillips, *Bastogne,* 72. Interview with General Hasso von Manteuffel, ETHINT 46, 5.

200. MacDonald, *Trumpets,* 265, 145. Phillips, *Bastogne,* 133.

201. Jodl, ETHINT 51, 20.

202. Dupuy, *Gamble,* 109. Cole, *Ardennes,* 186–87.

203. Cole, *Ardennes,* 224. Phillips, *Bastogne,* 167.

204. Cole, *Ardennes,* 192. MacDonald, *Trumpets,* 426–27.

205. 28th ID, Unit Report No. 6. Weigley, *Eisenhower's Lieutenants,* 514.

206. Cole, *Ardennes,* 487.

207. Report of VIII Corps, File 208-0.3.

208. Ibid. G-3 Journal, December 23, 1944.

209. From Gen. Middleton to Liaison Officers and All Units and Corps Staff, December 25, 1944, File 208-3.2.

210. MacDonald, *Trumpets,* 532. Cole, *Ardennes,* 480, 555, 621.

211. Interview with Generalmajor Heinz Kokott, ETHINT 44, 5.

212. Dupuy, *Gamble,* 248. Cole, *Ardennes,* 570, 673. Winton, *Corps Commanders,* 213.

213. Cole, *Ardennes,* 619. Dupuy, *Hitler's Last Gamble,* 297.

214. Danny S. Parker, *To Win the Winter Sky: The Air War over the Ardennes, 1944–1945* (Conshohocken, Pa.: Combined Books, 1994), 448.

215. VIII Corps G-2 Estimate of the Situation, December 29, 1944, File 328-3.2.

216. Steven J. Zaloga, *US Armored Divisions, The European Theater of Operations, 1944–1945* (Oxford: Osprey Publications, 2004), 45. Thomas E. Nutter, *Mythos Revisited: American Historians and German Fighting Power in the Second World War,* ch. 9.1, http://www.military historyonline.com/wwii/armies/default.aspx.

217. Winton, *Corps Commanders,* 234.

218. Cole, *Ardennes,* 603, 605, 610–12. Boog, *Germany and the Second World War,* 691–92. Winton, *Corps Commanders,* 204, 288.

219. Boog, *Germany and the Second World War,* 693.

220. Winton, *Corps Commanders,* 205–208. Dupuy, *Hitler's Gamble,* 322–23. Weigley, *Eisenhower's Lieutenants,* 542–44.

221. 28th ID, Unit Report No. 6. The division's historian stated that "28th Division losses amounted to 3,850 men killed and wounded, and 2,000 captured." Robert Grant Crist, *The First Century: A History of the 28th Infantry Division* (Harrisburg, Pa.: 28th Infantry Division, 1979), 176.

222. 109th Infantry, Unit Report No. 6.

223. 110th Infantry, Unit Report No. 6. Cole, *Ardennes*, 192.

224. 108th Field Artillery Battalion, Unit Report No. 6, January 1, 1945.

225. 109th Field Artillery Battalion, Unit Report No. 6, January 1, 1945, File 328-FA(109)-3.2.

226. Fairchild and Fergerson interview.

227. 707th S-3 Journal.

228. Lt. Jack Shea, HQ 1st U.S. Army, interview with Major General Norman D. Cota and Major Carl W. Plitt (no date, probably March 1945), 28th ID, CI. General Jodl took the opposite view, blaming the small road network for constricting their mobility. Jodl, ETHINT 51, 13.

229. Report of VIII Corps. Phillips, *Bastogne*, 265.

230. G-2 Periodic Report No. 2, TUSA, in 109th Infantry Regiment, Unit Report No. 6, January 4, 1945, File 328-INF(109)-0.3.

231. Field-Marshal The Viscount Montgomery of Alamein, *El Alamein to the River Sangro; Normandy to the Baltic* (London: Barrie and Jenkins in association with the Arcadia Press, 1948), 358.

232. Bradley, *A Soldier's Story*, 475.

233. Strickler, Action Report, 23. 110th Infantry, Unit Report No. 6.

234. Kemp, *The Regiment*, 293–94.

13. Winter Battles

1. History of the 28th Infantry Division, June 24, 1944. 28th ID, Unit Report No. 7. Headquarters 28th Division Artillery, After Action Report. February 5, 1945, File 585.028, July 1944 to February 1945, AFHRA.

2. Colonel G. M. Nelson, Unit Report No. 7, 112th Infantry, February 5, 1945, File 328-INF(112)-0.3, Aug–Dec 1944.

3. 28th ID, Unit Report No. 7, February 10, 1945, File 585.028, AFHRA.

4. History of the 28th Infantry Division, June 24, 1944. HQ Company 3–4 January 1945, History 3rd Battalion, 112th Infantry.

5. Unit Report No. 7, 28th ID.

6. Charles B. MacDonald, *United States Army in World War II, The European Theater of Operations: The Last Offensive* (Washington, D.C.: Office of the Chief of Military History, United States Army, 1973), 6.

7. Colonel James E. Rudder, 109th Infantry Regiment, Unit Report No. 7, February 4, 1945, File 328-INF(109)-0.3, Jan.–May 1945.

8. Colonel Daniel Strickler, 110th Infantry, Unit Report No. 7, February 3, 1945, File 328-INF(110)-0.3.

9. History of the 28th Infantry Division, June 24, 1944. HQ Company January 3–4, 1945, Fowler, 3rd Bn Unit History.

10. "The Vosges Mountains and the Colmar Pocket, 51," File 28 ID 328-INF(110)-0.1 to 0.3. Smith, "*Medic!*" 93.

11. Smith, "*Medic!*" 100–101.

12. History of the 28th Infantry Division, June 24, 1944. 28th ID, Unit Report No. 7. Headquarters 28th Division Artillery, After Action Report, February 5, 1945, AFHRA.

13. MacDonald, *Last Offensive*, 1–5, 18.

14. Clarke and Smith, *Riviera to the Rhine,* 533–34.

15. Weigley, *Eisenhower's Lieutenants,* 597. Eisenhower, *Crusade in Europe,* 374.

16. Clarke and Smith, *Riviera to the Rhine,* 534–35. The 28th ID transferred to XXI Corps, Maj. Gen. Frank W. Milburn.

17. Clarke and Smith, *Riviera to the Rhine,* 535–39.

18. Ibid., 539–47. "The Vosges Mountains," 52.

19. 28th ID, Unit Report No. 7. Clarke and Smith, *Riviera to the Rhine,* 547.

20. Colonel James E. Rudder, 109th Infantry Regiment, Unit Report No. 7, February 4, 1945, File 328-INF(109)-0.3.

21. "The Vosges Mountains," 53–54. 109th Infantry Regiment, Unit Report No. 7.

22. "History of 229th," 45.

23. Clarke and Smith, *Riviera to the Rhine,* 548–49, 557–58.

24. Kemp, *The Regiment,* 315–17.

25. Ibid. The seizure of Aachen was a bloody and difficult affair that destroyed much of the city.

26. 28th ID, Unit Report No. 8, March 13, 1945, File 585.028, July 1944–February 1945, AFHRA.

27. Colonel Gustin M. Nelson, Unit Report No. 8, 112th Infantry, March 1, 1945, File 328-INF(112)-0.3, Aug–Dec 1944. Colonel James Rudder, Unit Report No. 8, 109th Infantry, March 4, 1945, File 328-INF(109)-0.3, Jan–May 1945.

28. "Vosges Mountains," 54. 109th Infantry, Unit Report No. 8. Weigley, *Eisenhower's Lieutenants,* 598. General d'Armee deLattre de Tassigny, Order of the Day No. 7, February 14, 1945. MG-272, Henschen Collection, Box 19, PSA.

29. 109th Infantry, Unit Report No. 8.

30. Kemp, *The Regiment,* 319.

31. 110th Infantry, Unit Report No. 8, March 3, 1945, File 328-INF(110)-0.3.

32. Ibid.

33. Ibid. Smith, *Medic,* 102.

34. 28th ID, Unit Report No. 8. The division became a part of V Corps again on February 20.

35. Kemp, *The Regiment,* 297.

36. Weigley, *Eisenhower's Lieutenants,* 408–409, 500.

37. 28th ID, Unit Report No. 8. 109th Infantry, Unit Report No. 8. The division became a part of V Corps in First Army again on February 20.

38. Derek S. Zumbro, *Battle for the Ruhr: The German Army's Final Defeat in the West* (Lawrence: University Press of Kansas, 2006), 85.

39. History 110th Infantry Regiment, "The Monshau Forest," 58. Kemp, *The Regiment,* 329.

40. Toby Thacker, *The End of the Third Reich: Defeat, Denazification and Nuremberg, January 1944–November 1946* (Stroud, Gloucestershire: Tempus Publishing, 2006), 93.

41. Weigley, *Eisenhower's Lieutenants,* 619.

42. 2nd Lt. Ralph A. Larson, Capt. Michael Murphy, Lt. Col Carl W. Plitt, Maj Gen. Norman D. Cota, interview by Capt. William J. Fox, "From the Roer to the Rhine: 28th Inf. Div., 28 Feb–9 March 1945," CI. The combat interview does not say when the meeting took place, but it was probably March 2 or 3.

43. Larson, Murphy interview.

44. Ibid.

45. Colonel Gustin M. Nelson, 112th Infantry, Unit Report No. 9, April 2, 1945, File 328-INF(112)-0.3, Aug–Dec 1944.

46. Larson, Murphy interview.

47. Colonel James E. Rudder, 109th Infantry, Unit Report No. 9, April 4, 1945, File 328-INF(109)-0.3.

48. Kemp, *The Regiment*, 326.

49. Larson, Murphy interview. Kemp, *The Regiment*, 331.

50. "The Monschau Forest," 60.

51. 110th Infantry, Unit Report No. 9, April 2, 1945, File 328-INF(110)-0.3.

52. Larson, Murphy interview. "The Monschau Forest," 61.

53. Daniel B. Strickler, 110th Infantry, Unit Report No. 10, May 4, 1945, File 328-INF(110)-0.3. Unit Report No. 1-5, July–Nov. 1944. History 229th FA, 48.

54. 109th Infantry, Unit Report No. 9.

55. "Advance across the Rhine and Return," 63–66, File 328-INF(110)-0.1 to 0.3. It appears that the division crossed in the area between Weissenturm and Koblenz. The town of Honningen is not on extant maps, and several of the places named in the documents are nowhere near the Rhine.

56. April 23, 1945, Company History, Company G, 112th Infantry, File 328-INF(112)9-0.2.

57. Weigley, *Eisenhower's Lieutenants*, 627–28. "Advance across the Rhine and Return," 63–66, File 328-INF(110)-0.1 to 0.3. Field Order No. 42, April 30, 1945, File 328-3.9.

58. MacDonald, *Last Offensive*, 478.

59. James Lucas, *Last Days of the Third Reich*, with a foreword by Rt. Hon. Sir Bernard Braine, DL, MP (New York: William Morrow, 1986), 199. Thacker, *End of the Third Reich*, 96, 140.

60. "Across the Rhine," 64, 66; "Army of Occupation," 68–70, File 328-INF(110)-0.1 to 0.3. History 229th FA, 50. 110th Infantry, Unit Report No. 10. Earl F. Ziemke, *The U.S. Army in the Occupation of Germany, 1944–1946* (Washington, D.C.: Center of Military History, United States Army, 1975), 202–203.

61. Ziemke, *Occupation*, 202–203.

62. Colonel James E. Rudder, 109th Infantry, Unit Report No. 10, May 4, 1945, File 328-INF(109)-0.3, Jan–May 1945. The regiment's battalions were spread far and wide for occupation duty: 1st Battalion at Stolberg, 2nd at Monschau, 3rd at Dirmerzheim, headquarters in Bardenberg (just north of Aachen). Kemp, *The Regiment*, 338–39. Ziemke, *Occupation*, 186–89.

63. 109th Infantry, Unit Report No. 10. 109th Infantry, Unit Report No. 11, June 4, 1945, File 328-INF(109)-0.3, Jan–May 1945. Lt. Colonel A. D. Dugan became the 109th Infantry's commanding officer during the first week of May 1945. Ibid.

64. Peterson, *Faces of Defeat*, 40.

65. Zumbro, *Ruhr*, 80–87.

66. History 229th, 49. Ziemke, *Occupation*, 322, 324.

67. Thacker, *End of the Third Reich*, 137–38. Ziemke, *Occupation*, 97–98.

68. Smith, "*Medic!*" 109–10.

69. Ziemke, *Occupation*, 220. J. Robert Lilly, *Taken by Force: Rape and American GIs in Europe during World War II* (Houndmills, UK: Palgrave Macmillan, 2003), 117, 160.

70. Lilly, *Taken by Force*, 11.

71. "Monschau Forest," 73.

72. Ibid., 74.

73. 1,901 were killed, 9,157 wounded, 2,599 missing, 2,247 captured, 15,904 "battle casualties," and 8,936 "non-battle casualties." *Order of Battle of the United States Army, World War II: European Theater of Operations* (Paris: Office of the Theater Historian, 1945), 110. http://www.history.army.mil/documents/ETO-OB/ETOOB-TOC.htm

14. Conclusion

1. Horale Osterman, 1st Lt. Elmer S. Bundorf, Capt. George R. Dane, Roger Lee Farrand, Howard F. Harvier, Miner M. Lang, Morris G. Sykes, Christopher Sotiro, Marion Bedford Davis, Robert P. Probach, John F. Ritter; see also Edmund S. Lewis, Ivor William McKay, John R. Ricci, Veterans' Questionnaires, 28th Infantry Division, MHI.

2. Currey, *Follow Me,* 58.

3. Brown, *Draftee Division,* 159.

4. HQ 1st Battalion, 112th Infantry, to S-2 112th History, March 15, 1944, File 328-INF(112)0.1.

5. Rush, *Hell in Hürtgen Forest,* 96.

6. Mansoor, *GI Offensive,* 89–90.

7. Rush, *Hell in Hürtgen Forest,* 331, 342–43.

8. Mahon, *History of the Militia,* 219.

Appendix 1

1. William Bradford Huie, *The Execution of Private Slovik: The Hitherto Secret Story of the Only American Soldier since 1864 to be Shot for Desertion* (New York: Duell, Sloan, and Pearce, 1954). See also Edward Patrick Woods, *United States vs. Private Eddie D. Slovik (36896415), Company G., 109th Infantry, 28th Infantry Division: Trial by GCM, Convened at Roetgen, Germany, 11 November 1944: Sentence, To Be Shot to Death with Musketry: A Personal Review* (E. P. Woods, 1979). Charles Whiting, *American Deserter: General Eisenhower and the Execution of Eddie Slovik* (J. Whiting Books, 2004).

2. Kemp, *The Regiment,* 308, 311.

3. Huie, *Private Slovik,* 12.

4. Ibid., 81–88, 91–92, 97.

5. Ibid., 102–106.

6. Ibid., 107, 109–10.

7. Ibid., 114, 117, 119–23.

8. Ibid., 152.

Appendix 2

1. Chief of Staff, Memorandum for the Secretary of War, September 29, 1944, RG-107, Entry 74B, Box 7, Folder National Guard, NARA. Doubler, *Civilian in Peace,* 219–20.

2. War Department Public Relations Division, 13 June 1946, RG-19.17, Slot 14-2201, Box 3, PSA.

3. Hill, *Minute Man,* 498.

Bibliography

Archival Sources

Chester County Historical Society, West Chester, Pennsylvania
  West Chester Organizations
George C. Marshall Research Library, Virginia Military Institute Lexington, Virginia
  Papers of George C. Marshall
  Larry Bland Personal Manuscript Collections
Georgetown University Library, Washington, D.C.
  Ord Family Papers
National Archives and Records Administration, College Park, Maryland
  Record Group 107 Office of the Secretary of War
  Record Group 159 Office of the Inspector General of the Army
  Record Group 165 War Department General and Special Staffs
  Record Group 168 Records of the National Guard Bureau
  Record Group 337 Headquarters U.S. Army Ground Forces
  Record Group 338 Numbered Army Groups
  Record Group 407 Office of the Adjutant General
Pennsylvania National Guard Museum, Indiantown Gap, Pennsylvania
  Uncatalogued Collections
Pennsylvania State Archives, Harrisburg, Pennsylvania
  Record Group 7 Records of the General Assembly
  Record Group 19 Department of Military and Veterans Affairs
  Manuscript Group 156 Papers of Edward Martin
  Manuscript Group 272 Pennsylvania Military Museum Collection, Individual Collections: Papers of Robert H. Henschen
  Manuscript Group 356 Papers of Daniel Strickler
Pennsylvania State Library
  Journal of the House of Representatives of the Commonwealth of Pennsylvania for the Session Begun at Harrisburg on the Seventh Day of January, 1941, Part I. Harrisburg, Pennsylvania, 1941.
  Laws of the General Assembly of the Commonwealth of Pennsylvania Passed at the Session of 1941 in the One-Hundred and Sixty-fifth Year of Independence. Harrisburg, Pennsylvania, 1941.
  Laws of the General Assembly of the Commonwealth of Pennsylvania passed at the Extraordinary Session of 1942 in the One hundred and Sixty-sixth year of Independence. Harrisburg, Pennsylvania: 1942.

U.S. Army Military History Institute, Carlisle, Pennsylvania
World War II Veterans' Questionnaires
USAWC/USAMHI Senior Officer Oral History Program
   LTG Charles A. Corcoran Interview
   LTG Henry K. Fluck Interview
   MG Nicholas P. Kafkalas Interview
Henry K. Fluck Papers
John Fairchild Papers
Daniel B. Strickler Papers
U.S. War Department Bulletins
U.S. War Department Training Circulars
U.S. War Department Tables of Organization
Final Report III Corps Phase First Army Maneuvers, Manassas, Va., August 5–19, 1939
Unit History, 109th Infantry Regiment, 25 November 1945
U.S. Government Documents
   Amphibious Training Center, Study No. 22. Washington, D.C.: Historical Section, Army
      Ground Forces, 1946.
   Chief of Staff, United States Army. *Biennial Report of the Chief of Staff of the United States
      Army, July 1, 1939, to June 30, 1941, to the Secretary of War*. Washington, D.C.: United States
      Government Printing Office, 1941.
   Field Service Regulations; Operations: FM 100–5. Washington, D.C.: U.S. Government
      Printing Office, 1941.
   National Defense Act of June 4, 1920. Statutes at Large, Vol. 42, 1034 (1922).
   Official National Guard Register for 1943. Published by authority of the Secretary of War.
      Washington, D.C.: United States Government Printing Office, National Guard Bureau,
      March 1, 1943.
   U.S. War Department. *Annual Report of the Chief of the National Guard Bureau, 1939*, by
      Albert J. Blanding. Washington, D.C.: National Guard Bureau, June 30, 1939.
   ———. *Annual Report of the Chief of the National Guard Bureau, 1940*, by Albert J. Bland-
      ing. Washington, D.C: War Department, June 30, 1940.
   ———. *Annual Report of the Chief of the National Guard Bureau, 1942*. Washington, D.C.:
      War Department, 1942.
   ———. *Army Regulations No. 600–750, Personnel Recruiting for the Regular Army and Regu-
      lar Army Reserve* (April 10, 1939).Washington, D.C.: 1939.
   ———. *Field Service Regulations, United States Army, 1923*. Washington, D.C.: Government
      Printing Office, 1924.
   ———. *Mobilization Regulations No. 1–5. October 1, 1940, Procurement and Reception of
      Volunteers during Mobilization*. Washington, D.C.: War Department, 1940.
United States Air Force Historical Research Agency, Maxwell AFB, Ala.
   Army Air Forces Histories
   28th Infantry Division Records
   V Corps Records
United States Publications
   U.S. Bureau of the Census; Rogers C. B. Morton, Secretary, U.S. Department of Com-
      merce. *Historical Statistics of the United States, Colonial Times to 1970*. 2 parts. Washing-
      ton, D.C.: Bureau of the Census, 1975.
   United States Congress. *Records of the United States House of Representatives*. 1940.

United States Congress. *Records of the United States Senate*. 1939, 1940, 1941.
United States Congress. *Congressional Record*. Volume 84, 1939.
United States Department of Commerce, Bureau of the Census, *Sixteenth Census of the United States: 1940*. Washington, D.C.: Government Printing Office, 1943.

Newspapers

Allentown Morning Call
Harrisburg Telegraph
Lebanon Daily News
Lancaster Evening Gazette
New York Times
Philadelphia Evening Bulletin
Philadelphia Inquirer
Philadelphia Tribune
Pittsburgh Sun-Telegraph

Periodicals

Life
Newsweek
Army Navy Journal
Army Navy Register
Pennsylvania Guardsman
Time

Dissertations

Clevenger, Richard P. "Apprenticeship in Great Britain and the United States." M.A. thesis, University of Oklahoma, 1964.
Cockrell, Philip Carlton. "Brown Shoes and Mortar Boards: U.S. Army Officer Professional Education at the Command and General Staff School, Fort Leavenworth, Kansas, 1919–1940." Ph.D. diss., University of South Carolina, 1991. UMI Order Number AAT9200799.
Herrera, Ricardo Adolfo. "Guarantors of Liberty and the Republic: The American Citizen as Soldier and the Military Ethos of Republicanism, 1774–1861." Ph.D. diss., Marquette University, 1998. UMI Order Number 9901729.
McNally, Vincent Paul, Jr. "A Most Dangerous and Noble Calling: The Development, Organization and Operation of the American Volunteer Fire Service." Ph.D. diss., Temple University, 1979. UMI Order Number AAT7924008.

Published Sources

Alpers, Benjamin. "This Is the Army: Imagining a Democratic Military in World War II." *Journal of American History* 85, no. 1 (June 1998): 129–63.
Andidora, Ronald. *Home by Christmas: The Illusion of Victory in 1944*. Westport, Conn.: Greenwood, 2002.

Bacque, James. *Crimes and Mercies: The Fate of German Civilians under Allied Occupation, 1944–1950*. Vancouver: Talonbooks, 2007.

Bailyn, Bernard. *The Ideological Origins of the American Revolution*. Cambridge, Mass.: Belknap Press of Harvard University Press, 1967.

Balkoski, Joseph. *Beyond the Beachhead: The 29th Infantry Division in Normandy*. Harrisburg, Pa.: Stackpole Books, 1989.

Barbash, Jack. *The Practice of Unionism*. New York: Harper and Bros., 1956.

Barbier, Mary Kathryn. *D-Day Deception: Operation Fortitude and the Normandy Invasion*. Westport, Conn.: Praeger Security International, 2007.

Barnett, Correlli. *The Desert Generals*. 2nd ed. Bloomington: Indiana University Press, 1982.

Berryman, Sue E. *Who Serves: The Persistent Myth of the Underclass Army*. Boulder, Colo.: Westview, 1988.

Blair, Clay. *Ridgeway's Paratroopers: The American Airborne in World War II*. Garden City, N.Y.: Dial Press, Doubleday, 1985.

Blakeslee, Clarence. *A Personal Account of WWII by Draftee #36887149*. Rockford, Mich.: Clarence Blakeslee, 1989.

Blumenson, Martin. "America's World War II Leaders in Europe: Some Thoughts." *Parameters* 19, no. 4 (December 1989): 5.

———. *The Patton Papers, 1940–1945*. Boston: Houghton Mifflin, 1974.

———. *United States Army in World War II. The European Theater of Operations: Breakout and Pursuit*. Washington, D.C.: Center of Military History, United States Army, 1989.

Bond, Brian. *War and Society in Europe, 1870–1970*. New York: Oxford University Press, 1986.

Boog, Horst, Gerhard Krebs, and Detlef Vogel. *Germany and the Second World War: The Strategic Air War in Europe and the War in the West and East Asia 1943–1944/5*. Vol. 7. Oxford: Clarendon Press, 2006.

Bradley, Omar N. *A Soldier's Story*. New York: Henry Holt, 1951.

Bradley, Omar N., and Clay Blair. *A General's Life*. New York: Simon and Schuster, 1983.

Brinkley, Douglas. *The Boys of Pointe du Hoc: Ronald Reagan, D-Day, and the U.S. Army 2nd Ranger Battalion*. New York: William Morrow, 2005.

Brown, John Sloan. *Draftee Division: The 88th Infantry Division in World War II*. Lexington: University Press of Kentucky, 1986.

Chernitsky, Dorothy. *Voices from the Foxholes: By the Men of the 110th Infantry, World War II*. Uniontown, Pa.: By the Author, 1991.

Clark, Lloyd. *Anzio: Italy and the Battle for Rome—1944*. New York: Atlantic Monthly Press, 2006.

Clarke, Jeffrey J., and Robert Ross Smith. *United States Army in World War II, The European Theater of Operations: Riviera to the Rhine*. Washington, D.C.: Center of Military History, United States Army, 1993.

Clawson, Mary Ann. *Constructing Brotherhood: Class, Gender, and Fraternalism*. Princeton, N.J.: Princeton University Press, 1989.

Clifford, J. Garry, and Samuel R. Spencer Jr. *The First Peacetime Draft*. Lawrence: University Press of Kansas, 1986.

Coffman, Edward M. *The War to End All Wars: The American Military Experience in World War I*. New York: Oxford University Press, 1968; reprint, Madison: University of Wisconsin Press, 1986.

———. "The Duality of the American Military Tradition: A Commentary." *Journal of Military History* 64, no. 4 (October 2000): 967–80.

————. *The Regulars: The American Army, 1898–1941.*Cambridge, Mass.: Belknap Press of Harvard University Press, 2004.

Cohen, Eliot. *Citizens and Soldiers: The Dilemmas of Military Service.* Ithaca, N.Y.: Cornell University Press, 1985.

Colby, Elbridge. *The National Guard of the United States: A Half Century of Progress.* Manhattan: Kansas State University Press, 1977.

Cole, Hugh M. *United States Army in World War II, The European Theater of Operations. The Ardennes: Battle of the Bulge.* Washington, D.C.: Center of Military History, United States Army, 1994.

Cole, Wayne S. *Roosevelt and the Isolationists, 1932–45.* Lincoln: University of Nebraska Press, 1983.

Coles, David J. "'Hell-by-the-Sea': Florida's Camp Gordon Johnston in World War II." *Florida Historical Quarterly* 73, no. 1 (July 1994): 1–23.

Cooper, Jerry. *The Rise of the National Guard: The Evolution of the American Militia, 1865–1920.* Lincoln: University of Nebraska Press, 1997.

Copp, Terry. *Fields of Fire: The Canadians in Normandy.* Toronto: University of Toronto Press, 2003.

Cosmas, Graham A., and Albert E. Cowdrey. *United States Army in World War II, Technical Services. The Medical Department: Medical Services in the European Theater of Operations.* Washington, D.C.: Center of Military History, United States Army, 1992.

Cress, Lawrence Delbert. *Citizens in Arms: The Army and the Militia in American Society to the War of 1812.* Chapel Hill: University of North Carolina Press, 1982.

Crist, Robert Grant, ed. *The First Century: A History of the 28th Infantry Division.* Prepared Under the Direction of Colonel Uzal W. Ent. Harrisburg: 28th Infantry Division, 1979.

Current, Richard Nelson. *Lincoln's Loyalists: Union Soldiers from the Confederacy.* New York: Oxford University Press, 1992.

Currey, Cecil B. *Follow Me and Die: The Destruction of an American Division in World War II.* New York: Military Heritage Press, 1984.

Dallek, Robert. *Franklin D. Roosevelt and American Foreign Policy, 1932–1945.* With a new afterword. New York: Oxford University Press, 1995.

Daugherty, Robert L. *Weathering the Peace: The Ohio National Guard in the Interwar Years, 1919–1940.* Lanham, Md.: Wright State University Press, 1992.

D'Este, Carlo. *Decision in Normandy.* New York: E. P. Dutton, 1983.

Detwiler, Donald S., ed., and Charles B. Burdick and Jurgen Rohwer, assoc. eds. *World War II German Military Studies: A Collection of 213 Special Reports on the Second World War Prepared by Former Officers of the Wehrmacht for the United States Army.* Vol. 3, part 2: *The ETHINT Series Continued.* New York: Garland, 1979.

Doenecke, Justus D. *Storm on the Horizon: The Challenge to American Intervention, 1939–1941.* Lanham, Md.: Rowman and Littlefield, 2000.

Doubler, Michael D. *Civilian in Peace, Soldier in War: The Army National Guard, 1636–2000.* Lawrence: University Press of Kansas, 2003.

————. *Closing with the Enemy: How GIs Fought the War in Europe, 1944–1945.* Lawrence: University Press of Kansas, 1994.

Doughty, Robert Allan. *The Breaking Point: Sedan and the Fall of France, 1940.* Hamden, Conn.: Archon Books, 1990.

Dupuy, Trevor N., David L. Bongard, and Richard C. Anderson Jr. *Hitler's Last Gamble: The Battle of the Bulge, December 1944–January 1945.* New York: Harper Collins, 1994.

Eiler, Keith E. *Mobilizing America: Robert P. Patterson and the War Effort, 1940–1945*. Ithaca, N.Y.: Cornell University Press, 1997.

Eisenhower, Dwight D. *Crusade in Europe*. Garden City, N.Y.: Doubleday, 1948.

———. *The Papers of Dwight David Eisenhower*. Ed. Alfred D. Chandler Jr. Vol. 4: *The War Years*. Baltimore: Johns Hopkins University Press, 1970.

Ellis, John. *Brute Force: Allied Strategy and Tactics in the Second World War*. New York: Viking, 1990.

Finlayson, Kenneth. *An Uncertain Trumpet: The Evolution of U.S. Army Infantry Doctrine, 1919–1941*. Westport, Conn.: Greenwood, 2001.

First Troop Philadelphia City Cavalry. *History of the First Troop Philadelphia City Cavalry, 1948–1991. Together with an Introductory Chapter Summarizing Its Earlier History and the Rolls Complete from 1774*. Philadelphia: First Troop City Cavalry, 1991.

Flynn, George Q. *The Draft, 1940–1973*. Lawrence: University Press of Kansas, 1993.

Focht, Brown, ed. *The Pennsylvania Manual*. Vol. 85: *1941*. Published by the Commonwealth of Pennsylvania, Arthur H. James, Governor. Harrisburg, Pa.: Bureau of Publications, 1942.

Ford, Nancy Gentile. *Americans All! Foreign-Born Soldiers in World War I*. College Station: Texas A&M University Press, 2001.

Forty, George. *U.S. Army Handbook, 1939–1945*. New York: Charles Scribner's Sons, 1980.

Fredrickson, George M. *The Black Image in the White Mind: The Debate on Afro-American Character and Destiny, 1817–1914*. New York: Harper and Row, 1971.

Gabel, Christopher R. *The U.S. Army GHQ Maneuvers of 1941*. Washington, D.C.: Center of Military History, United States Army, 1992.

Gavin, James M. *On To Berlin: Battles of an Airborne Commander, 1943–1946*. New York: Viking, 1978.

Goda, Norman J. W. *Tomorrow the World: Hitler, Northwest Africa, and the Path toward America*. College Station: Texas A&M University Press, 1998.

Green, Constance McLaughlin, Harry C. Thomson, and Peter C. Roots. *United States Army in World War II, The Technical Services. The Ordnance Department: Planning Munitions for War*. Washington, D.C.: Office of the Chief of Military History, Department of the Army, 1955.

Greenfield, Kent Roberts, Robert R. Palmer, and Bell I. Wiley. *The United States Army in World War II. The Army Ground Forces: The Organization of Ground Combat Troops*. Washington, D.C.: Historical Division, Department of the Army, 1947.

Hadden, Alexander H. *Not Me! The World War II Memoirs of a Reluctant Rifleman*. Bennington, Vt.: Merriam Press, 1997.

Hall, Lawrence Percival, Jr. *My Brother's Letters Home: Blutiger Eigmer (28th Division) Field Artillery Officer's Letters Home*. Ed. John Milliken Hall. New York: Vantage, 1999.

Hamilton, Nigel. *Monty: The Battles of Field Marshall Bernard Montgomery*. New York: Random House, 1994.

Harrison, Gordon A. *United States Army in World War II. The European Theater of Operations: Cross-Channel Attack*. Washington, D.C.: Center of Military History, United States Army, 2002.

Hastings, Max. *Overlord: D-Day and the Battle for Normandy*. New York: Simon and Schuster, 1984.

Heinrichs, Waldo. *Threshold of War: Franklin D. Roosevelt and American Entry into World War II*. New York: Oxford University Press, 1988.

Hesketh, Roger. *Fortitude: The D-Day Deception Campaign.* With an introduction by Nigel West. Woodstock, N.Y.: Overlook, 2000.

Higgenbotham, Don. *The War of American Independence: Military Attitudes, Policies, and Practice, 1763–1789.* New York: Macmillan, 1971.

Hill, Jim Dan. *The Minute Man in Peace and War: A History of the National Guard.* With a foreword by George Fielding Eliot. Harrisburg, Pa.: Stackpole, 1964.

Hogan, David W., Jr. *A Command Post at War: First Army Headquarters in Europe, 1943–1945.* Washington, D.C.: Center of Military History United States Army, 2000.

Huie, William Bradford. *The Execution of Private Slovik: The Hitherto Secret Story of the Only American Soldier since 1864 to be Shot for Desertion.* New York: Duell, Sloan, and Pearce, 1954.

Jenkins, Philip. "'It Can't Happen Here': Fascism and Right-Wing Extremism in Pennsylvania, 1933–1942." *Pennsylvania History* 62, no. 1 (Winter 1995): 31–58.

Johnson, Charles, Jr. *African American Soldiers in the National Guard: Recruitment and Deployment during Peacetime and War.* Contributions in Afro-American and African Studies, number 149. Westport, Conn.: Greenwood, 1992.

Johnson, David E. *Fast Tanks and Heavy Bombers: Innovation in the U.S. Army, 1917–1945.* Ithaca, N.Y.: Cornell University Press, 1998.

Kemp, Harry M. *The Regiment: Let the Citizens Bear Arms! A Narrative History of an American Infantry Regiment in World War II* [109th Infantry Regiment]. Austin, Tex.: Nortex Press, 1990.

Kennett, Lee. *For the Duration . . . The United States Goes to War: Pearl Harbor—1942.* New York: Charles Scribner's Sons, 1985.

———. *GI: The American Soldier in World War II.* New York: Charles Scribner's Sons, 1987.

Kindsvatter, Peter S. *American Soldiers: Ground Combat in the World Wars, Korea, and Vietnam.* With a foreword by Russell F. Weigley. Lawrence: University Press of Kansas, 2003.

Kirby, John B. *Black Americans in the Roosevelt Era: Liberalism and Race.* Knoxville: University of Tennessee Press, 1980.

Knouff, Gregory T. *The Soldiers' Revolution: Pennsylvanians in Arms and the Forging of Early American Identity.* University Park: Pennsylvania State University Press, 2004.

Koskimaki, George E. *Battered Bastards of Bastogne: The 101st Airborne in the Battle of the Bulge, December 19, 1944–January 17, 1945.* Havertown, Pa.: Casemate, 2003; New York: Ballantine Books, 2007.

Kreidberg, Marvin A., and Merton G. Henry. *History of Military Mobilization in the United States Army, 1775–1945.* Department of the Army Pamphlet No. 20–212. Washington, D.C.: Department of the Army, 1955.

Kuhn, J. J. *I Was Baker 2: Memoirs of a World War II Platoon Sergeant.* West Bend, Wis.: DeRaimo, 1994.

Lee, Ulysses. *United States Army in World War II. Special Studies: The Employment of Negro Troops.* Washington, D.C.: Office of the Chief of Military History, United States Army, 1966.

Lender, Mark Edward. "The Social Structure of the New Jersey Brigade." In *The Military in America, from the Colonial Era to the Present,* ed. Peter Karsten. New York: Free Press, 1980.

Lewis, Adrian R. *Omaha Beach: A Flawed Victory.* Chapel Hill: University of North Carolina Press, 2001.

Lilly, J. Robert. *Taken by Force: Rape and American GIs in Europe during World War II.* Houndmills, UK: Palgrave Macmillan, 2003.

Lindermann, Gerald F. *The World within War: America's Combat Experience in World War II.* New York: Free Press, 1997.

Lucas, James. *Last Days of the Third Reich.* With a foreword by Rt. Hon. Sir Bernard Braine, DL, MP. New York: William Morrow, 1986.

MacDonald, Charles B. *A Time For Trumpets: The Untold Story of the Battle of the Bulge.* New York: William Morrow, 1985.

———. *United States Army in World War II. The European Theater of Operations: The Siegfried Line Campaign.* Washington, D.C.: Office of the Chief of Military History, Department of the Army, 1963.

———. *United States Army in World War II. The European Theater of Operations: The Last Offensive.* Washington, D.C.: Office of the Chief of Military History, United States Army, 1973.

MacDonald, Charles B., and Sidney T. Mathews. *United States Army in World War II. Three Battles: Arnaville, Altuzzo, and Schmidt.* Washington, D.C.: Office of the Chief of Military History, Department of the Army, 1952.

Mahon, John K. *History of the Militia and the National Guard.* Macmillan Wars of the United States. Louis Morton, general ed. New York: Macmillan, 1983.

Maier, Klaus A., Horst Rohde, Bernd Stegemann, and Hans Umbreit. *Germany's Initial Conquests in Europe.* Trans. Dean S. McMurray and Eward Osers. Vol. 2 of *Germany and the Second World War.* Militargeschichtliches Forschungsamt (Research Institute for Military History), Freiburg im Breisgau, Germany. Oxford: Clarendon, 1991.

Mansoor, Peter R. *The GI Offensive in Europe: The Triumph of American Infantry Divisions, 1941–1945.* Lawrence: University Press of Kansas, 1999.

Marshall, George C. *The Papers of George Catlett Marshall.* Vol. 1: *"The Soldierly Spirit": December 1880–June 1939.* Ed. Larry I. Bland and Sharon R. Ritenour. Baltimore: Johns Hopkins University Press, 1981.

———. *The Papers of George Catlett Marshall.* Vol. 2: *"We Cannot Delay": July 1, 1939–December 6, 1941.* Ed. Larry I. Bland, Sharon R. Ritenour, and Clarence E. Wunderlin Jr. Baltimore: Johns Hopkins University Press, 1986.

———. *The Papers of George Catlett Marshall.* Vol. 3: *"The Right Man for the Job": December 7, 1941–May 31, 1943.* Ed. Larry I. Bland and Sharon Ritenour Stevens. Baltimore: Johns Hopkins University Press, 1991.

———. *The Papers of George Catlett Marshall,* Vol. 4: *"Aggressive and Determined Leadership": June 1, 1943–December 31, 1944.* Ed. Larry I. Bland and Sharon Ritenour Stevens. Baltimore: Johns Hopkins University Press, 1996.

———. *George C. Marshall Interviews and Reminiscences for Forrest C. Pogue.* Rev. ed. with an introduction by Dr. Pogue. Ed. Larry I. Bland, Joellen K. Bland, and Sharon Ritenour Stevens. Lexington, Va.: George C. Marshall Research Foundation, 1991.

Marshall, S. L. A. *Bastogne: The Story of the First Eight Days.* Assisted by John G. Westover and A. Joseph Webber. Washington, D.C.: Infantry Journal Press, 1946.

———. *Men against Fire: The Problem of Battle Command in Future War.* New York: William Morrow, 1947.

Martin, Edward. *Always Be On Time: An Autobiography.* Harrisburg, Pa.: Telegraph Press, 1959.

Matloff, Maurice, and Edwin M. Snell. *United States Army in World War II. The War Department: Strategic Planning for Coalition Warfare, 1941–1942*. Washington, D.C.: Center of Military History, United States Army, 1990.

McManus, John C. *Alamo in the Ardennes: The Untold Story of the American Soldiers Who Made the Defense of Bastogne Possible*. Hoboken, N.J.: John Wiley and Sons, 2007.

McPherson, James M. *Battle Cry of Freedom: The Civil War Era*. New York: Oxford University Press, 1988; reprint, Norwalk, Conn.: Easton Press, 1989.

Miller, Edward G. *A Dark and Bloody Ground: The Hürtgen Forest and the Roer River Dams, 1944–1945*. College Station: Texas A&M University Press, 1995.

Moenk, Jean R. *A History of Large-Scale Army Maneuvers in the United States, 1935–1964*. Fort Monroe, Va.: Historical Branch, Office of the Deputy Chief of Staff for Military Operations and Reserve Forces, U. S. Continental Army Command, 1969.

Montgomery of Alamein, Field-Marshal, Viscount. *El Alamein to the River Sangro; Normandy to the Baltic*. London: Barrie and Jenkins in association with the Arcadia Press, 1948.

Mortensen, Daniel R., ed. *Airpower and Ground Armies: Essays on the Evolution of Anglo-American Air Doctrine, 1940–43*. Maxwell AFB, Ala.: Air University Press, 1998.

Nash, Douglas E. *Victory Was beyond Their Grasp: With the 272nd Volks-Grenadier Division from the Hürtgen Forest to the Heart of the Reich*. Bedford, Pa.: Aberjona Press, 2008.

Nenninger, Timothy K. "Leavenworth and Its Critics: the U.S. Army Command and General Staff School, 1920–1040." *Journal of Military History* 58, no. 2 (April 1994): 199–232.

Nutter, Thomas E. *Mythos Revisited: American Historians and German Fighting Power in the Second World War*. http://www.militaryhistoryonline.com/wwii/armies/default.aspx.

Odom, William O. *After the Trenches: The Transformation of U.S. Army Doctrine, 1918–1939*. College Station: Texas A&M University Press, 1999.

Ohl, John Kennedy. *Minuteman: The Military Career of General Robert S. Beightler*. Boulder, Colo.: Lynne Rienner, 2000.

Ossad, Steven L., and Don R. Marsh. *Major General Maurice Rose: World War II's Greatest Forgotten Commander*. With a foreword by Martin Blumenson. Lanham, Md.: Taylor Trade Pub., 2003.

Ottanelli, Fraser M. *The Communist Party of the United States: From the Depression to World War II*. New Brunswick, N.J.: Rutgers University Press, 1991.

Overy, Richard. *Why the Allies Won*. New York: W. W. Norton, 1995.

Palmer, Robert R., Bell I. Wiley, and William R. Keast. *The Army Ground Forces: The Procurement and Training of Ground Combat Troops*. Washington, D.C.: Historical Division, Department of the Army, 1948.

Parker, Danny S. *To Win the Winter Sky: The Air War over the Ardennes, 1944–1945*. Conshohocken, Pa.: Combined Books, 1994.

Pavalko, Ronald M. *Sociology of Occupations and Professions*. 2nd ed. Itasca, Ill.: F. E. Peacock Publishers, 1988.

Peterson, Edward N. *The Many Faces of Defeat: The German People's Experience in 1945*. New York: Peter Lang, 1990.

Phillips, Robert H. *To Save Bastogne*. New York: Stein and Day Publishers, 1983.

Pogue, Forrest C. *George C. Marshall: Ordeal and Hope, 1939–1942*. With a foreword by General Omar N. Bradley. New York: Viking, 1965.

Porter, David L. *The Seventy-Sixth Congress and World War II*. Columbia: University of Missouri Press, 1979.

Radtke, Terry. *The History of the Pennsylvania American Legion.* Mechanicsburg, Pa.: Stackpole Books, 1993.

Ralston, David B. *The Army of the Republic: The Place of the Military in the Political Evolution of France, 1871–1914.* Cambridge, Mass.: M.I.T. Press, 1967.

Reichelt, Walter E. *Phantom Nine: The 9th Armored (Remagen) Division, 1942–1945.* Austin, Tex.: Presidial Press, 1987.

Remini, Robert V. *The Battle of New Orleans.* New York: Viking, 1999.

Resch, John. *Suffering Soldiers: Revolutionary War Veterans, Moral Sentiment, and Political Culture of the Early Republic.* Amherst: University of Massachusetts Press, 1999.

Reynolds, David. *Rich Relations: The American Occupation of Britain, 1942–1945.* New York: Random House, 1995.

Riker, William H. *Soldiers of the States: The Role of the National Guard in American Democracy.* Washington, D.C.: Public Affairs Press, 1957.

Robertson, John. "Re-enlistment Patterns of Civil War Soldiers." *Journal of Interdisciplinary History* 32 (2001): 15–35.

Roosevelt, Franklin D. *The Public Papers and Addresses of Franklin D. Roosevelt.* Compiled with special material and explanatory notes by Samuel I. Rosenman. Vols. 1–13. New York: Harper and Bros., 1938–1950.

———. *The Public Papers and Addresses of Franklin Delano Roosevelt.* With a special introduction and explanatory notes by President Roosevelt. 1940 vol.: *War—and Aid to Democracies.* New York: Macmillan, 1941.

———. *The Public Papers and Addresses of Franklin D. Roosevelt.* Compiled with special material and explanatory notes by Samuel I. Rosenman, 1941 vol.: *The Call to Battle Stations.* New York: Harper and Bros., 1950.

Rosswurm, Steven. "The Philadelphia Militia, 1775–1783: Active Duty and Active Radicalism." In *Arms and Independence: The Military Character of the American Revolution,* ed. Ronald Hoffman and Peter J. Albert. Charlottesville: Published for the United States Capitol Historical Society by the University Press of Virginia, 1984.

Royster, Charles. *A Revolutionary People at War: The Continental Army and American Character, 1775–1783.* New York: W. W. Norton, 1979.

Rush, Robert Sterling. *Hell in Hürtgen Forest: The Ordeal and Triumph of an American Infantry Regiment.* Lawrence: University Press of Kansas, 2001.

Russell, Henry D. *The Purge of the Thirtieth Division.* Macon, Ga.: Lyon, Marshall and Brooks, n.d.

Schrijvers, Peter. *The Crash of Ruin: American Combat Soldiers in Europe during World War II.* Washington Square: New York University Press, 1998.

Shy, John. *Toward Lexington: The Role of the British Army in the Coming of the American Revolution.* Princeton, N.J.: Princeton University Press, 1965.

———. *A People Numerous and Armed: Reflections on the Military Struggle for Independence.* Ann Arbor: University of Michigan Press, 1990.

Skeen, C. Edward. *Citizen Soldiers in the War of 1812.* Lexington: University Press of Kentucky, 1999.

Skelton, William B. *An American Profession of Arms: The Army Officer Corps, 1784–1861.* Lawrence: University Press of Kansas, 1992.

Sligh, Robert Bruce. *The National Guard and National Defense: The Mobilization of the Guard in World War II.* With a foreword by Roger Beaumont. New York: Praeger, 1992.

Smith, Graham. *When Jim Crow Met John Bull: Black American Soldiers in World War II Britain.* London: I. B. Taurus, 1987.

Smith, John Richard, and Antony L. Kay. *German Aircraft of the Second World War.* With drawings by E. J. Creek. London: Putnam, 1972.

Smith, Robert L. *"Medic": A WWII Combat Medic Remembers.* Berkeley, Calif.: Creative Arts Book Co., 2001.

Smoler, Frederic. "The Secret of the Soldiers Who Didn't Shoot." *American Heritage,* March 1989, 40–43.

Sobel, Robert, and John Raimo, eds. *Biographical Directory of the Governors of the United States, 1789–1978.* Vols. 1–3. Westport, Conn.: Meckler Books, a division of Microform Review, 1978.

Spiller, Roger J. "Calhoun's Expansible Army: The History of a Military Idea." *South Atlantic Quarterly* 79, no. 2 (Spring 1980): 189–209.

———. "S. L. A. Marshall and the Ratio of Fire." *RUSI Journal* 133, no. 4 (Winter 1988): 63–71.

Stanton, Shelby L. *Order of Battle, U.S. Army, World War II.* With a foreword by Russell F. Weigley. Novato, Calif.: Presidio Press, 1984.

Steele, Richard W. *Free Speech in the Good War.* New York: St. Martin's, 1999.

Stentiford, Barry M. "The Meaning of a Name: The Rise of the National Guard and the End of a Town Militia." *Journal of Military History* 72, no. 3 (July 2009): 727–54.

Stouffer, Samuel A., Edward A. Suchman, Leland C. DeVinney, Shirley A. Star, and Robin M. Williams Jr., eds. *The American Soldier: Adjustment during Army Life.* Vols. 1, 2. Princeton, N.J.: Princeton University Press, 1949.

Sylvan, William C., and Francis G. Smith, Jr. *Normandy to Victory: The War Diary of General Courtney H. Hodges and the First U.S. Army.* Ed. John T. Greenwood. Lexington: University Press of Kentucky, 2008.

Thacker, Toby. *The End of the Third Reich: Defeat, Denazification and Nuremberg, January 1944–November 1946.* Stroud, Gloucestershire: Tempus Publishing, 2006.

Thomson, Harry C., and Lida Mayo. *United States Army in World War II, The Technical Services. The Ordnance Department: Procurement and Supply.* Washington, D.C.: Office of the Chief of Military History, Department of the Army, 1960.

Toland, John. *Battle: The Story of the Bulge.* New York: Random House, 1959.

Trask, David F. *The War with Spain in 1898.* New York: Macmillan, 1981.

———. *The AEF and Coalition Warmaking, 1917–1918.* Lawrence: University Press of Kansas, 1993.

Van Creveld, Martin. *Fighting Power: German and U.S. Army Performance, 1939–1945.* Westport, Conn.: Greenwood, 1982.

Watson, Mark Skinner. *United States Army in World War II. The War Department, Chief of Staff: Prewar Plans and Preparations.* Washington, D.C.: Historical Division, Department of the Army, 1950.

Weaver, Michael E. "The Volunteers of 1941: The Pennsylvania National Guard and Continuity in American Military Policy." *Pennsylvania History* 72, no. 3 (Summer 2005): 347–68.

Weigley, Russell F. *The American Way of War: A History of United States Military Strategy and Policy.* New York: Macmillan, 1973.

———. *Eisenhower's Lieutenants: The Campaign of France and Germany, 1944–1945.* Bloomington: Indiana University Press, 1981.

———. *History of the United States Army*. New York: Macmillan, 1967.

———. *Towards an American Army: Military Thought from Washington to Marshall*. New York: Columbia University Press, 1962.

Wesbrook, Stephen D. "The Railey Report and Army Morale, 1941: Anatomy of a Crisis." *Military Review* 60, no. 6 (June 1980): 11–24.

Westbrook, C. H., ed. *The Pennsylvania Manual*. Vol. 84: *1939*. Harrisburg: Commonwealth of Pennsylvania, 1940.

Westbrook, Robert B. *Why We Fought: Forging American Obligations in World War II*. Washington, D.C.: Smithsonian Books, 2004.

Whiting, Charles. *The Last Assault: The Battle of the Bulge Reassessed*. New York: Sarpedon, 1994.

Wiebe, Robert H. *The Search for Order, 1877–1920*. The Making of America series, ed. David Herbert Donald. New York: Hill and Wang, a division of Farrar, Straus, and Giroux, 1967.

Wieviorka, Olivier. *Normandy: The Landings to the Liberation of Paris*. Trans. M. B. DeBevoise. Cambridge, Mass.: Belknap Press of Harvard University Press, 2008.

Wilmot, Chester. *The Struggle for Europe*. New York: Harper and Bros., 1952.

Wilson, John B. *Maneuver and Firepower: The Evolution of Divisions and Separate Brigades*. Army Lineage Series. Washington, D.C.: Center of Military History, United States Army, 1998.

Winders, Richard Bruce. *Mr. Polk's Army: The American Military Experience in the Mexican War*. College Station: Texas A&M University Press, 1997.

Winton, Harold R. *Corps Commanders of the Bulge: Six American Generals and Victory in the Ardennes*. With a foreword by Dennis Showalter. Lawrence: University Press of Kansas, 2007.

Zaloga, Steven J. *US Armored Divisions, The European Theater of Operations, 1944–1945*. Oxford: Osprey Publications, 2004.

Ziemke, Earle F. *The U.S. Army in the Occupation of Germany, 1944–1946*. Washington, D.C.: Center of Military History, United States Army, 1975.

Zumbro, Derek S. *Battle for the Ruhr: The German Army's Final Defeat in the West*. Lawrence: University Press of Kansas, 2006.

Index

Harrisburg, Pa., 14, 95, 96, 97, 123
Harry James Orchestra, 85
Harvier, Howard F., 257
Harwell, Gerald A., 226
Hasbrouck, Robert, 236
Haskell, William N., 80
Hazlett, Robert T., 188
Hedgerows. *See Bocage*
Heilman, John L., 124
Henbest, Ross C., 261, 318n54
Hill, Jim Dan, 117
Hinkson, DeHaven, 112, 301n92
Hitler, Adolf, 18, 26, 106–107, 166, 212, 213, 235, 239, 240, 246, 247
Hoban, Thomas, 225, 334n137
Hodes, Henry I., 176, 318n54
Hodges, Courtney H., 177, 179, 187, 188, 192; leadership failures, 196–200, 227, 228, 235, 258, 318n64, 324n79
Hogan, David W., 199
Homanich, Andy, 181, 319n86
Hotel Claravallis, 224
Hubbs, Edward, 122–23
Huebner, Clarence R., 250, 251, 252
Hughes, James R., 225
Huntley, Theodore A., 25, 118

Ideals and values of Pennsylvania National Guard, 10, 86, 90, 95, 97, 106–12, 113, 122, 159, 258
Illinois National Guard, 17, 42, 81, 112, 135, 309n112
Infantry Divisions, United States: 1st, 26, 63, 163, 218; 3rd, 143, 246; 4th, 127, 176, 241; 9th, 187, 199; 28th, ix, 6, 7, 8, 10, 12, 20, 23, 26, 35, 42, 43, 45, 46, 48, 50, 56, 57, 58, 59, 61, 64, 67, 70, 73, 74, 77, 79, 95, 97, 99, 116, 118, 119, 124, 128, 132, 138–39, 144, 157, 160, 165, 168, 169, 170, 172–73, 181, 187, 188, 195, 200, 210, 211, 214, 216, 218, 222, 230, 238–39, 243, 246–48, 251, 253–54, 256, 258, 260, 265, 305n7, 329n198; 29th, 131, 166; 30th, 22, 73, 117, 120, 131, 170; 35th, 120; 36th, 120; 38th, 122, 139; 41st, 22; 42nd, 12; 43rd, 60, 63, 74, 76; 44th, 22, 25, 60, 63, 64, 69, 70, 72, 74,

75, 76; 45th, 22; 79th, 127, 166; 80th, 236; 83rd, 126, 166; 85th, 134; 106th, 235, 237, 244, 336n179; Provisional Division (Manassas Maneuvers), 55, 56, 58, 59; square division, 54, 270n25; triangular division, 14, 129, 151, 270n25
Infantry Regiments, United States: 18th, 65; 22nd, 326n117; 57th, 132; 109th, 23, 26, 32, 41, 51, 63, 64, 65, 72, 84, 85, 87, 88, 89, 90, 91, 94, 96, 101, 105, 107, 125, 130, 137, 141, 148, 149, 157, 162, 163, 164, 165, 171, 173, 177, 180, 181, 195, 200, 207, 209, 210, 221, 229, 230, 234, 235, 236, 243, 244, 248, 249, 251, 252, 254, 261; 110th, 31, 35, 42, 46, 51, 54, 62, 64, 70, 71, 85, 88, 91, 104, 121, 135, 139, 140, 142, 146, 153, 173, 177, 183, 192, 200, 203–204, 209, 212, 214, 215, 216, 219, 224, 226, 228, 232, 240, 241, 249, 250; 111th, 37, 49, 51, 52, 62, 67, 76, 84, 85, 87, 89, 91, 95, 108, 124, 128, 305n7; 112th, 41, 42, 45, 50–51, 54, 65, 71, 81, 84, 85, 87, 104, 105, 124, 130, 141, 147, 148, 159, 161, 162, 165, 181, 185, 188, 197, 198, 202, 209, 212, 221, 230–31, 233–34, 236–37, 243, 251, 258, 337n194; 152nd, 140, 141; 174th, 25; 176th, 71; 182nd, 71; 372nd, 112
Initial Protective Force, 34
Inman, Horace J., 48

James, Arthur H., 37, 55, 79, 83, 109, 111, 112, 289n4
Jewish Welfare Board, 132
Jodl, Alfred, 213, 237, 338n228
Johnson, Annie B., 93
Johnson, Clyde, 201
Johnson, Dave, 185
Johnson, Everett, 112
Jones, Alan W., 234
Jones, Benjamin C., 46, 133

Kafkalas, Nicholas, 94, 126
Kean, William B., 199
Keehn, Roy D., 136
Kelley, Fred H., 67, 118
Kelly, Raymond J., 112

MICHAEL E. WEAVER is Associate Professor of Comparative Military History at the U.S. Air Force Air Command and Staff College. He completed his doctorate at Temple University in 2002 under the guidance of Russell F. Weigley.

www.ingramcontent.com/pod-product-compliance
Lightning Source LLC
Chambersburg PA
CBHW060324100426
42812CB00003B/878